Norton All-in-One
Reference For Dum

M000291115

When to Use Which Program

Use This Program	When You Need to . . .
LiveUpdate	Update all your Norton tools.
Norton AntiSpam	Get control over all those unsolicited ads flooding into your electronic mailbox; it can defeat many pop-up ads when Web browsing, too.
Norton AntiVirus	Scan for, detect, and repair computer infections and remove adware and spyware.
Norton CleanSweep	Remove rarely used files and programs yet not lose them; CleanSweep can compress and store your programs until you need them again, saving space.
Norton CleanUp	Clean your drives of a surplus of temporary files, leftover Internet files, and more.
Norton Disk Doctor	Check your drives — especially your hard disks — for problems and attempt repairs.
Norton Ghost	Back up your hard disks or copy the contents of your current hard disk to a new one.
Norton GoBack	Return to the way your system looked and worked at a previous point in time; the AutoBack feature within GoBack lets you return to the same setup every time you restart.
Norton Internet Security	Protect you and your family and your privacy while enjoying the bounty the Internet has to offer.
Norton Parental Control	Keep your kids from content that's not appropriate for them to view.
Norton PartitionMagic	Partition, repartition, format, or otherwise adjust your hard-disk partitions; this tool is great for preparing a new hard disk for use.
Norton Password Manager	Keep track of your Internet passwords along with your home and office mailing address and credit-card information; store it in Password Manager, and you won't need to type it over and over again.
Norton Personal Firewall	Protect yourself during your Internet sessions, making it harder for hackers, crackers,and phishers to attack you or reach your confidential information.
Norton Privacy Manager	Keep your confidential information from spying eyes.
Norton Speed Disk	Optimize your hard disk, a regular feature of good drive maintenance.
Norton System Doctor	Monitor your system and its changes to try to spot and repair problems as they appear.
Norton SystemWorks	Have a comprehensive package solution to troubleshooting and maintenance for your PC.
Norton Unerase Wizard	Recover files you've accidentally removed from your system; Norton even offers its own version of the Recycle Bin to keep your files extra safe.
Norton WinDoctor	Diagnose and cure Windows-based problems on your PC.
One Button Checkup	Perform a fast diagnostic scan of your system with repair options.

For Dummies: Bestselling Book Series for Beginners

FOR DUMMIES
BESTSELLING
BOOK SERIES

Norton All-in-One Desk Reference For Dummies®

Cheat Sheet

What to Do When Problems Arise

If You Have . . .	Take These Steps . . .
A conflict between Norton and another program	Use the options available from the Help menu in each Norton tool.
A disk about to die	Back up the problem drive using Norton Ghost or Windows Backup but store the backup somewhere off the hard disk where you're having the problem; contact the support number for your hard-disk manufacturer.
A new hard disk	Run Norton PartitionMagic to partition and format it (your Windows XP install CD can do this, too).
A problem drive	Run Norton Disk Doctor.
A problem preventing Windows from starting	Restore using Norton GoBack or Norton Ghost.
A virus	Run Norton AntiVirus and its LiveUpdate tool.
Adware or spyware	Run Norton AntiVirus and its LiveUpdate tool.
An incompletely installed Norton product	Open Windows Control Panel, be sure you're in Classic view (click Switch to Classic view in the left pane), and then double-click Add or Remove Programs, select your Norton product, click Remove; then reinstall it.
An insecure Internet connection	Run Norton Personal Firewall or Norton Internet Security.
An e-mail with an attachment	Don't open the attachment until you check it with an antivirus tool, such as Norton AntiVirus.
A missing file or folder	If you're using Norton Ghost, use the Restore Files and Folders feature to try to recover the individual files and folders without restoring the entire disk.
People using your PC without your permission	Begin to use better, stronger passwords and use a product like Norton Password Manager to create profiles and store passwords securely.
A slow-running PC	Use Norton Speed Disk and then try Norton System Doctor or One Button Checkup.
Someone spying on your PC	Run Norton AntiVirus and Norton Personal Firewall.
Strange Windows problems	Run Norton WinDoctor.
Contents that you want to copy from one hard disk to another	Use Norton Ghost to copy the drive.
A PC that is beginning to make loud noises or you smell burning	Turn off your PC and disconnect it from power; contact your PC tech-support line or a local repairperson.

For Dummies: Bestselling Book Series for Beginners

Norton

ALL-IN-ONE DESK REFERENCE

FOR

DUMMIES®

Norton
ALL-IN-ONE DESK REFERENCE

FOR
DUMMIES®

by Kate Chase

WILEY

Wiley Publishing, Inc.

Norton All-in-One Desk Reference For Dummies®

Published by
Wiley Publishing, Inc.
111 River Street
Hoboken, NJ 07030-5774

For general information on our other products and services, please contact our Customer Care Department within the U.S. at 800-762-2974, outside the U.S. at 317-572-3993, or fax 317-572-4002.

For technical support, please visit www.wiley.com/techsupport.

Wiley also publishes its books in a variety of electronic formats. Some content that appears in print may not be available in electronic books.

Library of Congress Control Number: 2005921600

ISBN: 0-7645-7993-2

Manufactured in the United States of America

10 9 8 7 6 5 4 3 2 1

1B/RV/QT/QV/IN

WILEY

About the Author

Kate J. Chase is a technical support engineer, online community manager, and author who has written, co-authored, or revised 20 technical books. An expert in Windows, PC hardware, and applications, she has a passion for cutting through the computerese to let normal people get the most out of their PC dollar.

Kate also writes for magazines, newspaper, and online publications on a variety of non-technical subjects. She lives in the wilds of north-central Vermont with her six PCs, family, and satellite-based Internet connection.

Dedication

This book is dedicated to my friends and neighbors in north-central Vermont. They bless me with help when it's needed and quiet afternoons in which to work.

Author's Acknowledgments

My utmost appreciation goes to all the people who came together to turn this book from a concept into a reality. You see my name on the book's cover but a number of talented folks have their work buried here in the binding.

Thanks to Tom Heine, Acquisitions Editor at Wiley, and to Elizabeth Kuball, the Project Editor who willingly took my questions on weekends and helped keep the work humming along despite a very tight schedule. Kudos also to Peter Davis who served as Technical Editor for this project, catching problems for correction so you won't. Last but not least, let me applaud the good folks in Wiley's Production Department who work so diligently to assemble the finished manuscript into the book you're reading now.

My agent, David Fugate of Waterside Productions, is always great about trying to find just the right projects for me and working out most of the wrinkles.

More locally, I want to express my extreme gratitude to my family — John and Ben — who tolerated my late nights in the office and both the over- *and* undercooked meals.

Publisher's Acknowledgments

We're proud of this book; please send us your comments through our online registration form located at www.dummies.com/register/.

Some of the people who helped bring this book to market include the following:

Acquisitions, Editorial, and Media Development

Project Editor: Elizabeth Kuball

Acquisitions Editor: Tom Heine

Technical Editor: Peter T. Davis

Editorial Manager: Robyn Siesky

Media Development Supervisor: Richard Graves

Editorial Assistant: Adrienne Porter

Cartoons: Rich Tennant (www.the5thwave.com)

Composition Services

Project Coordinator: Maridee Ennis

Layout and Graphics: Andrea Dahl, Lauren Goddard, Stephanie D. Jumper, Melanee Prendergast, Heather Ryan

Proofreaders: Vickie Broyles, John Greenough, Joan Griffitts, Jessica Kramer, Sossity R. Smith, Brian Walls

Indexer: Joan Griffitts

Publishing and Editorial for Technology Publishing

    Richard Swadley, Vice President and Executive Group Publisher

    Barry Pruett, Vice President and Publisher, Visual/Web Graphics

    Andy Cummings, Vice President and Publisher, Technology Dummies

    Mary Bednarek, Executive Acquisitions Director, Technology Dummies

    Mary C. Corder, Editorial Director, Technology Dummies

Publishing for Consumer Dummies

    Diane Graves Steele, Vice President and Publisher

    Joyce Pepple, Acquisitions Director

Composition Services

    Gerry Fahey, Vice President of Production Services

    Debbie Stailey, Director of Composition Services

Contents at a Glance

Table of Contents

Introduction

The fastest way to get your day off to a nasty start is to find your PC isn't ready or able to do what you want. The experience can quickly make you feel impatient, scared, and oh so very alone in your troubles.

If only you knew more about your PC hardware and software. If only you had a better idea of what's wrong and how to fix it.

Not everyone has a degree from the Massachusetts Institute of Technology or has the time to become a PC troubleshooting guru. For them — and for you — there's Norton. These products were designed to fix or tweak things like you might if you were a PC technician, able to look for issues large and small that can affect whether your PC boots, how it responds, and how well you can run your applications and games.

About This Book

Sometimes, even the best tools require you to get a little savvy to use them to your best advantage. This is true about the new saw you buy for a home workshop, for a rug cleaner you get to clean those carpets, and for troubleshooting, repair, and protection tools such as you find in Norton products.

See, because of the kind of jobs your PC lets you do (a huge number), there's always the possibility that the same tool designed to help you when used correctly could create some chaos and even harm if used improperly. You know how dangerous a simple kitchen knife is. Used correctly, a knife can cut through the toughest meat and otherwise make your food-prep tasks easier. Used incorrectly, you run the risk of losing a fingertip, or rushing to the emergency room for stitches and a tetanus shot.

This book is all about helping you use these Norton tools to your maximum advantage while trying to reduce your risks. It was written in part by researching the kinds of questions people like you are asking or struggling with in regard to Norton products, and then trying to get you the answers you need.

Wherever possible, this book presents some alternative products you can use if you need the functions of a particular Norton product you don't currently have. Some of these alternatives are found right within Microsoft Windows itself, so you may not need to go buy anything. Or you can try one of the 15-day trials suggested in this book to see how a Norton product does for you before you buy it.

Foolish Assumptions

Without trying to make too many assumptions (everyone is a bit different), it's very possible you fit into one or more of the following types:

✦ You may be relatively new to Windows-based PCs with little or no experience in troubleshooting and PC security.

✦ You don't want to just call a technician (or you already have and feel less than helped) or send your PC in for repair every time you hit a bump in the road.

✦ You're looking for a way to troubleshoot and protect your system that doesn't require you to become an expert in order to get better results.

✦ You're concerned about what may be at risk — your kids, your confidential information like credit-card details, the data and programs you have that could be devastated by a virus or Trojan — when you and your family are online.

✦ You don't want to feel helpless when your PC doesn't work right. You want to get it fixed with minimum hassle.

✦ You don't necessarily have all the Norton products. You may have either a suite with a number of different products (such as the popular Norton SystemWorks) or you may have purchased separate Norton products (like Norton AntiVirus and Norton PartitionMagic).

One thing this book does not assume is that you're a dummy. You proved that in trying to find a solution to problems or insecurities you're having with your PC and Windows. A dummy might just sit and hope for rescue; *you* know you have to find the answers. This book attempts to bridge the gap between the tools and your knowledge, so you can feel more comfortable in using them and see better results.

Conventions Used in This Book

Although you're welcome to read this book, page by page, in order from cover to cover, that's not what you must do. That's how most people read a great novel but it's not usually how we approach problem solving.

Instead, this book has been created as a reference guide where you can jump in at a specific product, such as Norton AntiVirus, and find out what you need to do. Topics and concepts are presented in plain English, and not computerese designed to make pros sound smart while leaving you hopelessly confused.

You'll see keyboard shortcuts in several places in the book. These usually require you to press one key and hold in while pressing another, such as Ctrl+X. This means you press and hold the Ctrl key while you press the X key.

When I tell you to click or double-click or right-click on a choice, the book assumes you haven't tweaked your mouse or pointer settings to respond differently from how Windows works by default. Normally, to click or double-click, you press the left mouse button. To right-click, you press the right mouse button.

One more point and it's a small yet important one. I assume that if you're using Windows XP, you're using Classic view rather than the cutesy regular Category view for most work. Classic view presents some options immediately available that Category view doesn't. Here's how to switch from Category view to Classic view:

1. **Choose Start ⇨ Control Panel.**

2. **When the Control Panel opens, look near the top of the left pane and click Switch to Classic View.**

This redraws the Control Panel as shown in the figure.

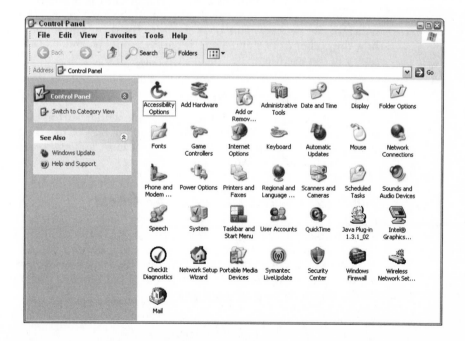

How This Book 1s Organized

Each of the nine minibooks in *Norton All-in-One Desk Reference For Dummies* is designed to stand alone. For example, you don't have to read the chapters in Book IV, dealing with Norton GoBack, to make sense of Book VIII's coverage of Norton PartitionMagic. I do include cross-references to other books and chapters, however, where it makes sense to check for other information.

The following sections give you a description of what each minibook contains.

Book 1: Norton Essentials

This book not only introduces you to the wide variety of Norton home and small-business programs and tools, it also gives you important facts about what can go wrong with your PC that requires assistance or repair. Because you may not have every single Norton package, this book also suggests other programs you can use when you need a tool you don't currently have. You'll also find out how to try certain Norton products free for 15 days.

Book 11: Norton Suites

Norton SystemWorks (and its deluxe version, Norton SystemWorks Premier) and Norton Internet Security roll a bunch of the most helpful Norton products into one package. This book provides the details about both suites and how they differ from stand-alone separate products, and also shows you how you can use them.

Book 111: Norton Utilities

This book covers all the major tools available within Norton Utilities, part of the Norton SystemWorks suite. You'll find out how to use the doctors to diagnose, One Button Checkup for a quick cure, and extra features you won't find in any other Norton package.

Book 1V: Norton GoBack and Ghost

Like the Boy Scouts always say, be prepared. Norton's major fall-back recovery tools, Norton GoBack and Norton Ghost, share the spotlight in this book. You'll see how to use GoBack to revert back to a working setup after you come face-to-face with disaster. Then you'll discover how Norton Ghost can not only prepare backups of your hard disks, but also lets you copy one hard disk's contents to another hard disk.

Book V: Norton AntiSpam

Exhausted and frustrated by the mountain of unsolicited ads in your electronic mailbox? This book is all about using Norton AntiSpam to wrest control back from the dreaded spammers. Discover what extra features this tool offers to reduce the overall amount of unwanted e-mail you get.

Book VI: Norton AntiVirus

This is the book to read when you're wondering whether a computer infection has invaded your hard disk. But you'll find that Norton AntiVirus does so much more, including the ability to seek out and destroy spyware and other nasties that may be snooping on your online activities.

Book VII: Internet Control Tools

Here's the book for understanding how to manage your online pursuits. From watching what your kids do and where they go online to protecting your private information and shielding you and your files behind a personal firewall, you'll find what you need here.

Book VIII: Norton PartitionMagic

Installing a hard disk is a lot easier than most people think. Where they often experience problems is in preparing a new hard disk for use. Whether you have a new hard disk or you're trying to better organize an existing one, this book shows you the ins and outs along with the extra helping hand provided by the ultra-friendly Norton PartitionMagic.

Book IX: Norton CleanSweep

Did you know that unwanted temporary and leftover files and unused programs can clog your hard disk, reducing space for the things you really want to keep? This book covers all the basics to let you identify and kill — or safely protect but in a smarter compressed format — all the stuff gathering virtual dust on your hard disk(s).

Icons Used in This Book

Icons are the little pictures you see in the margins throughout this book. They're there to draw your attention to particular types of information:

Whenever you see the Tip icon, you're sure to find some handy hint or piece of information that will help you work with the Norton product or your computer better and faster.

You don't have to memorize this whole book — thank God! — but the pieces of information I attach the handy Remember icon to are ones that you'll want to file away in your brain for later use. They're *that* important.

Whenever you see this bomb in the margin, you can be sure I'm warning you of something that you want to avoid.

This icon flags information that's interesting but not absolutely necessary to your knowledge of the task at hand. Use it to impress your friends.

Where to Go from Here

This is a reference book, which means you don't have to read it from cover to cover. You can hop around from one chapter to the next, pulling pieces of information that you need. Keep it on your desk and make use of the table of contents and index to track down what you're looking for.

Book I

Norton Essentials

The 5th Wave   By Rich Tennant

© RICHTENNANT

"So, someone's using your credit card info to buy stylish clothes, opera tickets and exercise equipment. In what way would this qualify as 'identity theft'?"

Contents at a Glance

Chapter 1: Getting to Know Norton Products

In This Chapter

✔ Appreciating Norton's long history in the PC help biz

✔ Figuring out exactly who Norton is

✔ Getting to know Norton products by type

*E*ven if you're brand-spankin'-new to computers, and before you purchased your Norton software, you probably heard or read the name Norton many times. In fact, Norton is one of the relatively few PC-industry names that has been with us since early on in the history of personal computers. If you only knew how many companies have gone bust or been bought up by bigger firms over the last two-plus decades, you would be astounded!

This chapter introduces you to the various tools that are available under the Norton name (plenty!). Here, I focus in on the type of software, because you have so many different ones to choose from. Just as finding and using the right tool in your household tool chest is important when you're wanting to do a specific repair, choosing the right Norton product for the PC protection, repair, or maintenance job you face is important — and in this chapter, I help you do just that.

Norton: A Name Long Associated with PC Care

IBM's name is still associated with the original PC-class computer that rolled out in 1981. This is true even though so many other manufacturers have joined the PC design and rollout industry.

Not very long after the debut of the IBM PC, the name IBM was joined by the name Norton for some of the first utilities created to help consumers work with those PCs. Those initial offerings not only eventually developed into a broad range of additional products under the Norton name, but they also helped spawn the creation of similar tools by other software developers. Some of those competing titles and the companies who published them have actually been rolled into Norton products as they exist now.

Yes, Virginia, there really *is* a Norton

Getting jaded about product packaging and advertising is easy, because you've learned over time that there really isn't a great baker named Betty Crocker or a buttery-tasting pancake aficionado named Mrs. Butterworth.

But Norton products are a bit different, because there really *is* a man named Norton. His name is Peter Norton, in fact, and his name has become synonymous with PC utilities. Grizzled vets in the PC industry remember him as the guy who wrote all those books that were the first to explain the inner workings of the IBM PC and how to use it. Even today, his name still appears on new books.

Just as Oprah's image shows up on the cover of every issue of her magazine, Peter Norton graced the covers of almost all his books (rare in PC help books, where the computer is the star). He usually wore a proper office shirt with rolled-up sleeves and a slightly loosened tie, giving you the distinct impression that this fellow was no stranger to hard work at the office.

But don't speak of him in the past tense, because he's alive, well, and still active. His name remains an icon in the PC world and he still writes for a number of publications. However, his bestselling utilities have long been produced not by him but by the talented folks working at the software publisher, Symantec.

Although today, you can choose from a whole shelf of various utility software in a large electronics superstore, you'll always see the name Norton (that is, unless they've sold out). People who can't correctly name one other disk utility can identify Norton Utilities and all the tools within it. The same holds true for antivirus software and other products.

If you've happened to use Windows for a bit, you've probably seen tools initially designed by the Norton folks rolled into the system tools packed into the operating system. So the influence Norton has had over the entire industry — and we, those lowly end users they work for — has been nothing short of phenomenal.

Knowing Your Norton Products

The very first thing you need to understand is that Norton makes a *lot* of different products. That's the good news, because they offer a little something for everyone, regardless of your particular needs.

Yet on top of that, many of the Norton products are available as *standalones* (meaning just a single product, sold individually), many are sold both in home (or small-business) and professional versions, and some are packaged into *suites* (three or more products packed into one).

The result is often that people mix up which Norton package is which. But don't worry, because you won't. Before you're finished here, you'll know them well.

One of the smartest ways you can easily identify and remember what different Norton products do is by understanding the type of job they're designed to handle. With this in mind, in the following sections I examine each of those products covered within this book.

But before I do that, keep in mind that most of your installed Norton products have an option you can use to further explore the wealth of other Norton options. To view those other Norton options, first be sure you're connected to the Internet. Then follow these steps:

1. **Choose Start➪All Programs, and then point to your Norton product in the list (such as Norton AntiVirus).**

2. **From the submenu that appears, choose More Symantec Solutions.**

3. **Your Web browser launches and opens the page shown in Figure 1-1.**

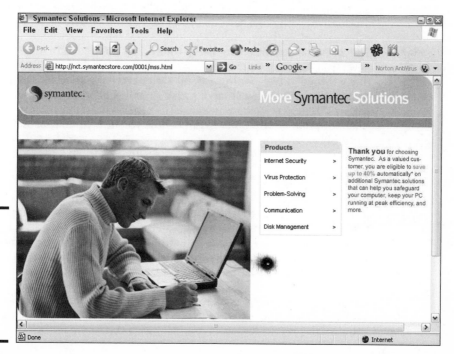

Figure 1-1: Explore some of the other recommended Norton products.

While you're at the Norton Web site, take a moment to see if any new versions have been released for the Norton products you already have. I tell you more about what happens when you mix and match different versions of the various Norton tools as we go along. But knowing when a new version is available and what it offers is always a good idea.

Antivirus protection

For protection from viruses, you want Norton AntiVirus, available either as a standalone product or packaged into both Norton Internet Security suite or Norton SystemWorks suite. Before Norton AntiVirus even installs, it does a special scan to be sure your system isn't infected in some way that may make it difficult for AntiVirus to install and work.

Also, the LiveUpdate tool within Norton AntiVirus means you can keep up-to-date on protection for the most recently released computer viruses, Trojans, and worms. If you're not up on your infected PC terminology, fear not — Book VI, especially Chapter 1 of that book, tells you everything you need to know.

Right now, all you need to know is that very strange people are sitting in front of a monitor somewhere around the globe, every day, creating all new problems and twists they can try to send into unprotected PCs. In fact, many viruses are designed to try to kill your antivirus software before they do anything else. Because these no-goodniks are so determined (and all too productive), you need serious protection against them.

The antivirus software you install today may not be ready for tomorrow's new virus. Keeping your antivirus software updated — and with Norton, that's through LiveUpdate — along with exercising good PC behavior is your best chance of keeping someone else's nasties off your precious system.

Oh, about that good PC behavior: I show you how to do that in Chapters 1 and 2 of Book VI.

Comprehensive Internet security

The Internet is the greatest library on the globe and provides some of the best fun you can have legally, but it also presents some real dangers. It can take a security wiz to try to sew up all the holes in PC security so that your personal information (like credit card or Social Security numbers stored on your PC) doesn't get revealed, your kids don't wind up on a sleazy site, and you don't inadvertently advertise your e-mail address to the world.

Thankfully, Norton has packaged up your very own security wizard (he was a tight fit in that little box) to protect you from things you may not even know exist.

Consider Norton Internet Security suite, a comprehensive package that includes the most popular and necessary tools for safe Web surfing and online sessions. For example, Norton Internet Security 2005 packages together:

✦ **Norton AntiSpam** for controlling e-mail ads and annoyances

✦ **Norton AntiVirus** (see "Antivirus protection," earlier in this chapter), which includes a special tool added directly to your Web browser to scan files and other things that can cause you problems online

✦ **Norton Personal Firewall** for creating a virtual moat around your PC and Internet connection to keep unwanted visitors out

✦ **Norton Parental Control** to help you keep your kids safe from some of the Internet's shady characters and dimly-lit back alleys

✦ **Norton Privacy Control** to block certain private information from being transferred to strange Web sites and services, sometimes without your knowledge

Beyond what you can find in Norton Internet Security, there is another tool available called Password Manager. I bet you can guess its job: to keep track of the many passwords you likely use on the Internet. It does more, however. You can store your credit card information and your work and/or home addresses and phone numbers within Password Manager. Then, when needed, the tool can automatically copy your details directly into Web forms. This is a must for anyone who loves the convenience of online shopping but really hates having to fill out all the blanks on the virtual order forms. At the same time, Password Manager *encrypts* (scrambles) this confidential info you store within it, so the bad guys have a harder time stealing it.

Norton AntiSpam, AntiVirus, and Personal Firewall are also sold as standalone packages, but you pay less if you buy them as part of the Internet Security 2005 suite. If you don't already have one or more of these products, you may want to consider buying the suite rather than buying them separately.

Drive diagnosis, management, maintenance, and repair

For all of the above, think Norton Utilities, one of the original names in handling a multitude of drive checking and repair jobs. The title — utilities — is apt because it rolls together a number of tools into one spiffy interface.

Within Norton Utilities, you'll find a tool to make your drives run faster and more efficiently by cleaning up any messes created on them by system lock-ups, power outages, and those times you hit the Off button rather than properly shut down. Later in the book, I explain how information gets written to your disk when you save files. If the files don't get written correctly, the results can be very much like a big filing cabinet in which hundreds of pieces of paper have been tossed with very little rhyme or reason.

If you've ever run the Windows Disk Defragmenter utility (choose Start⇨All Programs⇨Accessories⇨System Tools⇨Disk Defragmenter), you may have seen a mess. Check out Figure 1-2 and you see a large drive with a lot of disorganized data written all over the place. This phenomenon is called *fragmentation* (and the cleaning of it is known as *drive defragmentation* or *optimization*).

 Let a drive stay badly fragmented, and it will only get worse. Fragmentation increases the time it takes for Windows to locate and open the programs and files stored in that clutter. Eventually, some of the files won't load at all or may seem damaged.

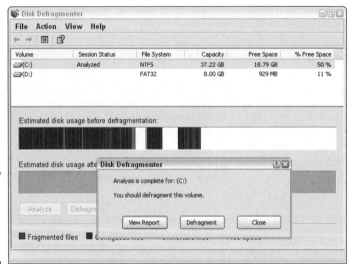

Figure 1-2: Running Windows Disk Defragmenter.

Norton Utilities is only the premier product in this category. There are others, too, including

✦ Norton AntiVirus, which protects against the kinds of viruses that can make your drive about as useful as a dead goldfish or turn the files stored on that drive into garbage

✦ CheckIt Diagnostics, which allows you to perform a thorough examination of your drive against a standard list of common problems

✦ Norton CleanSweep, a tool that helps removed unneeded files from your system, including the ton of virtual dust bunnies left behind by Web browsing

✦ Norton Ghost, which creates what is called a *drive image* that you can copy onto a brand-new PC or a newly-installed hard drive to start the new system or drive off where your old system/hard drive left off

✦ Norton Partition Magic, which does many different jobs, and also creates smaller drive sizes to reduce the time required to perform routine drive maintenance

Norton SystemWorks, one of the Norton suites, includes several of these utilities. You'll find out more about this package in the next several chapters.

E-mail management and protection

If you're like 103 percent of PC users and now feel like your e-mail inbox has turned into Grand Central Station, where anybody and everybody can walk in, shout things at you, and entice you with goodies you don't want, check out Norton AntiSpam.

AntiSpam was designed to give you a great deal more power over whose e-mail can actually make it into your inbox. It does this by bolstering the simpler, less effective tools already present in e-mail software such as Outlook Express (all of which, as you may have noticed, still allow way too many ads in). Look at Figure 1-3 and you'll see that I've set up several special rules in Outlook Express to try to reduce the 500 to 700 pieces of spam I get each day. But even with all my efforts to stop the spam, Outlook Express lets a lot of unwanted e-mail in.

The Norton AntiSpam tool also has a special built-in feature that performs an analysis of the type of e-mail you send to try to help it guess what type of e-mail you may *want* to receive. Although you'll need to tweak AntiSpam settings for best results — I show you how to do that in Chapter 3 of Book V — you may be pleasantly amazed at how much fewer "buy this" and "just give us your bank information so we can steal from you" e-mails you receive.

Beyond AntiSpam, Norton AntiVirus can scan the e-mail you receive — and send — to cut down on the likelihood that you and those you communicate with may fall victim to a computer virus or mail worm. This feature is great when you consider how much unwanted mail you receive with files attached to them. Even if you know the rules (don't open a file from anyone you don't know), you're human and you probably make mistakes occasionally (we all do). AntiVirus can keep the mistake from morphing into disaster.

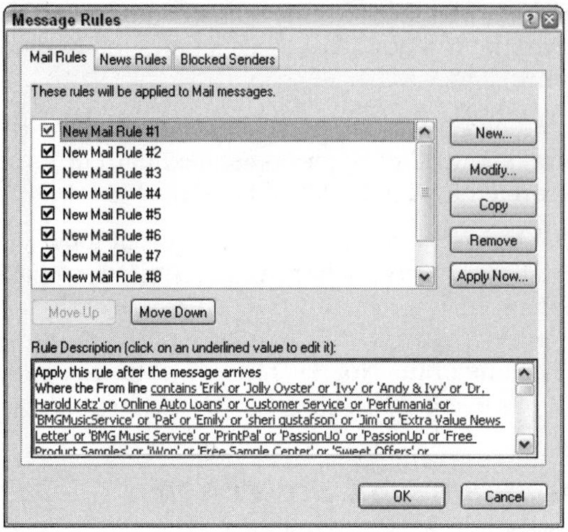

Figure 1-3:
Outlook
Express
Message
Rules.

Keeping Windows happy

It can be startling how fast Windows can morph into that really fussy old aunt who doesn't like anything — not the new mattress you bought just because of her visit and not the box of candy you wrapped yourself. You want to have a good time while she visits, but you just can't imagine how.

But unlike the fussy aunt who probably isn't really upset with you, you usually bear a certain amount of responsibility when your operating system begins to behave poorly. Think of what you do to it from the moment you unpack a new PC from its box!

If you're anything like me, you install all sorts of strange software and keep trying to get another month or two of use out of hardware someone else would have tossed ages ago. On top of it, you're usually better about checking the oil in your car and cleaning out the fridge than you are about doing proper PC maintenance. And if you're honest about the fridge, you know how many times you've found fuzzy tuna and mystery meat. So yeah, Windows often has legitimate cause to grouse.

With this in mind, several Norton products work to keep Windows running well and to make necessary maintenance both easier and more productive for you to perform:

✦ **Norton Utilities** (see "Drive diagnosis, management, maintenance, and repair," earlier in this chapter) offers WinDoctor, a special tool designed to look for common problems and less-than-great settings you've tweaked. Then the good doctor makes its best guess about what needs to be done to resolve it. Other tools it offers, like SpeedDisk, can keep Windows and your PC running at good speed.

✦ **Norton AntiVirus** protects Windows from viruses and little software gremlins that may let a hacker through a hole in the operating system's screen door. This is important, especially because some viruses are written specifically to hurt Windows or turn one of its features against you.

✦ **Norton Personal Firewall** can prevent problems from getting through your Internet connection to lock up your Windows session or foul up your online connection.

✦ **Norton GoBack** gives you the ability to jump back to the way your Windows ran at an earlier point in time, to rescue you from a mistaken change in settings or other issue that may prevent Windows from loading or running properly.

✦ **Norton Ghost** can take a smart snapshot of your system when everything is working well, so that you have a way to get back to normalcy faster after a drive disaster or complete Windows failure.

✦ **PartitionMagic** lets you divide a large-capacity hard drive into smaller parts through a process known as *partitioning* (no Ginsu carving knives required) for better organization. But did you know that, if you wanted, you could run a different operating system from each of those partitions? For example, on the PC I'm typing on right now, I have three different Windows versions installed, because I use them for different purposes.

✦ **System Optimizer,** part of Norton SystemWorks, evaluates your entire system and then tweaks it to try to improve overall PC speed and performance.

Beyond all these specifics, it just makes sense that when you have a well-maintained PC that you've properly protected from viruses and Internet intrusions, Windows will run better. Now if Norton only had a product to manage that refrigerator, eh? Alas, there is no Mold Doctor or AntiMush tool.

Making the best choice

Just because you see all these different Norton products listed in this chapter doesn't mean I expect that you're going to have each and every one of them. Almost no one does. This book has been designed to help people who have any of these major products, but presented in a way so that you can pick and choose what you read based on what applies to you. However, thinking about whether you need additional products based on what you've already read (and will read throughout this book) is smart. Determine your needs and your problems, and then decide which Norton product or products you want to buy.

If you've become something of an expert around Windows, you probably realize that Windows includes utilities to do some of the same jobs mentioned here. For example, System Restore in Windows is the same basic type of tool as Norton GoBack. In upcoming chapters, I fill you in on the differences between some of the Windows tools and those in Norton.

Chapter 2: Norton Products and PC Health

In This Chapter

✓ **Identifying some of the most common PC problems**

✓ **Figuring out how Norton products can help**

*B*ecause your PC is a great tool, you need to keep this tool in great shape. If you don't, difficulties will crop up that either rob you of precious time trying to overcome them or make your work or recreation sessions at the keyboard far less productive and enjoyable. Who wants that?

This chapter is devoted to the subject of how specific PC issues like poor maintenance and privacy can affect the time you spend on your PC. Where applicable, I tell you about the tools Windows includes to help. Then I compare the Windows tools to the Norton products, which may do a much better job for you.

The moment you unpack a new PC from its box, set it up, and begin to use it, that PC is at risk for all sorts of messy problems and failures. Many of these are caused by your own goofs (don't worry — you're not alone in this). Others may occur because of new software or hardware you install.

Over time, and depending on how much time you spend at your system, your PC can begin to demonstrate signs of wear. No, I'm not just talking about the crumbs from lunch and snacks collecting in your new keyboard or little scratches on the case either. These are more serious issues, such as:

✦ An increase in the amount of time it takes for Windows to load after you turn on your PC

✦ Odd little error messages that seem to report a problem (but aren't necessarily written in plain English so you can understand them)

✦ Windows becoming flaky and more prone to crashes or requiring more restarts to work properly

✦ Slowness in opening files and programs

✦ A hardware device that used to operate beautifully but that no longer works as it should

✦ Suspicion that you may have picked up a virus

Even a great doctor can't save everyone

Ever notice that you're not always at your most rational when you're faced with what seems like impending doom? You begin hoping for miracles. Sometimes, you even extend "the miracle network" out to your PC. You buy utility software thinking it can make that grinding noise or that faint burning smell go away.

One thing you're going to find true as you move ahead in your knowledge of PCs (ah, don't you hate it when the mystery fades?) is that there are limitations to what software can do in terms of curing some PC issues. This is particularly true when the leading suspect is an actual hardware failure, like a dying hard drive or the-bargain-modem-from-hell.

Even if you were to have the best software utilities ever created, none of them is apt to fix every single possible component (hardware, software, or the beloved "user error") that can and does go awry. What they can do — as Norton products do — is give you a fighting chance at a correct diagnosis, sometimes coupled with at least a work-around if not an all-out repair.

When the diagnosis is accurate, you can usually narrow the list of suspects from 200 to a few. That helps.

Just as when people ignore problems with their own health, pretending not to notice PC issues rarely makes them go away. All too often, the problems increase in scope and magnitude to the point where the system no longer works as needed. When you finally have to sit down and try to figure them out, the problems can be so compounded that figuring out what's happening or what you should do is difficult.

Obviously, you don't want to reach that desperate moment, which is almost guaranteed by fate to happen at the time it's least convenient (like when a big paper or report is due, or you must print a document). One of the ways to prevent this from happening is to perform proper and frequent maintenance on your system and to use helpers in the form of utilities to analyze your system and make necessary changes.

Many of the tools offered by Norton assist you in just these ways. Let's examine some of the most serious ones, and how various Norton products can rescue you from those desperate moments.

Diagnosing Drive Problems

Windows isn't terribly helpful with problems you may have with your various drives, especially your hard drive. The error messages range from the very specific to the reasonably confusing, and there is little within Windows itself to fix drive issues except for some of those caused by bad fragmentation or bad maintenance practices. (See the following section, "Cleaning Up Drives from Poor Maintenance," for more details.)

Safety in numbers

One of the beauties of using popular tools like many of the Norton products is that they've been around so long and used by so many people. That's not insignificant, either to you or within the PC industry where many companies start up and go under at blazingly fast speed.

Go online to some of the PC troubleshooting online resources and you can usually draw on the experience of a large number of folks who've already gone before you in trying to problem-solve. Another bonus is that utility developers and publishers like Symantec, the people who produce the Norton line, have used comments from many of these people to help improve their products over the years. You get the benefit of that.

Norton Utilities with its Norton Disk Doctor has been one of the leading drive diagnostic-and-repair tools available for the better part of two decades. As such, it's pretty reliable for assessing many common drive issues and will repair several that aren't actually hardware-related.

You can also use CheckIt Diagnostics, a tool included with Norton System Works to perform an evaluation of your drives along with other hardware attached to your PC.

Norton Utilities is only available as part of Norton SystemWorks for PCs; only Macintosh users can purchase it separately.

The next chapter provides you with a brief crash course in the many varied parts — hardware and software — that make up your PC.

Cleaning Up Drives from Poor Maintenance

Your drives — particularly your hard disk — are in constant use when you're working at your keyboard. Just like any device, they need maintenance to keep running properly. The longer a drive goes without adequate maintenance, the more problems it's likely to develop later on.

Here are some examples:

+ Temporary files left over from Web surfing can sit on your drive forever, consuming valuable space; they can also build up to the point where your Web browser won't run properly (you can't go forward or back), and they can affect overall system performance as well.

+ Other temporarily files created while you're working with open files on your desktop can do the same thing.

✦ Files that are open at the time Windows or a program you're running locks up or your PC powers down unexpectedly can become damaged and may not open without repair.

✦ A drive can become fragmented (more about this in a moment), which slows down the drive, the time it takes to access files stored there, and eventually, begins to drag on overall PC performance.

Disk or drive fragmentation happens to just about every hard drive. Every time your PC is turned off without properly shutting down (like when the power fails) and a program or your desktop locks up with work unsaved, the files may be written haphazardly to the drive rather than in a neat, consecutive order. Over time, this can lead to increasing slowness with which both programs and files open on your system. In extreme cases, the programs or files won't load at all. Look at Figure 2-1, and you see a drive that has a fair amount of fragmentation present, even though maintenance was performed less than a week before.

Windows provides a few utilities to help with maintenance such as Disk Cleanup and Disk Defragmenter. You can access them by choosing Start ⇨ All Programs ⇨ Accessories ⇨ System Tools and then selecting either Disk Cleanup or Disk Defragmenter.

However, the Windows utilities aren't as robust as many third-party or commercial disk utilities, like those found in Norton Utilities. In some cases, the Windows versions are stripped-down versions of commercial utilities provided merely as a convenience.

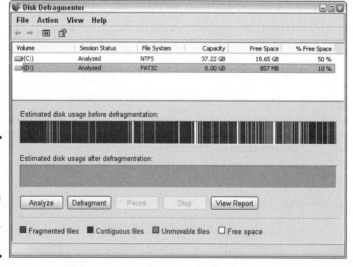

Figure 2-1:
A view of fragmented files through Windows Disk Defragmenter.

Norton SpeedDisk, for example, has often been used as the base for the Windows defragmenting tool (called Disk Defragmenter, or Defrag in different

Windows versions). But you'll find SpeedDisk itself more powerful and better able to be customized. Norton also makes it easier to automate the process (although Windows allows for automation, you have to take a couple extra steps). Automation is important because disk defragmentation, also called optimization, should be done when you're not at your desktop working.

If you have Norton SystemWorks with CleanSweep, you'll also see that this works more powerfully than the Windows tool Disk Cleanup. CleanSweep not only removes unneeded temporary and backup files, it analyzes what else you may be able to toss out because you don't use it. It can also make recommendations for software to uninstall when you never use a program or feature.

Through Norton SystemWorks, there is also a special version of the Windows Recycle Bin that makes it much easier to recover files you've deleted only to discover you actually need them (and this happens to all of us, trust me).

Wrestling with Windows Issues

Windows is a highly-integrated operating system. This means it does more than just run your software; it also manages just about every minute detail of PC operation. Through the Windows Registry (which you can find more about in Chapter 4 of Book I), Windows keeps track of your hardware, your programs, and even what type of desktop color you like. Install a printer to Windows once, and it's available in all your programs.

But that integration, which helps so much when Windows works well, can turn into a real nightmare when Windows *doesn't* work well. A bad change made in one part of Windows, like the Registry, can reverberate through whatever you try to do — that is, if you're lucky enough to get Windows to load at all.

Norton Utilities WinDoctor (discussed in detail in Chapter 5 of Book III) analyzes your Windows setup and operation to try to seek out any of a host of common problems and improper settings. It can then correct these for you automatically, often making a "best guess" at what needs to be done to repair or improve the situation at hand. It also provides you with a report of what it has diagnosed. When you suspect a problem lies primarily within Windows, this may be the best tool to use first.

After you've run WinDoctor, you may want to move on to Norton System Doctor, which examines the entire system rather than just Windows. Besides recommending or executing repairs, System Doctor gives you a fairly comprehensive analysis of everything connected to your PC.

You may want to compare both WinDoctor's and System Doctor's analysis to information present when you run the Microsoft System Information utility. To run the Microsoft System Information utility:

1. **Choose Start ⇨ Run.**

2. **In the Run window, type** msinfo32, **and then click OK.**

The System Information window, shown in Figure 2-2, appears.

3. **Explore the different screens of information by moving down and opening different listings available from the left task pane.**

But Norton products offer more than just WinDoctor and System Doctor. As I cover in the "Messed-Up PC Syndrome" section, later in this chapter, you can use products like Norton GoBack to restore your Windows setup to a previous point in time (for example, just before you made an unfortunate change). Norton Ghost lets you make a "copy" of your disk setup with Windows so you can obtain a new hard drive, and then copy this image to it to mirror your previous setup.

Also, if you need to divide a very large hard drive into multiple parts (called *logical drives* or *partitions*), either for better organization or to run more than one operating system at a time, a Norton tool called Partition Magic can help you do this without losing all the data on your drive. This is a big change from FDISK, the Windows-based partition tool, which automatically wipes out all your data as part of the partitioning process. FDISK can be pretty tough to use by less experienced folks. FDISK's replacement in Windows XP, called DiskPart, isn't much easier (see Figure 2-3). By comparison, Partition Magic is relatively friendly.

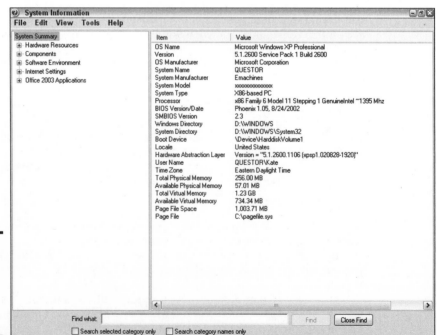

Figure 2-2:
The System
Information
tool in
Windows
XP.

Comparing notes

I've worked with tens of thousands of people needing PC help. I've also used a slew of different utilities over the years as part of my work (as much for review as for troubleshooting and repair). I want to share with you something I find very useful.

Windows includes a number of different utilities that can help you assess your system and Windows — that is, if you understand what you're looking at (the utilities don't always make it easy to comprehend). The Microsoft System Information tool is an example of this (refer to Figure 2-2).

So consider this. Try comparing notes between reports you get through Norton Utilities and those reported by Windows tools like Microsoft System Information and MSConfig. One report

may help you understand the other. Also, one utility may spot a problem that the other won't.

However, one interesting thing you'll discover is that not all the information will look identical. One utility may report your video adapter correctly, while the other one identifies it as something else altogether. Likewise, one may pick up the right amount of memory you have installed while another does not.

When you begin to notice that one utility (either Windows, Norton, or another tool) has a tendency not to report information accurately in various categories, you may not want to depend on that utility for repairs. Some utilities just seem to work better assessing certain configurations than they do others.

Did you realize that you can check through each individual change made to your system and its settings? To do this from the Windows System Information tool (run msinfo32), open the View menu and select System History.

Figure 2-3:
Windows
DiskPart for
partitioning
drives.

```
D:\WINDOWS\System32\diskpart.exe
On computer: QUESTOR

DISKPART> /?

Microsoft DiskPart version 1.0
ADD        - Add a mirror to a simple volume.
ACTIVE     - Activates the current basic partition.
ASSIGN     - Assign a drive letter or mount point to the selected volume.
BREAK      - Break a mirror set.
CLEAN      - Clear the configuration information, or all information, off the
             disk.
CONVERT    - Converts between different disk formats.
CREATE     - Create a volume or partition.
DELETE     - Delete an object.
DETAIL     - Provide details about an object.
EXIT       - Exit DiskPart.
EXTEND     - Extend a volume.
HELP       - Prints a list of commands.
IMPORT     - Imports a disk group.
LIST       - Prints out a list of objects.
ONLINE     - Online a disk that is currently marked as offline.
REM        - Does nothing. Used to comment scripts.
REMOVE     - Remove a drive letter or mount point assignment.
RESCAN     - Rescan the computer looking for disks and volumes.
RETAIN     - Place a retainer partition under a simple volume.
SELECT     - Move the focus to an object.

DISKPART>
```

Messed-Up PC Syndrome

Have you ever had those moments when you felt extreme gratitude that the PC starts up in the morning? I have, and it's really no way to begin the day.

Unless you're profoundly fortunate, you will, at one time or another, come face-to-face with a PC that seems fouled up beyond all possible redemption.

Because people tend to get fairly impatient when their systems don't operate properly, they may take drastic measures. Some immediately format the hard drive (many without backing up their data first, so the contents of the hard drive are lost). Others keep reinstalling Windows again and again. Then there are those who just go buy a new PC. But how many new PCs can you buy in a year before your budget — if not your spouse — screams?

The reality is that these "quick fixes" often involve a lot more work than people expect, sometimes far more than getting to the real source of the problem. Yet most people don't have endless free time to spend troubleshooting.

Norton product features like the SystemWorks One-Button Checkup can do a very swift analysis and perform simple repairs. This may be enough to get you back to normal operation or improve things enough so you can do more than just fret. You'll discover that most of the Norton products shave time off your troubleshooting and make up for any lack of technical expertise you feel.

 If you feel you absolutely, positively must try to start over fresh, make use of a previous snapshot of your drive made with Norton Ghost to take some of the pain and time away from the process. Use such a drive copy along with data backups you perform, and you cut your losses even more.

Saving Yourself from Sputtering Performance

Ever notice that a new car may not seem as fast or dependable after a year or two of heavy use but little maintenance? The same thing happens with your brand-new PC, although sometimes far faster (a matter of months rather than years).

Some issues take time to become noticeable. Others can be rather dramatic, leaving you saying, "But it seemed to run great yesterday! What happened?" However, so much happens on your system — usually below your radar — as you work that determining exactly what changed to cause the performance loss can be nearly impossible.

Book I
Chapter 2

Norton Products
and PC Health

An assortment of Norton tools make it possible for you to:

✦ Troubleshoot without advanced technical expertise (Norton Utilities WinDoctor and System Doctor)

✦ Perform maintenance routines like those discussed earlier (Norton Utilities SpeedDisk)

✦ Measure how well your PC measures up to the speed averages of similar systems (Norton PerformanceTest)

✦ Identify and remove viruses and other infections that affect proper operation (Norton AntiVirus)

✦ Back out of the problem so that you can get back to work (Norton GoBack)

✦ Boost overall system performance and stability (Norton Utilities System Optimizer)

Will these products catch and fix everything? Again, the answer is no. But it's worth a try before you resort to PC replacement or reformatting.

Doing Battle against Viruses, Pop-up Ads, and Spam

There isn't just one computer virus and there isn't just one type of destruction or disability caused by them. Even similarly named viruses that act roughly alike can do different types of damage. Some do no real damage at all — they just announce themselves or change the home page for your Web browser (annoying but not fatal).

Yet not every virus broadcasts the news that you've contracted it. Some viruses lurk on your system until a specific date and time and then wreak havoc (meaning that if you catch it first, you can prevent it from harming your PC). Many viruses can hurt performance, steal passwords, and even wipe out everything on your hard drive(s). Ouch!

Norton AntiVirus is probably the best known of all virus-checking utilities. It's also one of the oldest in continuous release. If you've used it before but not recently, you'll see that its coverage has expanded to help protect you when you're using instant messaging services like AOL Instant Messenger or MSN/Windows Messenger.

Norton AntiVirus can check your e-mail — both outgoing and incoming — to cut the possibility you either send or receive a virus as a file attached to e-mail. With its new Internet (mail) worm protection, you reduce your risk of becoming one of the statistics cited next time the TV news anchor reports that millions of users have received and been harmed by a new mail-based specialty virus that sends copies of itself to all the people in your address book.

Kill pop-ups before they kill you

You can't afford to treat pop-up ads as just an annoyance. Most do nothing but get in your way. However, some are designed in such a way that they can make you do something you don't want to do or won't notice you've done.

For example, when you visit a certain Web site, a pop-up ad appears, announcing, "We've detected a serious problem with your PC. Do you want us to fix it?" It's never smart to respond to these anyway. But this one is minor league genius, because regardless of whether you click "Yes" or "No," it opens a strange Web site and begins to download a file. This file could do just about anything to your system and you probably won't even know whom to blame.

Rather than respond at all to a pop-up, close it. You can usually do this by clicking the small *x* in the top-right corner of the pop-up window.

That coverage extends also to Microsoft Internet Explorer and other Web browsers. The Norton AntiVirus icon is added to Internet Explorer and provides options for your Web sessions.

If you have Norton AntiSpam, either by itself or as part of Norton Internet Security suite, take advantage of its ability to help you block unwanted e-mail. Left unchecked, unsolicited e-mail fills up your electronic mailbox. Some people get hundreds of these everyday, which makes a dent in your free hard-drive space and tries your patience. Even with special tools in place, my mailbox overflows today.

Yet that overflow isn't necessarily your biggest problem.

These messages sometimes include file attachments, which, if opened, can launch a virus or open a Web site that tries to capture unprotected information from your PC. Even without file attachments, much of what they offer — like sexually-oriented material, questionable "get rich quick" or financing schemes, and "no prescription needed" painkillers — can give you a serious case of the creeps. Why let it ruin your day, much less your hard drive?

Norton AntiSpam also blocks those miserable pop-up ads that seem to come out of nowhere when you're surfing the Web. Some of them can be hard to close and you can receive dozens of them during an otherwise pleasant evening of browsing.

Never open a file attachment from anyone you don't know. Then treat the rest with special care. Norton AntiVirus can scan your e-mail attachments before you even read your messages.

Stopping Password Insecurity

Is your head overflowing with all the passwords you need on a regular basis? Join the club!

Most basic-level computer security of any kind — whether it's access to Windows or to a special spreadsheet you use at work or using the ATM at your bank — is tied to the use of passwords or pass codes and PIN numbers, which amounts to essentially the same thing. A recent study reports that the average American may have to juggle more than two dozen of these on a semi-regular basis.

But your brain really isn't trained to remember dozens of passwords. At best, you can come up with two or three you use frequently. So, if you're like most people, you do one of three different but equally bone-headed things to compensate:

✦ Use whatever ways you can to avoid using passwords, even when you know this results in less security

✦ Choose the same passwords again and again for everything, never change them, and make those passwords incredibly simple to remember (and for others to guess)

✦ Write down your passwords somewhere you can find them again (like jotted on a sticky note attached to your monitor or keyboard), meaning that others can read them

So in the name of computer and account security, people completely defeat it by making it much easier for someone to guess or hijack their passwords. In some company settings, you can lose your job for doing something like this.

Enter Norton Password Manager, a tool designed to let you store your passwords so that you can easily access them again. While stored, these passwords are encrypted, meaning they're strategically scrambled, so that others with access to your system can't simply open Password Manager and look at your passwords.

One smart way to use the tool is for Web sites where you've had to register with a user name and password for access, as is the case with members-only and some shopping sites. You can store your passwords in Norton Password Manager and then retrieve them.

Password Manager also makes much faster work of shopping online, allowing you to establish profiles (up to three, for work, home, and another) where you can keep your name, billing and shipping addresses, and credit card numbers. Then, when you go to purchase, Password Manager can either automatically plug these in for you or make it simple to copy the information in place so you don't have to type it. For people who hate filling out forms — virtual or not — this is a big plus.

Securing Your Privacy

It's hard not to absolutely adore the Internet, because there is always something new to see or learn, with access to so very much. Web browsers and related software make it fairly simple to perform all these cool Internet-based activities without knowing your TCP/IP from your NetBEUI (before you scratch your head, these are two types of network protocols used on networks, and the Internet is the mother of all networks).

But easy-to-surf doesn't necessarily mean very private. Without realizing it, almost every time you use an Internet store, chat with friends old and new, or read the virtual edition of *The Chicago Tribune,* you're exposing private details about yourself. These details range from your geographic location to your e-mail address to what account you use on which Internet service.

Unfortunately, there are people out there who make their living — or at least entertain themselves — by trying to obtain your private data. Information about the account you use to access the Internet, for example, could give those people access to the credit card you use to pay for that account. If your Social Security number gets exposed, this gives such folks the golden access key to your financial and private life, as well as your job.

But there are also holes in the software you use for the Internet, too, that can allow people to get access to files stored on your PC. What's there to steal? You'll be amazed, even if you mostly just use your system for games and Web browsing. The credit card number you typed in at an online store may be stored in temporary browser files left behind. Perhaps you check your bank account balances online, where you also leave a record behind along with your account numbers and passwords.

By installing Norton Internet Security Suite as well as some stand-alone products, you can effectively lock out those prying eyes. Privacy and Parental Control Manager, both available from this suite, allow you to configure your system for better privacy for yourself and to limit the kinds of sites your kids can visit.

Norton Personal Firewall, available alone or as part of the suite, erects a safety buffer between your PC or home/office network and everyone else on the Internet. Norton AntiVirus can check files you download — intentionally or forced surreptitiously through a Web site. It even adds scanning options to your Web browser, as noted earlier. Norton AntiVirus can seek out and destroy spy programs that watch your every keystroke and remove adware that monitors where you travel on the Internet.

Even smaller tools such as Norton Cleanup can enhance your privacy. Cleanup will remove temporary Internet files left behind from Web surfing, files that may contain private data like account numbers or can be used to piece together an electronic record of where you've been. Earlier, you learned about how cutting down on spam and pop-up ads can help, too, which you can do through Norton AntiSpam.

When Fear of Disaster Limits What You Do

Yes, this is less of a problem with your PC and one that more directly afflicts you. Yet it's a common phenomenon, especially after you've had a few PC crises set you back with losses of time, money, and confidence. You just don't want to get in a similar jam again.

Knowing that you can depend on the Norton programs can give you some much-needed breathing room because they can either catch a disaster before it occurs, limit your damage when it does, or give you a way to start over again that involves less chaos and cursing.

Wait. Are you still unsure you want to venture down the darkly lit boulevard named Experimentation? You may have tried it before, perhaps when you heard Windows began to offer a feature called System Restore to rescue you from bad changes. Then System Restore didn't work right — or you forgot to turn it on first — and salvation never came.

You should find that using Norton GoBack rather than the Windows System Restore tool is a bit more — yet not perfectly — foolproof. It overcomes some of the limitations of System Restore.

GoBack also features a rather cool feature called SafeTry Mode, which allows you to create a special environment in which to test new software or hardware with more safety. It prevents you from making permanent changes until you get a chance to see what happens. Think of it as having someone "check" you while you exercise on a trampoline or having the driver's ed teacher with his own separate brake pedal and/or steering wheel sitting next to you as you learned to drive.

Other tools, including Norton Ghost, also lend a hand in case the safety net breaks.

System Restore, like Norton GoBack, creates a copy of your Windows setup as it exists at a particular moment in time. If you want to use programs like System Restore or Norton GoBack to record vital system information for retrieval, choose one or the other. Trying to use both simultaneously, as you'll learn in Chapter 1 of Book IV is a mistake.

When monitoring performance slows you down

Sure, that title might sound contradictory, yet it's true.

Many Norton products — including Norton Utilities and Norton AntiVirus — allow nearly constant monitoring of your system. This can be highly useful because it aids you to identify potential problems before they get past the initial stages.

However, such monitoring can create its own drag on overall PC performance. They consume desktop resources as they go. If you use more than one simultaneously, your Windows sessions may seem a lot slower when performing certain tasks.

This isn't just a problem with Norton products. Although there are some utilities out there that use very little overhead so they aren't as quick to become memory hogs, they may account for just a fraction of all the utility types out there.

Thus, throughout this book, I suggest ways you can try to use your Norton products successfully, be selective in what you choose to run continuously (often referred to as *running in the background*), while not over-burdening your PC with resource hogs that rob performance.

Chapter 3: PC Anatomy 101

In This Chapter

- Identifying your PC's major parts
- Understanding what lies between your hardware and you
- Knowing your BIOS
- Understanding why drivers are so important
- Appreciating the role of the operating system

Many of the Norton products you're reading about in this book have a lot to do with your hardware, or at least with how your PC and operating system interact with your hardware.

In some cases, a Norton product actually analyzes and attempts to repair the "software" side of your drive contents. In other cases, a Norton product can test and compare your overall system performance and that of its components against other PCs like yours. You see aspects of this with Norton Utilities, which can check your drives, your overall components and system, and how well your Windows operating system runs; with Norton Antivirus, which scans your drives and protects your system from infection; and with Norton Personal Firewall, which protects your system from intrusion.

Norton products have been designed so you don't need some great technical knowledge to get assistance. However, having a basic idea of what a PC is composed of (and I don't mean lead, plastic, alloys, and copper) and how all the major parts work together will be helpful. In this chapter, I show you what's inside that PC of yours. I also show you some common-sense solutions for fixing or troubleshooting issues that Norton products aren't likely to identify or fix.

Adding Up the Sum of the PC Parts

You've no doubt heard that there are only two parts to a PC: the hardware and the software. Others joke that the breakdown (and I mean breakdown) is more like, "the working parts and the broken parts."

Actually, I think of a PC as having four distinct parts:

✦ The hardware, beginning at the core components like the motherboard (through which almost everything else is installed) and its brain, the CPU, is installed out to your speakers and keyboard (called peripherals)

✦ The basic input/output system (BIOS), which plays team captain to your hardware

✦ The operating system (here, that's likely Windows)

✦ The applications installed (the software)

How well your PC performs for you is directly dependent on how compatible each of these parts are in working together. If they're very compatible, they'll allow you to do your thing without having to pay attention to error messages, device failures, and the occasional alarm bell. That doesn't mean everything will be perfect, but no PC should give you a coronary as you sit down at the keyboard.

In the following sections, I show you the basics of how all these parts need to work together for you. I don't get down to the nuts-and-bolts — just what matters to you in trying to manage it all. You'll find smart tips for trying to keep all parts of your PC compatible, so a new piece of hardware doesn't have to become an exercise in frustration.

Hardware

The job of hardware is to work, plain and simple. If your hardware doesn't, then you need to either fix it or replace it. I'm mentioning this because some people buy utilities like those found in the Norton products hoping that a tool will fix a broken hard drive or an aging CPU when it probably won't.

It's important to understand a few facts about today's hardware, because they relate to how you install equipment additions to your system. Today's hardware is smart; it often contains some virtual label within it to identify itself to the PC in which it's installed. Such hardware is known as Plug and Play compatible. Plug and Play is a type of technology designed to make it easier to install hardware that can work with the operating system.

When you physically install a new component, Windows should automatically detect that new hardware is present and guide you through the installation process. Plug and Play can help tremendously when you install new components, because you're not left with the job of trying to introduce a new keyboard or DVD drive to Windows. The "U.N. translator" between the hardware and your operating system is known as a *driver*. Drivers are special software created to help Windows (or other operating system) and the newly installed equipment communicate with one another.

If Windows doesn't detect new hardware automatically, you can try to help the process along by using a wizard within Windows to perform a manual scan for new attachments. To do this:

1. **Physically install (for example, plug in) your new hardware.**

2. **Locate the software that came with the hardware (usually a CD that contains drivers for the hardware as well as management and maybe even testing software), and place the CD into your CD/DVD drive.**

3. **With Windows up and running, choose Start ➪ Control Panel (or Start ➪ Settings ➪ Control Panel).**

4. **Double-click the Add New Hardware icon in the Control Panel (see Figure 3-1).**

The New Hardware Wizard launches (see Figure 3-2), and steps you through the process.

Figure 3-1:
Control
Panel's
Add New
Hardware
option.

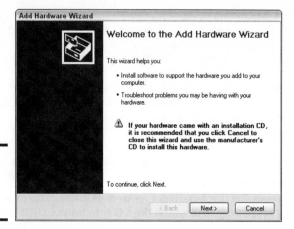

Figure 3-2:
The New
Hardware
Wizard.

BIOS

The BIOS is actually the programmable part of your PC's *motherboard,* the central circuit board to which everything else (like your CPU and memory, your hard drives, your PC display system, and the power supply) connect.

Attached to the motherboard as a chip, the job of the BIOS is to keep track of the hardware installed to the PC and assign needed resources to it. Resources are the virtual equivalent of giving each new worker a desk area and a phone line to work from.

After new hardware is installed, the BIOS juggles the equipment around everything else that is installed. Then, as Windows loads, the BIOS passes this information along to your operating system, so Windows knows what you have. This kind of information coordination is vital to having everything work well, without conflicts.

You can make changes to your BIOS, as needed. However, this is not done directly through the BIOS but through its interface, called CMOS Setup. When you first start your PC, you may notice that for just a second, you see a message displayed saying, `Press [this key] to enter Setup.` That's CMOS Setup.

Are you the designated PC repairman in your home or office? You may feel like you don't know that much more about computers than others around you, but someone always gets pressed into service as the designated troubleshooter. If you fit that description, consider taking a tour of CMOS Setup. Doing this helps acquaint you with what's set there and what it looks like. This can help a lot if you do it when the PC's behaving great so you can better spot a bad or changed setting when something goes wrong. Too often, people's first look at CMOS is when all hell is breaking loose (or instructions order them in there).

Check your PC manual or your startup screen for instructions on how to access CMOS Setup. Usually, you simply need to press a single key or set of keystrokes when the PC is first booting.

Look but don't touch or change any settings within CMOS Setup unless you're absolutely sure of what you're doing.

Operating system

Do you think you have to juggle a lot of details as part of your job? Well, you haven't seen anything until you get some idea of how much Windows must handle.

Every little setting you change, every program you install, every piece of hardware you connect all comes under the scrutiny of Windows as PC traffic cop and police chief. Because it's such a fussy cop, the printer you install once is available to all the programs in Windows and can even be shared on a network at your home or office. If Windows doesn't like something, it will let you know loudly and often. Just like a tough parent, you don't want to upset Windows, because that can make your use of the PC more difficult.

Recent versions of Windows, such as Windows XP, play a bigger and bigger role with the overall management of the PC. For example, Windows XP takes some of the detection and management of the hardware away from the BIOS. Another change is that versions like Windows XP can actually step you through preparing a new hard drive to work with your PC. This takes a lot of techie details out of the process. After you physically install the hard drive, restart the system using your Windows XP install CD, and the CD's setup walks you through steps like partitioning the drive and formatting it. If you've ever had to fool around with a boot disk and DOS commands like FDISK and FORMAT, you're going to love the ease.

Easy is a relative term

I know you may have read my comment about hardware being much easier to install now, and found yourself shaking your head. It's still not always so easy, you think.

We're both right, however. Hardware is much easier to install than it was just five or ten years ago. Then, you could be forced to do some really outlandish things trying to get a newly-installed hard drive or modem to work on your PC. However, even with the advances, every item won't install easily or work well after you install it.

The "easy install" technology isn't perfect yet, so you still may need the occasional bandage, ice pack, or headache remedy. But you can improve your odds of an easy install if you follow the advice offered later in this chapter, in the "Taking the Hard out of Hardware" section.

The keeper of all the details in Windows is called the Windows Registry, a massive index containing information about your system, hardware, and software and all the settings you've adjusted.

Applications

Working well is all most applications want to do. They depend on Windows to provide support services like the ability to print, or display certain types of fonts to display a document the way it should look, and to allow them to save and open files.

Turn to "Keeping Your Applications Running," later in this chapter, to find a few tricks to keep your applications running smoothly and to resolve problems that crop up.

Taking the Hard out of Hardware

Installing and working with hardware doesn't have to be some big challenge. To keep it from becoming so, let me tip you off to some key points that can make a difference, such as getting the right drivers and checking for compatibility ahead of time.

Checking compatibility

Before you shop for new equipment, you want to check for its compatibility with the version of Windows you're running. When you're actually in the bricks-and-mortar store or looking at an online shop, you definitely want to check the "minimum system requirements" listed for the product you purchase.

Yet meeting these minimum system requirements may not be enough. For one, manufacturers give you the *minimum* system requirements, but you probably don't want the minimum from your new product. Also, they give a range of Windows versions for which the product should work. But you want to determine that your product actually should install fine under your Windows version.

So let me show you one way to shop smarter. Microsoft has a special site called the Windows Catalog, which allows you to look up products for compatibility with Windows XP. For versions of Windows older than XP, you'll use a similar tool called the Hardware Compatibility List (HCL). You can reach both from the same Web page (www.microsoft.com/whdc/hcl/default.mspx), as shown in Figure 3-3.

To use the Windows Catalog, click See the Windows Catalog, choose your country, select the Hardware tab, and then search by product category or manufacturer, as shown in Figure 3-4.

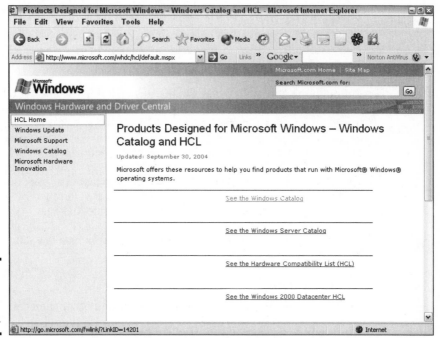

Figure 3-3:
Microsoft's
hardware
checker site.

Figure 3-4:
Using the
Windows
Catalog.

Understanding why drivers matter so much

Earlier in this chapter, I call hardware drivers the "U.N. translator" between your equipment and your operating system. Drivers do so much more than just translate.

Although the actual power lies in the device itself, the ability to tap into that power is decided by the driver. A good driver allows you to make changes through Windows — turn a feature on or off, for example — that affect how the hardware performs. Yet a bad driver can make a perfectly working piece of hardware act like it's dead as the proverbial doornail.

When you install a new piece of equipment, you install at least one driver with it. That driver helps it get picked up and correctly identified by Windows, and helps the device get listed in the Windows Device Manager.

So how do you get a bad or wrong driver? It happens a few different ways, including the following:

+ Your hardware shipped with the wrong one.

+ You somehow managed to install something other than the right driver.

+ The driver was fine to start, but an upgrade to Windows or to a new browser or another program requires a new driver to keep the device working correctly.

+ Something happened to corrupt your existing driver.

What you experience when any of the preceding happens can also vary. Some of the more commonly seen symptoms of a bad driver include the following:

+ The equipment won't work or doesn't work like it did before. You may think the device is dead.

+ The hardware is no longer seen in Windows or through Windows Device Manager.

+ An error message displays when Windows first loads or when you first try to use the device.

+ Even if the problems with a specific device seem light but flaky, Windows runs badly.

Checking for driver updates at least occasionally is smart. Some computers ship with utilities that actively scan for driver updates for hardware installed on your PC and alert you when they find them. Updates for some drivers can be found through Windows Update, a tool in Windows that lets you check Microsoft's special update site to keep your operating system current.

I show you how to perform driver updates manually in the "Updating drivers with the Device Manager" section, later in this chapter.

Putting yourself in the driver seat

Time is likely to elapse from the time a piece of hardware is manufactured and packaged with its driver and the time you purchase it. In that intervening time, the device driver for it may have been updated two, three, or more times. Drivers often get updated when a new version of Windows is released, when new applications come out, or simply to fix a problem with the last driver.

Do yourself a favor. When you buy new hardware, check the manufacturer's Web site to see if there's a later driver for your new device than what you got in the package. Be sure to look for the driver that matches your new equipment's name and model or you could get the wrong driver by mistake.

Search for an updated driver *before* you try to physically install the new device itself. If you don't do this ahead of time, you certainly want to do it if you notice a problem with the hardware after you've installed it.

Keep your drivers updated so they continue to work with you rather than against you. The difference can be between a piece of hardware that works and one that doesn't.

More about BIOS

You need to know a couple of additional things about your BIOS and how to keep it healthy and working well for you. I let you know the details in the following sections.

Keeping your BIOS healthy

One frequently-encountered problem with adding new hardware to the system or upgrading to a more recent version of Windows revolves around the age of your BIOS.

Because your BIOS plays such a key role in identifying your hardware and assigning resources to it in those seconds before Windows loads on your desktop and takes over the job, the BIOS needs to work. But at least three problems can prevent a BIOS from working properly:

✦ A virus or rogue software making changes to your BIOS, which can corrupt it. Norton AntiVirus helps protect you there.

✦ A dead CMOS battery. Located on the motherboard, this small battery stores your hardware settings and information even when the PC is turned off; if it fails, it must be replaced. You can find CMOS batteries at any store that sells batteries for consumer electronics; they cost about $3 to $7.

✦ The BIOS being out-of-date.

Because you have solutions for the first two, I'm going to zero in on the out-of-date BIOS. Your PC's first BIOS is installed at the time the motherboard is manufactured. Special software containing the BIOS is then written to a storage cell on the BIOS chip that gets mounted on the motherboard.

Normally, you don't need to worry about the age of your BIOS. Some people have the same PC for years without needing to update the BIOS. But if your BIOS is older than three to four years (and it may be about the same age as your PC), you could need an update. Without the update, your BIOS may not be ready to accept the most recent versions of Windows or work with some of the newest types of hardware.

Here's a common situation. You add one of the new high-capacity hard drives (40GB to 80GB or greater). But you discover that your PC doesn't seem to recognize all the drive real estate you have. This may be because the BIOS is too old to recognize a drive of that size. Yet you don't want to waste the space the BIOS can't see.

The best solution is to update your BIOS (see the following section).

Use a BIOS update to repair a corrupted BIOS, too.

Some drive manufacturers help you out by providing disk management software with these big drives to help an old BIOS in recognizing your new drive. But these disk managers, called *overlaps,* can get messy to work with if you need to make a change to your drive. I recommend avoiding them.

Updating your BIOS

Performing the update is a pretty easy procedure after you get the update. Because there are big differences between motherboards and BIOSes, you need to get the right BIOS for your motherboard. If you bought a name-brand PC like Dell or Gateway, the first place to check for a new BIOS is through your PC manufacturer. They can help you identify which motherboard you have and what BIOS update you need, if any.

If you can't get help through the PC manufacturer, you can use online services (like www.mrbios.com) that will help you determine your BIOS type and locate the needed update for you. The cost is often between $30 and $60.

After you get the BIOS update, you simply follow the directions for installing it. The software supplied usually makes a copy of your existing BIOS settings so that you can return to your old BIOS if you hit a snag in the updating process. With the BIOS updated, you can then breathe easier with installing new hardware and Windows upgrades.

The process of updating your hardware through the use of software, as you do with a BIOS, is called *flashing*. In this case, you're flashing your BIOS.

Knowing Your Operating System

Although this book isn't just about fixing Windows, the operating system plays a huge role with your PC. Problems with Windows can cause headaches throughout your PC use. So let's look at what Windows provides you to keep it running well. But let's start at a very basic step: knowing your Windows version and PC type.

Figuring out which version of Windows you're running

If you're one of those people who isn't even sure which version of Windows you're running, join the large club. Yet Windows can answer this question for you in a couple of steps. You can also see what type and speed of CPU you have, as well as how much memory is installed.

Here's how to check:

1. **Choose Start ⇨ Control Panel (or Start ⇨ Settings ⇨ Control Panel).**

2. **From the left side task pane, choose Classic view. Then double-click the System icon.**

    A multi-tabbed window opens to the General tab, shown in Figure 3-5.

3. **Look for your details there.**

Figure 3-5:
The General
tab offers
system info.

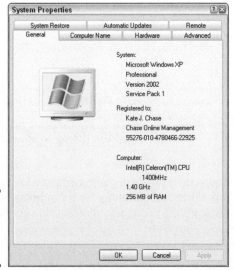

Using the Device Manager

Another tool in Windows you need to know is called Device Manager. It's where Windows keeps track of most of the hardware installed on your PC. From there, you can remove a device's driver (when you're removing the device, too) and look for warning signs of conflicting hardware.

To open Device Manager:

1. **Choose Start ⇨ Control Panel (or Start ⇨ Settings ⇨ Control Panel).**

2. **Double-click the System icon.**

3. **Select the Hardware tab (see Figure 3-6).**

4. **Click Device Manager.**

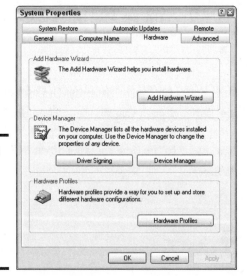

Figure 3-6:
The Hardware tab gives access to hardware details in Windows.

With Device Manager open, as shown in Figure 3-7, note that you see your hardware divided up into major categories.

5. **Click the + sign next to each to expand the listing to show all devices in that category.**

Windows has a way to alert you to problems with certain equipment listed in Device Manager. You just need to look carefully. Two symbols may appear on device listings here. These are

✦ **A red x:** This indicates a device has been disabled or doesn't seem to be working. Figure 3-8 shows a red x appearing on the entry for the standard game port. If I tried to connect gaming hardware like a joystick to the game port on the back of my PC with this red x in place, I probably wouldn't be able to use the hardware.

✦ **A yellow exclamation point:** This is seen with devices that may be in conflict (the resources they're assigned to use may be the same resources being used by another piece of hardware).

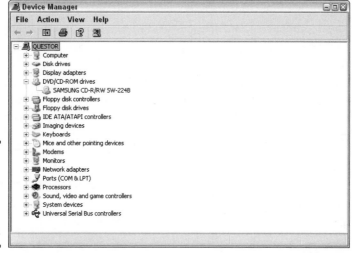

Figure 3-7:
Device
Manager
lists most
of your PC
components.

Figure 3-8:
A red x
alerts you to
a disabled
device.

Fixing problems in the Device Manager

Unfortunately, how to resolve problems you notice in the Device Manager could take a book of its own, but let me show you a couple of tricks that can help. When you see a red x, you can try to re-enable the device to see if it's just a temporary problem that disabled it. To do this:

1. **With Device Manager open, select the device with a red x, and right-click on it.**

2. **Point to Enable (see Figure 3-9).**

3. **Now look back at the Device Manager listing. Is the red x gone?**

If so, problem solved! If not, repeat these steps, but this time, select Scan for Hardware Changes.

If you still have no luck in removing the red x, you can also try updating the driver for this device (see "Updating drivers with the Device Manager"). But there's another method to try, removing the existing driver and then letting Windows redetect the device and reload the driver. This approach is what I particularly recommend for situations where you have a yellow exclamation mark.

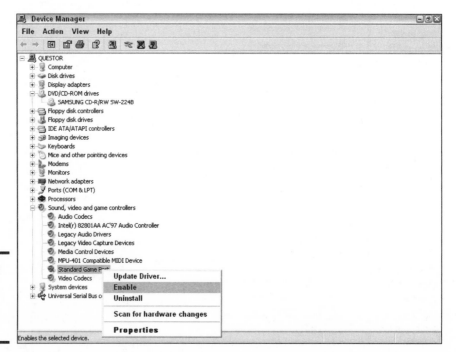

Figure 3-9:
The sub-
menu lets
you make
choices.

Before you do this, there are a few things to know. Be prepared to restart your PC, which means saving any work on your desktop and closing open applications. Also, have the disk that came with the equipment handy in case you need it to reinstall the driver after you reboot your PC.

After you're covered, here's what to do:

1. **Right-click on the problem listing in Device Manager.**

2. **Click Uninstall.**

3. **You may be asked to confirm the removal; click Yes.**

4. **Click OK to close Device Manager.**

5. **Choose Start ➪ Shutdown ➪ Restart.**

   After Windows restarts, it should detect that a new piece of hardware (actually, your old one) is installed. It should then launch the process to install it and configure it for use with Windows.

6. **As soon as Windows finishes working, return to the Device Manager and check the listing again.**

   If there's no mark on the device now (note that the red x is now gone from the game port listing in Figure 3-10), you may be OK. But try to test the hardware in some way to make sure it's working.

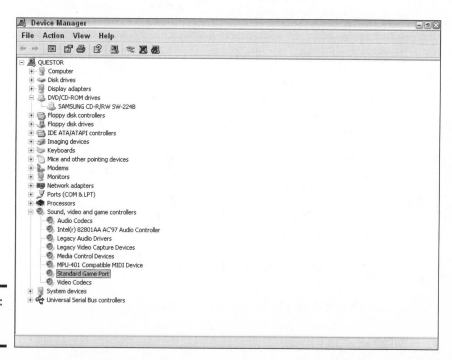

Figure 3-10:
No more
red x!

The real power of Windows

Windows is more than a choice of operating systems. It's a whole platform with really specific standards for how everything — hardware and software — must work.

With so many different hardware manufacturers and software publishers out there, it could be nearly impossible to make sure everything works together. After you buy your PC and start using it, you probably add things to it. The result is that no two PCs are identical. Your PC is apt to have very different equipment and programs installed on it than mine does, and every one of the six PCs in my office has a configuration unique to it.

I just told you two systems are rarely alike. But here's a way you can try to create a set of twins, so to speak. You can use Norton Ghost (covered in Book VIII) to make a copy of your entire setup then place that copy on the hard drive of a second PC. That other system will them have the same files, version of Windows, installed application, and custom settings as the first PC.

When you have all these differences available, you have to make sure that the similarities meet basic standards. Microsoft, as the developer of Windows, requires that all programs that call themselves Windows-compatible meet certain standards for how they install and operate. This helps you, as the person at the bottom of the PC-industry food chain, because all your programs will share common functions like printing.

Beyond that, Microsoft works with Intel, the major manufacturer of CPUs and other equipment, to create standards that must be met by hardware before any device, from modem to full PC, can call itself Windows-compatible. The Windows Catalog I show you in the "Checking compatibility" section, earlier in this chapter, is an example of the results of those tough standards. You'll only find products listed in the catalog that Microsoft says meets its criteria to work with Windows.

Updating drivers with the Device Manager

After you obtain a driver update — for example, by following my suggestion to check your hardware manufacturer's Web site for them — you'll need to install it.

First, know where your driver update is located on your drive — or have the CD available — because you'll need to tell Windows where to find it. Then follow these steps:

1. **Open Device Manager, then locate and select the device you want to update.**

2. **Right-click the device listing and choose Properties (on some Windows versions, there may be a Properties button right in Device Manager itself).**

3. **Select the Driver tab (see Figure 3-11).**

4. **Click Update Driver.**

5. **You have a choice here (see Figure 3-12): Use the default selection (install the software automatically) or install from a list or specific location. If you have the disk for the hardware, let Windows automatically install after you place the driver install disk in the appropriate drive. Click Next.**

If you chose to let it install automatically, Windows tries to look for a new driver among your files. If it doesn't find it, then go back and choose install from a list or specific location, then point Windows to the new driver you obtained.

6. **When the process says it's finished, click OK to close Device Manager.**

Figure 3-11:
Most —
but not all
devices —
have a
Driver tab.

Figure 3-12:
The Update
Driver
Wizard.

What happens if the new driver doesn't work very well? See the following section, "Going back to the previous driver."

Going back to the previous driver

Sometimes, new drivers don't work well or simply aren't compatible with other parts of your system. This experience can leave you wishing you never updated.

Here's how to return to your previous driver version.

1. **From Device Manager, select the device in question, right-click on it, and choose Properties.**

2. **Select the Driver tab again.**

3. **Click Roll Back Driver**

4. **Click Yes (see Figure 3-13).**

   Now Windows tries to remove the new driver and restore the previous driver, so you can get back to work.

Check Device Manager whenever you're having a problem with hardware, or you notice that a new driver may be working poorly.

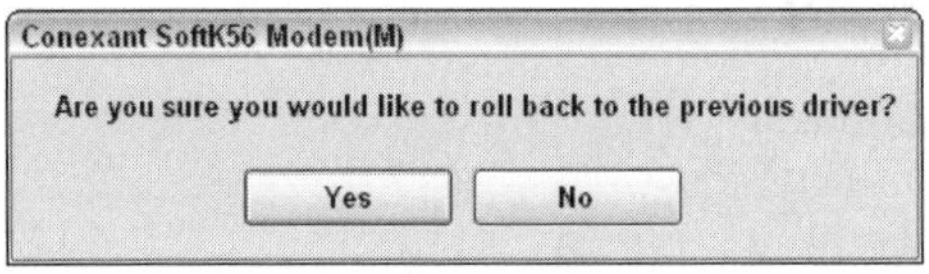

Figure 3-13: Go back to your previous driver version.

> **Conexant SoftK56 Modem(M)**
>
> Are you sure you would like to roll back to the previous driver?
>
> [Yes]   [No]

Using Windows Update

If you haven't yet acquainted yourself with Windows Update, you're missing out on security patches, driver updates, and other files that can help Windows stay healthy and well protected. This feature, available since Windows 98 Second Edition, takes a lot of the guesswork out of what files you need when you hear about a security hole in the Internet Explorer Web browser or Outlook Express that needs repair.

You'll need an available Internet connection, already on. Then choose Start ⇨ Programs or choose Start ⇨ All Programs, and note that Windows Update appears near the top of the Start menu. Click this, and the Windows Update site opens, as shown in Figure 3-14. The site scans your system to see which updates are needed, and then reports them to you. For this, choose Express Install and then click Install to let Windows and this update site decide what you need.

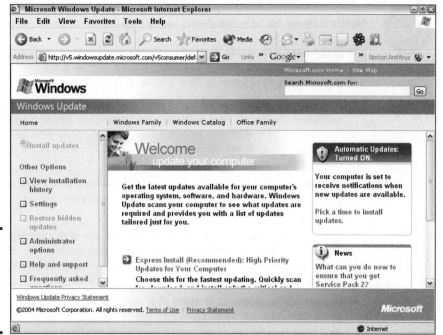

Figure 3-14:
The
Windows
Update
site scans
your PC.

Keeping Your Applications Running

Almost nothing in the PC world is worse than trying to use a program only to find that it won't run or behaves pretty strangely when it does. This gets even worse if you begin to notice problems with many other applications.

Here's a little PC truth: If one program doesn't run well, it's probably the program itself or some incompatibility between your system and this program. In this situation, you may want to uninstall the program from Windows until you can figure out where the problem lies. Or you can try uninstalling and then reinstalling it to see if it improves on the second try (which means the first install probably didn't go so well). You'll see how to uninstall a program in just a minute.

However, if multiple applications don't work, you have to start looking at the entire system. Is something happening with Windows that may be at fault? Tools in Norton products like WinDoctor or Norton System Doctor may be able to tell you whether Windows is having a core meltdown.

Here's a smart list of suggestions to try to get around problem programs:

✦ **If the problem starts during your current session, try closing all your applications and restart your PC.** It may just be a temporary issue relating to desktop resources that a fresh start will fix.

✦ **If the problem appeared right after you installed some new type of software, uninstall that software and see if the problem disappears.** If it does, check with the publisher or author of the problem software for ideas (an address is usually provided in the manual or other documentation).

✦ **Be sure you have enough memory.** If you run a lot of heavy-duty programs at once, you may be running out of desktop resources to juggle them all. Adding memory can help.

✦ **Try closing all the other applications and see if the problem persists.** Sometimes, two programs just don't like each other; they'll work fine if opened alone but not if you open the other program at the same time. Try to avoid having both programs open at once.

✦ **If a problem program is quite old, consider updating it.** The old program just may not be terribly compatible anymore with your system.

✦ **Run disk utilities like Windows Disk Defragmenter or Disk Cleanup (discussed in Chapter 2) or Norton Utilities to see if poor disk maintenance is causing problems for these applications.**

✦ **As suggested before, try removing and then reinstalling programs that don't run well.**

To remove a program and reinstall it:

1. **Be sure that you have access to the setup CD or file needed to reinstall the software.**

2. **Choose Start ⇨ Control Panel or Start ⇨ Settings ⇨ Control Panel.**

3. **Double-click the Add or Remove Programs icon.**

4. **After the list of programs opens (as shown in Figure 3-15), select the program you want to temporarily remove.**

5. **Click Change/Remove.**

6. **When asked, confirm the removal, then close the window.**

7. **Restart your PC.**

8. **Run Windows Disk Defragmenter or Norton SpeedDisk.**

9. **Reinstall the program and try it again.**

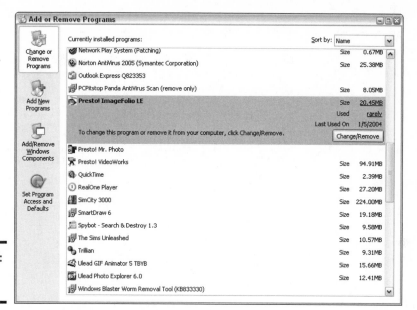

Figure 3-15:
Remove a
program.

Chapter 4: Overcoming Your Windows Pain

In This Chapter

✔ **Understanding the complexity of Windows**

✔ **Recognizing the symptoms of a fouled Windows setup**

✔ **Identifying how Norton WinDoctor and other Norton tools can diagnose and cure**

*E*ver get a new PC with Windows and just find yourself basking in the relative ease of having everything work well, respond quickly, and seem so wonderfully fresh and uncluttered? Yet after just a few months, you start to notice that the PC equivalent of the new car smell has faded. Your desktop is overflowing with icons for programs you may not even remember installing. You get these odd error messages with the kind of language that worries you but doesn't exactly tell you what to do. Nothing seems quite as fast, and it seems as though Windows startup and shutdown are stuck in molasses.

If you don't take measures to stop the decline, the situation can get so bad that you start gnashing your teeth whenever you have to start or restart your PC. But what do you do? How do you troubleshoot like a pro when you're not a Windows cardiac or brain surgeon? Maybe you even wonder if you need to buy another new PC before you remind yourself you just got one.

This chapter is all about a way you can put a team of doctors to work for you to help nurse Windows and your overall system back to health. These doctors come equipped with their own aspirin, PC x-ray devices, and suture kit.

Understanding How Windows Seems Deceptively Simple

Believe it or not, Microsoft goes out of its way to try to make the Windows operating system easy to use for any person with any level of skill. Colorful icons, wizards designed to walk you through complicated operations, and other assistants are all built in to make it possible for a novice to do many of the same things a grizzled vet can.

But good software designers will tell you that the minute a company tries to — and oh, what a phrase — "dummy software down" so that everyone can use it, the company usually also makes it much tougher to fix problems. Why? Because it has to build in safeguards to make it difficult for someone with less experience to make a fatal error that can result in transforming his big hard drive into toast or his neat Windows operation into a crazy kaleidoscopic mess.

Although Windows looks very simple from the desktop, it actually has several layers of complexity to it that can drive you nuts trying to root out the source of a problem — or multiple problems, because trouble loves to travel in packs. Part of that complexity has to do with *integration,* or the ability of everything you install to your PC and Windows to get micromanaged and be immediately available to you through your operating system. Windows strives to sweat every little detail for you so you don't have to.

Integration is great because when you hook up a new printer, digital camera, or sound system to your PC, you can take advantage of them throughout Windows. Having Windows playing mother hen and social worker to make certain things work well in unison is nice.

Yet that same integration works against you when you have a problem in Windows. Make a mistake in one place and the trouble can echo through your PC. Mess up a new printer installation and you can't print from any program. Turn off your PC without shutting down even just one time, and you can scramble everything you had open at the time into the worst plate of eggs you ever tasted.

In Chapter 2 of this book, I show you how to keep Windows healthy to prevent getting to the point where everything appears hopeless. When you reach that mark, you feel stuck. Windows help sites are great at suggesting you make a Registry change to fix a problem (Figure 4-1 shows just a tiny part of the ultra-strict Registry). Yet navigating the Registry is like entering a no-man's-land or minefield. You don't know where you can step safely. The smallest typo can send your desktop into a coma or a seizure.

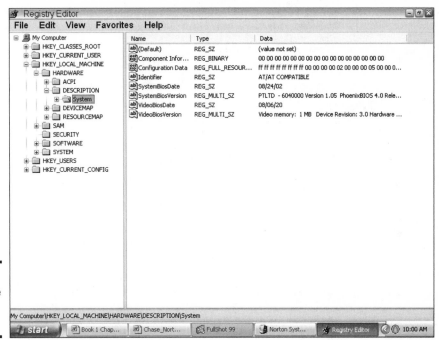

Figure 4-1:
A look at the
Windows
Registry.

If your PC were a member of the family (and mine practically is), you'd probably call in a specialist to consult. So here, you're going to hand off diagnosis and treatment to programs that are designed to spot common and uncommon problems, look for confusing or wrong Registry entries, locate missing files, and otherwise restore Windows to its former vim and vigor.

Recognizing the Mess That Can Be Left Behind

Some of the common "messes" and symptoms you can see with a troubled Windows installation include (and go ahead and get yourself some coffee, because it's a sizable list)

✦ The PC starts but Windows refuses to load.

✦ You see Registry error messages at startup.

✦ You see error messages about missing files or services or features that can't load.

✦ The Control Panel won't open or you can't click to open any of its options.

✦ You can't get on the Internet or run your Internet programs such as your Web browser — or you can't do so for long without problems.

✦ You have missing *shortcuts* (links to files placed on your desktop or in other folders to help you find and open them quickly).

✦ Double-clicking files or programs to open them does diddly-squat.

✦ All or many of your installed programs behave badly and are prone to lock up or otherwise crash.

✦ Windows won't shut down properly anymore, so you have to turn off the PC.

✦ Your hard drive churns away every time you try the simplest task.

✦ You have problems installing software and/or making changes to your settings.

✦ Whenever you try to do something, you get the *blue screen of death* (an error message indicating a potential nightmare of a problem with Windows) or you get a box telling you Windows needs to shut down.

✦ Windows only loads in *safe mode* (a protective mode used either when Windows had some serious error during its last session that it can't fix on its own or some issue cropped up during startup that prevented full loading).

Where Norton Provides Assistance

For all of the griping people do about it, Microsoft Windows usually takes a fair amount of use and abuse before it starts to cough or you begin to plan its funeral. Abuse it you do: You throw some really strange and old software and hardware onto it, try to cut every corner you can, and otherwise behave like you're trying to collect on a life insurance policy (that is, if you treat Windows the way I do).

Yet just like the person who takes a lot of guff before he really gets mad, Windows has a way of screaming bloody murder when you've fouled it enough that it really can't continue to operate without causing more harm than good. Whenever you can, you want to avoid reaching that point, as recommended in Chapter 2. When you can't, you want to consider using utilities like Norton WinDoctor (see Figure 4-2) available within Norton Utilities from the Norton SystemWorks suite.

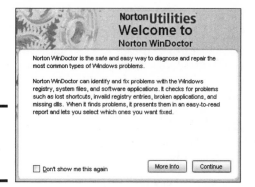

Figure 4-2:
The
WinDoctor
is in!

Using WinDoctor to cure what ails you

You can ask for your first Norton WinDoctor house call right after SystemWorks installs on your system. Let WinDoctor run, and it performs a full diagnostic workup. It evaluates your system settings and operations against its internal wisdom about optimal settings, then delivers up a full report of its findings.

You may be installing Norton SystemWorks specifically because you have a toasted system or Windows setup, so you're probably inclined to jump right into a repair. After Norton SystemWorks installs, Norton WinDoctor may load auto-magically, because it's spotted such serious issues that it can't wait to get your setup into the treatment room. If not, that's great, but you can launch it manually. You'll see that WinDoctor runs from a wizard to step you through each stage of the diagnosis and cure efforts.

Follow these steps to launch WinDoctor:

1. **Choose Start ⇨ All Programs ⇨ Norton SystemWorks (or SystemWorks Premier) ⇨ Norton Utilities ⇨ Norton WinDoctor.**

   The doctor welcomes you into his office.

2. **Click Continue.**

3. **Select how you want it to run (see Figure 4-3).**

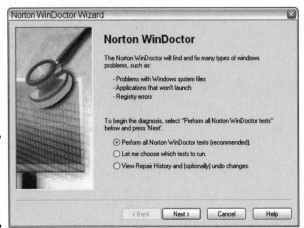

Figure 4-3:
Tell the doctor want you want to test.

I second Norton's listed recommendation: Perform all Norton WinDoctor tests.

The scan and diagnosis procedure starts; you see a status screen showing you the list of issues the doctor will help for, including drive problems, Windows Registry foul-ups, and important missing files.

When the process finishes, you see a screen reporting how many problems were found in the various diagnostics categories (see Figure 4-4).

4. Click Finish.

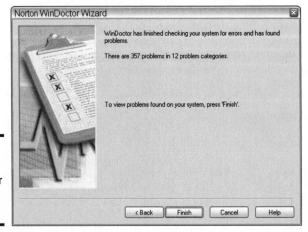

Figure 4-4:
The doctor reports your number of problems.

The treatment was a success, but the patient died

Not all repairs turn out well. WinDoctor tries its best, but the fix either doesn't fix the original issue or (worse) it created new ones.

When you spot Windows misbehaving or otherwise can tell that a newly-fixed repair is making the rest of your system seem ill, you can click the History button on the WinDoctor toolbar, select the repair you want to undo (see the figure), and then click the Undo toolbar button. Click Yes to confirm.

The wizard will then try to reverse the changes it made as part of the repair. It will also return the "fixed" to its former problem status. You can then select it and click Repair again but this time try one of the other solutions recommended there to see if you have better luck the second — or third or fourth — time around.

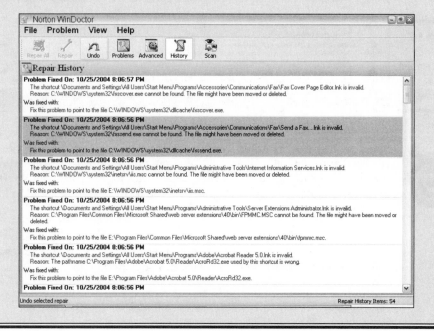

With the wizard finished, it's time to investigate the bad news. A window opens showing a category of problems (see Figure 4-5). The problem window actually gives you the tools you need to find out more information about your issues as well as to repair (or even ignore) them. Click on a problem listing and see what's there. With the listing selected, click Details to have additional information about the issue appear at the bottom of the screen.

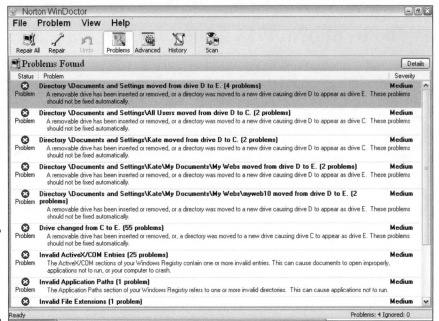

Figure 4-5:
Your
problem and
repair
window.

Some problems — as noted from their listings — suggest they not be repaired automatically. When you see that, you simply select the listing you want to work on and then click Repair (not Repair All) to let WinDoctor start its treatment on that particular problem (the one that shouldn't be done automatically).

Choose Repair, and a Repair Solutions window appears like that shown in Figure 4-6. It usually offers two or more possible repair options to resolve the problem. Select the one you want and click Repair.

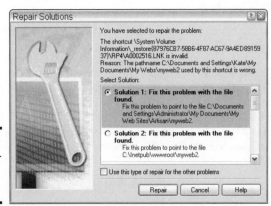

Figure 4-6:
Choose your
suggested
solution.

When the repair is complete, you'll notice the problem category listing changes from problem to a green checkmark labeled Fixed. Proceed through to address other problems that recommend *not* using automatic repair then, when you're down to just the simple ones, click the Repair All button on the toolbar to fix the rest.

Right after you fix problems and make Windows run better is an excellent time to back up your files, record your system as it is right now using either Windows System Restore or Norton GoBack, or create a drive image. Chapter 6 shows you how to back up and restore, while Book IV takes you through Norton Ghost.

You can find out far more about using Norton WinDoctor in Chapter 5 of Book III.

Taking a look at your other options

There are other tools in Norton SystemWorks that can help both Windows and your overall system in general. These include Norton System Doctor and Norton Disk Doctor. Norton AntiVirus can help keep your system free of computer infections and malicious software, which keeps Windows up and running every day.

Other helpful Norton Utilities' tools like Norton System Doctor are covered elsewhere in Book III.

Chapter 5: Detecting the Differences between Norton Suites and Standalones

*V*isit your Norton product site at www.symantec.com. Look under Products and Services, and you'll see they've been very busy. They offer an incredible array of products aimed at specific audiences (such as the corporate or enterprise versus the home/small-business folks), addressing particular needs like virus protection, system diagnostics, and drive utilities.

Even for those who use these products daily and have for many years, keeping them straight can be difficult. The product name isn't all that matters either, because some of the differences relate to which version you use (like 2003 or 2005) or which tools are included in which *suites* (packages of multiple tools). This chapter is designed to help you get a handle on important differences among the Norton products as well as on how to figure out which product and version you have.

Understanding How Norton Products Are Packaged

I'm not talking about the pretty boxes these products come in, but what's inside each. Norton products come one of two ways:

✦ As a separate package (called a *standalone*)

✦ As a *suite,* which amounts to a bundle of separate packages

In addition, the products are packaged to reflect the type of environment where you'll use them. These include

✦ Home and small office

✦ Small business (usually larger than a few people)

✦ Enterprise (usually large businesses and organizations where operations are directly tied to and depend on computer services)

The products aren't always exactly the same; each product is engineered specifically for the needs of that group. For example, the virus-checking in a busy corporate environment has to take into account situations in which e-mails and files are passing among hundreds or thousands of people simultaneously — as opposed to just the handful of people operating in a home or home-office environment. Corporate and company *servers* (where computing services are based) may handle all the virus-checking for every employee, because the company doesn't want anything to get out to their workers' individual PCs.

Figuring out the differences between standalones and suites

Except for the fact that a suite may have complementary extra tools available to you, there usually is no real difference between using a product like Norton AntiVirus as a standalone or as part of a suite. This is great because you don't have to relearn the tool or the *interface* (the look of the desktop application as you use it). In fact, the only differences you'll usually encounter are between versions. Even then, smart software producers try not to reinvent the wheel too much with each new version, because that just makes it harder for loyal, longtime customers to get acquainted with the new layout.

Many Norton products are available both in a separate package as well as bundled into a suite. Examples of these include

✦ Norton AntiVirus (standalone or bundled both in SystemWorks and Norton Internet Suite)

✦ Norton Personal Firewall (standalone or bundled in Norton Internet Suite)

✦ Norton Password Manager (standalone or bundled in Norton Internet Suite)

However, a small number of products are only available rolled into one of the suites; they aren't packaged separately for purchase. Only a few products are like this (for example, the Privacy Control and Parental Control tools found in different versions of Norton Internet Suite). One famous package also falls into this category: Norton Utilities. Norton Utilities is a very popular set of tools that was always available as a separate product. No more! If you're on a PC, you have to buy Norton SystemWorks to get Norton Utilities.

Like most software companies, Symantec experiments with its packaging to try new combinations in its suites. Sometimes it takes a product that is only available as part of a suite and makes it available as a standalone. So it's possible that next year Norton Utilities may be available again as a separate package. You never know. . . .

Deciding whether to buy a suite or a standalone

One major advantage of suites for the home or small-office user is that suites allow you to get a number of utilities at once. You'll probably pay less for them in these bundles than you would if you bought each product separately.

If you find you need or want to add to your Norton products, you may wonder whether it makes more sense to buy a tool separately or as part of a suite. So let me offer you a few suggestions:

✦ If you're absolutely interested in just one product, buy that product in a separate package (if it's available).

✦ If your current Norton tools are older and you're shopping for an additional tool to add to what you already have, investigate whether you can buy a suite that gives you not only the new tool you want, but also an upgrade of your older tools.

✦ Compare the products available in each suite. If you know you want one of the suite's tools, but you think there's a good chance you may wind up using two or three others, then purchasing the suite is a better move.

✦ Shop aggressively for the best pricing. I've seen online stores sell a suite containing a product I wanted at a special price that was 10 to 20 percent less than it would have cost me to purchase that one product alone.

Identifying Which Products You Already Have

Don't have any idea which Norton products you're running? If so, you may not know which versions of these products you have either. In this section, I show you two ways you can see what products you have and which version you have (short of hunting down the original package to look, of course).

Through the Start menu

If you choose Start ➪ All Programs, the tried-and-true All Programs menu appears. Scan down the list for your Norton product name. After you locate your first Norton product, you can click to look at its submenu. The version — like 2004 or 2005 — is usually listed right within the product name.

Products installed as part of a suite, like Norton SystemWorks, will probably be listed in the All Programs menu as Norton SystemWorks. Click on this and you'll see the individual products, such as Norton Utilities, listed on a submenu.

Keeping track of what you've got

I've been using different Norton products since the mid to late 1980s (there really *were* computers back in those dark ages). I've also helped users learn and work with them for well over a decade.

Until recently, you could walk almost anywhere in my office complex (and here, that's two or three buildings at my home), and discover so many different versions lying around that locating the right one could be a challenge.

You want to be smarter than that. Keep your Norton products together and organized. If you choose to keep some older versions around, label them and place them away from your most current versions. In Chapter 1 of Book II, I share why you have to be careful using older Norton versions mixed with newer ones on recent versions of Windows.

From the About window

If you have trouble finding your product version through the Start menu (see the preceding section), you can go through the About window for your product. Exactly how you find your About window in Norton differs slightly among products and product versions, but here's the bottom line: Open the product, and at the top-right of the window you'll see either Help or Help & Support. Choose whichever one of these you see. Figure 5-1 shows the menu that appears if you have the Help & Support option. Then choose About *<this product>* (where *<this product>* is the name of the product you're using). A new window opens, as shown in Figure 5-2. Here, it reports I'm running Norton AntiVirus 2005.

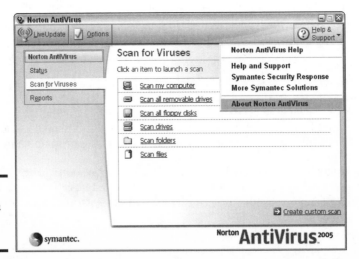

Figure 5-1: The Help & Support menu.

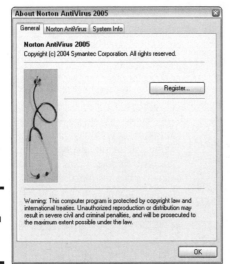

Figure 5-2:
Details from
the About
window.

Some Norton products' About windows have a feature that you won't see everywhere. Glance back at Figure 5-2 and you see there is more than one tab in the About window. Click the System Info tab, and you see details about your PC, as shown in Figure 5-3. These details include how busy your memory is (memory utilization %) and how much disk space you have available on the drive where Norton is installed. Just some interesting information you may be curious about.

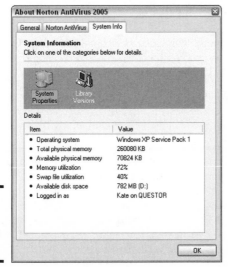

Figure 5-3:
Norton's
System Info
window.

TIP

Get organized

Sure, some Norton products you install and use all the time. But you may have others that you don't use all that often. That's likely true for many of your special utilities.

The problem comes when you have an emergency. You need to quickly locate critical items like a particular Norton product, maybe your Norton AntiVirus emergency disk set, or even your Windows install CD.

But where are they? Scattered to the wind? This isn't going to make coping with your emergency any easier, is it?

Try this: Set aside a shelf, a cabinet, a large drawer, or even a little closet space somewhere in your office or home office to put together everything you need for an emergency. Make sure everything you store there is properly labeled, too. The following table shows a list of some of the items you'll want to bring together into this one location for easy access — sort of an emergency first-aid kit or your PC.

Tool Category	What You Need
Emergency disks	Includes the emergency disk set you create with Norton AntiVirus, boot disks, or an emergency disk that may have come with your computer.
Installation CDs	Make sure you have the installation CD for your copy of Windows, along with the master CDs for Norton products and other utilities you use. Some of these can be used to boot the PC when it won't start on its own.
Backups and drive copies	If you create backups of your files (as you should) or make a drive image using a product like Norton Ghost, keep these together in your emergency kit and be sure they're fully labeled (date, contents) so you don't have to guess what you have.
Driver and device software	Be smart — keep in this emergency kit all the CDs or disks that come with new hardware you install, so that if you have to reinstall a device after a problem, you can do so without fuss.
PC manual or documentation	Not all PCs come with a great manual, but they usually offer some kind of documentation. This can help you identify its parts. Keep this handy. But if you can't find it, you can visit the PC manufacturer's Web site and locate details about your model.
Hardware tools	Whether you need to remove the cover on your PC or just firmly attach some external device, having a small set of tools available that aren't part of some large, messy household tool collection makes sense. A good tool kit to start with includes a small but powerful flashlight; a couple of screwdrivers, including one with a Phillips head (the one with the cross); and perhaps a can of compressed air (used to remove dust from internal PC components where dust can gather and be tough to remove).

Chapter 6: Taking Precautions

In This Chapter

✔ **Understanding what safety measures you can take**

✔ **Checking for compatibility**

✔ **Backing up your files**

✔ **Restoring your PC after a problem**

*E*ver notice that Murphy's law ("everything that can go wrong will") seems to apply beautifully to PCs? Not only that, but you can almost count on having a crisis happen on an evening, weekend, or holiday when the tech-support lines are closed or it's otherwise tough to find help.

With this in mind, you have to prepare to deal with some glitch or change that some part of your system won't like whenever you install any new hardware or software. If you don't, you're stuck up the creek without that proverbial paddle — and Murphy won't be there to help either.

Even though Norton products are carefully designed and tested before they're released and even though many of these provide tools to protect or fix your system, you may hit a snag with them. That snag could be anything from an Internet account that won't connect anymore, to Internet tools that won't run, all the way to Windows screaming error messages at you.

This chapter is all about taking precautions such as looking for potential problems before they blow up on you. Oh yeah, about that backup you keep meaning to run? It's time. That backup could help you get back up and running the way you were before you installed your Norton product(s) or tweaked the way it operates.

Checking Compatibility

Unless you're a big fan of surprises, you probably want to avoid getting into a jam. Although you're going to run backups on your system and be able to restore them, if needed, steering around trouble is just easier.

Not everyone buys the latest version of a Norton product. At any given time, it's usually easier — and cheaper — to buy older versions even after a brand-spanking-new version has just been released. In fact, when an update becomes available, many stores immediately discount their older copies and place them in a discount rack where they hope you'll spot it and lighten their old inventory.

Getting a previous version doesn't have to be a problem. To be sure it doesn't turn into one, you need to check compatibility between any product you buy and your Windows version, as well as other programs and tools you already have installed.

Between Norton and your Windows version

Whether you shop online or in a store, you'll usually see information listed in an ad or on the product box labeled "Minimum System Requirements." That box tells you what versions of Windows the software is designed to run under. Take a moment to check this to be sure the product and your version of Windows will be happy together.

Besides the Windows version itself, it helps to know what file system type your PC uses. Normally, the file type is something you don't have to worry about too much because Windows takes care of it all. However, certain Norton products (like the disk tools available in Norton SystemWorks — especially with older versions) may not be compatible with your file system type. In these cases, the file system type will be noted under the Minimum System Requirements or compatibility info on the package or in the online product details.

The two file system types in regular use with Windows today are

✦ **FAT32:** The most common file system type

✦ **NTFS:** A more secure file system type used in Windows NT, Windows 2000, and Windows XP

Here's how to check for the file system type used on your PC:

1. **Go to My Computer and right-click on the icon for your C: or primary hard drive.**

2. **Select Properties.**

3. **Look at the Properties window, under File System, to see the type you have (see Figure 6-1).**

4. **Repeat Steps 2 and 3 for any additional hard drives.**

   If you happen to have two or more hard drives and have more than one version of Windows installed, it's possible that one hard drive uses one file system type while the second uses another.

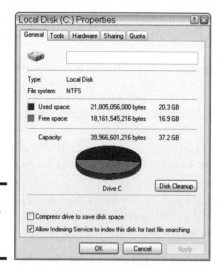

Figure 6-1:
Check your
file system
type.

Compare the file system type against the information for your Norton product or before you install any *disk-based utility* (a utility that acts to try to diagnose or fix one of your disk drives). Using a disk tool not designed to work with your file system type is more dangerous than playing Russian roulette: In extreme cases, it can turn the contents of a hard drive into Egyptian hieroglyphs, but with your files rendered nowhere near as precious.

Between Norton and what else you have installed

With many tens of thousands of programs available in the marketplace, there's always a chance you'll happen to combine two that really, truly, and loudly hate one another. Who wants to have the virtual equivalent of a marital spat playing out while you're trying to work or at least advance to the next level of Doom 3?

The beauty of Norton products is that they've been around a long time, with lots of testing, so they've been designed and retooled around known issues with other software. Yet with new software released every day, you still have no take-it-to-the-bank guarantee.

Also, because many Norton products — including Norton Personal Firewall and Norton AntiVirus — load each time you start your PC, and run in the background while you work with other programs, your risk that you'll load an incompatible program with Norton running is even greater.

Here's how you can find out about and prepare for incompatibilities:

✦ **When you buy or download new software, look in the documentation —
sometimes a printed booklet and sometimes a README file installed**

with the program — to locate a section marked **"Known Issues"** or **"Read Before You Run."** This documentation often spells out known conflicts and can suggest workarounds.

+ **After you install a new program, run it to see how it performs.** If it immediately begins to lock up or cause problems, you may want to temporarily uninstall or remove the program until you can determine what's wrong. Use Add or Remove Programs in the Control Panel to remove installed software.

+ **Use precautions like backing up and using tools like System Restore noted later in this chapter to revert back to an old setup if the conflict is severe.**

+ **Don't run programs or tools that do the same type of jobs as Norton products while the Norton tool is loaded.** Disable or close one while you run the other.

Most of these recommendations are pretty self-explanatory, but let me tell you a bit more about the last one. Several Norton tools perform a very similar function to Windows utilities or to programs from other software publishers. When this is the case, you probably don't want to run two or more of the same tools at once, regardless of whether you spot a problem, because they can eat up desktop resources you need to do other things.

Some examples of Windows utilities that do the same job as Norton products are shown in Table 6-1. When you know you want to run one tool, be sure to turn off the other.

Table 6-1	Similar Windows and Norton Tools	
Windows Tool	*Norton Tool*	*Job It Performs*
Disk Defragmenter	Speed Disk	Optimizes your hard drive for better performance
Internet Connection Firewall	Norton Personal Firewall	Protects your Internet connection
System Restore	GoBack	Records system settings you can later restore

Backing Up Your System

When you back up your system, you copy some or all of the files into one special larger file, called a *backup archive*. The files are all stored together and compressed into a smaller size. The difference between backing up and just copying files is that some types of backups can be used to completely restore your system after a problem stops Windows from running properly.

What utility you use to back up your files is entirely up to you. Your choices include the following:

✦ The Windows Backup tool

✦ Backup software that came with your recordable or rewritable CD or DVD drive

✦ Other products like the backup tool in SystemWorks

I don't spend much time discussing using Norton products in this chapter, because you may not have a Norton backup tool and because making a backup before you make any big change, like adding and running utilities, is smart. So you may want to create your first major backup *before* you install your Norton products.

After your Norton software is installed, you can use:

✦ Norton Ghost to create a drive copy

✦ Norton Ghost to perform backups

✦ Norton GoBack to restore your system to an earlier point in time

Did you know you can schedule a backup of files to happen when you're away from the keyboard? You can have your backup software run automatically to make copies of key files which you can then store on a recordable CD or DVD (you can copy the files onto a disc later on, after you get back to the PC). I show you how to schedule using Windows Backup here, but you can also refer to Book V to see how to schedule backups using Norton Ghost.

Don't have time to back up?

If you're like most PC users, you probably don't have a regular system in place to back up your files in case a crisis strikes. Maybe you keep telling yourself you should, but you're having trouble finding 30 minutes or an hour to do it. The funny thing about time is that you lose more of it when a new installation causes you problems or a hard-drive failure hits and you don't have a backup. Some productivity studies tell us that having access to a backup of your files can get you back to work 5, 10, or 20 times faster than it takes to troubleshoot a problem preventing you from using your PC.

Still think you don't have time?

Data-recovery services aren't cheap

If you're tempted to avoid doing a full backup before you install your Norton products or soon thereafter, reconsider.

Many companies provide data-recovery services. These businesses specialize in pulling files and bits of information off damaged drives. They can do a remarkable job, too, recovering material from drives that have been wiped clean, flooded, burned, and even run over by a vehicle (believe it or not, it happens).

But these services can be very time-intensive and that usually leads to a big bill. The tab can start at a few hundred dollars then easily jump into the thousands for a large drive where you need to restore as much as possible. That's really priced out of the range of most people and most situations. Even if the some of the drive contents can be recovered, you may face trying to salvage your work by piecing bits back together like a puzzle. Ouch!

Unless you have a lot of money or you create or store very few important, one-of-a-kind files on your PC and have a system for regularly copying these few files elsewhere for safety, do the backups. They take far less time and effort than what you'll expend if you get caught without them.

When to back up

Think of backups as something you need to do regularly, sort of in the same league with flossing your teeth and getting routine exercise. If you're a very busy person at the keyboard, you may want to perform a full backup once a week or so, and then do intermediate backups (see the "Types of backups" section) in between. In addition, plan to run a backup before you make any big change to Windows or your PC.

Performing a backup becomes especially important before you use a Norton tool that makes serious changes to your system. The best example of this is Norton PartitionMagic. Although PartitionMagic is designed to let you create, change, or delete partitions on your hard drive without accidentally or deliberately messing with the contents of any files stored on the drive, why take unnecessary risks? Sure, you can cross your fingers and hope all goes well but if you lose that big paper for school or the only copy of your great American novel, you won't be a happy camper.

Using Windows Backup

The Windows Backup tool is available to everyone, so I'll start by showing you how to use it to perform your backup. If you want to use another backup tool, start it according to its directions.

Follow these steps to begin your backup:

1. **Choose Start ➪ All Programs ➪ Accessories ➪ System Tools ➪ Backup.**

This launches the Backup or Restore Wizard (shown in Figure 6-2) which steps you through the process of creating backups and using those backups to restore the system (when needed).

Figure 6-2:
The Backup
or Restore
Wizard.

2. **If you have a floppy drive, find a good, blank floppy disk, and insert it in your floppy drive. If you don't have a floppy drive, look for the Backup Type, Destination, and Name window and select a different drive such as a second hard disk.**

Even if you're not backing up to a floppy drive (which you probably won't), Windows wants to store certain information on a floppy when you choose to back up all information on your system. You'll need this floppy to restore your backup regardless of where your backup file itself is stored.

3. **Click Next.**

4. **Make sure that Back Up Files and Settings is selected, and click Next.**

5. **From the What to Back Up window (shown in Figure 6-3), choose the type of backup you want to perform, and click Next.**

If this is your first backup, you probably want All Information on This Computer.

Now you're asked where to store the backup. If you have a floppy drive, this is selected automatically (although a floppy disk won't hold much information).

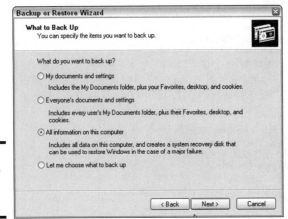

Figure 6-3:
Select your
desired
backup.

6. In the Choose a Place to Save Your Backup drop-down list, select Let Me Choose a Location Not Listed Here (see Figure 6-4).

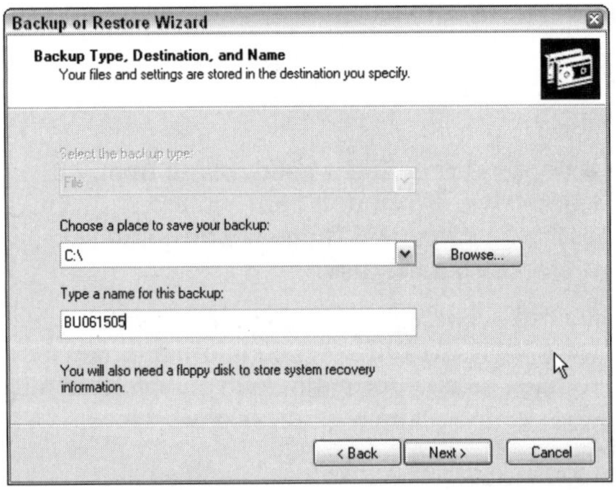

Figure 6-4:
Choose
where to
store the
backup.

7. Click Browse and locate the drive or folder where you want to store your backup.

8. Click within the box below Type a Name for This Backup and type something descriptive (for example, BU061505 would automatically tell you that you created the backup on June 15, 2005).

9. Click Next.

A final window appears with the information about this backup file (see Figure 6-5).

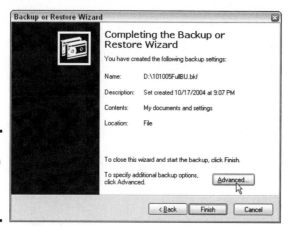

Figure 6-5:
Your backup
info before
the backup
begins.

10. **Click Advanced and you can set your backup type.**

See "Types of backup" for more information.

11. **To start your backup, click Finish.**

A backup progress window opens on your desktop, like the one shown
in Figure 6-6.

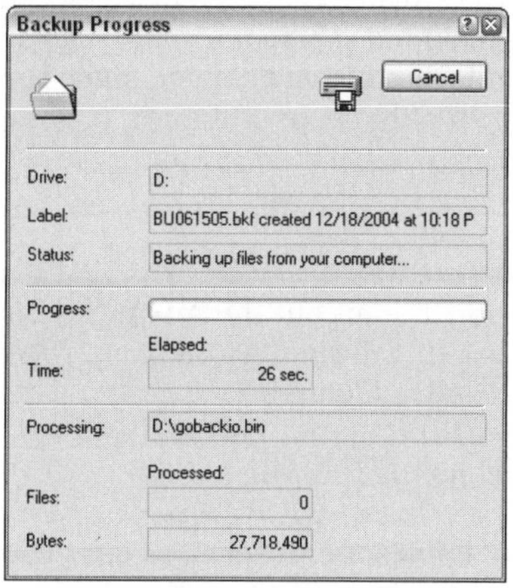

Figure 6-6:
Chart your
progress.

At the end of the process, you receive a message stating your backup is
complete.

12. **Click Close to shut the backup window or, to see details about your
backup, click Report.**

Details open in a Notepad window (see Figure 6-7).

Backup files in Windows are saved with the file extension *.bkf. If you use the name BU061505 for your backup, the full file name is BU061505.bkf. This is important to know if you need to use the Windows Search tool (choose Start ➪ Search) to locate a backup you created.

When you back up files on your PC, Windows sets a mark — called the *archive attribute* — on each file included. This information is used to decide which files have been copied and which have changed since the last time they were backed up. Not all types of backups will mark your files, as I explain in the following section.

Types of backup

In Step 10 of the preceding section, I point out the Advanced button on the backup information window. Click this during the backup procedure and you can set your backup type, as shown in Figure 6-8.

The Windows backup types include the following:

✦ **Normal:** Creates a full set of copies for all selected files; the most recent Normal-type backup can be used to restore your system.

✦ **Copy:** Use this to copy selected files but not mark them as backed up (helpful when you're spot-copying files yet want these same files included in a later backup).

✦ **Incremental:** Choose this when you want to back up files that have been added or changed since your last normal backup; if you need to restore your system; you'll need your last normal backup plus any incremental backups.

Figure 6-8:
Choose your
backup
type.

♦ **Differential:** Copies only those files that have been added or changed
since you last did a normal or incremental backup, but doesn't mark
these files as backed up; they'll be picked up during your next Normal/
Incremental backup.

♦ **Daily:** Use this between normal or incremental backups when you want
to regularly back up new files created each day (great when you start
many new files on a daily basis).

If you don't select a specific type, Normal is used by default.

After you choose your type, follow these steps:

1. **Click Next.**

The How to Back Up window opens (see Figure 6-9).

Figure 6-9:
Choose
Verify Data
After
Backup to
have
Windows
check the
data on the
backup.

2. **Select Verify Data After Backup, then click Next.**

This step adds a few extra minutes to the process but helps make sure you have a reliable backup in hand if disaster strikes.

3. **From Backup Options, choose whether to append (add to) this backup to an existing backup file or use it to replace an existing backup with the same name, then click Next.**

The When to Back Up window appears (see Figure 6-10).

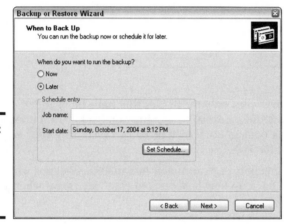

Figure 6-10: Back up now or later, on a schedule you set.

4. **Select Now to run immediately or select Later.**

If you click Now, jump to Step 5. If you select Later, type a name for the "job" (backup) and then click Set Schedule to assign a time and date to perform the backup as shown in Figure 6-11.

5. **Click OK and then click Next.**

A window pops up asking you to type your password (see Figure 6-12). This refers to the password (if you use one) needed to log on to Windows; by supplying the password, Windows can come back from a screensaver or idle mode when you aren't around and start the backup even if you're not there to type your password.

6. **Type your password and confirm it, then click OK, or just click OK if you don't use a logon password.**

7. **Click Finish.**

If you use a floppy, CD, DVD, or other type of removable disc to back up, remember to label it with the backup name and date. Then store it safely away with your other important, must-keep discs.

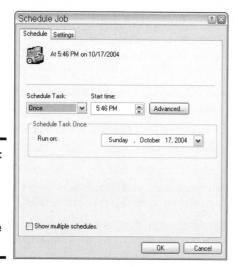

Figure 6-11:
Select a
time, date,
and how
often to
perform the
backup.

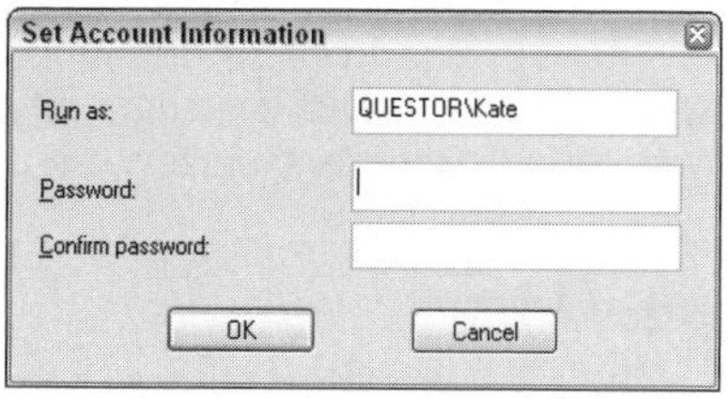

Figure 6-12:
Type in your
password
when you're
scheduling
later
backups.

Scheduling Windows Backup

Putting your backup routine on a schedule means it remembers to run even when you don't. Though Book V shows you how to set this up if you're using Norton Ghost for backups, here you're going to be blown away by how easy this is to set up for Windows Backup. Because performing backups at least once a week is the smart way to go, that's what I do here.

Follow these steps:

1. **Choose Start ➪ All Programs ➪ Accessories ➪ System Tools ➪ Scheduled Tasks.**

The Scheduled Task window opens.

2. **Click Next.**

3. **From the list of applications you can schedule (gosh, I'm starting to sound so organized), select Backup and then click Next.**

The name of the task will be listed near the top of the next window as Backup.

4. **If you want a different title for it, click inside the window and type a new name.**

5. **Below, select Weekly to set this for once-a-week operation, and click Next.**

6. **Select a time (preferably when you're not at your desktop) then select the day of the week you want to run this.**

    My favorite is Friday or Saturday. Just be sure it's a time when your PC is up and working even if you aren't

7. **Click Next.**

8. **Type the user name and password you supply whenever Windows (re)starts, then type the password again to confirm this.**

    By setting these up ahead, you don't have to be at your keyboard to provide them, so the backup can run in what's called "unattended mode."

9. **Click Next.**

10. **Click Finish.**

Remember the Scheduled Task option in Windows for any kind of utility or tool that needs to run regularly, like Windows Disk Defragmenter. Norton products, by comparison, have their own schedule setter and keeper.

Where to store your backups

When you make a copy of your house key, you don't store the spare on your main key ring, do you? You set it aside somewhere safe so you can get to it if you lose your main key. The same idea holds for your backups.

Even if you've got enough free hard-drive space and/or more than one hard drive installed on your PC, you don't want to store your only backup copy right on the system itself. Sure, you can keep one copy on your hard drive, but have another one available off the drive, such as written to a CD or DVD disc that you can store safely in another room, another building, even at the office (if you back up at home) or at home (if you back up at your office).

Be sure to label your backups by date with notes about anything especially important stored in that backup. This way, you can easily find your most recent backup or spot a backup that contains a really crucial file you need.

Add a fine or medium point Sharpie or other permanent marker to your pot of pens and pencils. They do a great job of labeling CDs and DVDs. A thick-point marker makes it tough to write crisply in the small space. You can also find specialty pens just for writing on CDs and DVDs; check an office supply store.

Restoring from a backup

The same Backup or Restore Wizard you used to create your backup also steps you through what you need to restore one of these backups to recover from bad changes or a system problem. To launch the wizard:

1. **Choose Start ➪ All Programs ➪ Accessories ➪ System Tools ➪ Backup, and click Next.**

When you restore from a backup, you may lose any changes to files or programs made since you last performed a backup.

2. **Have your backup files handy.**

If they're stored on a separate disc like a floppy or CD, insert the disc in the appropriate drive.

3. **Click Restore Files and Settings.**

4. **In the What to Restore window, select the backup file to restore from those listed on the right-hand side, as shown in Figure 6-13.**

If you don't see your backups listed there, click Browse and locate them.

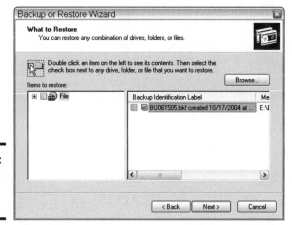

Figure 6-13:
Choose the backup to restore.

After you choose your backup, the files or drives included in that backup appear in the right-hand window. Keep scrolling down until you see what you want to restore.

5. **Click to check any or all files to restore (see Figure 6-14), then click Next.**

6. **Click Finish.**

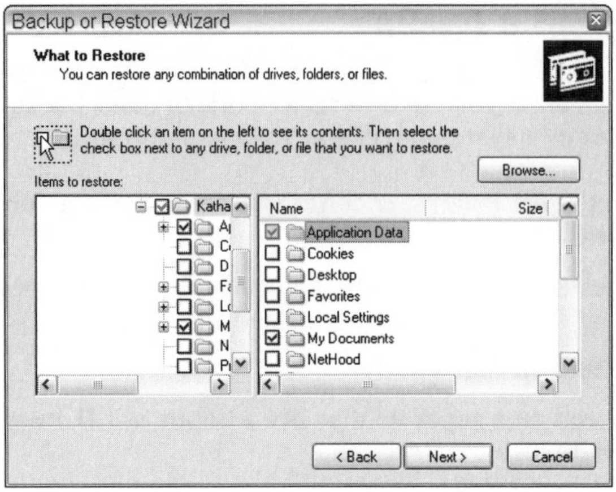

Figure 6-14:
Click to
check files
you want
restored.

7. **From the How to Restore window, choose the option you want to use (Leave Existing Files is your best choice), as shown in Figure 6-15.**

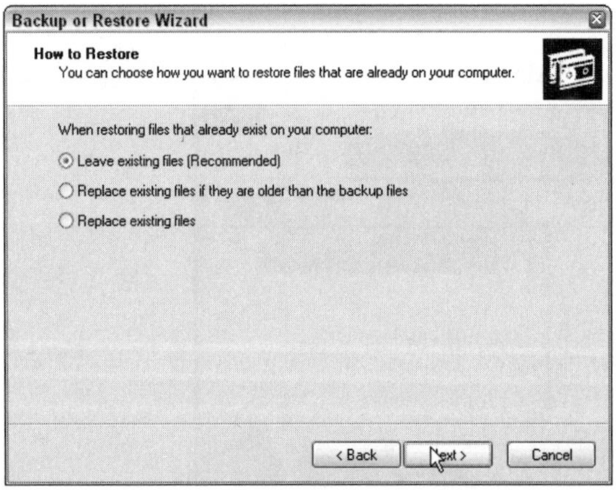

Figure 6-15:
Select
whether to
leave or
overwrite
existing
files.

8. **Make any needed changes (click to uncheck) any options you don't want from the Advanced Restore Options window.**

9. **Click Next and then click Finish.**

A Restore Progress window appears giving you an idea of what's happening. When it's done, it tells you that, too.

Using System Restore

"If only I could go back in time and live that moment over again, I would do it all differently."

You can't go back to age 16 and live your prom over again, but you can ask Windows to jump back to the way it worked last Tuesday or last month. Recent Windows versions come with a tool called System Restore that records copies of your system at points in time known as *restore points.* These restore points let you go back in time to the way your PC was before you installed the software equivalent of the *Titanic* or decided to doodle in your Windows Registry.

Creating a restore point

To make System Restore available to toss you a life preserver, it has to be turned on and you need to have at least one restore point to choose. Here, I show you how to use the tool from start to finish. If you're not sure whether System Restore is already running, don't sweat it. Just follow along.

Follow these steps to turn on System Restore and create a restore point:

1. **Choose Start ⇨ All Programs ⇨ Accessories ⇨ System Tools ⇨ System Restore.**

If System Restore is already enabled, you'll see a windows that says "Welcome to System Restore." If it's not running, you're asked if you want to turn it on (see Figure 6-16). Click Yes.

Figure 6-16:
Turn on
System
Restore.

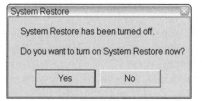

At this point, System Restore may close and you'll need to restart it. Or you may simply see the window shown in Figure 6-17.

2. **Click Create a restore point and then click Next.**

3. **Type a name to help you identify the restore point, and click OK.**

4. **When you see a confirmation window, click Close.**

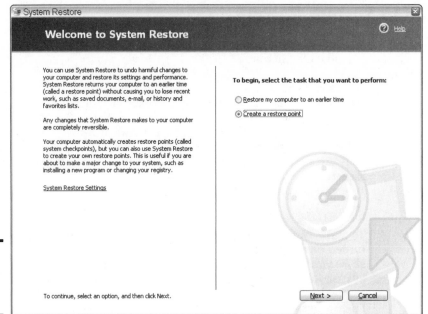

Figure 6-17:
Create your
restore
point.

Create a new restore point before you make any big change to make sure that you don't have to go too far back in history if you need to restore. Because Windows only keeps a certain number of restore points (to conserve space), very old ones get deleted as fresh ones are added.

Restoring your system

Okay, assume for a moment that the great new free game you just downloaded and installed turned out to be hackerware instead. Although you aren't seeing smoke spiral up out of the PC speakers, Windows seems hopelessly fouled.

With any luck, System Restore will run. If it will and you have your good restore point, you can go back to where you were before that nasty surprise. Here's how:

1. **Save any open work and close all programs.**

To restore, Windows will restart itself after you start the process and there's no easy way to stop it.

When you restore your system with a restore point, you may lose any changes or additions to your setup made since you created the restore point you use.

2. **Choose Start ➪ All Programs ➪ Accessories ➪ System Tools ➪ System Restore.**

3. **Choose Restore My Computer to an Earlier Time and click Next.**

4. **Select the restore point you want to use from the list, like that shown in Figure 6-18, and click Next.**

Don't be surprised if a moment or two passes before Windows begins to shut down any programs you may have open and then restarts your PC. After it does, the restore point gets applied and you'll see a window telling you it's finished.

If you choose the wrong restore point or just want to undo the restoration you just finished, simply run System Restore again, and choose Undo My Last Restoration.

Turning off System Restore

Some people really don't like the hard drive space that the created restore points take up, while others may decide they never use it so why run System Restore? You also may need to turn off System Restore because you want to use a similar product, like Norton GoBack.

All restore points are deleted or at least made no longer available when you disable System Restore. Turning it back on again usually won't recover previous restore points.

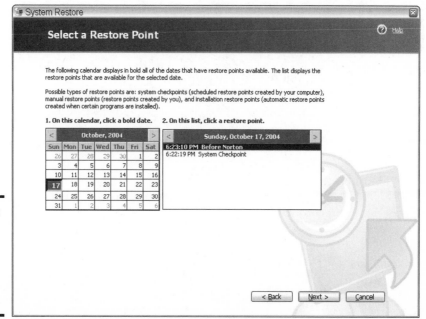

Figure 6-18:
Decide
where
you want
your com-
puter to be
restored to.

To turn off System Restore:

1. **Choose Start ➪ All Programs ➪ Accessories ➪ System Tools ➪ System Restore.**

2. **Click System Restore Settings (on the left half of the window).**

3. **From the Settings window, select Turn Off System Restore on all drives (see Figure 6-19), click Apply, and then click OK.**

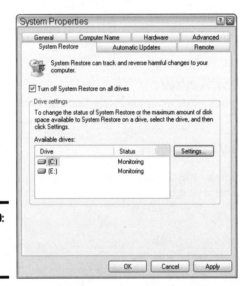

Figure 6-19:
Turn off
System
Restore.

4. **When you're asked to confirm, click Yes.**

Chapter 7: Coping with Activation Woes

In This Chapter

✔ Defining product activation

✔ Stepping through the product activation process

✔ Troubleshooting problems with activation

*H*ave you noticed that some of the software you get these days tends to boss you around from the minute you try to install it?

A big trend among software publishers is to use a practice called *activation* to require a piece of software to connect to the Internet and notify the publisher that it's been installed on your system. The chief reasoning behind this is to reduce software piracy, which costs the PC industry — and you, in the form of higher prices and added time spent during installation — billions each year.

This situation isn't unique to Norton products. Microsoft software, including recent versions of the Windows operating system, also use activation, as do a bunch of others. Some of the tips offered here can help you beyond just your Norton products.

The problem is that activation with some products doesn't always go well. If you install software on a PC not connected to the Internet, you have to call a phone number to activate the software manually. Even if you're connected, you can hit a problem accessing the activation Web site or in getting the software to recognize that it's ready to use.

Why a whole chapter on Norton product activation? Because some people have serious problems with the process. In some online technical support message boards, where people ask questions looking for help, activation woes account for a large number of the problems discussed.

Also, many people simply hate the idea that they have to perform this activation — it's a little like asking for permission to use software you've already paid for. Yet, if you go beyond the time period (usually 15 days) you can get locked out of your product altogether. And you aren't going to be happy.

Because you absolutely must activate your Norton goodies before you use them, this chapter is designed to knock down any hurdles you encounter on your way.

Need help with some other part of the Norton product installation process? Connect to the Internet and visit www.symantec.com/techsupp.

What Is Activation?

Think of product activation like a cyber security checkpoint. When you enter a different country, you usually have to register as a visitor so the authorities know you're there or can send you back if they think you're a problem or your papers aren't quite right.

That's the basic idea between activation. Each piece of software has a unique ID, and activation connects the software back to the publisher (Symantec) to report that this specific product is in now in use and to check that it's a valid copy.

Don't confuse activation with product registration. The difference is that activation identifies a specific copy of the software (called a *license*), while registration (in which you supply your name and address along with other details) identifies you as the specific owner of that copy. You also usually need to register your products before you can get technical support for them.

The Basics of Norton Product Activation

Open your Norton product box and you spot a few things along with the booklet and CD. Among them is a card that loudly proclaims "IMPORTANT Product Activation Required." Check the CD and you notice the product activation warning there as well.

Your activation clock starts counting down the minute you install your Norton product. You have 15 days to activate the software — or to pay for a trial version — before you can't use it anymore. If you reach the 15-day mark and you get locked out, all you have to do is activate the software (or pay to make the trial software the real deal), and you're back in.

Most pieces of software — and this applies to virtually all the Symantec Norton products — provide you with a product key that serves as an ID unique to you and the product you have. No one else should have the same one. When you install the software, that product key gets written into the Windows Registry and onto your drive usually through the product key you have to provide to install it.

No tricks, please

Don't fool yourself into believing that if you tweak the date on your PC —by double-clicking the time stamp in the Windows System Tray at the bottom-right corner of your desktop and choose a different date, as shown in the figure — you can buy more time before your activation deadline runs out.

Any smart software publisher — and Symantec, which makes Norton products is one of them — knows this trick all too well, so they've prepared against it. When your Norton software installs, the program writes information to your disk so it can tell how long the product has been used without activation, even if you play with the date.

Every product key is different. The software is smart enough to spot invalid product keys as you enter them, so you can't even install the software without the right key. But activation is designed to catch other problems, like a valid product key but one already in use elsewhere or from a product shipment reported stolen. The activation site can determine whether the same product key or unique ID has been activated more than a certain number of times, something you expect to see if people are sharing illegal copies.

This is why software publishers give you a fairly short time in which to activate: They want to know you've got a legitimate copy before you use the product for too long.

Sometimes, the software gets it wrong, announcing that the activation or trial period is up before 15 days pass. I ran into this a few different times in writing this book and the software doesn't notice when you curse at it. Be prepared. In the "Before you call for help" section, I show you what else you can try before you have to resort to calling Symantec for assistance in activating the product.

Activating Your Norton Product

If you're about to install your Norton product, take special care in typing in the product key. One wrong letter or number typed makes the difference between a simple installation and one you can't start. Figure 7-1 shows the license agreement and product key window.

After you run the setup for your Norton software and most of the installation is complete, you're usually asked to restart your PC. After it restarts and the installation is done, you're immediately asked if you want to activate the product (see Figure 7-2).

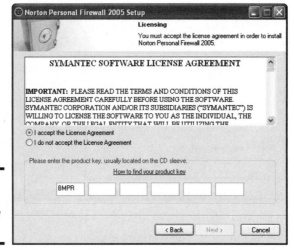

Figure 7-1:
Enter your
product key
with care.

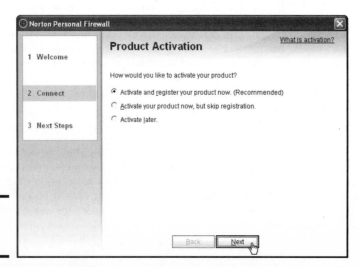

Figure 7-2:
Start
activation.

Now you have a choice. You can activate and register now (or activate without registering) and have it behind you, or you can wait up to that 15th day to do it. If you expect to use the product and don't want the bother of having to go back later to activate, choose Activate and Register Your Product Now. However, if you aren't sure whether you plan to keep the product or you don't have an available Internet connection, choose Activate Later. If you choose to do it later, every time the Norton tool loads after you install it, you'll see a reminder screen counting down the number of days you have left. Just click the Activate Now button and click OK when you're ready to boogie.

Before you start activation, make sure you're connected to the Internet.

Here's what happens after you choose activate:

1. **The software connects to the Symantec site automatically.**

2. **The software transmits the product key or the unique ID.**

3. **Data services on the Symantec site instantly check the database to be sure the ID is valid (see Figure 7-3).**

4. **After the ID is verified and recorded, a notification is sent back into your software that the activation is successful.**

With the activation behind you, you should be exempt from nagging reminders. But notice I said *should.* One of the problems with activation is that, every once in awhile, something happens and the activate process doesn't work as it should. You can activate your product today and get asked to activate it again tomorrow. The following section gives you some suggestions for getting past this problem.

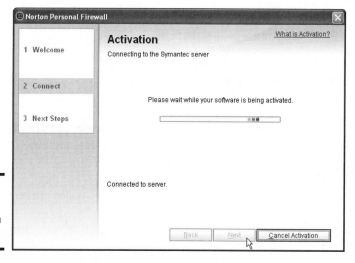

Figure 7-3:
Activating
your Norton
product.

TIP

Getting a trial version

To download trial versions of some of the most popular Norton products such as Norton AntiVirus and Norton Internet Security, here's how to find them:

1. **Go to** www.symantec.com.

2. **Click Downloads.**

3. **Choose either Home and Home Office Trialware (for consumers) or Enterprise Trialware (if you're trying this at the office).**

4. **Look for the product you want to try from the list, like that shown in the figure.**

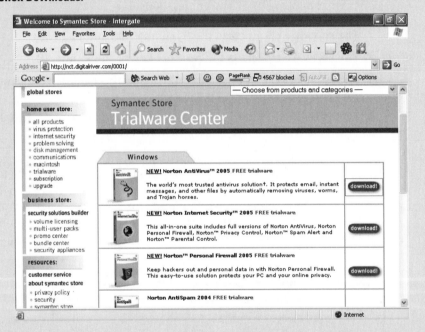

5. **Click the Download! button corresponding to the product you want.**

   A page opens up with details about that product.

6. **Click the link labeled FREE 15-Day Trialware (see the figure).**

The next page asks you to specify what country you're from and for your e-mail address.

7. **Choose your country and type your e-mail address, then click Submit.**

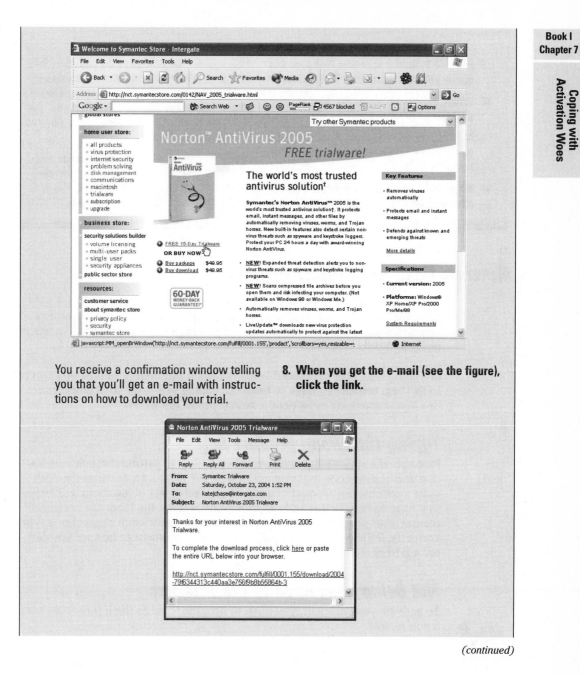

You receive a confirmation window telling you that you'll get an e-mail with instructions on how to download your trial.

8. When you get the e-mail (see the figure), click the link.

(continued)

(continued)

9. **From the Symantec download Web page that opens, click the link to start the download.**

10. **When prompted, save the file to your desktop.**

   Navigate to your desktop if you need to, when you're choosing where to save the file.

11. **After the download completes, double-click the file on your desktop.**

After you run the download, as you do in Step 11, the installer loads and guides you through the process to install your Norton trialware. Mostly, you'll just have to click Next until you reach the point where the software is ready to use for your 15-day trial.

Remember: If you're using a trial version and it expires or you later purchase the actual package to install, you need to remove the trial. Book II Chapter 2 shows you the steps.

Getting Past Activation Problems

Activation woes account for a major percentage of people looking for help with Norton and other products. They're particularly frustrating because you've already paid your money for the package and you just want to use it, unencumbered.

In this section, I tell you about some common problems and how you can try to fix them before you have to resort to calling Symantec to activate your product (something most people would prefer not to do).

Typing the wrong product key

Probably the single biggest non-techie problem in getting through installation and activation is that you fail to type the product key correctly. With most versions, the product key is a 24 character mix of numbers and letters that have to be typed exactly as they're printed on the label. Go back and reenter your product key taking your time to be sure each character is typed correctly. If the printing isn't very clear, take a moment to be sure you can tell a *B* from an *8* or an *I* from a *1*.

Not being connected to the Internet

To activate your product, you have to be connected to the Internet. So what if you're not?

Use the Activate by Phone feature when:

✦ You can make it as far as the activation process but can't ever get past it

✦ You don't have or can't get connected to the Internet

The Activate by Phone option appears when your Norton software can't get a connection to the Symantec Web site. Just follow the steps on your screen. But if you're one of those folks (and there are many) who hate having to call and sit waiting on the line for assistance, try the steps in "Before you call for help" up next.

If all else fails, you can go online to get help at www.symantec.com/techsupp or you can call Symantec's technical support lines at either of the numbers listed on the back of your User's Guide. However, these support lines charge for your call.

Before you call for help

If you're stuck because you can't get your product activated without calling Symantec, let me suggest one more set of tips to try:

+ **Check your system date by clicking on the time display in your Windows System Tray.** Clicking on the time opens the Date and Time Properties window. Although you can't try to fool your Norton products by setting back the date, a wrong date displayed here may cut short the time you have until you activate your product. Games and some older types of software can sometimes play with the time and date, either speeding your time forward or not catching up to today's date. When you fix your time and date to the proper schedule, your Norton product and its activation clock should respond accordingly.

+ **If you have a second means of connecting to the Internet, and if activation fails online using your primary Internet connection such as DSL or cable modem, try a dialup connection instead (or vice versa).** I've run into problems using my satellite Internet account for activation that got resolved using my standby dialup account.

+ **Shut down and restart your system and try activation again.** You know what they say about "when at first you don't succeed. . . ." It's not uncommon to have to try three or more times before the activation takes.

+ **Try to restart your system with nothing running on your desktop.** This means don't start your instant messaging software, your e-mail client, or any other tool that requires your Internet connection to run. In some cases, having these types of programs running can make it difficult for you to connect properly with Symantec's activation servers.

If none of these work, then it's time to try to activate by phone.

Book II

Norton Suites

The 5th Wave   By Rich Tennant

ROCKET SOFT
DESIGN AND CONSTRUCTION

The feeling is, we may not have all the Internet security we should.

Contents at a Glance

Chapter 1: Getting Started with Norton SystemWorks

In This Chapter

✔ Knowing what's in the SystemWorks package

✔ Understanding the differences between packages and SystemWorks Premier

✔ Putting the extra features of SystemWorks to work for you

*N*orton SystemWorks and SystemWorks Premier are two of the most comprehensive system diagnostics and system checking packages available to you as a home or small office PC user. It's also probably one of the best buys in terms of how many tools you get within the package, including some old standards.

This chapter explores what's inside these packages and how to start them. You also see how to use some of the extra tools available only within SystemWorks/SystemWorks Premier such as CheckIt diagnostics and Connection Keep Alive.

What's in the Package?

Before I show you all the neat extras you get — and there are many of those — you need to know what's contained in your basic Norton System-Works package. There's a little something here for every part of your PC — whether you're addicted to surfing the Web or you just want to make your system run better.

Norton Utilities

One of the "grandfathers" of PC utilities, Norton Utilities features Norton Disk Doctor, Norton System Doctor, and Norton WinDoctor. You'll also find utilities that are better than the Windows version, like Speed Disk (which is superior to Windows Disk Defragmenter). You can find out more about Norton Utilities in Book III.

Norton AntiVirus

Today, a virus detective program that can also annihilate infections and worms is not a luxury but a necessity for your PC, whether you regularly connect to the Net or you simply share files back and forth with your coworkers. Norton AntiVirus can constantly update itself using the LiveUpdate tool to do battle against the newest destructive computer viruses and other infections. Book VI tells you all about using the virus scanner.

Norton Ghost

Ever wish you could take a snapshot of your system at a particular moment in time when everything's installed and running picture perfect? You can with Norton Ghost, an often-recommended feature that lets you take drive images you can then use to get back up and running in record time. Book IV shows you everything you need to exercise and summon your Ghost.

Norton GoBack

If you've ever hoped you could go back in time and *not* install or change something on your system that turned out to make a super-duper mess, then consider Norton GoBack, a tool that lets you do just that. Explore how you can put this tool to work for you in Book IV.

Norton Cleanup

No matter how neat you try to be, your drive fills up with junk from temporary files, left over debris from your Web surfing, and too many other files you don't want. Before long, your hard disk can overflow, sending you in a desperate search to reclaim some of that drive real estate. Norton Cleanup is designed to help you slay the junk-file dragon and get control again over your disk space. More about this in Book IX.

Differences between SystemWorks Versions and Stand-Alone Packages

SystemWorks and SystemWorks Premier include some tools you can't buy as stand-alone packages. Norton Utilities and all its diagnostic doctors is an example — you can't purchase this as a separate product. Of the available tools, you can acquire Norton Ghost, Norton GoBack, and Norton CleanSweep (which features more tools than Norton Cleanup, available in SystemWorks) separately.

Also, the major difference between Norton SystemWorks and SystemWorks Premier is the addition of Norton Ghost in the Premier package. If you already have Norton Ghost, you just need SystemWorks to have the same basic package as Premier.

Starting Norton SystemWorks

Out of the box, Norton SystemWorks and SystemWorks Premier place an icon right on your Windows desktop. Just double-click it to start SystemWorks. It opens to the System Status window as shown in Figure 1-1, which gives you these choices:

✦ **One Button Checkup:** A fast system diagnostics checker you can find out about in Book III, Chapter 1.

✦ **Norton AntiVirus:** This option typically listed the last time your virus checker was updated using the LiveUpdate feature.

✦ **Windows Update:** Choose this and click Configure to let Norton take care of your necessary Windows Updates for you.

✦ **UnErase Protection:** Turned on by default, this tool adds a layer of protection to your Recycle Bin (repository of deleted files) so you can more easily recover unintentionally erased files before they get purged.

✦ **Free Disk Space:** Reports the amount of available, free drive space on your main hard drive (usually, this is your C: or primary hard drive).

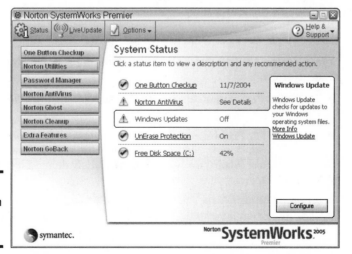

Figure 1-1:
Your System
Status
window.

Looking over the Norton selection

Although this book is a soup-to-nuts explanation of all the Norton products you're most likely to use or need, you may just have one or two Norton tools right now. Do you have the exact one you need? That's a good question. Chapter 2 of this book tells you about some of the common PC problems and how Norton products can help, but you can find online help, too.

You can see the entire selection of Norton products if you visit the Symantec Web site. Click Products and Services. Click the down-arrow next to Symantec Products A–Z to look at the entire selection.

If the Symantec Products A–Z list is a bit overwhelming, try this instead: Look for the "Not sure what you need?" section, lower on the page. Click the Home & Home Office Product Selector link. This opens a new browser window (it can take a few moments to load if you have a slow connection). Move your pointer over the words *I want...*, and a drop-down list appears. Move your mouse over the kind of protection or help you're looking for. Many menu options open a submenu. After you click on what you need, you'll be given some suggestions of product(s) that can handle the job.

Or you can follow these steps to load an individual tool within SystemWorks:

1. **Choose Start ➪ All Programs ➪ Norton SystemWorks or SystemWorks Premier.**

2. **Select the tool you want to use.**

There are some specific tool categories you can put to work for you, too. To see them, follow these steps:

1. **Open SystemWorks or SystemWorks Premier.**

2. **Select Norton Utilities from the buttons on the left, which gives you three options:**

- **Optimize Performance:** Choose this and you can run Norton Speed Disk.

- **Find and Fix Problems:** Select this to access all the Norton doctors (Norton Disk Doctor, Norton System Doctor, and Norton WinDoctor), plus UnErase Wizard for restoring previously deleted files (see Figure 1-2).

- **System Maintenance:** Click this to select between the many different tabs in System Information (shown in Figure 1-3) or Wipe Data to permanently remove files from your PC.

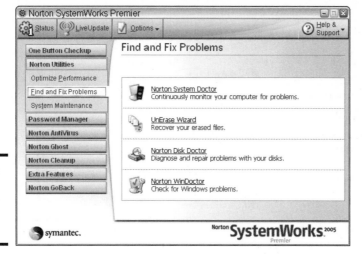

Figure 1-2:
Your Find
and Fix
Problems
choices.

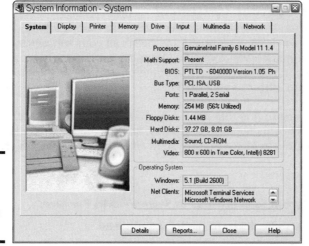

Figure 1-3:
The Norton
System
Information
window.

Using the Extra Features in SystemWorks

Norton SystemWorks bundles some additional tools into its package, each with a specific diagnostic or performance-optimizing job. Figure 1-4 shows you your options from SystemWorks including the much-recommended CheckIt Diagnostics package.

Note: A few of these special features aren't installed automatically with Norton SystemWorks or SystemWorks Premier. I've noted these.

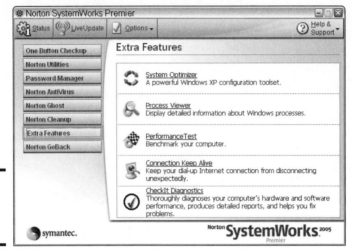

Figure 1-4:
Your roster
of extra
features.

Running System Optimizer

Running Norton System Optimizer is a little like having a Windows efficiency expert sit down at your keyboard and tweak all your settings to get the best overall performance out of your PC. From your mouse to your display to your drives and back through to your memory, System Optimizer looks for anything it can adjust to your benefit.

Yet you're going to find that not every change has quite the great effect you might want. For this reason, I beg (okay, not beg but definitely urge) you to proceed cautiously. Making one system adjustment at a time is smart.

Follow these steps:

1. **Open Norton SystemWorks or SystemWorks Premier.**

2. **Select Extra Features in the left-hand menu.**

3. **Click System Optimizer.**

4. **Click Continue to read a short help file (I strongly recommend you read it so you're informed), then click the X at the top-right corner of the help file window to close it.**

5. **From the System Optimizer main screen, click on the category you want to use at the left side of the window, as shown in Figure 1-5.**

   Choose from one of the following and (with most) click Start:

   • **System Optimizer settings:** Specifies how the optimizer should run.

   • **General:** Lets you adjust details about Optimizer, like whether to present the categories as text or icons.

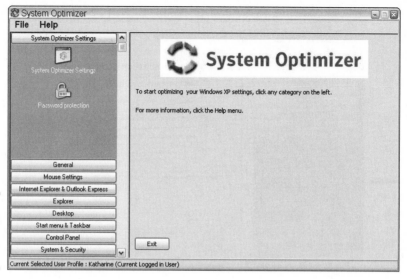

Figure 1-5:
Choose your
optimization
category.

- **Mouse Settings:** Lets you tweak your cursor and mouse speed.

- **Internet Explorer & Outlook Express:** Allow for special adjustments just for the Microsoft Web browser and its Gal Friday, the e-mail software.

- **Explorer:** Allows you to change how Windows Explorer operates when you're looking for files on your drive.

- **Desktop:** Lets you modify settings related to your desktop workspace.

- **Start Menu & Taskbar:** Helps you find wasted resources among less-than-necessary startup programs.

- **Control Panel:** Explores the main switchboard for Windows.

- **System & Security:** Offers special choices that apply throughout the system and to Windows protection schemes (see Figure 1-6).

- **Information:** Provides the details about your Windows setup.

6. **After you've made a single change or two, you can close System Optimizer by choosing File ⇨ Exit.**

Looking at Process Viewer

Process Viewer is another take on the information provided by Windows Task Manager (which you can open at any time by using the three-fingered salute, or Ctrl+Alt+Delete), giving you the lowdown on services, processes, and applications running on your desktop. This feature is part of Norton's System Optimizer tool.

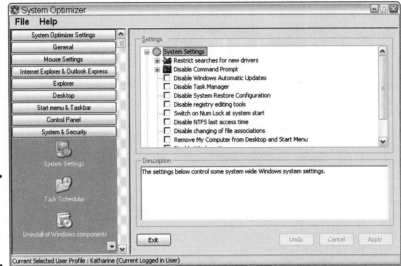

Figure 1-6:
System &
Security
optimization
tweaks.

Although Process Viewer doesn't tell you in plain English what each process is or what it does, you can get clues from it. Click on a listed process and then look at the bottom of the Process Viewer window (see Figure 1-7). This status bar usually tells you what program or company provided the file in use. Expect to see several entries from Microsoft Corporation (maker of your Windows operating system) and Symantec Corporation (publisher of your Norton software).

Refresh your processes list at anytime by pressing your F5 key on your keyboard. To save a list of your processes — useful when you're contacting technical support to ask for help — choose File ➪ Save As, and then type a name for your saved process list.

Figure 1-7:
Check the
status bar at
the bottom
of the
viewer.

TIP

Keep an eye on the patient

Not every system — or one of its distinct separate parts — takes performance tweaks graciously.

Just like the little kid who kicks at the doctor when being given a shot, your PC may stage a revolt when System Optimizer has made a change. Your video display could get flaky, the hard drive may start to sound like a coffee grinder, or a sound file may get stuck right in the middle of the really annoying part.

Besides my suggestion before about making a single change at a time, you also want to keep a careful eye on your system after making these tweaks. If it misbehaves, go back into System Optimizer and try to reverse that change (by checking or unchecking an option selected).

Comparing your PC speed with PerformanceTest

PerformanceTest gives you a way to test your system performance — along with special subsystem parts like your CPU, memory, video, and Windows desktop — and then measure it against the results of similar systems or individual components. Heard the term *benchmark?* Benchmarks provide the performance markers for comparing your system or one of your components against others.

PerformanceTest is not installed automatically when you set up Norton SystemWorks or SystemWorks Premier. You may have to go grab your Norton install CD, insert it into your CD or DVD drive, and then follow the on-screen prompts to get it installed before you first use it.

Then follow these steps:

1. **Open Norton SystemWorks.**

2. **Click Norton Extra Features and then PerformanceTest.**

3. **Click Next twice, then click I Agree, and click Next again.**

4. **Choose Tests ⇨ Run All Tests.**

The Test Status window appears (see Figure 1-8) to keep you apprised as to what's being done. Don't be surprised if you see some wild screens as PerformanceTest gives your PC's video subsystem a real triathlon-level workout.

When the tests are finished, you see a PassMark Rating window like that shown in Figure 1-9. Click Explain to find out more about your particular rating. You can also look back at the report screen to see how each part of your system did, but it may not make a lot of sense until you compare your results against a similar PC. Before you do that, though, you want to save a baseline.

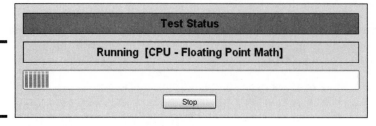

Figure 1-8:
Your Test
Status
window.

Figure 1-9:
Your
PassMark
test score.

A *baseline* is a gauge against which to measure all future test results. Similarly, you might have a baseline test done at your doctor's office when you're 35, and another test at 40, the first test gives your doctor something to compare the second test to. Here's how to save your own baseline:

1. **Choose File ⇨ Save as Baseline.**

The Save as New Baseline window (shown in Figure 1-10) appears.

2. **From the Save as New Baseline window click in Notes and then type some identifying information about your system for later reference.**

3. **Click Save.**

With your baseline saved, you can open this baseline again to test later PerformanceTest results. But you can also use some of the test's included benchmark results to measure yours against other systems. Just follow these steps:

1. **From PerformanceTest, choose Baselines ⇨ Select Baseline.**

2. **Select a baseline from the list that seems closest to the type of PC you have (see Figure 1-11).**

3. **Click Add and then OK.**

Now you see your performance results (in green) measured against the baseline you selected (with its markers in red), as shown in Figure 1-12.

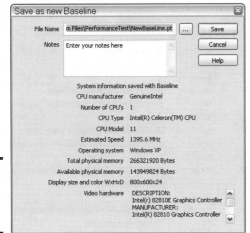

Figure 1-10:
Save your
baseline
with notes.

Look for situations where your (green) measurements are noticeably different
from the others in red: These may indicate you either have a problem (because
your system runs nowhere near as well) or your PC is super-charged and does
much better than the baseline you chose.

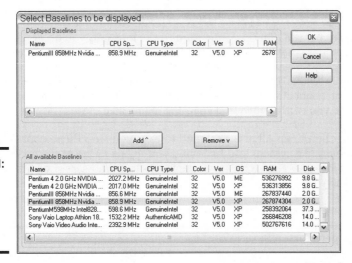

Figure 1-11:
Choose a
baseline
study to
measure
against.

From PerformanceTest, choose the Advanced menu and select from special
tests to measure your home network, multitasking capabilities, or give your
3-D graphics subsystem (which is ever so important when you're a gamer) a
real workout.

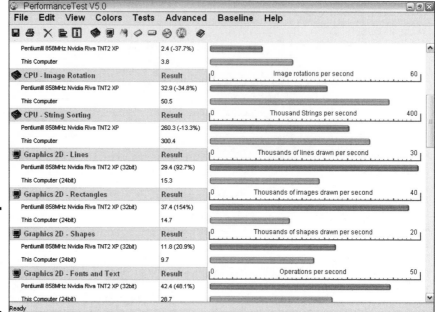

Figure 1-12:
Compare
your test
results
against the
baseline.

Using Connection Keep Alive

If you're using a dial-up connection to the Internet, you no doubt know the unhappiness of having your connection close on you somewhere about 80 to 90 percent through a long, arduous download. Your connection might close for several reasons, but all too often, it happens just because your system detects that the connection is idle — there's not enough activity to make your system believe you're actually doing anything online so it closes the connection. Ouch.

Connection Keep Alive is designed to help you stop those connection drops by fooling the system into believing you're busy. One of the ways it does this is to *ping* — or send a message packet — to a Web server or otherwise simulate busyness.

To turn on Connection Keep Alive:

1. **Open Norton SystemWorks.**

2. **Click to open Extra Features.**

3. **Click Connection Keep Alive.**

The Options window (shown in Figure 1-13) appears.

4. **Select Enable Connection Keep Alive.**

Make any other changes you want (see the following for details).

5. **Click Apply and then OK.**

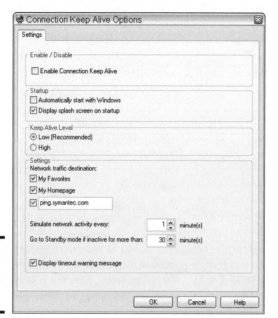

Figure 1-13:
Turn on
Connection
Keep Alive.

After Connection Keep Alive is turned on, a connection icon appears in your System Tray. Now what about the options you have under Connection Keep Alive? The following applies to those items you have checked (enabled):

✦ **Automatically Start with Windows:** Launches your connection tickler whenever Windows (re)starts.

✦ **Display Splash Screen:** Shows the special screen as Windows launches (not really necessary unless you're just totally in love with the gold-and-white screen).

✦ **Keep Alive Level:** Determines how often your software *pings* (the cyber equivalent of paging another computer) the network to which you're connected to let it know you're still online and want to stay there; the low setting pings less often than high.

✦ **Simulate Network Activity Every *x* Minutes:** Lets you specify how often to "fake" online busyness to keep your connection alive. (***Note:*** Don't fake any more frequently than necessary.)

✦ **Disable When Inactive for *x* Minutes:** Lets you specify how long before Keep Connection Alive quits after it stops detecting you typing away at the keyboard or moving the mouse.

✦ **Display Timeout Warning Message:** Use this to nudge you when you're about to lose your connection due to inactivity.

Speed isn't everything

Don't get obsessed with speed and benchmarks and the eternal pursuit of making some part of your PC outpace the test results of another computer. If you've ever tried weight lifting or some super-duper exercise routine, you know how easy it is to fall into a groove where you're constantly trying to outdo either your old record or the speed demon who exercises with you. But you also know what a punishment that can inflict on your body.

The same thing holds true for your PC. If you follow all the tips and tweaks you find posted online to drastically improve your overall system performance, you can actually find yourself with a pretty unstable computer that is now adjusted for speed rather than for what you really want: a nice crash-retardant desktop. If the darned thing becomes too rocky to let you browse the Internet without error messages or begins to lock up during your favorite game, how will speed help?

If you genuinely notice that a part of your system (for example, your drives) seems too slow, you can run a diagnostics test like Norton Disk Doctor or Norton System Doctor to try to improve that. But you may be better off replacing hardware or even the whole PC than you would be tweaking your settings into oblivion.

Now your connections shouldn't die during long downloads or extended periods when you're away from the keyboard. If you want to turn the feature off again, just repeat the previous steps, but uncheck Enable Connection Keep Alive in Step 4.

Scanning with CheckIt Diagnostics

If you've ever had to troubleshoot some thorny issue with your PC, you may have already heard of CheckIt Diagnostics, a recognized name in system checking. Unlike PerformanceTest, CheckIt doesn't just look for overall performance issues but for anything that can cause a problem.

It can review and test your CPU, your memory, your audio and video plus graphics subsystems, your drives, your modem, and your shortcuts and report back. I'll take you through the tests then show you how to perform a video calibration to adjust your display.

CheckIt Diagnostics isn't installed automatically. Have your Norton SystemWorks CD handy and place it in your CD or DVD drive, then follow on-screen prompts to install it when you go to use it for the first time.

After CheckIt Diagnostics is installed, follow these steps to run it:

1. **Open Norton SystemWorks.**

2. **Click to open Extra Features.**

3. **Click CheckIt Diagnostics.**

   Your roster of tests opens on the left side.

4. **Click System Information.**

   Complete details about your PC opens in the larger window on the right (see Figure 1-14).

5. **Click on a tab to view details about each component.**

6. **Click on one of the tests listed on the left below System Information and then click Start.**

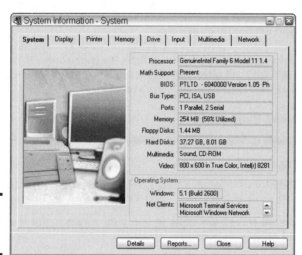

Figure 1-14:
Your system
information.

You can also choose tests by opening the Tools menu and choosing one. Man, do you have a full menu of exams to select from (choose a test and click Start), including

✦ **Processor:** Run a working evaluation of how well your PC's CPU handles different types of calculations as well as measure its performance and speed.

✦ **Memory:** Choose from a battery of tests designed to check the speed and accuracy of your system's installed memory (RAM).

✦ **Audio:** Play different types of sound files (click Select Files to choose specific ones like some complicated, longer recordings) to determine how well your PC sound system performs.

✦ **Video:** Similar to audio, but tests your system's ability to properly run digital movies such as AVIs and MPEGs.

✦ **Modem:** Check your installed modem to see if it can properly detect dial tone and handle the kinds of commands sent to the modem to dial, hang up, and generally communicate when you try to go online.

✦ **Graphics:** Different from basic video, the tests here challenge the heck out of your PC video subsystem's ability to draw, render, and otherwise manipulate the kind of super-duper graphics you see with games, animations, and more.

✦ **Hard Disk:** Rates your hard disk's ability to be read from or written to.

✦ **Removable Disk:** Runs the same type of tests as for hard disks but specifically on your removable disk drives.

✦ **CD-ROM:** Puts your CD drive through its paces to determine how quickly and efficiently it operates

Video calibration is a nifty trick to pull from up your sleeve if you notice your display is a little off after you play a really graphics-intensive game. To perform a video calibration on your system:

1. **Start CheckIt Diagnostics.**

2. **Choose Tools ➪ Video Calibrate Test.**

3. **Click Next.**

CheckIt takes you through a long series of screens like that shown in Figure 1-15.

4. **Follow the on-screen prompts to test your video to get it displaying as sharp and crisply as possible.**

5. **When you're done, click Finish.**

Click Stop to stop any CheckIt test before it's done. To print a report of your test results, press Ctrl+P.

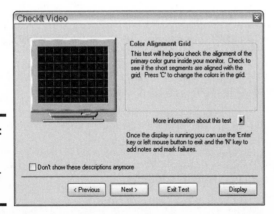

Figure 1-15: Testing every little part of your display.

Chapter 2: Upgrading from an Older Version

In This Chapter

✔ Knowing the *hows* and *whys* of smart upgrading

✔ Protecting yourself and your PC from problems

✔ Uninstalling Norton trialware

Norton products have been around so long and are installed — at least in trial version — in so many new PCs when they're first sold that you can pretty easily end up with a mishmash of products and versions. This can sometimes lead to problems in upgrading your Norton products or in just simply using them after you install them.

This chapter is all about upgrading without tearing your hair out or wishing you could do it all over again. There's just no need for that! The information in this chapter will work for any Norton product and many of the suggestions work for just about any upgrade you may get.

Getting Smart about Upgrading

People upgrading their software often fall into two categories. There are those who just can't wait, then there are others — like me — who still have a bitter taste in their mouths from the last update from hell where a simple little revision left the PC silent while smoke wafted from the user's ears (or vice versa).

The first group has the right attitude but probably isn't going to take precautions, while the second group is apt to linger too long on old versions of software, letting fresher copies pile up on the desk not installed. In this section, I show you the ways you can upgrade to protect both you and your PC as well as get you up and running with that new version quickly and successfully.

Here's your checklist for upgrading success:

✦ **Make sure your PC meets the eligibility requirements for the upgrade (usually noted under "Minimum Requirements" on the product box or in the online description).** Your PC probably does, but checking to be sure is a good idea.

✦ **Read the instructions.** I know that reading the instructions seems like a bother, but you may find valuable tips that can warn you about what may bite you.

✦ **Exercise care.** Don't just cross your fingers or don your lucky socks when you're about to perform an upgrade. I've tried those and I'm here to tell you as a grizzled vet that they don't work. Give yourself a security net instead. The suggestions offered in Chapter 6 of Book I give you the tools you need to protect your system if the upgrade goes badly. Back up your files and use tools like Windows System Restore — or if you already have it installed and working, Norton GoBack — to get your system back in shape.

✦ **Restart your PC.** If your system has been up and running for a while, restart it to clear the decks before you try to upgrade.

✦ **Close any open windows on your desktop before you start the upgrade.**

✦ **Follow the steps outlined in the instructions.**

✦ **If the upgrade bombs, restart your PC and try it again.** If the upgrade fails a second time, stop and look for help; there's usually a Web address in your documentation to tell you where to find it. For information about using Symantec's help site, see the following section.

Even if you already have your Norton upgrade installed, you can put this kind of information to work for you with almost any other software or upgrade you have.

Getting Help Online with Symantec

Symantec's Web site at www.symantec.com is the place to go if you have problems with your Norton product or upgrade. They make it fairly simple to find information in just a few clicks. They also give you a choice between using:

✦ An automated assistant that steps you through the help you need

✦ A special database of help called a knowledge base where you can get help with a particular product or feature

You may need both. If the automated assistant doesn't provide what you need, you just go back to use the knowledge base. Here's how:

1. **Go online and type** www.symantec.com **into your Web browser.**

2. **At the Symantec site, click Support.**

3. **Choose your product type: Home and Home Office/Small Business or Enterprise.**

**Book II
Chapter 2**

Upgrading from an
Older Version

Oh, those baffling error messages!

Few things are more annoying than getting an error message right after you upgrade or otherwise use your software. These error messages can leave even seasoned pros scratching their heads, wondering what they mean and why they got the error.

But the Symantec Knowledge Base gives you a way to decipher Norton error messages through a help file they have online. All you need to do is follow Steps 1 through 3 in the "Getting Help Online with Symantec" section,

then jump to Step 5 and select Error Message Issues. Top error support issues are displayed first, but you can click the Search tab, as shown in the figure, to type in the text of your error message. Then click Search.

Help I found here let me resolve a really vexing problem with Norton Password Manager that temporarily hung up my PC whenever I went to shut down and restart. Try it! You may like your results.

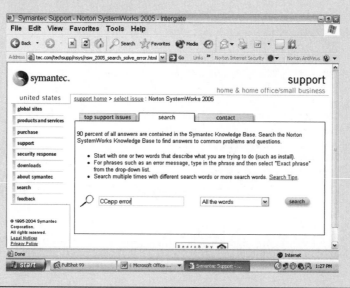

4. **Select Access Free Online Support.**

5. **Click the Automated Support Assistant button and follow the instructions.**

6. **If you don't get what you need, return to the support window and select your Norton product and version (see Figure 2-1).**

7. **From the Knowledge Base page, click to open one of the set links, such as "installation" tips or type a phrase into the search window and click Search, as shown in Figure 2-2.**

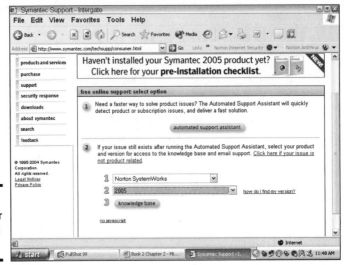

Figure 2-1:
Choose your
product and
version.

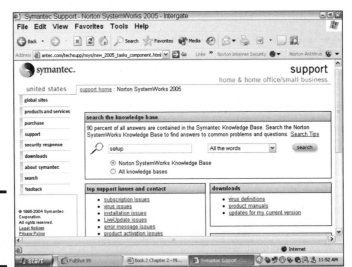

Figure 2-2:
Search for
a word
like *setup.*

Norton product support costs money when you call by phone. Whenever possible, save yourself the money and just jump online to see if you can grab the exact help you need.

Removing Norton Trialware

The free 15-day trialware of popular Norton products is a super way to test out software like Norton AntiVirus before you put down the cash to buy them. Yet you have to remove trialware before you can successfully install the purchased version from the CD.

Follow these steps to uninstall your trialware:

1. **Choose Start ⇨ Control Panel (or Start ⇨ Settings ⇨ Control Panel).**

2. **Double-click the Add and Remove Programs icon.**

3. **Select the Norton trialware you want to uninstall from the list of Windows programs and click Remove (see Figure 2-3).**

The Norton product setup screen (shown in Figure 2-4) appears.

4. **Click Remove All.**

5. **When asked to confirm your decision to remove, click Yes.**

Book II
Chapter 2

Upgrading from an
Older Version

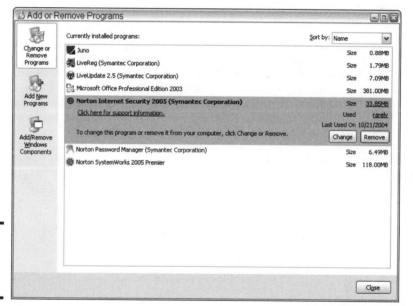

Figure 2-3:
Choose the
trialware to
remove.

Although you usually need to remove Norton trialware before you install a full, purchased copy, there are two key exceptions:

✦ **If you're upgrading your trialware into a paid version:** If you use the Norton trialware to upgrade to a paid version directly through the software itself (like through the screen shown in Figure 2-5 that appears every time you start your trialware during your 15-day period and follow onscreen prompts), you can simply type the product key Symantec provides you when you pay for it online. You don't want to remove the trialware first.

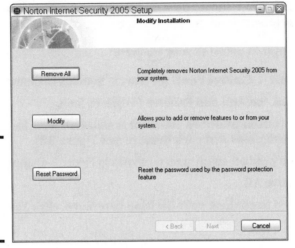

Figure 2-4:
Click the
Remove All
button to
start the
process.

✦ **If the Norton product you're installing is *not* the exact same one as you're using in trialware:** You don't need to remove trialware for one product if you're installing a full version of a different Norton product. For example, if you're installing Norton SystemWorks or SystemWorks Premier, you don't have to remove the trial version of Norton Internet Security to do this. The two will happily coexist, at least until your test period runs out.

The need to remove a trial version of software before you install the full version isn't unique to Norton products. You'll find this with Microsoft products and those from a number of other software publishers as well.

Figure 2-5:
If you're
upgrading
trialware
into a paid
version, you
don't have
to get rid
of the
trialware.

Chapter 3: Using Norton Internet Security

In This Chapter

✔ Identifying the products included in the package

✔ Understanding problems in mixing and matching Norton product versions

✔ Knowing how to configure products together

✔ Customizing which products install

*E*verywhere you go online, you can find someone telling you of the dangers of the Internet, warning you about the real problem of identity and data theft, and offering you lots of complex ways to try to reduce your risk. But some of the stuff recommended can make your head swim. Some people tell you to download five or six different tools and juggle them. Others suggest you tweak the Windows Registry (that master index that Windows keeps — the Registry doesn't like to be messed with). If you don't know what you're doing, you can lock yourself out of the Internet altogether and maybe foul up Windows besides.

Norton Internet Security (NIS) is designed as a one-stop shopping way to solve or at least neutralize a bunch of the most common problems that can clobber you online. These include viruses and spyware, spam, controls to keep the kids away from porn sites, and having your browser or Internet account hijacked and maybe your identity stolen as well.

In this chapter, you grab your flashlight to look inside the Norton Internet Security suite and see how to customize what gets installed. You launch the suite, configure it, and find out how to disable it (temporarily) as needed.

Looking Inside

You're going to find out all the nitty-gritty details about configuring and using the products included in Norton Internet Security. This comes in Book VII.

Right now, let's zero in on what these different tools are, how you choose to use them when you install them, and get an understanding of some problems you might see if you try to mix and match too many different Norton product versions at the same time.

Norton AntiVirus

Easily one of Norton's best-known and widely used products, Norton AntiVirus scans your system for all of today's latest types of computer infections, including the CPU flu known as a virus or worm. With it, you can scan your entire system, including key Windows startup files, memory, e-mail attachments, and deep inside your Zip files.

Not only do you want to keep this program installed, you also need to keep it prepped to defend against the most recently released cyber nasties by using the LiveUpdate tool. Book VI takes you through everything you need to know about using Norton AntiVirus and tweaking it the way you want.

Norton Personal Firewall

Just as its name suggests, a firewall is designed to place itself as a security buffer between you and everyone else out there on the Internet.

A firewall acts as a gatekeeper, checking what programs are trying to access the Net and who's trying to connect to your PC. It can be either your best friend when it saves you from cyber Darth Vader or your worst enemy when it blocks you from getting where you want to go online.

To keep you on speaking terms with your Internet connection when using a firewall, you usually need to watch what happens when you first install the firewall. When you know how comfortable a fit it is, you can adjust your firewall settings until you have a balance between keeping everyone else out and keeping you online.

Norton Privacy Control

Norton Privacy Control helps keep you from unwittingly exposing information about yourself, such as your e-mail address, as you browse online. This tool is helpful because most people don't even realize how many little details they drop as they go.

This is the rare Norton product that is only available as part of Norton Internet Security. You can't purchase it separately.

Norton to the rescue

Here's a scary and really frustrating situation you may run into if you use Windows XP or Windows 2000. It happened to me as I was installing Norton Internet Security on a new hard drive where I had just installed Windows XP.

Before I configured any kind of Internet protection or ran Windows Update (see Book I), I connected to the Internet so I could activate my copy of Windows XP. Yet before I could do that and within a couple seconds of going online, I got hit with a Windows error message telling me LSASS.EXE had some kind of problem and had to close.

Because I know LSASS is important to system security, I was worried because this file has to run for Windows to operate properly and securely. (The figure shows Windows Task Manager's process window where you see LSASS loaded as it should be.) I also happened to know that LSASS is a file often attacked by viruses and worms (more about these in Book VI, Chapter 1) like the Sasser Worm.

Almost as suddenly, a Windows security warning popped up telling me that the system would have to shut down and didn't give me a way to stop it. When Windows asked to report the error (as it does almost anytime a program crashes), I chose yes, and when I clicked More Information, I was taken to a Microsoft help page just long enough to learn LSASS was under attack. But before I could read what to do, my PC shut down.

I went through this same thing three times, never getting enough time to read the Microsoft help page to learn what to do because my PC cycled through the error-warning-shutdown process on me each time. Then I remembered I had installed but not enabled Norton Internet Security, which provides protection for LSASS. The NIS icon was sitting there in my System Tray.

Rats, I thought. I got a new Windows error message on part of Norton after I right-clicked the NIS icon! But I was able to enable NIS, download a LiveUpdate to make sure I was protected against the most recent threats. With NIS loaded, I was able to get back to work in just a minute or two. No more crashes or shutdowns. Whew! Crisis averted, thanks to Norton.

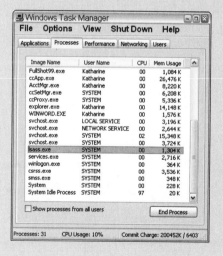

Norton AntiSpam

Remember those great old days when you used to say, "Gee, why doesn't anyone send me any e-mail?" You promptly stopped grumbling about that when you got your millionth unwanted ad in your virtual mailbox.

Norton AntiSpam does more than just try to catch obvious ads before you do. It's designed to perform a smart analysis of the kinds of e-mail you send and the legitimate mail you receive; this can outwit savvy spammers who are always looking for a new way to slip in beneath the radar.

Other ways to protect yourself

If NIS or Norton Personal Firewall doesn't happen to be one of the Norton products you have (but you're savvy enough to read this chapter anyway), you can prevent some pretty nasty scenarios.

When you first install Windows on a PC that connects either directly to the Internet or to your home or small office network, configure the Windows XP Internet Connection Firewall (also called the Windows XP Firewall). Also, even if your PC or Windows isn't new but you haven't yet installed any kind of firewall, you can set up a firewall by following these directions.

To do this, choose Start⇨Network Connections. Choose your Internet or network connection, and then under Network Tasks from the left-hand task pane (see the figure), select Change Settings of This Connection. From the multi-tabbed window that opens, click the Advanced tab and at the top of the window, under Internet Connection Firewall, select Protect My Computer . . ., as shown in the figure. Click OK until you close all the windows.

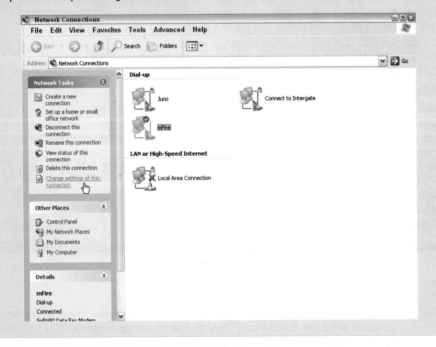

When the firewall is turned on, go online and use Windows Update (choose Start ⇨ All Programs ⇨ Windows Update) to immediately identify, download, and install the latest critical fixes for your PC. Although other issues might still crop up at some point, this gives you a decent basic layer of protection, and it's a lot better than sending your PC out onto the Internet naked and exposed.

Like the firewall already mentioned, Norton AntiSpam usually needs some careful tweaking so it doesn't intercept important messages from work or a warning that your beloved mother-in-law is about to visit. With a little careful training, you won't miss much — except the junk in your mailbox.

Norton Parental Control

Here's the product to use when you want to set limitations for the things your kids can do or reach online. If you've tried Microsoft Internet Explorer's Content Advisor tool or the parental controls from America Online, you'll be familiar with the concept of this software, which offers the same basic idea by turning you into the supervisor of your Web browser controls. You can get past the blocks if you choose, but your kids hopefully won't.

Are You Mixing and Matching Sets and Packages?

You're probably going to get your best results if you don't mix and match one version of this Norton product with an elderly version of another. This is true whether you're talking about Norton Internet Security or something else. For example, if you're using a two-year-old version of Norton Personal Firewall and now you install Norton AntiVirus, the two may not operate in perfect unison.

One bit of good news: If you're using an older version of a Norton product and want to upgrade, you can usually get the update for a lower price than you can a whole new version. Also, you may not notice a huge difference or incompatibility unless there is more than a year or two between the versions.

You can check your Norton version from the Help window by selecting About or by checking Help and Support from the main Norton tool window. You can also click the Norton Internet Security globe icon and choose About from the menu.

For example, if you have an old version of Norton AntiVirus installed — maybe one you haven't been so careful to keep updated for best protection — when you first install Norton Internet Security, one of the first operations it performs is to render that dinosaur of yours extinct and install its own new version.

Even if you happen to decide you liked the look or feel of the previous version of Norton AntiVirus, resist the temptation to try to reinstall the older version over the top of the NIS copy. Not only will it probably not work but the old copy may not be designed to take advantage of all the latest LiveUpdate options.

Here's something else to expect. If you do have a previous Norton AntiVirus setup and you have quarantined files stored within it (see Book VI, Chapter 4 for details), you're asked if you want to keep these files shielded from your PC. I suggest keeping them, because Norton AntiVirus will just pick these files up again and add them to the quarantine of your new Norton AntiVirus version.

Norton Accounts and Customizing What You Install and Use

Norton gives you some choices for how you install and set up certain features, including Parental Controls and Privacy Control. Some of these tools and features require you to establish and use accounts where each person sharing a PC gets a user name and password assigned. That account information must be supplied whenever the person goes to use a Norton tool that needs him to be logged on to access.

If you set up accounts when you install Norton, you can log on and log off NIS to change users without logging off Windows altogether. This way you can take advantage of personalized security settings. When you install Norton Internet Security, choose a Custom install to add support for accounts and for Parental Control. (For more information on Parental Control, see the "Norton

Parental Control" section, earlier in this chapter.) Click to check Accounts as one of the options you want installed. This account — called a Supervisor account — then becomes the main account. Additional accounts for other people can then be added.

After it's installed and when Norton Internet Security loads with Windows, the main account is automatically logged on. To log off, just right-click the Norton Internet Security icon in the System Tray and choose Log off. The same steps are available to log on again.

In this section, I walk you through accounts.

If more than one person shares your PC, setting up accounts in Norton Internet Security lets each of you decide exactly what settings you want to use. Adults can choose their preferred security level while parents can tweak their kids' settings.

**Book II
Chapter 3**

**Using Norton
Internet Security**

Here's how to add accounts:

1. **Open Norton Internet Security.**

2. **Click User Accounts.**

3. **Click Create an Account.**

4. **Type a name and password for the account you're adding, then type the password again to confirm it.**

5. **Click to select the account type (adult versus supervisor, or child versus teen).**

6. **Click OK.**

One thing you don't get to do during the setup process is choose exactly which programs within Norton Internet Security to include. You also can't go back and remove one program — like Norton Personal Firewall — separately.

What you can do is to go back to modify your settings to add accounts and Parental Control if you didn't do so during setup. To do this, follow these steps:

1. **Choose Start ⇨ Control Panel.**

2. **Double-click the Add or Remove Programs icon.**

3. **Locate and point to Norton Internet Security in your list of programs and click Change.**

4. **From the Modify Installation window, click Modify (see Figure 3-1).**

5. **Click Yes and then Finish to complete the change.**

You probably noticed that from the Add or Remove Programs window, you also have the option to remove Norton Internet Security. Use this if you want to completely remove the package from your PC.

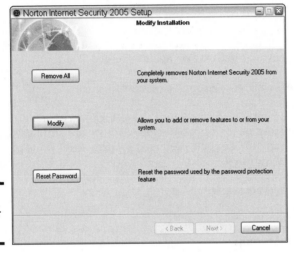

Figure 3-1:
Modify your
NIS setup.

Launching Norton Internet Security

After Norton Internet Security installs, you need to restart your PC (Norton Internet Security asks whether to do this now or later — choosing now is your best bet). When you do restart, the suite is available to use and it's running in the background on your desktop when Windows loads.

To launch it, either click the Norton Internet globe icon in Windows System Tray and choose Open Norton Internet Security. Or Choose Start ➪ All Programs ➪ Norton Internet Security ➪ Norton Internet Security.

The Norton Internet Security main window (shown in Figure 3-2) opens to the status and settings screen. Each of the top three buttons is critical:

✦ **Block Traffic/Allow Traffic:** Click this when the button reads Block Traffic, and you can halt all Internet traffic to and from your system (useful if you have a problem with your connection and you want to disconnect); click it when the button says Allow Traffic and you restart your ability to move around the Internet.

✦ **LiveUpdate:** This option is available in many Norton products and allows you to update your software to handle the latest threats as well as upgrade to newer Norton product components or features.

✦ **Options:** Here you can choose your personal preferences for how Norton Internet Security works.

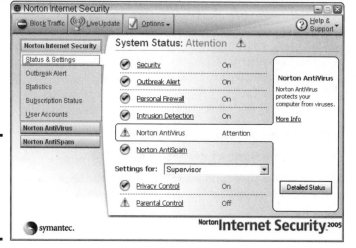

Figure 3-2:
Norton
Internet
Security's
main status
screen.

Notice that at the left of the window, you see menu options. Right now, Norton Internet Security is chosen so you see the options listed beneath it, including

✦ **Status and settings:** This is the main window that opens each time you launch Norton Internet Security.

✦ **Outbreak Alert:** Click this to see any notifications about current Internet outbreaks such as viruses and worms (see Book VI, Chapter 1 for more information).

✦ **Subscription Status:** This option is usually used most when you're taking advantage of a Norton trial version; it reminds you of the date by which you must register the software to get full and continuous protection, as well as when your subscription period expires requiring you to resubscribe before you can continue to receive new updates.

✦ **User Accounts:** This displays information for the different people who may use your PC (one of the things you configured when you installed Norton Internet Security).

Go down the left-hand side of the screen and you discover menu options for Norton AntiVirus and Norton AntiSpam, too, because they're part of the suite. Book V tells you what you need to know to tweak Norton AntiSpam, while Book VI shows you how to configure and use Norton AntiVirus.

Other features available in Norton Internet Security such as the firewall and the parental and privacy controls are managed directly through Norton Internet Security.

Disabling Norton Internet Security

At any point, you're free to temporarily turn off Norton Internet Security. Why would you want to? If you're having trouble staying connected or accessing a site on the Web and want to see if NIS has anything to do with this problem, you might turn it off briefly to see.

To turn off Norton Internet Security:

1. **Right-click the NIS icon in System Tray.**

2. **Select Disable Norton Internet Security.**

3. **When the Disable window appears, select the time period during which you want it to remain off before switching back on (see Figure 3-3).**

4. **Click OK.**

Figure 3-3:
Disable
Norton
Internet
Security.

After NIS is disabled, you can wait until it turns itself on automatically or you can click the NIS icon again and select Enable.

When NIS is disabled, much of your basic protection goes with it. However, scheduled virus scans with Norton AntiVirus continue to run as does the LiveUpdate.

Configuring Norton Internet Security

When you open Norton Internet Security, you land right at the main status and settings window. Click on the underlined options such as Security to see a submenu open at the right of the window, allowing you to turn a feature on or off or check its settings, as shown in Figure 3-4.

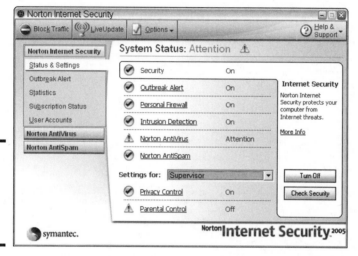

**Book II
Chapter 3**

**Using Norton
Internet Security**

Figure 3-4:
Turn on/off
features
from the
NIS status
window.

Notice that, in Figure 3-4, there is a button marked Check Security. Click this with a live connection to the Internet, and you're magically transported to Symantec's security site to let you test your security setup to see how effective it is (see Figure 3-5). Click Go and the test is performed, with your report card given out at the end.

Use the Check Security option after you've configured Norton Internet Security and regularly (maybe once a month) thereafter, just to be sure you're properly protected.

Now I want you to peer deeply into the NIS settings to see what's there. Follow these steps:

1. **Open Norton Internet Security.**

2. **Click Options and choose Norton Internet Security.**

   A multi-tabbed window opens to the first tab, General (see Figure 3-6).

3. **Check your current settings to see if they make sense to you.**

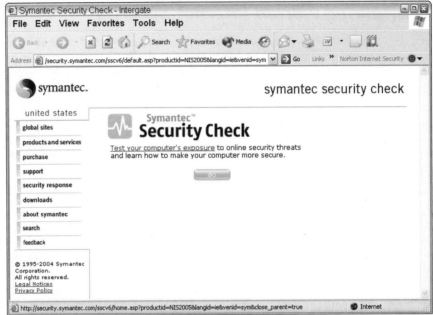

Figure 3-5:
Test your PC security online.

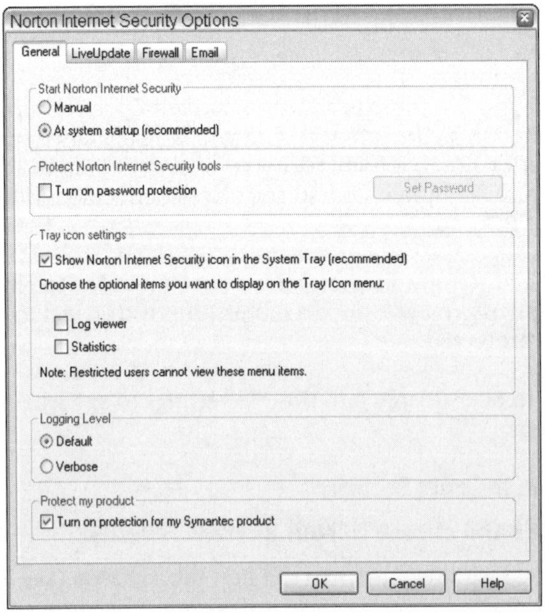

Figure 3-6:
Your General Norton settings.

These settings include the following:

- How NIS starts (automatically rather than manually)
- Whether to require a password to open and change NIS (select to add a password)
- Whether to show the NIS icon in the System Tray
- How much information should go into your Norton log (a special file created that records all the details about what NIS does — select to check Verbose if you plan to use the log and want the most detail)
- Whether to protect your Norton product (checked automatically)

4. Make any changes desired, and click OK.

**Book II
Chapter 3**

**Using Norton
Internet Security**

Look back at the tabbed window seen in Figure 3-7 and you notice the other tabs read LiveUpdate, Firewall, and Email. Each tab lets you configure the basics for each tool.

You'll find out more about these in some detail as you begin to work with individual Norton products in Book III. In the following sections, I give you a peek at what's there to customize.

Checking your LiveUpdate settings

How does LiveUpdate work to keep your Norton products current for the latest threats and file fixes? The answer is as automatically as you want it to work.

What happens here is that Symantec sends its own version of an interoffice memo around to its software through your Internet connection, so your setup always knows when new files are ready. This takes all the pesky work of having to go check periodically for yourself. If you're anything like me, you'll forget to do that for months on end.

Follow these steps to check your NIS LiveUpdate settings:

1. In Norton Internet Security, click Options.

2. Select Norton Internet Security.

3. Select the LiveUpdate tab.

Most options listed here are designed to work pretty automatically, but you can reset anything to specify that NIS handle it as it wants or to notify you so you can decide how you want to run LiveUpdate each time updates become available.

Viewing your firewall setup

You can view or adjust your firewall settings in different ways — one with a more general emphasis and the other more specific.

First, open Norton Internet Security and click on Personal Firewall. To the right, you see that you have your choices of buttons: Turn Off (which does exactly that; if the firewall is already off, this button reads Turn On) and Configure.

Click Configure and you see a master control panel, as shown in Figure 3-7 with five tabs, each offering specifics about the way Norton is running your firewall. For complete details about these various settings, see Book VII, Chapter 1.

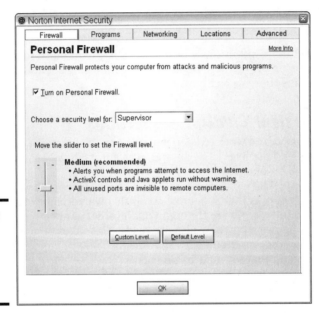

Figure 3-7:
Norton
Personal
Firewall
control
settings.

You can make other choices from within Norton Internet Security as well. To view these:

1. **In NIS, click Options and then Norton Internet Security.**

2. **Choose the Firewall tab.**

What you see here may seem hopelessly complicated, but most of it refers to how much your PC gets locked down and away from unwanted access from the outside or from programs on your PC — perhaps operating under the direction of a virus or spyware — trying to access the Net to deliver information. Click the Help button to get the lowdown on some of the settings here.

With any firewall, including Norton Personal Firewall, you'll sometimes see mentions of ports. A port is used for PC communications. Windows offers hundreds of them, many tied to specific port numbers (Web servers use port 80, for example). You'll find out more about this in Book VII, Chapter 1 where I cover Norton Personal Firewall in detail. Normally, you don't need to worry about setting up or excluding specific ports.

Locating your e-mail settings

Because Norton AntiSpam is controlled through its own menu in Norton Internet Security, the only options under the Email tab when you click Options and then Norton Internet Security allow you to:

+ Specify whether to show a "scanning e-mail" icon in your System Tray during mail checks

+ Display a progress meter

To find out about configuring Norton AntiSpam, see Book V, especially from Chapter 3 on.

Reviewing Your Norton Internet Security Log

Logs are a great tool when you're troubleshooting some kind of problem or assorted weirdness with a program or other PC component. Because of this, many applications and Windows functions actually create similar logs; look in the online help for them and you can usually figure out where the log — often saved as a text file that can be opened by any text editor such as Notepad — is stored.

Norton Internet Security keeps a log of its activities. This can help if you want to go back and review the log later to see if you can stop problems or attempted intrusions. You may want to take a moment to find out how to review this log and see what you find there.

To review your NIS log:

1. **Open Norton Internet Security.**

2. **Select Statistics from the left-hand menu.**

3. Click the View Logs button (see Figure 3-8).

4. When Log Viewer opens as shown, click on any option from the left navigation pane to have details open at the right.

For example, click Connections under Norton Internet Security to see a summary of your Internet connections as seen by NIS (see Figure 3-9).

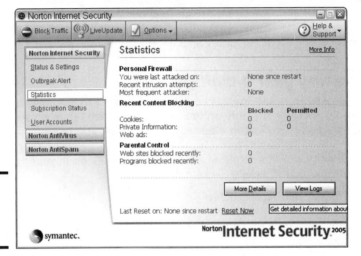

Figure 3-8:
Click View
Logs from
Statistics.

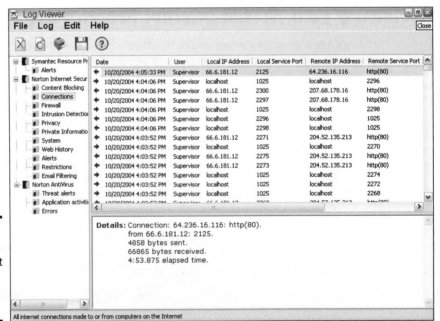

Figure 3-9:
Reviewing a
log of recent
Internet
connection
sessions.

Notice that the Norton Internet Security section alone is broken down into 11 different categories. When you click on a category on the left, then an entry on the right, specific details about the selected entry appear in the bottom-right window.

Norton gives you these categories:

✦ **Content Blocking:** Records information about any sessions in which controls like Parental Control you've configured have blocked questionable content from view.

✦ **Connections:** Provides a history of your recent online sessions.

✦ **Firewall:** Summarizes any kind of situation where Norton had to intercept what it saw as an attempted unwanted access onto or from your system.

✦ **Intrusion Detection:** Gives you a breakdown of what intrusion threats are being monitored and how many signatures — suspect IDs for worms and other problems — are in effect.

✦ **Privacy:** This section notes Norton Internet Security's efforts to block files being sent to your PC from the Internet; this can include *cookies* (small files that rot your privacy rather than your teeth but can be used in helpful ways to note what you've already read on a Web site or to save your password so you won't have to type it in during your next visit).

✦ **Private Information:** Look here for any attempts to access private information about you stored on your system.

✦ **System:** The "housekeeping" of connection information and when someone's logged in to Norton is found here (see Figure 3-10).

✦ **Web History:** Notes any unique issues to report about your Web browsing sessions (many of the entries are apt to relate to LiveUpdate and its efforts to keep your Norton software up-to-date).

✦ **Alerts:** Look here for details about any changes made or rules set for Norton operation.

✦ **Restrictions:** Provides data about any restricted situations that are noted (often blank unless you have strong privacy and parental controls set).

✦ **Email filtering:** Details data about anything "picked up" in a scan of your incoming e-mail for problems or spam attacks.

Note, too, that Log Viewer has a menu bar. Open the Log menu and you see options for refreshing (updating) your Log and for clearing entries to start fresh. You can also select Disable All Logging (something you can do if you're sure you'll never look at the logs) here.

To close Log Viewer, simply click the X in the top-right corner or choose File ➪ Exit.

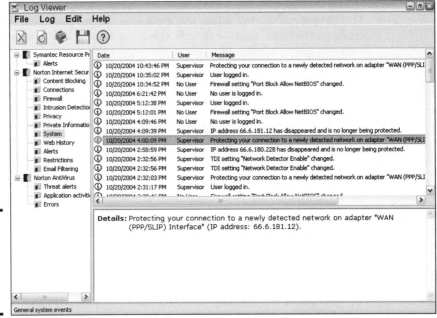

Figure 3-10:
The System section lists house-keeping notes.

Cookies aren't always best crumbled

Cookies — the Internet rather than the Toll House variety — have a pretty bad reputation. The biggest gripe is that they're passed around on the sly with most people having no idea of exactly what ingredients that little bite of computer dough contains.

Web sites you visit send them to you when your Web browser opens their sites, where the cookies get stored on your hard drive in a Temporary folder. They usually take up very little space individually, but if you're addicted to the Net, you can wind up with hundreds upon hundreds of these files. The figure shows a bunch of them on my drive when I use Windows Search (Start ⇨ Search) and search on the word "cookie" in files on my drive. And wouldn't you know? Not one of these files is a recipe for snickerdoodles.

Exactly what's in that cookie differs from site to site — and sometimes, from page to page on the same Web site. Some Webmasters design them to help recognize you when you return (it helps them keep track of their site visitors to distinguish unique visitors from happy returnees, among other possibilities) and others store little markers in your cookie to identify where you've already been on the site. Some can get more invasive.

Although Web cookies can irritate the sweet tooth out of some Web surfers, understand that not all cookies rot your privacy or your free disk space. Some are created with the main goal being to help give you a better experience when you revisit a Web site so you don't have to plough through all the same screens or messages again.

Also, there are some sites that simply won't let you visit them — or may not give you access to some features on the site — if you refuse all cookies. You end up stuck: Crumble all cookies and you may be locked out of your favorite Sports page or shopping site, but let all cookies in, and your drive begins to get littered with these "treats," not all of which may be good for you.

So don't worry about busting every cookie you get unless you have some real reason to suspect that you're the recipient of some truly awful ones. If the latter description fits you, then you may want to raise your security to block all cookies.

To block all cookies, open Norton Internet Security (or Norton Personal Firewall), then click on Privacy Control and then Configure. Here, if you move the slider bar up to raise the security level to high, you effectively block all cookies. Choose Medium instead, and Norton (through your browser) will warn you each time a site attempts to pass a cookie so you can decide "yea" or "nay" on the fly. Click OK when you're done configuring.

One more thing: If you block all cookies but want to permit one from specific sites, go back into Privacy Control (just as you did in the previous paragraph) and choose Advanced.

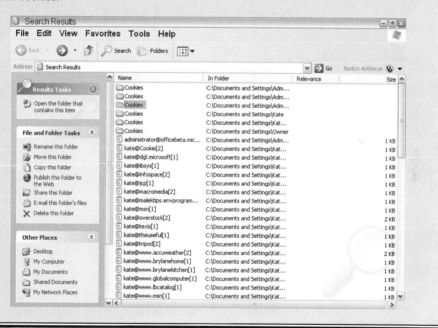

Book III

Norton Utilities

The 5th Wave   By Rich Tennant

©RICHTENNANT

"We take network security very seriously here."

Contents at a Glance

Chapter 1: Giving Your PC a One Button Checkup

In This Chapter

✔ Understanding what the checkup looks for

✔ Running your One Button Checkup

✔ Customizing and reviewing your checkup

✔ Putting the checkup on a schedule

✔ Handling problems the checkup reports

✔ Knowing where to go from here

*N*orton SystemWorks and its Norton Utilities tools work something like a PC emergency room and triage center trying to identify and fix the things that go bump and beep on your system.

But what if you just want a quick spot check to see if there is something actually wrong before you call out the bigger guns? After all, you might want to be sure to run a backup or use either Windows System Restore or Norton GoBack before you launch one of the big tools. You know, just in case.

As it happens, Norton includes a special tool just designed for rapid identification and repair of typical conditions. One Button Checkup is its name and speed is its game.

When you're planning to see the doctor, it's easy to think to yourself, "Boy, I hope it's fast and that the good doc doesn't poke and prod too much!" That's sort of the concept behind the Norton Utilities One Button Checkup: a quick evaluation that looks for typical PC woes and alerts you to what it finds. It's all done without you needing a stethoscope or asking your PC to put on a silly gown and then to turn and cough.

One Button Checkup won't look at everything on your PC and it may not fix all the ills. But it's a smart first step when you first install Norton SystemWorks with Norton Utilities or when you want to check your system between running the full-fledged doctors available.

In the following sections, I show you what it checks, then take you through the steps to run it. I show you how to put your checkup on a schedule as well as what you need to do if the checkup can't successfully treat and fix everything it reports as problematic.

Knowing What Gets Checked

Just as an emergency room crew gets a patient and does a fast evaluation of vital signs and what needs to be done, so does One Button Checkup. It's pre-programmed to go through your system looking for problems typically seen with Windows and the system in general.

Specifically, it checks for common types of:

✦ Windows Registry foul-ups and mismatched entries

✦ Problems arising from a buildup of leftover Internet browsing files

✦ Missing desktop and other shortcuts

✦ Disk-based problems

✦ Performance and system woes

After you run One Button Checkup, you'll see what it finds wrong. Then you have the option of letting it try to fix what things it can. You can also look at details about the errors discovered.

One Button Checkup also looks at the status of your Norton AntiVirus software if you also have that installed.

Starting One Button Checkup

Trust me — four years of medical school aren't required to perform this checkup. All you need is a few clicks. The very first time you run it, however, you probably want to pay close attention so you get an idea of what it does as well as to evaluate what it finds.

Follow these steps:

1. **Double-click the Norton SystemWorks icon on your desktop.**

2. **From the System Status window (shown in Figure 1-1), click One Button Checkup and then Scan Now.**

3. **When the One Button Checkup window opens, notice that all the options like Windows Registry Scan and Program Integrity Scan (shown in Figure 1-2) are checked.**

4. **If you don't want to run a particular section, such as Last Virus Scan Check, deselect it.**

5. **Click Start Scan.**

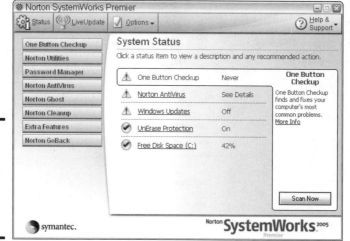

Figure 1-1:
Choose
Scan Now
from the
One Button
Checkup
window.

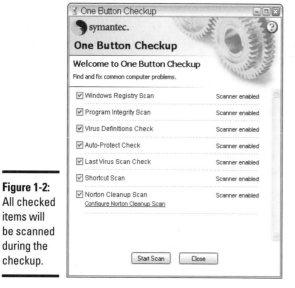

Figure 1-2:
All checked
items will
be scanned
during the
checkup.

After you start the scan, you'll see a status window telling you what stage the scan is at, such as Scanning or Analyzing. Don't be surprised if the checkup takes some time, even just from one item to another. Later in this chapter, I show you how to schedule your checkup to run when you're not sitting at the PC working or playing.

When the checkup is complete, you see a report card of sorts like that shown in Figure 1-3. Problems are shown in red, while "No Errors Found" messages are displayed in green.

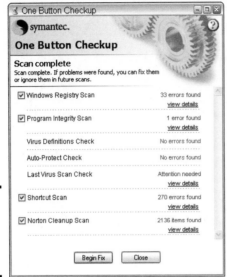

Figure 1-3:
Your
checkup
diagnostics
sheet.

Review your report and click View Details to see the additional info about an item that reports an error. Figure 1-4 shows an example of these details.

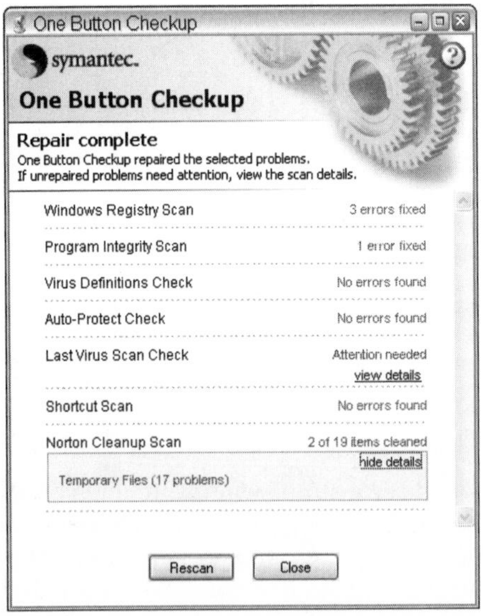

Figure 1-4:
Click View
Details to
find out
more about
the problem
diagnosed.

To let One Button Checkup try to repair the problems it's found, click Begin Fix. Check the "Handling problems reported" section of this chapter to see

Problems running One Button Checkup?

If you hit a problem running One Button Checkup, restart your PC and try again. It's possible that something running elsewhere on your desktop when you perform the checkup is hanging up your system and this can lead to the checkup freezing.

If the checkup continues to die on you, you may want to try one of three things:

✔ Close everything down on your desktop before you start the checkup.

✔ If that doesn't work, deselect one or more options from the One Button Checkup scanning window.

✔ If that doesn't help, you may want to run one of the doctors first. Norton WinDoctor and Norton System Doctor do more aggressive diagnostics than the checkup, so they may be able to clear a hurdle and then let you use checkup later.

what you need to do when One Button Checkup can't fix everything it finds, as shown in Figure 1-5. You can click Rescan if you want to try it again to see if it can resolve anything during a second pass that it didn't resolve during the first pass.

Need to halt the scan before it's finished? Just click Stop Scan at any time. You can then start it again when you're ready.

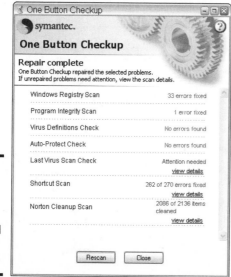

Figure 1-5:
One Button
Checkup
reports
what it fixed
and what it
could not.

Pay particular attention when you see the message "Attention Needed" from the diagnosis window. Use the View Details option whenever this happens and turn to "Handling problems reported," later in this chapter.

Customizing and Reviewing Your Checkups

One Button Checkup is a simple, straightforward tool, but it still offers some helpful options. Included is the ability to schedule your checkups, to customize them (say, if you never want it to check your antivirus software status because you monitor that yourself), and to review past problems and even undo repairs.

Here's how to customize and review your One Button Checkup:

1. **Open Norton SystemWorks.**

2. **From the left-hand menu, click One Button Checkup.**

The One Button Checkup configuration window opens as shown in Figure 1-6, with the following choices:

- **Start One Button Checkup:** Runs the checkup as you did before

- **Scheduling:** Lets you set up a specific time to run the checkup

- **Repair History:** Gives you the ability to check previous checkup histories and undo changes made (helpful when One Button Checkup makes a repair that doesn't seem to go well)

- **Options:** Allows you to customize your scans and when they occur

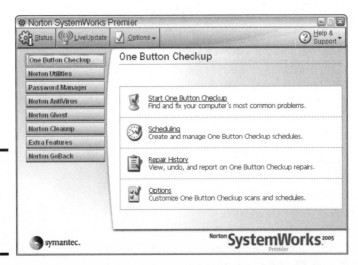

Figure 1-6:
Set your options for using One Button Checkup.

3. Click Options.

A multi-tabbed window appears:

- From the Scans tab, deselect any scan you normally don't want to include in the checkup.

- Select Ignored Problems to review any issues checkup couldn't repair and which you set to ignore.

- Click Repair History (see Figure 1-7) to make changes to how long a log of the checkup's repairs are kept (set by number of days, number of sessions, or forever if you want to keep everything). Click the + sign to see a list of all the fixes. You can select one of these and select Undo if you want to reverse the repair.

- Select the Scheduling tab to establish a time for your checkup to run (see "Scheduling Your Checkup" in this chapter for all the details).

4. Click OK and close Norton SystemWorks.

Figure 1-7:
Choose how long to save your checkup Repair History.

Book III
Chapter 1

Giving Your PC a One Button Checkup

Scheduling Your Checkup

You may not want the checkup to run while you're busy working or enjoying a game on the PC, because it can grab your attention and sometimes make the desktop seem just a tiny bit slower. To keep this from happening, you may want to set up a schedule so that the checkup runs at a specific time, such as during lunch or at the end of the day.

Actually, you'll usually discover that Norton has already set up a checkup schedule for you designed to run overnight on Mondays. However, that may not be too useful to you if you usually turn your PC off at night, so you'll want to edit the schedule and/or add additional scans (you can run checkup more than once each week, if you like).

When checkup runs on schedule, it does so in an automated mode that doesn't require you to sit right there and watch it. But if you choose to schedule your checkups, you'll want to take advantage of that Repair History option discussed in the previous section to keep track of what One Button Checkup has been doing.

Follow these steps to edit your checkup schedule:

1. **Open Norton SystemWorks.**

2. **Click One Button Checkup in the left-hand menu on the System Status screen.**

3. **Click Scheduling.**

4. **Select the single item listed under Schedule Name and click Edit.**

5. **From the Schedule tab (shown in Figure 1-8), follow these steps:**

   - Click on the drop-down list box beneath Schedule Task to set a frequency (example: daily, weekly, or monthly).

   - Under Start Time, click in the drop-down list box and choose an hour.

   - Click to check the day or days on which you want the checkup to run.

6. **Click OK.**

You can go back at any time to edit this schedule again.

You can also add custom One Button Checkup scans to your schedule. To do this, just open One Button Checkup, choose Scheduling, and click New. Select the scans you want to include (as you did before) through the Scans tab, and then establish its schedule through the Schedule tab.

To permanently remove One Button Checkup from this schedule, repeat Steps 1 through 3 in this section, and then, in Step 4, choose the scan you want to remove and click Delete.

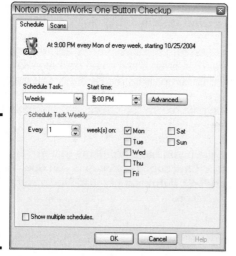

**Book III
Chapter 1**

**Giving Your PC a
One Button Checkup**

Figure 1-8:
Tell Norton
exactly
when to run
checkup
when you'll
be away
from the PC.

Getting a Second Opinion

In life as well as PCs, there's a price to be paid for speed. A fast doctor's exam isn't always the best — the doc may only check your eyes, ears, and lungs and take a look at your blood pressure. A fast exam may mean the doctor will miss things that could be wrong under the surface.

That's the case with One Button Checkup: It only looks so deeply into your system and it only identifies what it's designed to check. It also can't fix everything that can be wrong with your system.

But, luckily, you're not limited to just these rapid checkups. Norton Utilities and SystemWorks give you a whole ambulance gear box full of tools that can examine various parts of your system — including Windows, disks, and overall system performance. Where needed, these doctors and wizards can perform delicate surgery or suck clogging fat or defects from a bloated Windows Registry.

Handling problems reported

It's a bummer when One Button Checkup finds a few — or even a few hundred — problems but it can't fix them all. However, there's no reason to think your PC is terminal and needs life support.

Chances are that if your PC seemed to operate pretty well before the checkup, it will continue to run even when not all necessary repairs are done. Also, some of what checkup looks for includes rather simple errors that aren't apt to result in a dead system if they don't get fixed.

Yet, with that said, getting outstanding issues corrected so they don't multiply or grow in size is a good idea. Even a few small problems can sap overall performance and cause at least minor headaches. Also, you may get a harsher diagnosis with lots of serious problems not corrected by checkup. Worse, you may not even be able to run the checkup thoroughly because your system is so fouled up.

The first thing you can try when you have problems that aren't getting fixed is to rescan using One Button Checkup. If checkup is still open on your desktop, click Rescan (see Figure 1-9). If not, simply load Norton SystemWorks and go through the checkup again.

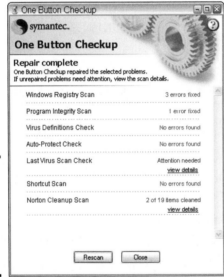

Figure 1-9:
Click
Rescan to
go through
the checkup
routine
again.

If a rescan still shows errors when it completes — and especially if they're serious ones under Windows Registry or Program Integrity Scan — you may want to call on the doctors. I point you to the right one in the "Doing your homework" section at the end of this chapter.

After you run checkup, the date is recorded on the System Status screen when you open Norton SystemWorks. Check there first if you're wondering when you last ran it.

TIP

"Why do I keep getting errors?"

Don't be enormously surprised if you run One Button Checkup again not long after you last ran it and find a whole new roster of errors. That's pretty common in my experience. The figure shows a checkup report on my system done just a few hours after I ran checkup previously, and yet I've got new problems.

You can develop new issues just in working with Windows, especially if you're trying other fixes around your system as part of your overall doctoring effort. Windows may not like every change you make and some of these changes may show up under checkup as an error.

Still, be sure to consider what may be causing frequent errors, particularly if you notice that whenever you run checkup after playing a game or running a program or game on the Web, checkup finds new problems. Simple measures such as defragmenting your hard drive (using Windows Disk Defragmenter or

Norton SpeedDisk) or cleaning up your hard drive (using Windows Disk Cleanup or Norton Cleanup) may be able to solve them.

One Button Checkup	
symantec.	
One Button Checkup	
Scan complete	
Scan complete. If problems were found, you can fix them or ignore them in future scans.	
☑ Windows Registry Scan	3 errors found
	view details
☑ Program Integrity Scan	1 error found
	view details
Virus Definitions Check	No errors found
Auto-Protect Check	No errors found
Last Virus Scan Check	Attention needed
	view details
Shortcut Scan	No errors found
☑ Norton Cleanup Scan	19 items found
	view details
Begin Fix	Close

Doing your homework

No, no! You don't need to go running for some 1,400-page PC reference book to try to resolve the errors that One Button Checkup can't fix. You just need to turn elsewhere in Norton SystemWorks and Norton Utilities for help.

If you encounter Windows Registry errors, it's time to call upon Norton WinDoctor detailed in Chapter 5 of this book.

For Program Integrity woes, Norton WinDoctor may help, too. But you should also consult with Norton Disk Doctor and Norton System Doctor. These are covered in Chapters 3 and 4 of this book, respectively.

If the problems show up under Cleanup, then run Norton Cleanup before you re-run checkup to see if you can clear the cobwebs out of your drive.

Chapter 2: Improving Disk Performance with Norton Speed Disk

In This Chapter

✔ **Understanding how disk fragmentation hurts your system**

✔ **Configuring Norton Speed Disk**

✔ **Optimizing your hard drives with Norton Speed Disk**

✔ **Scheduling your disk maintenance**

✔ **Knowing how often to optimize**

*I*f you're busy, your hard disk is frenetically so. It not only has to keep up with your frantic pace, it has to keep track of every little file you write to them so you can find these files again.

So much can happen to your drive as you work. Your hard drive has to put up with your incomplete PC shutdowns and restarts and tolerate the way you run it when it's over- or underheated.

Yet one of the very best things you can do for your beleaguered hard disk is also one of the easiest: You can properly maintain it using special software designed to reorganize how data is written to the drive. It's almost faster than flossing your teeth and the whole operation can be done while you're away from the keyboard.

That's my focus here in this chapter, using the Norton Speed Disk utility included with Norton Utilities in Norton SystemWorks and SystemWorks Premier.

The Lowdown on Drive Fragmentation

It's easy to underestimate how poorly a badly fragmented hard disk performs. Like tooth decay, a little problem that can be ignored also may grow into a much more significant one without much effort at all. Also like a tooth going bad, a little attention can go a long way in preventing bigger bills and more trouble.

You'll notice that Norton Speed Disk calls what it does *disk optimization*. But it means the very same thing as defragmenting.

How your drive becomes fragmented

Hard drives, just like almost everything else that occurs in life, cry out for organization. If you gave a hard drive a choice, it would always want files written to it neatly, in proper order, so it could find the files you store there.

Yet the ways in which people abuse these precious drives defeat the drive's natural sense of order. Drives become fragmented through a number of different uses and misuses of our PCs, including

✦ PC crashes and improper shutdowns

✦ Badly-behaved software

✦ Working with files from the MS-DOS command line (as shown in Figure 2-1) rather than Windows

✦ An overfilled hard drive where you're constantly fighting for free space

✦ Abruptly terminating programs open on your desktop rather than closing them normally

Only hard disks and floppy disks need to be defragmented. Removable media drives like recordable CDs and DVDs do not.

Figure 2-1:
Deleting
files from
the
command
prompt can
increase
fragment-
ation.

Diagnosing common symptoms

Believe it or not, a badly fragmented hard disk can behave very much like one that's about to take the long dirt nap. The good news is that unlike a dying hard disk, a heavily fragmented one can often be cured or at least brought under control.

When you crash

Ever have the PC lock up during a session, only to restart and find yourself facing a disk check before Windows can reload? If you do, go through the disk check. Doing so can help repair small problems created during the crash and can reduce (but not eliminate) your urgent need to defragment. But if you begin to notice that the disk check has to run almost every session, definitely defragment using Norton Speed Disk and consider advice later in this chapter to follow this up with a session with Norton Disk Doctor.

Some of the symptoms you may experience with a fragmented drive include the following:

✦ Overall slowness with accessing files

✦ Constant low noise from the hard disk as it churns and works to find and save files

✦ A certain funkiness when loading programs on your desktop (yes, that's the technical description — funkiness)

✦ Low memory errors (not from low installed memory but the special area of the hard disk used as virtual memory)

✦ Difficulty in Web browsing (your browser may seem sluggish as you try to move back and forth between Web pages)

If any of these sound familiar, it's time to defragment using Norton Speed Disk.

You don't have to wait until the symptoms become so obvious either. Defragmenting once a week — especially if your hard disk gets a hard workout — is smart. It can also keep these symptoms from ever rearing their ugly heads to roar at you.

How often is too often?

People often ask the question, "How often is too often with disk defragmenting?" In truth, most people probably don't do it enough. Yet there are others who defragment almost as often as they shower, meaning on average at least once per day.

There's rarely any need to defragment even a busy hard disk more than once a week. The most important thing about defragmenting is to do it. Then you need to keep doing it regularly.

Later in this chapter, I show you how you can schedule your disk defragmenting, so you won't have to wonder *if* you remembered to do this maintenance. Instead, you can set it up to run while you're away from your desk.

Defragmenting while you're not trying to use your computer is critical because disk defragmenting — whether you're using Norton Speed Disk or Windows Defragmenter — works best when files aren't open and programs aren't busy on your desktop. Also, the process of defragmenting your data can take a good long while, especially if you have a very large drive or you're checking multiple drives. So you don't want Norton Speed Disk open while you're otherwise engaged.

Revving Up with Speed Disk

Put down the screwdriver and place those latex gloves back in a drawer. These aren't needed to defragment or optimize your drive.

Now follow these steps to prepare to defragment:

1. **Close all open windows and programs on your desktop.**

2. **If you've had a rocky or unstable Windows session prior to disk defragmenting, you may want to restart your system first.**

You have a couple of choices for how you start Norton Speed Disk. You can:

1. **Open Norton SystemWorks.**

2. **Click Norton Utilities from the left-hand menu.**

3. **Select Optimize Performance and then click Speed Disk.**

4. **Click Continue.**

Or you can follow these steps:

1. **Choose Start ⇨ All Programs ⇨ Norton System Works ⇨ Norton Utilities ⇨ Norton Speed Disk.**

2. **Click Continue.**

Norton Speed Disk opens on your desktop just as shown in Figure 2-2. Now follow these steps:

1. **Select the drive you want to defragment (you can always return after the first drive is done to do another).**

2. **Open the Actions menu and click Start Optimizing.**

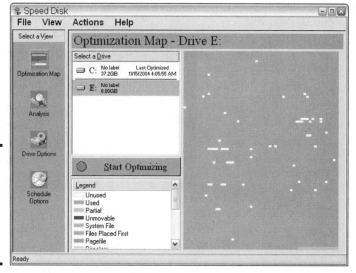

Figure 2-2:
Norton Disk
Doctor
ready to
diagnose
and
reorganize.

Bingo! The process begins. First, Speed Disk analyzes your drive. Then it begins to sort out your files and other data. Then it begins to move those file chunks around for better organization.

Look at the legend at the bottom-left corner of the Norton Speed Disk window (see Figure 2-3) and you can tell what you're seeing at the right side where colors change and little chunks move. White areas show unused space while dark-gray areas show used chunks. Partially used chunks are displayed in light gray while system files appear in pink.

Exactly how long the process takes depends on a number of factors, including

 ✦ The size of your hard disk

 ✦ The last time you defragmented

 ✦ The overall speed of your PC

 ✦ How much use-abuse the PC has suffered since the last defragmentation

Don't be shocked if it takes between 15 and 45 minutes during the first round. Although Norton Speed Disk normally optimizes faster than Windows Disk Defragmenter, it still takes a while to scan, sort, move, and otherwise optimize. So now's the time to raid the kitchen, go read your kid a bedtime story, or catch the end of a movie.

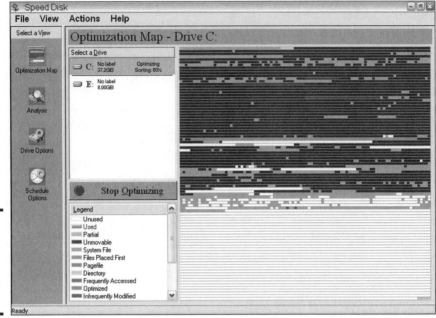

Figure 2-3:
Your hard
disk legend
reports
what Speed
Disk sees.

 It may appear as though Norton Speed Disk is just sitting there, seemingly doing nothing, for periods of time. Although it's actually working, you may not be able to tell this. Don't panic and restart your system or try to close Norton Speed Disk until you're sure there has been no activity for several (more than five) minutes.

 One thing you don't want to do right now is load a program or get on the Internet. Let Norton Speed Disk work without interruption. It works best and fastest when it doesn't have to work around open files and programs. Interrupt Speed Disk too much and you may have to start all over again.

When Norton Speed Disk finishes and alerts you to this, you're ready to look at the right side of the screen where you see the final results. This shows a picture of your data reorganized. Click the Analysis button at the left and look at your drive post-optimization, as shown in Figure 2-4. This gives you the lowdown on how well the disk optimization went, how much free space fragmentation you may still have, as well as how much of your drive is being used.

At this point, you can click the Optimize Map on the left and defragment another drive. Or you can set your options for both your drives and to run Speed Disk.

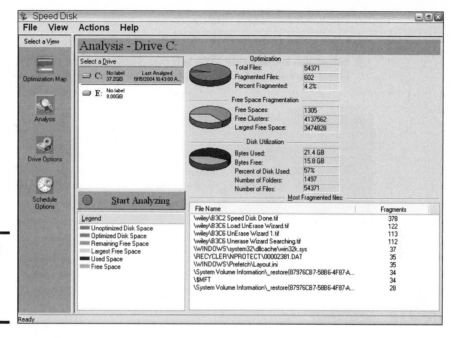

Figure 2-4:
Analyzing your post-optimized drive.

Setting your options

Norton Speed Disk gives you some choice in how it should work. With it, you can designate certain files that shouldn't be moved around as part of disk optimization and you can schedule your Norton Speed Disk sessions to run when you're not around.

Marking your files

You can assign certain files — probably files that are particularly important to you — a special location either at the physical beginning of your free hard disk space or at the end so that these files don't get changed around a lot in the optimization process.

Normally, you don't have to worry about assigning space to files. In fact, you probably don't want to do anything with this feature unless it becomes necessary. You may want to do this if you hit a problem where important files become damaged or corrupted or you can't find them immediately after you defragment.

Let's say you have a very important paper due for work or school called My Report.doc. You've had a previous problem with this file after disk defragmenting so you want to protect it from harm. Here's an example of what you can do to assign it a special space during disk defragmentation:

1. **Open Norton Speed Disk.**

2. **Click Drive Options from the left-side menu.**

3. **Select the Unmovable Files tab (see Figure 2-5) to specify that any files listed here won't be moved about as part of the disk defragmentation.**

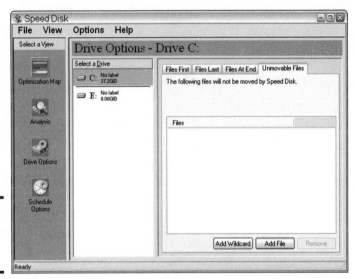

Figure 2-5:
Select
Unmovable
Files.

4. **Click Add File.**

5. **Locate and select the file you want to add to this list and click Open (see Figure 2-6).**

Figure 2-6:
Add a file to
the list.

With this file now added to your "unmovable list," you've told Norton Speed Disk *not* to touch this file as it defragments your drive. This should keep it from any possible problem.

Now you're ready to run Norton Speed Disk with this one file designated as unmovable. You can also specify where other files should be resituated on the disk, such as:

✦ **Files First:** Any files placed here are positioned at the very beginning of the drive, ahead of other data.

✦ **Files Last:** Designated files are placed behind all other data on the drive.

✦ **Files At End:** Specified files are placed at the very end of the disk, behind all other data as well as free space.

If you later want to remove a file you've added to your unmovable list, follow these steps:

1. **Open Norton Speed Disk.**

2. **Click Drive Options.**

3. **Select the first tab where you've added files.**

4. **Choose the file from the list and click Remove (see Figure 2-7).**

5. **Repeat as needed to remove other specially added files.**

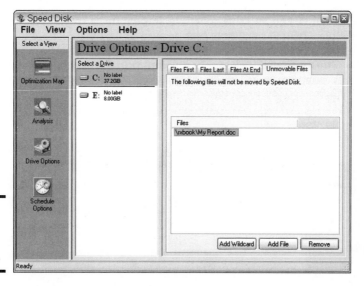

Figure 2-7:
Remove
specially
added files.

Setting schedule options

You can place your disk defragmenter on a schedule so you don't have to remember this maintenance routine on top of the 300 other details you juggle every day. Just keep in mind that you want Norton Speed Disk to run while you're away from the PC but at a time when you know the PC will be on and available.

Here's how to do this:

1. **Open Norton Speed Disk.**

2. **Click Schedule Options from the left-hand menu.**

3. **From the Schedule window (shown in Figure 2-8):**

- Click to check Enable Schedule.

- Select the Frequency drop-down list and choose a time period such as Weekly.

- Click to check a day of the week to run the scan.

- Set a start time, such as 1:00 AM.

- Select Optimized Based on Threshold and then select Only Optimize Drive If Fragmentation Exceeds and specify a percentage (for example, 40%).

4. **Click Apply.**

There! You're set to boogie — or at least defragment your selected drive — at a set time each week. Now if only you could floss and do aerobics while you sleep.

You're not locked into this schedule. Repeat these steps to change the schedule whenever you like. Just be sure to designate a time when your PC will be available. If the PC happens to be turned off or otherwise engaged when Norton Speed Disk is scheduled to run, the disk defragmentation simply won't happen. It's okay to go an extra week between optimization, but you don't want to repeatedly miss doing it.

Figure 2-8:
Scheduling
your disk
scan and
defrag-
mentation.

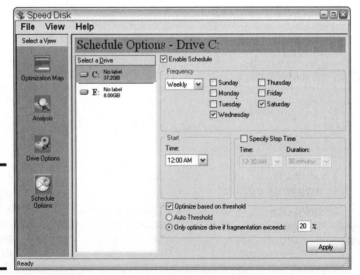

Handling problems

Yes, problems can happen. Norton Speed Disk may encounter a situation it can't immediately fix or work around. It may stall out or keep restarting.

The first thing you should do in such situations is to make sure everything else on your desktop is closed. If programs are open and running in the background, click or right-click on their icons in the Windows System Tray (bottom-right corner of your desktop at the far end of your task bar) and temporarily disable them as shown in Figure 2-9.

Occasionally, Norton Speed Disk may hang up while it's working. If this happens, try to close Speed Disk. If that doesn't work, restart your entire system and then reload Norton Speed Disk to try again.

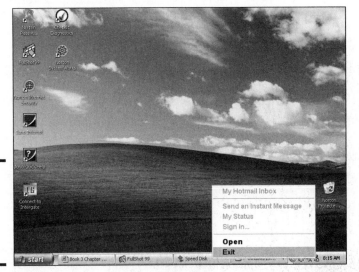

Figure 2-9:
Close open programs from the System Tray.

Overcoming Issues with Use

What happens if you hit repeated problems trying to run Norton Disk Doctor? More aggressive medical intervention may be required.

If you haven't done so already, consider running Norton Disk Doctor (covered in Chapter 3) before you try to defragment again. If Norton Disk Doctor says it's found a problem it can't fix that session, go ahead and schedule it to perform the repair when your system restarts. Then be sure to restart and let that fix happen before you run Speed Disk.

If you suspect the problem lies with Windows itself rather than the drive, you also may want to run Norton WinDoctor and perhaps even Norton

System Doctor before you try to optimize your drives again. If you've set up files as unmovable or assigned them a special space at the beginning or end of your drive (see the "Marking your files" section earlier in this chapter), try removing these files through Norton Speed Disk to eliminate the possibility that one of these is hanging up the process.

Getting Help

Norton Speed Disk is a maintenance program and not a fix-it-all solution. But even Norton Disk Doctor won't be able to repair serious problems with a hard disk, at least not the ones that affect the drive's ability to work as it normally should.

If your drive has become very noisy or you see repeated errors ("Cannot write to Drive x" or "Cannot read from Drive x"), you can try to use both Speed Disk and Disk Doctor. Yet you should also be prepared to investigate other possibilities.

Repeated errors like those discussed may be a sign that the drive is operating at a high temperature because hot air is building up inside your PC case. Buying and installing a special drive fan may help this. It also may be time to replace the drive.

Is your hard drive under warranty? Many drives today ship with either a one- or two-year warranty. If you hit a significant problem with the drive during that time, the manufacturer will usually ship you another drive to replace it (that replacement may be new or it could be refurbished). Contact your manufacturer, explain the situation, and find out what to do next.

Team up with Norton Disk Doctor

Having a particularly pesky problem you think may be disk-related? If so, you may want to double-team your system's medical care. To do this, you want to run both Norton Speed Disk followed by Norton Disk Doctor.

Just the act of defragmenting your hard disk using Norton Speed Disk may overcome certain issues before you ever run Disk Doctor. Then the doctor can focus on the real problems at hand because the drive has already been reorganized through disk optimization.

Chapter 3: Diagnosing Drive Symptoms with Norton Disk Doctor

In This Chapter

- ✔ Figuring out the basic operation of Norton Disk Doctor
- ✔ Configuring Norton Disk Doctor's operation and appearance
- ✔ Conducting your drive tests
- ✔ Checking your problem details and recommendations
- ✔ Repairing problems

*O*ur PC drives take an incredible amount of abuse. We overwork them, overfill them, occasionally overheat them, and sometimes overwhelm them. All too frequently, we remember to perform routine maintenance on our drives only after they begin to scream or slow down.

Along with primary PC components like the CPU and memory, your drives — particularly your hard disks — are the real workhorses of your computer setup. Even though we store tens if not hundreds of thousands of files on them, our PCs usually manage to find that important document or that very special one-of-a-kind video.

But because these drives are almost always working, they're subject to problems. When your PC locks up, data from files left open on the desktop may get written to the hard disk rather haphazardly. Or two open files can become merged together to create what are called *cross-linked files*. Hard drives are also one of the favorite victims for PC viruses and other infections.

With all that to contend with, it's nice to know that you've got a long-recognized drive specialist at your disposal. Norton Disk Doctor was created to fully test your drives as well as to correct some of the problems it finds. Although Disk Doctor can't cure every patient, it's always worth a try to see if it can help.

Visiting the Doctor

Of all the doctors contained within Norton Utilities in Norton SystemWorks and SystemWorks Premier, Norton Disk Doctor should always be your first choice when you're concerned about how well your drives are running and whether something may be wrong.

In the following sections, I start by giving you a look at exactly what the doctor does. Then I help you put the doctor's superior diagnostic and healing skills to work for you.

Understanding how Disk Doctor works

Norton Disk Doctor performs a complete audit of your drives and the files and file structure contained within them. The doctor begins with the drive *partitions* (each hard drive has at least one partition) and then at the file allocation table (FAT) on each. The FAT provides the basic organizational structure of the drive and acts as a sort of master card catalog for the contents of that drive. Besides FAT, there is also NTFS, a more professional-style and secure type of file system used by Windows XP. Norton Disk Doctor can work with either FAT or NTFS drives.

Norton Disk Doctor also looks at file integrity, scans for the kinds of problems that can lead a drive's contents to become corrupted, and checks to be sure that hard drives are set up properly to be booted from when the PC first starts. This is a much more exhaustive series of tests than you can get through Windows all by itself — even in pre–Windows XP versions that include the ScanDisk utility — and it's designed to try to correct most of the problems it encounters.

You have two basic ways you can run Norton Disk Doctor: as needed or placed in your Start menu so it loads whenever Windows starts or restarts. Unless you have a situation where you need to watch a problem drive all the time, I recommend you just load Norton Disk Doctor on an as-needed basis. Running the doctor all the time puts a drain on desktop resources.

Opening Norton Disk Doctor

You page Disk Doctor for a house call in a couple ways. You can choose Start ➪ All Programs ➪ Norton SystemWorks Premier ➪ Norton Utilities ➪ Norton Disk Doctor. Or you can go through Norton SystemWorks if you follow these steps:

1. **Double-click your Norton SystemWorks desktop icon.**

2. **From the left-hand menu, click to open Norton Utilities.**

3. **Choose Find and Fix Problems.**

4. **Click Norton Disk Doctor (see Figure 3-1).**

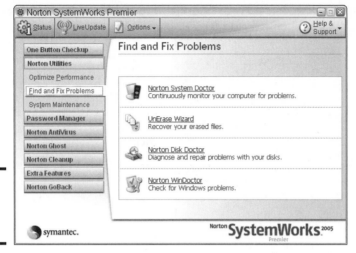

Figure 3-1:
Launching
your Disk
Doctor.

Configuring Norton Disk Doctor

If you're having — or suspect you have — disk problems and you want to at least temporarily load Norton Disk Doctor so it opens automatically every time you start or restart Windows, you simply need to add the doctor to your Windows Startup.

Follow these steps:

1. **Open Norton SystemWorks.**

2. **Click Options and select Norton Utilities (see Figure 3-2).**

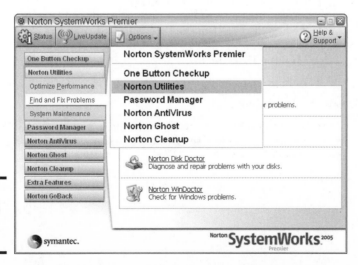

Figure 3-2:
Set options
for Norton
Utilities.

**Book III
Chapter 3**

**Diagnosing Drive
Symptoms with
Norton Disk Doctor**

3. **In the Norton Utilities Options window, select the Startup tab and then click to check Norton Disk Doctor (see Figure 3-3).**

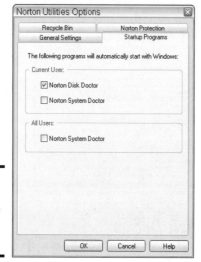

Figure 3-3:
Tell Norton
Disk Doctor
to load with
Windows.

4. **Click OK.**

Your new setting takes effect the next time you restart Windows. Later, when you want to turn it off again, just follow the same basic steps, this time clicking to uncheck Norton Disk Doctor from the Startup tab.

Adding Disk Doctor to Windows Startup

You can add Disk Doctor to your Windows Startup and specify which drives are checked when Norton Disk Doctor loads. Here's how:

1. **Launch Norton Disk Doctor.**

2. **Click Options.**

3. **Select the General tab.**

4. **Under Startup Options, click to check Start Automatically with Windows, and then click to check the drives you want automatically checked (see Figure 3-4).**

5. **Click OK.**

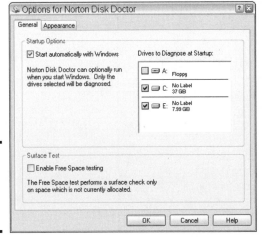

Figure 3-4:
Load at
Startup and
specify
drives.

Changing the doctor's appearance

Norton Disk Doctor lets you modify how it appears. By default, the doctor displays animation while it works. Although the animation can be visually appealing and can temporarily take your mind off your drive woes, this animation eats up some desktop resources and you may not want to look at it for long periods of time.

You can also set up a sound file to play as an alert when a drive problem is diagnosed. Or you can add your own custom message to display when the doctor is doing diagnostics.

To change your doctor's appearance:

1. **Start Norton Disk Doctor.**

2. **Click Options.**

3. **Select the Appearance tab (see Figure 3-5).**

Do any of the following that appeals to you:

- **To turn off animation,** deselect Enable Animation.

- **To play a sound file,** select Play Music and then browse to the sound file you want to play.

- **To have the system display a custom message,** click to select Show Custom Message and then click Edit. When the Custom Message opens, type the wording you want to display, as shown in Figure 3-6). Click OK.

4. **Click OK.**

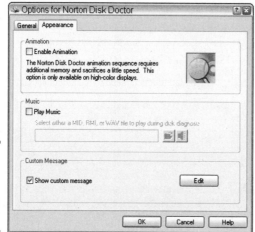

Figure 3-5:
Disk
Doctor's
Appearance
tab.

Figure 3-6:
Add your
own custom
message
to alert.

Taking your tests

As I walk you through the diagnostic tests, keep in mind that Norton Disk Doctor can just scan or it can scan and fix. In this section, I just show you how to scan (or diagnose the problems). To both find and fix problems, jump to the "Curing your problems" section.

TIP

Getting rid of the extra screens

Annoyed by the extra screens in Norton Disk Doctor that make you press Continue to get to the tool? Banish them by following these steps:

1. **Load SystemWorks.**

2. **Click Options.**

3. **Choose Norton Utilities.**

4. **Select the General tab.**

5. **Deselect both Display Splash Screens and Display Program Introductions, as shown in the figure.**

Next time you load Disk Doctor, you won't have these screens running interference.

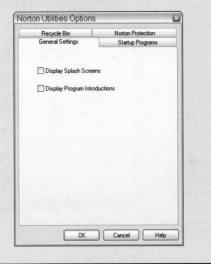

TIP

Start by closing any open windows you don't absolutely need to have open. Avoid transferring files to other people over the network or downloading files from the Internet while you're running your tests. You'll notice some system slowdown while Disk Doctor is scanning.

Follow these steps:

1. **Open Norton Disk Doctor.**

2. **Select your drive(s).**

3. **Click Diagnose.**

 A progress window opens.

4. **If you need to halt the scan before it finishes, click Stop; otherwise, wait until the doctor reports the testing is complete or until you see an error message like the custom one you may have set up in the "Changing the doctor's appearance" section, earlier in this chapter.**

5. **Click Next.**

6. **Read the test results for the (first) drive you checked (see Figure 3-7).**

**Book III
Chapter 3**

Diagnosing Drive
Symptoms with
Norton Disk Doctor

Click the Details button to get more information. Figure 3-8 shows the Details screen telling me what to do for an error encountered.

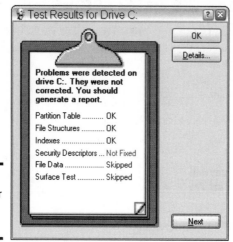

Figure 3-7:
Review your
drive test
results.

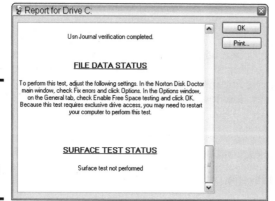

Figure 3-8:
Click to
check
Details for
recom-
mendations
on errors.

7. **Click Next.**

8. **If you chose to check a second drive, review the test results for this, and click Next.**

When you're done, just click Close to exit Norton Disk Doctor. Next, I show you how to fix errors the doctor may diagnose in its exam.

Curing your problems

The first time you run Norton Disk Doctor — unless you're really up against a problem that seems to threaten your system — you may want to just let it scan your drives and report back problems. This way, you have the information about what may be wrong before Norton tries to fix it. Then you can run Disk Doctor again to fix the problems.

To tell the doctor to repair this time, follow these steps:

1. **Load Norton Disk Doctor.**

2. **Be sure the drive(s) you want to examine are checked.**

3. **Select the Fix Errors check box (see Figure 3-9).**

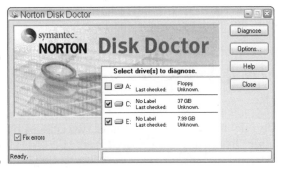

Figure 3-9:
Check Fix
Errors to
repair
problems
discovered.

4. **Click Diagnose.**

As the drive tests are performed, you may see a warning screen (like the one shown in Figure 3-10), alerting you to a problem found that cannot be fixed immediately because the files involved are currently locked. If this happens, click Yes to schedule the repair for a later time. Norton then fixes the drive problem as soon as it can get access to the drive and the files.

If you don't see such a message and don't see any other types of warning screens, your drives have passed their tests. The doctor can safely escape back to an afternoon of PC golf. This means you can close Norton Disk Doctor and get back to more fun yourself.

5. **Click Close to exit Norton Disk Doctor.**

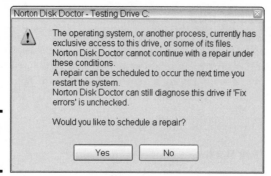

Norton Disk Doctor - Testing Drive C:

⚠ The operating system, or another process, currently has
exclusive access to this drive, or some of its files.
Norton Disk Doctor cannot continue with a repair under
these conditions.
A repair can be scheduled to occur the next time you
restart the system.
Norton Disk Doctor can still diagnose this drive if 'Fix
errors' is unchecked.

Would you like to schedule a repair?

[Yes]   [No]

Figure 3-10:
Schedule a
later repair.

You may see the phrase *surface scan* used to describe some of that Disk Doctor does. A surface scan means an overall superficial scan that does not look at down-deep disk issues and file integrity. A surface scan is faster to run than a full scan, but it isn't as thorough.

Knowing What to Do If You Can't Get Disk Doctor to Run

What if Norton Disk Doctor won't run? You have two choices here. You can try to run the utilities from the Norton SystemWorks CD or — if you're having trouble just starting Windows — you can use a special recovery CD.

The System Recovery CD that packs along with Norton SystemWorks (check your package — it should be in there along with your Norton installation CD) may be able to help you run Norton Disk Doctor when you can't load it otherwise. If you still can't get access to the troubled drive, it's probably past time to replace it (see the nearby sidebar, "When to replace the drive").

Your Norton SystemWorks CD is more than just the way you install your Norton suite. It allows you to run your Norton Utilities, including Norton Disk Doctor, when you can't load them as you would other programs from Windows (such as when you're having a problem running Windows). But a second CD, called the System Recovery disk, is included; it has a repair and rescue setup built into it to help you get out of a jam that either won't let you run the PC as usual or one that prevents you from loading Norton from Windows.

Follow these steps if Windows can load:

1. **Place your Norton SystemWorks CD into your CD or DVD drive.**

2. **If the CD does not launch automatically, go to My Computer and double-click on your CD or DVD drive (see Figure 3-11).**

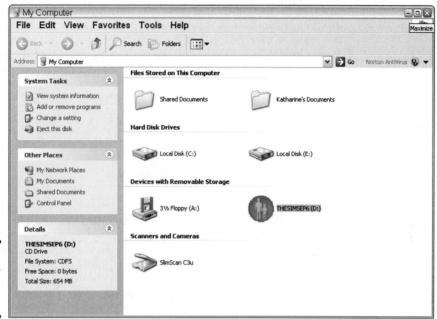

Figure 3-11:
Choose your
CD or DVD
drive.

3. **From the SystemWorks CD screen (shown in Figure 3-12), click Launch Utilities from CD.**

Figure 3-12:
Launch
Utilities
from your
Norton CD.

4. **Click Norton Disk Doctor.**

This starts the doctor and examines your drive setup, reporting any abnormalities such as that shown in Figure 3-13. If you click No in response to a suggestion, Norton asks you if you want to mark the problem as ignored so it won't ask again. Click Yes to ignore it or No to leave as is.

Figure 3-13: Disk Doctor reports problems.

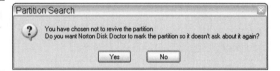

5. Continue to run Norton Disk Doctor as outlined earlier in this chapter.

If you can't get the PC to start as it should or you can't do anything in Windows, the steps vary a bit. Here's how to proceed:

1. Insert the Norton CD into your CD or DVD drive.

2. Restart your PC.

The system should start from the Norton CD.

3. Choose Launch Utilities from CD and then Norton Disk Doctor.

The Norton Disk Doctor opens, as shown in Figure 3-14.

4. Be sure the drives you want it to examine are checked; then click Diagnose.

Disk Doctor will walk you through the rest just like you've already seen when we used the installed Norton Disk Doctor.

When to replace the drive

What if the prognosis Norton Disk Doctor gives is poor?

You may go through all the steps in the preceding section where errors are discovered, and a later repair is scheduled, only to find that the same errors crop up again and again.

Or perhaps a drive you have is causing so much trouble that you can run neither Norton Disk Doctor nor Norton Speed Disk successfully. If that's the case, you probably want to see if you can immediately back up the files contained on that drive and store them on another drive, such as a second hard disk or a recordable CD or DVD drive where they'll be safe if the drive gives up its ghost.

Running out of disk space?

You may want to try another tool from the Norton System Recovery CD if you find you're in trouble because you're running out of free disk space.

Follow the steps in the "Knowing What to Do If You Can't Get Disk Doctor to Run" section for using the Norton System Recovery CD, but when you select Launch Utilities from CD, choose Fast & Safe as shown in the figure. This opens CleanSweep to perform an emergency file purge (sort of like rapid surgical liposuction on your hard disk) and clear some space for you.

Look at the CleanSweep Fast & Safe Cleanup window (see the figure) and what it reports. It tells you exactly what drives have free space and how much additional space can be liberated through the cleaning operation.

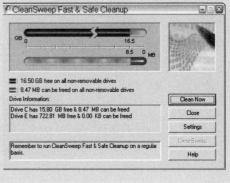

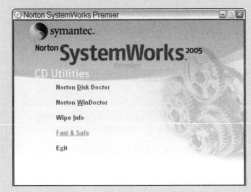

**Book III
Chapter 3**

**Diagnosing Drive
Symptoms with
Norton Disk Doctor**

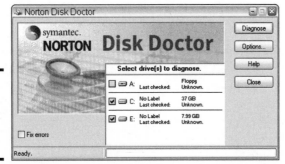

Figure 3-14:
Running
Norton Disk
Doctor
from CD.

You can also run WinDoctor from your CD. This can be extremely helpful when you're having serious issues with Windows and the way it runs to such a degree that you can't even load your installed Norton Utilities like Norton WinDoctor or Disk Doctor.

When you see reference to the Norton System Recovery CD, this is actually your Norton SystemWorks or SystemWorks Premier installation CD.

Chapter 4: Consulting with Norton System Doctor

In This Chapter

✔ **Finding out how to run Norton System Doctor**

✔ **Knowing how this doctor operates**

✔ **Configuring for alarms and auto-fixes**

✔ **Identifying how frequently to run the doctor**

*H*ave you ever wished before you dropped your car off at the repair shop that you could grab the mechanic and make him or her ride around with you for 15 or 20 minutes? This way, instead of you having to find a way to explain all the problems, the mechanic could experience every strange little noise and every hesitation first-hand.

If so, you'll be happy to learn that Norton System Doctor rides along with you as you work in Windows, keeping an eye on each little detail, staying on top of each potential problem. The doctor sounds an alarm when it detects something you need to be aware of and it can automatically go into repair mode, as needed, to fix problems.

In this way, Norton System Doctor performs like your own private physician, turning every Windows session into a professional consultation. Yet you can also tell the doctor to back off a little and give you more elbow room to work, as needed.

This chapter explores everything you need to know about Norton System Doctor but were afraid to ask.

Giving Your System the Once-Over

Think back to those health films you used to see in school or on public television. Remember how you'd see fluoroscopes where you watched the function of the human stomach or heart illuminated by radioactive dye? Getting to see up close a process that happens in your own body, of which you usually aren't even aware, was both scary and fascinating.

Well, that's sort of the idea behind Norton System Doctor. This virtual physician looks at all the important details of how fast your PC is transmitting and receiving packets of information over a network or the Internet, how busy your installed system memory (also called physical memory or RAM) is at any moment in time, and how overworked your hard drive is becoming.

Understanding how Norton System Doctor operates

I warned you that Norton System Doctor doesn't work quite the same way as WinDoctor or Norton Disk Doctor. WinDoctor and Disk Doctor are used to perform spot checks of your Windows or your drives. By comparison, Norton System Doctor wants to run all the time so it can constantly monitor your PC and make adjustments on the fly.

You may really like that idea — or you may be appalled. Operating Norton System Doctor all the time takes desktop resources. If you have 128MB of RAM or less installed, you may feel pinched. With 256MB installed, I still felt the impact.

Here's how Norton System Doctor works. You load Norton System Doctor and configure it to customize it for how you want to use it, telling System Doctor whether to alert you to specific problems or to try to fix them automatically without bothering you. Norton System Doctor runs in the background, sending alarms to the desktop (as shown in Figure 4-1) when it sees an issue like too much drive fragmentation or that you're getting low on available memory. For other issues — depending on how you configure it — the doc automatically schedules repairs, probably for odd times like 3 a.m., when you're not sitting at the keyboard.

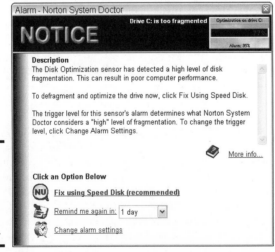

Figure 4-1:
An alarm telling you to run Norton Speed Disk.

You probably don't need to run Norton System Doctor all the time. Instead, you may only want to load it when you're testing your system or troubleshooting a problem. For example, Norton System Doctor may be helpful in determining when you start to get low on desktop resources such as memory.

A good alternative to running Norton System Doctor constantly or frequently is to use One Button Checkup (discussed in Chapter 1 of this book). Norton System Doctor and One Button Checkup share the same types of monitors and can do very similar diagnostic jobs. If you want to get a feel for what Norton System Doctor monitors but need some time to understand all the nitty-gritty details, you may want to switch back and forth. You can eyeball system performance using this doctor. Then you can run One Button Checkup once a week to see how the kind of reports you get through System Doctor translate into problems Checkup needs to repair.

Knowing what Norton System Doctor examines

Norton System Doctor analyzes various specific parts of your system, from the PC's brain (the CPU), to the memory, to your drives, to your home or small-business network.

Speed and *throughput* (how much data gets moved or copied in a set period of time) tend to factor into many of the details System Doctor watches. Then, through readings updated in the sensors appearing in the doctor window, you can see what's going on throughout your system while you're at work.

If you've ever run Windows Performance Monitor, available with professional versions of Windows including Windows XP Pro, then using Norton System Doctor will seem a little like old-home week. The two are pretty similar in what they monitor but some of the terminology is a bit different. Instead of Performance Monitor's counters, System Doctor calls them *sensors*. A bigger difference is that System Doctor can perform some repairs automatically.

**Book III
Chapter 4**

**Consulting with
Norton System
Doctor**

Opening Norton System Doctor

Ready to open up the patient and let the real diagnostics begin? Thankfully, you won't need a sterile gown for this. In fact, you don't even need to don gloves or pull the blasted cover off the system. Instead, you simply start Norton System Doctor. Then you can configure it just the way you want.

There are two different ways you can start Norton System Doctor: You can choose Start ⇨ All Programs ⇨ Norton SystemWorks ⇨ Norton Utilities ⇨ Norton System Doctor. Or you can follow these steps instead:

1. Open Norton SystemWorks.

2. Click Norton Utilities in the left-hand menu.

3. Select Find and Fix Problems.

4. Click Norton System Doctor.

Getting the Diagnosis

Unlike Norton Disk Doctor and Norton WinDoctor, which give you formal reports, System Doctor is constantly sending information to your desktop.

If you want Norton to handle everything for you, skip Norton System Doctor and use One Button Checkup in addition to the other doctors.

Running Norton System Doctor

Figure 4-2 shows the Norton System Doctor window as it appears on the desktop. Below the title bar at the top you see the menu bar (with the File menu, Edit menu, and so on). Under the menu bar are your *sensors,* or the special modules used to watch different parts of your total PC system.

Figure 4-2:
Your Norton
System
Doctor
window.

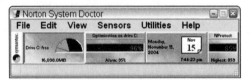

You can add new sensors, remove existing ones, update them, and specify exactly what they're monitoring. The ones shown in Figure 4-2 show how much free disk space is on my C: drive, how fragmented that drive is, the time and date, plus the number of files currently protected through Norton (see Chapter 6 for more details).

Notice that the Norton System Doctor window is what is known as a *floating window,* meaning that you can move it anywhere you want on your desktop by selecting and dragging it. However, you can *dock* it (position it at a particular place on your desktop where it stays until you un-dock it or otherwise move it). To dock your System Doctor, choose View ➪ Dock. Your Norton System Doctor is now fixed at the top of your window, as shown in Figure 4-3. To access the now-missing menu bar, just point to the gray area to the right of the doctor and right-click. Your menu bar choices are there. If you don't like your System Doctor being docked, just repeat the previous steps. The window will turn back into a floater.

Figure 4-3:
The System
Doctor is
docked.

Adding or removing sensors

Norton System Doctor sets you up with three sensors to start:

+ **Disk space:** Gives you a visual as well as a MB reading of how much disk space is free on a specified drive.

+ **Disk optimization:** Measures how fragmented the drive is and alerts you — or runs Norton Speed Disk — when you reach a set percentage

+ **Time and date**

To determine which sensors you're currently using:

1. Point and right-click on a sensor in Norton System Doctor.

2. Select Sensor Information.

This opens a box that identifies the sensor and explains its purpose, as shown in Figure 4-4.

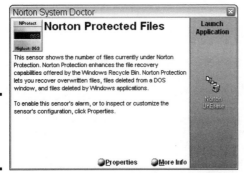

Figure 4-4:
Right-click
for sensor
information.

At the right of the sensor information window is a link to the Norton tool that can help you address the problem this sensor monitors. Just click it to run the utility.

Book III
Chapter 4

Consulting with
Norton System
Doctor

To add a sensor:

1. **Right-click on the Norton System Doctor and choose Add Sensor.**

2. **Select the category of the sensor type you want to add and then the sensor (see Figure 4-5).**

The sensor mini-window is then added to Norton System Doctor.

Figure 4-5:
Choose the sensor category and type.

Removing a sensor is even easier:

1. **Point and right-click on the appropriate sensor in Norton System Doctor.**

2. **Select Remove.**

Poof! That sensor is outta there.

Funny thing about watching system performance: Anything you use to monitor it acts as a drain on those same resources. Every sensor you add to Norton System Doctor saps it just a little bit more. Try to run no more than three or four sensors at any one time. Be sure you really feel you need to watch a particular issue before you set it up as a sensor. If you don't understand why you need to monitor an issue all the time, then don't run that sensor.

TIP

Choosing your sensors wisely

Wondering which sensors may be most useful for you in evaluating your system performance? Here are some suggestions. Use the:

✔ Disk Space sensor to monitor a particular drive that may be starting to fill up (less than 200MB available and you can begin to experience real system slowness)

✔ Disk Throughput to see how fast information is being transferred back and forth to your hard drive

✔ CPU Usage to determine times when your CPU is being overtaxed (at or near 100 percent usage)

✔ Paging File Size, Paging File Utilization, and Physical Memory to see if overworked virtual or physical memory may be slowing down your system

✔ Battery Power for laptops to watch how close you are to exhausting your battery's charge

Updating sensor readings

Sensors can be set to update their information at regular intervals, like every specified number of minutes. But you can also perform a manual update anytime you want. Here's how:

1. **Point and right-click on the desired sensor in Norton System Doctor.**

2. **Select Update.**

Now you have up-to-the-nanosecond information from that sensor.

Follow these steps to adjust the interval period between automatic sensor updates:

1. **From Norton System Doctor, right-click on the sensor you want to tweak.**

2. **Select Properties.**

3. **Select the Measurement tab.**

4. **Drag the slider bar to increase or decrease the time between updates, as shown in Figure 4-6.**

5. **Click OK.**

TIP

Symantec recommends that you keep intervals close to the default settings, noting that increasing or decreasing intervals too widely may not give you good results.

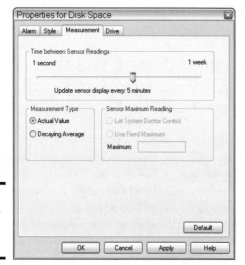

Figure 4-6:
Tweak your time interval.

Checking sensor history

Need a bit more detail to put a current sensor reading in some perspective by showing you a history of what other readings for this have shown? You can get that, too. Here's how you do it:

1. **Point and right-click on the sensor in System Doctor.**

2. **Select Sensor History.**

   A window opens like that shown in Figure 4-7, detailing your other recent historical sensor readings. Here, the history tells me how much physical memory I have available for programs at any given moment over the period of time monitored. If I saw I really had no physical memory free, I might consider upgrading my PC to add more memory.

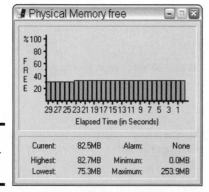

Figure 4-7:
Your sensor history.

To reset your sensor history, choose Edit ⇨ Reset.

Configuring Norton System Doctor

You may feel like Norton System Doctor is all-knowing, but you actually control how it operates. In this section, I fill you in on the general settings for how Norton System Doctor loads and operates.

To see your options as they're currently set, from within Norton System Doctor, choose View ⇨ Options.

If you're interested in appearance, most sensors allow you to point, click, and drag them into a new position within Norton System Doctor. Also, those that have a Style tab allow you to change the appearance of the sensor — change it to a histogram or a bar chart or a similar type of layout, whichever makes it the easiest for you to read and understand quickly.

Setting Norton System Doctor to start automatically

If you want Norton System Doctor to start each and every time Windows loads, follow these steps:

1. **Choose View ⇨ Options.**

2. **Select the Windows Settings tab, and select Start Automatically with Windows.**

3. **Click Apply and then OK.**

Having Norton System Doctor send alerts

Want Windows to beat down the door letting you know when there's a problem? If you do, you want to tell Norton System Doctor to send an alert to the top of all your open windows. Just follow these steps:

1. **Choose View ⇨ Options.**

2. **Select the Alarms tab.**

3. **In the Alarm Type drop-down list, choose the level of warning you want to use.**

4. **Click to select Show Alarm on Top of All Windows.**

5. **Click Apply and then OK.**

Telling the doctor what to do

Now let's dig deeper into the ways you can order your doctor about (ah, sweet payback for that cold stethoscope when you were 12). Sometimes you can tell the good doctor to fix an issue automatically or whether to alert you so you can choose your own solution. Just follow these steps:

1. **Right-click on the sensor in Norton System Doctor.**

2. **Select Properties.**

A multi-tabbed window opens (like the one shown in Figure 4-8), but exactly which tabs are available differs from sensor to sensor. Some have a Measurement tab, some an Alarm tab, and so on.

3. **Select the Alarm tab.**

4. **Choose the options you want.**

For example, move the slider bar to adjust the system to send an alarm when you have 60MB of memory left.

5. **Select the Style tab and select a style to display the alarm.**

TIP

Getting help with the Norton Recovery Disk

Can't get your PC to load Windows or run stably enough to use Norton System Doctor? Here's an idea. The Norton Recovery Disk (see the preceding chapter for information on how to use it) can be called in on emergencies with your system as well. If Windows will load, you can read the help files contained on the recovery CD by placing the CD into your CD or DVD drive and choose Browse CD. If it doesn't automatically load, go to My Computer to browse the contents of the CD, looking for `\\I386\START\HELP\EN`. Double-click on the file `help.hlp`. This help file directs you to the options you have for working with it.

Here's an example of how you can put it to work. Let's say you're using Norton Ghost to create drive images that back up your drive. One day, after installing new hardware or software, Windows won't load. This is what you can do:

1. **Place the Norton Recovery CD into your CD or DVD drive.**

2. **Restart your system and, as directed, press a key to boot from the CD.**

   You'll see a menu of options.

3. **Choose Restore Drive.**

4. **Select the location of your Ghost drive image and follow on-screen instructions to restore the contents of the drive image to your hard disk.**

5. **When the restore process finishes, restart the system as directed (removing the Recovery CD from your CD drive).**

   Your PC should now boot just as it did when you recorded that drive image.

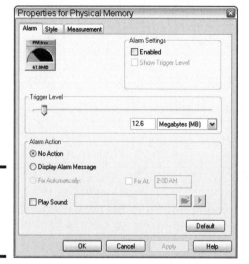

Figure 4-8:
Physical
Memory
sensor
properties.

6. **Select the Measurement tab and adjust the time between sensor readings.**

7. **Click OK.**

When you set up a situation where an alarm or notice appears when conditions match the criteria you set (such as when you reach a certain percentage of disk fragmentation), the appropriately-named warning appears on your screen. Figure 4-9 shows a notice about disk optimization and it warns me to run Norton Speed Disk to resolve it.

Figure 4-9:
An example
notice when
Norton
System
Doctor
spots a
problem.

Chapter 5: Curing Windows Coughs with Norton WinDoctor

In This Chapter

✔ **Identifying what Norton WinDoctor diagnoses and corrects**

✔ **Running Norton WinDoctor**

✔ **Dealing with reported problems**

✔ **Repairing problems and reviewing your WinDoctor repair history**

✔ **Using advanced options**

✔ **Reversing WinDoctor repairs**

*I*f there's anything more aggravating and unproductive in computerdom than a seriously fouled-up operating system, we probably don't want to encounter it. Yet the very normal acts of using a PC and installing or removing hardware and software can create unwanted trouble.

With your newfound knowledge about the complexity of Windows beneath its colorful, simple, graphically oriented desktop, you understand how tough it can be to sort out all the ways Windows can break even if you're not a novice. It can make you feel as though you either have to become a Windows expert or stop using your PC altogether.

But if you have Norton WinDoctor — part of Norton Utilities included with Norton SystemWorks or SystemWorks Premier — you have a powerful friend who can take over when you're not sure what to do. This chapter focuses in on how Norton WinDoctor can do the troubleshooting detective work and then perform repairs for you.

Understanding What WinDoctor Does

You wouldn't begin to believe how many thousands of lines of computer programming code go into making Windows load and run on your PC. Every little detail in Windows represents another little thing that can become messed up, too.

To try to scour the endless nooks and crannies of your Windows setup, Norton WinDoctor gives you the diagnostic power of not one but many different scanners. Each scanner is designed to peer into a specific area of your setup and test it.

These scanners include ways to check:

✦ Many different parts of the Windows Registry, like entries for help and font files, for shared resources like those files used by more than one Microsoft program, and ActiveX- or Web-based mini-programs

✦ Program integrity to be sure your installed programs pass medical muster

✦ Shortcuts

✦ For missing files

✦ For drive and directory changes, such as when you move a folder (another name for a directory) to a different drive

Running WinDoctor

How often you run WinDoctor is up to you, but running it at least once a week is a good idea.

How long the WinDoctor tests will take really depends on your system, how much software you have installed, and how mucked up your Windows setup may be. You'll probably have at least time enough to go grab a cup of coffee or raid the fridge. But you want to get through Step 3 in the following list before you make that snack attack.

To run WinDoctor, follow these steps:

1. **Choose Start ➪ All Programs ➪ Norton SystemWorks ➪ Utilities ➪ Norton WinDoctor.**

2. **Click Continue.**

3. **With Perform All Norton WinDoctor Tests (Recommended) already selected (as shown in Figure 5-1), click Next.**

You see the scanning progress window, as shown in Figure 5-2.

4. **When WinDoctor reports it's done, click Next and then click Finish.**

The Norton WinDoctor problem report window opens.

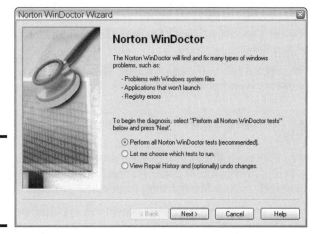

Figure 5-1:
Let
WinDoctor
perform all
its tests.

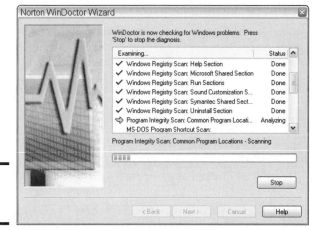

Figure 5-2:
Watch the
progress.

To stop your scan at any time you want, click Stop Scan from the scanning progress window.

Responding to Problems

When you've run Norton WinDoctor and problems are found and reported, you have some choices for how to proceed in trying to repair them. Figure 5-3 shows Norton WinDoctor open to Problems view. Pay attention to the toolbar's icons, because your basic choices are there for how to proceed, including the following:

+ **Repair All:** Use this to attempt to fix all displayed problems.

+ **Repair:** Select a problem in your list and click this to fix types of problems one at a time.

+ **Undo:** This option lets you undo a repair. This choice is normally grayed out in Problems view because nothing has been fixed yet in this session to undo.

+ **Problems:** Displays the default view you see in Figure 5-3 when your scan finishes.

+ **Advanced:** This view allows you to view problems based on symptoms, severity, or which WinDoctor scanners were used to detect them and make advanced choices like ignoring a specified problem.

+ **History:** Here you get a view of your previously repaired problems, from which you reverse a fix by choosing Undo.

+ **Scan:** Choose this to rerun Norton WinDoctor on the spot.

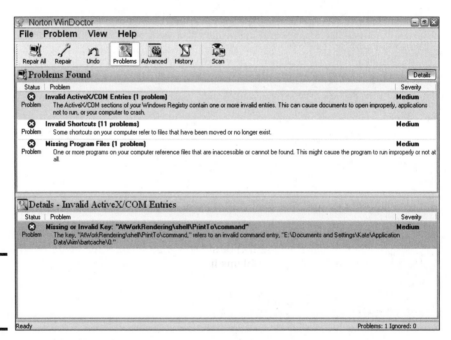

Figure 5-3:
Your
WinDoctor
report.

As you get to work, you'll see additional choices you can make by opening menu options such as Problem or View.

Each listing in Problems view represents a specific type of problem found by a particular WinDoctor scanner, like the Registry scanner. Some listings may show just one problem, while others may show multiple flaws (like the 11 problems shown back in Figure 5-3 in the Invalid Shortcuts problem category).

Now that you know the toolbar, let's zero in on the Problems Found entries (see Figure 5-4). Notice that there are three headings:

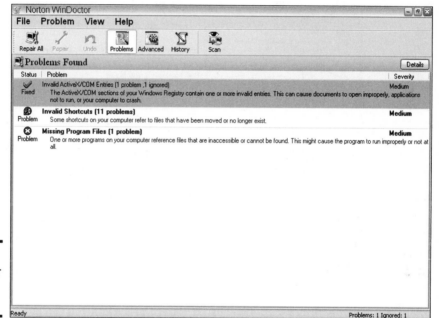

Figure 5-4:
Review your problem report.

Book III
Chapter 5

Curing Windows
Coughs with Norton
WinDoctor

✦ **Status:** Tells you whether the problem or problem category is fixed (green checkmark) or still a problem (red circle with an x). When only some of the problems in a problem category have been repaired, you'll see a green checkmark shown on a red circle with an x.

✦ **Problem:** This lists the category of trouble (for example, Invalid Shortcuts or Missing Program Files) with blue text beneath it, reporting the exact nature of the reported error.

✦ **Severity:** Reports whether the problem represents a low, medium, or high risk to Windows and your use if it's allowed to go unfixed.

To get more information about a problem or problem category, select it in the list and then click Details. Exact details about the highlighted problem category then display in the bottom half of the main problem window, as shown in Figure 5-5. Click the Details button again if you want to hide the summary. Press Ctrl+D to toggle Details on and off quickly.

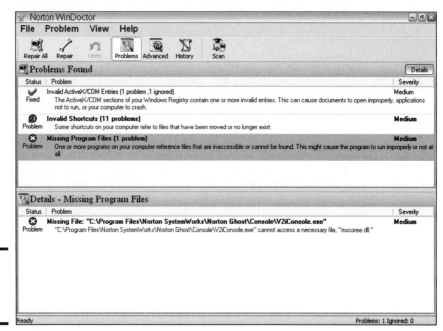

Figure 5-5:
Get your
problem
details.

Right-click on a problem listed under Details and you can choose to either Repair or Ignore a specific problem.

Repairing all problems at once

If you like quick fixes, Repair All is your tool. It's the fastest way to try to clear all the issues WinDoctor reports as presenting some kind of problem with your Windows setup. It's also the most automated way to handle the job if you don't want to be bothered with details or just feel like you're in over your head.

Follow these steps to repair all the problems at once:

1. **In Problems view, click Repair All.**

A window tells you WinDoctor will automatically decide which of all possible solutions to repair each reported problem.

2. **Click Yes.**

Look back at your problem list and you *should* see everything displayed now with a green checkmark and the "Fixed" label. You may not see all the problems fixed (see Figure 5-6). If this happens, you may need to do a spot repair that WinDoctor lets you choose (see the following section).

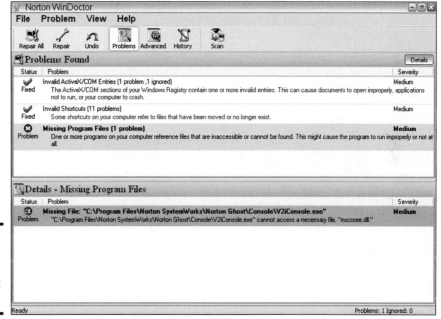

**Book III
Chapter 5**

**Curing Windows
Coughs with Norton
WinDoctor**

Figure 5-6:
Uh oh —
there's a
problem left
behind.

Repairing problems one at a time

You may want to see what's happening rather than just place your faith in WinDoctor to hit the right cure the first time around. Or, like in the previous section, you could end up with a lonely leftover problem after using the Repair All tool. For these situations, you want to use the Repair option instead.

To do this, follow these steps:

1. **When your scan is finished and WinDoctor opens in Problems view, select the first problem you want to repair.**

2. **Click the Repair icon on the WinDoctor toolbar.**

   The Repair Solutions window opens, as shown in Figure 5-7, with (usually) multiple choices and one selected by default.

3. **Click Repair to choose the default solution, or select the solution you prefer and then click Repair.**

4. **Repeat Steps 2 and 3 as needed until you're done.**

Now look back at your problem list. The issue you just cured with WinDoctor now displays with a green checkmark saying "Fixed" instead of that grumpy-looking red circle with an x.

Ignoring a problem

You may run into a situation where a problem that you've tried to repair keeps reappearing in your WinDoctor reports. This can also be something you've repaired previously only to have to undo that fix because you noticed some new problem arising from the mending job; you don't necessarily want to try to repair it again based on past history.

Yet you also don't want to make a decision on this same problem — repair or not? — every time you run WinDoctor. So for this kind of situation, you can tell WinDoctor to simply ignore the specific problem.

Follow these steps to ignore an identified problem:

1. **When your WinDoctor tests have run and you're at the problem report view, click Advanced from the toolbar.**

2. **Locate and select the problem you want to ignore to highlight it.**

3. **Click to open the Problem menu and choose Ignore Specified Problem (see Figure 5-8).**

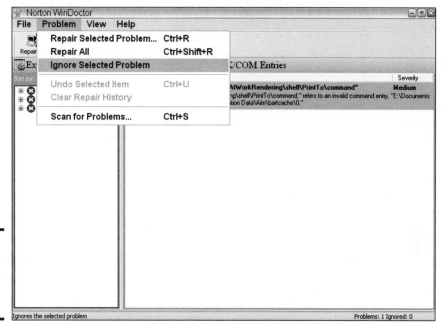

Figure 5-8:
Choosing to
ignore the
selected
problem.

When you finish Step 3, the problem disappears from your WinDoctor view
(if it's the only problem in that category) or it's shown as an ignored problem
in a problem category. If and when you want to redisplay ignored problems,
choose View ➪ Show Ignored Problems.

Ever notice that ignoring a problem only works for just so long? Then you
usually need to do something about it. When you choose to ignore problems
in Norton WinDoctor, you aren't resolving the cause or removing the trouble.
Instead, you're placing them in limbo. A note on each ignored issue gets written
into the Windows Registry where it stays until you clear the ignored file list.

However, there are some problems apt to be listed under Ignored Problems
that aren't really problems: Instead, they're something you may have set up
purposely or that may have been put in place by another program you're
running. So you may want to clear them by clearing your ignored file list.

Here's how to clear that ignored list:

1. **From WinDoctor Problems view, choose View ➪ Options.**

2. **From the General tab (see Figure 5-9), click Clear Ignore List.**

3. **Click OK.**

Figure 5-9:
Zap your list
of ignored
files.

Taking an Advanced view

Norton WinDoctor's Advanced view offers some additional choices in how you view and work with problems reported in your Windows setup. This allows you to sort and organize your problems based on certain criteria such as:

✦ **Symptoms:** Sorts your problems based on the way the problem causes Windows to respond (for example, not being able to load a desktop shortcut or not being able to locate a missing file).

✦ **Severity:** Whether the problem or problem category represents a low, medium, or high threat to your overall Windows stability and operation.

✦ **Scanners:** Sorts your problems by the type of WinDoctor scanner test used to detect the issue, like one of the Windows Registry scans or the Program Integrity Scan.

For example, follow these steps to sort your problems by severity:

1. **From Norton WinDoctor Problems view, click the Advanced icon on the toolbar.**

2. **When the Advanced view opens, open the Sort By drop-down list and select Severity (see Figure 5-10).**

3. **To expand listings marked with a plus (+) sign, click on the plus sign; to collapse them again, click the minus (–) sign.**

Notice, too, that when you drill down through your problem listings, as you do in Step 3 when you expand them, additional information appears in the large right-hand pane.

"What if I do nothing?"

So what happens if you close Norton WinDoctor without doing anything more than viewing the problems the tool has spotted?

The answer is nothing — and I mean, *nothing*. The next time you load Norton WinDoctor, the issues it found on your last pass won't show in the Problems Found window like the empty one shown in the figure. This will be true at least until you rerun WinDoctor, when those same issues should be picked up again along with any newly-developed troubles.

WinDoctor only keeps track of the problem repair history (and I tell you about that in the "Rewriting History" section, later in this chapter). It doesn't keep a running tally of the issues you chose not to fix.

So if you continue to not fix a problem, it's going to reappear again and again each time you run WinDoctor. A better way to handle this might be to tell WinDoctor to ignore a problem you specifically don't want it to fix.

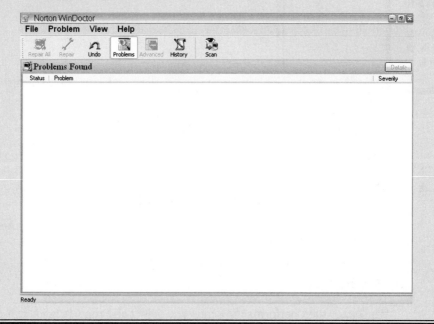

Deciding Which Tests to Run

No large nurse will come in to threaten you if you don't want to run the full battery of WinDoctor tests every time you check for troubles. Instead, you can pick and choose — a good idea when you want to look specifically for Registry problems or some other specific pest without having to go through the full diagnostic routine.

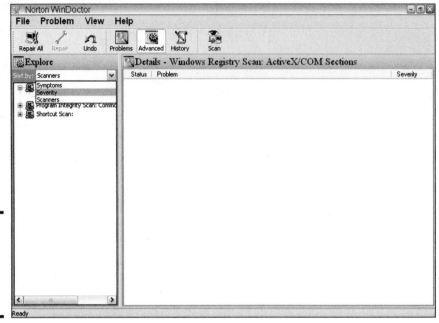

Figure 5-10:
Sort by
symptoms,
severity, or
scanner
type.

Here's how to choose which tests to run:

1. **Start Norton WinDoctor.**

2. **Click Continue.**

3. **Select Let Me Choose Which Tests to Run.**

A list of the various tests appears with each automatically checked, as
shown in Figure 5-11.

4. **Deselect any you don't care to run this time.**

5. **Click Next.**

WinDoctor then performs the scans you select and reports back as it does
when you run the full gamut of tests.

If you only want to run one or two tests, click Deselect All and then click to
recheck the few tests you do want before you click Next.

Figure 5-11:
Only
checked
tests will
run.

Rewriting History

Norton WinDoctor gives you control over how much of a repair history it keeps. Right out of the box, before you touch anything, the good doctor is configured to keep seven days' worth of repairs. Go longer than that, and you lose access to undo fixes made to the oldest problems.

You can change the repair history storage duration to a greater or lesser number of days, or you can save it based on number of WinDoctor sessions. A third option lets you save your repair history forever, but that can be pretty excessive, even for the most health-conscious of PC owners.

Follow these steps to adjust your repair history:

1. **From WinDoctor's Problems view, choose View ⇨ Options (or press Ctrl+O).**

The Options window opens.

2. **Select the Repair History tab.**

3. **Click on the history length you choose, and then set the number of days or sessions, as shown in Figure 5-12.**

4. **Click OK.**

**Book III
Chapter 5**

**Curing Windows
Coughs with Norton
WinDoctor**

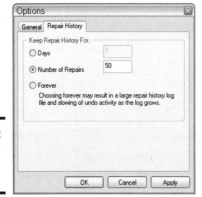

Figure 5-12:
Customize
your repair
history

Clear your Repair History at anytime by opening the Problem menu and
selecting Clear Repair History.

You can run into a pesky situation where a repair made by Norton
WinDoctor doesn't seem to agree with your system. This happens for an
assortment of reasons, including the fact that something "tweaked" on your
PC may be set a particular way by design, while WinDoctor sees it as an
issue in need of a fix. Your way of doing things may differ slightly from the
way WinDoctor is trained to see something configured, sort of like how you
and a friend may not quite agree on everything.

But unlike the situation with a friend, there's no need to get snarky or have
a fight. Norton WinDoctor allows you to go back in your repair history and
undo a fix to try to set things back they were before. Just follow these steps:

1. **Start Norton WinDoctor.**

2. **Click Continue.**

3. **Select View Repair History (see Figure 5-13) and click Finish.**

 The Repair History window opens.

4. **Point to the repaired problem you want to undo and click Undo on
 the WinDoctor toolbar (see Figure 5-14).**

5. **Click Yes when you're asked to confirm your decision.**

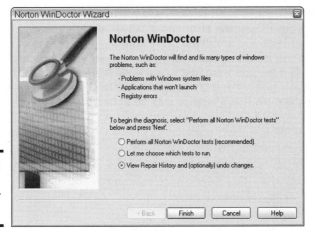

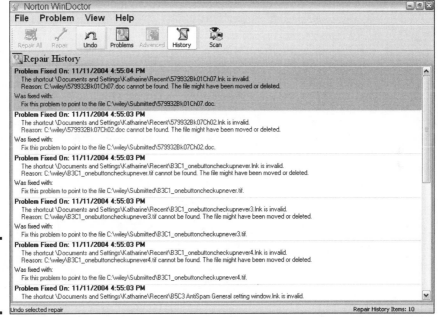

**Book III
Chapter 5**

**Curing Windows
Coughs with Norton
WinDoctor**

After the repair is reversed, you'll see a final window advising you to rescan
to detect the error and select another repair method. Take the doc's advice
and try to repair this problem again, this time choosing a different solution
than last time until you can clear the issue without causing a different type
of trouble to appear on your system.

Exactly when you may need to reverse a Norton WinDoctor repair is a tough call. Watch your PC shortly after you make some repairs using WinDoctor to see if you can spot any problems. For example, you could click on a desktop shortcut that no longer opens a program, or your word processor may be unable to find a file you were just working on before the fix. If that happens, go to the repair history and try to make your best educated guess about which of the last session's repairs may be at fault for the problem.

Chapter 6: Trimming Down Unnecessary Files

In This Chapter

✔ **Knowing the basics of file deletion and recovery**

✔ **Understanding the differences between Windows and Norton Recycle Bins**

✔ **Emptying Norton Protected Files and Recycle Bin**

✔ **Using Norton UnErase Wizard to restore needed files**

*J*ust like our seemingly constant need to try to lose a few pounds off our waistlines or hips, PC users know all too well the need to keep their systems clear of junk files they no longer want or use. Leaving them in place on a drive doesn't just contribute to lots of extra screens to wade through when you're trying to find a specific file, it can slow down your system in more ways than you can comfortably imagine.

But before you start the touchy task of putting your drive on a junk-free diet, you need to understand more about the file deletion process. With it come some protections afforded to you by installing and using Norton SystemWorks and Norton CleanSweep. After all, you may delete a badly needed file and you have to get it back.

Consider this chapter an introduction to the topic of truly weeding out your unwanted files that I walk you through in Book IX.

What Happens When You Delete Files

So you're trying to clean up your system and get rid of the virtual dust bunnies and unwanted files to recover some much-needed hard-disk real estate. As part of this, you delete some files.

Or do you? More happens beneath the Windows' surface than you may think. In the following sections, I fill you in on what goes on.

The mechanics of file removal

Deleting files was probably one of the first things you learned to do on a PC, whether you intended to or not. You know the drill:

1. **Select an icon or file from My Computer or Windows Explorer.**

2. **Press your Delete key (or right-click on the file and select Delete).**

   You're asked to confirm your choice.

3. **Click Yes.**

If you're using normal Windows — and unless you've specified otherwise — the file you've deleted is moved to the Recycle Bin on your desktop. The Recycle Bin acts as a temporary storage area or a keeper of unwanted files. For a period of time (this depends on how the Recycle Bin is configured to work), Recycle Bin holds on to your deleted files giving you the opportunity to rescue those you discover you still want or need.

Just double-click on the Recycle Bin icon and you see the files that have been slated for removal. If you want to recover a file, you select the file in the Recycle Bin, then click Restore This File from the left-hand menu, as shown in Figure 6-1. The file will be restored to the location it was in before you deleted it.

Figure 6-1:
Recovering a file from Recycle Bin.

When you're ready, you can empty your Recycle Bin. Emptying your Recycle Bin removes all the files contained within it and usually makes recovering these files using normal file-recovery utilities fairly difficult. To empty your Recycle Bin, just double-click to open it and then click Empty Recycle Bin from the top-left menu (or right-click on the Recycle Bin on your desktop, and select Empty Recycle Bin).

Thinking before you click

Before you think of file recovery as some magical form of salvation, think again. You won't always be able to rescue every file you've deleted. The longer you wait — and the fuller your hard drive is — the less chance you'll have in getting important files back.

Over time, the file-recovery mechanisms built into the Windows Recycle Bin and provided by the Norton UnErase Wizard (discussed later in this chapter) release older files to allow them to actually be removed from the system altogether. Also, the actual space on the hard disk used by that file will become overwritten by new data.

This means that either you can't get an older file recovered or the file you recover now may be garbled. In the latter case, you may open up a word processing document only to find it contains symbols and "text garbage" rather than your important letter home or the first draft of your novel. You may be able to cut and paste some of the text from the file into a new document. But you never know until you recover the file and try. If you see a File Conversion window like the one shown in Figure 6-2, your file may indeed be corrupted.

**Book III
Chapter 6**

Trimming Down
Unnecessary Files

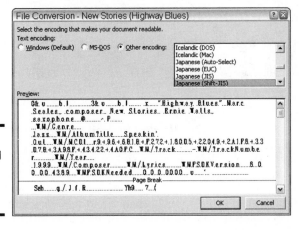

Figure 6-2:
A corrupted
file unsuc-
cessfully
recovered.

The sooner you discover a file is missing, the better your chances are of bringing it back. You still need to be very picky about which files you delete, because you may not be able to recover them.

Using Norton Protected Recycle Bin

When you install Norton SystemWorks, your normal Windows desktop Recycle Bin icon is replaced by the Norton Protected Recycle Bin icon, shown in Figure 6-3. Even though the icon's image is the same (only the label changes), there's an important difference between them: the ability to customize Norton's Recycle Bin and the extra layer of protection it adds. In my testing, for example, I noticed I was able to recover documents going back for a longer period of time using Norton's version than I was with the Windows version.

Figure 6-3: Norton Protected Recycle Bin on the desktop.

Double-click on Norton Protected Recycle Bin and you automatically open the Norton UnErase Wizard. This utility helps you recover accidentally deleted files before they're lost and does so a bit more aggressively than the standard Recycle Bin.

You can perform basically all the maintenance and recovery efforts you did with your old Recycle Bin. You just do them slightly differently as you'll see in the next section.

Configuring Norton Protected Recycle Bin

Out of the box, Norton SystemWorks sets up Norton Protected Recycle Bin to keep seven days' worth of deleted files in a protected holding area. Any files still there on the eighth day will be purged, making them harder to delete.

But you can modify how long a time period to keep these protected files. Just follow these steps:

1. **Right-click on the Norton Protected Recycle Bin icon on your desktop.**

2. **Select Properties.**

The Norton Protected Recycle Bin Properties window appears.

3. **Select the Norton Protection tab.**

4. **To increase or decrease the number of days before protected files are actually removed from your system, click the up/down arrow next to the number of days and set it to the length of time you want, as shown in Figure 6-4.**

5. **Click OK.**

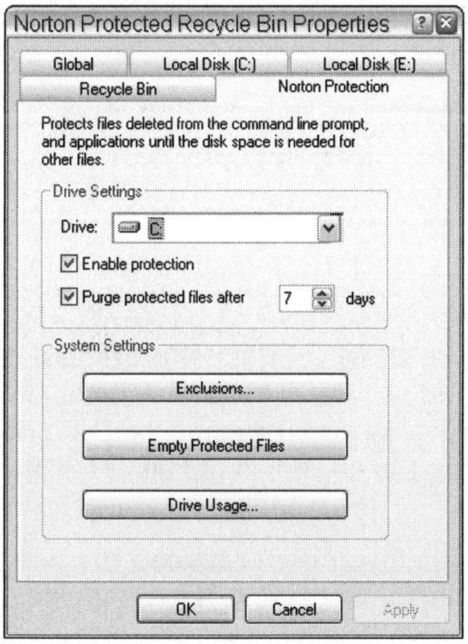

Figure 6-4: Set the time period to hang onto deleted-yet-still-protected files.

Look back at Figure 6-4 and you'll see you can make some additional choices in the Norton Protected Recycle Bin Properties window. For example, you can choose a different drive letter if you want the protected files stored on a different drive (perhaps one with more free space). You can also click Empty Protected Files to purge files you're sure you don't want. Finally, click Drive Usage and you can set up Norton Protected Recycle Bin to hold onto no more files than would occupy a certain percentage (say, 10 percent) of your hard drive (see Figure 6-5). Just use your mouse to adjust the slider bar to the left (to reduce the space devoted) or to the right (to increase the percentage).

Figure 6-5:
Set how much drive space to devote to protected files.

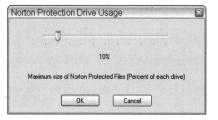

You can also specify exactly what appears when you click on the desktop Recycle Bin icon. Here's how:

1. **Right-click on Norton Protected Recycle Bin and choose Properties.**

2. **Select the Recycle Bin tab (as shown in Figure 6-6).**

Here are your options:

- Leave UnErase Wizard checked (by default) if you want to leave it as is.

- Click All Protected Files to show your list of protected files (which looks similar to your Windows Recycle Bin options before you installed Norton SystemWorks and the same as if you right-click on Norton Protected Recycle Bin as shown in Figure 6-7, and choose Open.

- Click Standard Recycle Bin if you prefer to load the Windows Recycle Bin (choose this if you decide to disable Norton file protection).

3. **Click OK.**

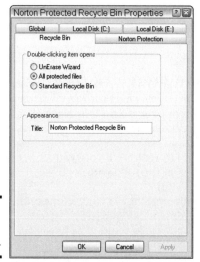

Figure 6-6:
Configure
Recycle Bin.

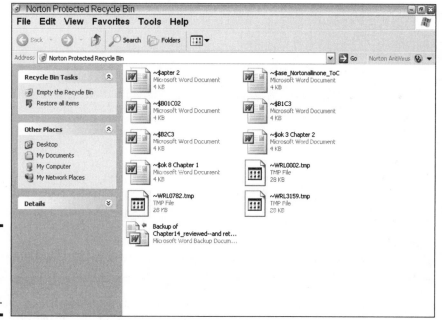

Figure 6-7:
Open
Norton
Protected
Recycle Bin.

To disable file protection, follow the preceding steps but in Step 3, uncheck Enable Protection before clicking OK. This turns off all file protection so your deleted files are directly purged.

Specifying a time period much longer than 14 days probably isn't a good idea, especially if you don't have a lot of free disk space. The longer a time period you set, the more room has to go to holding these no-man's-land files.

Empty Recycle Bin and protected files

Before you empty your Norton protected files through Norton Protected Recycle Bin, you want to look them over. To do this, right-click on the Norton Protected Recycle Bin icon on your desktop and choose Open.

Be sure there is nothing you need to restore. If you want to recover one or more files, follow the instructions in the following section.

When you're sure you don't need anything else, click Empty the Recycle Bin from the top left-hand menu, as shown in Figure 6-8.

Figure 6-8:
Empty your Norton Recycle Bin.

Purge your files even faster by right-clicking on your Norton Protected Recycle Bin icon and choosing Empty Protected Files.

After these files are deleted, you're probably going to need to use extreme measures to recover them. There are special utilities, usually quite expensive and some available only to data-recovery experts, that can recover long-deleted files, in whole or at least in part. Just like the utilities, the cost of a data-recovery specialist is very high, often starting at a price of several hundred dollars.

Recovering Files through the UnErase Wizard

The issue isn't *if* you'll accidentally delete a file you want to keep, it's a matter of *when* it will happen. We've all done it.

Thankfully, you have the Norton Protected Recycle Bin and the Norton UnErase Wizard to lobby on your behalf in trying to recover that deleted file and restore it to its former place of honor — or at least residence — on your drive. Just double-click on the Norton Protected Recycle Bin on your Windows desktop to open UnErase Wizard.

Here's another way to start the UnErase Wizard, useful if you've removed — accidentally or through tweaking — Norton's Recycle Bin from your desktop:

1. **Open Norton SystemWorks.**

2. **Select Norton Utilities from the left menu.**

3. **Click Find and Fix Problems.**

4. **Click on UnErase Wizard (see Figure 6-9).**

5. **Click Continue.**

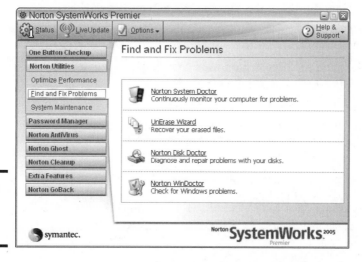

Figure 6-9: Launching UnErase Wizard.

Book III
Chapter 6

Trimming Down
Unnecessary Files

The UnErase Wizard loads, as shown in Figure 6-10. Now you're ready to try to find unintentionally deleted files. Follow these steps:

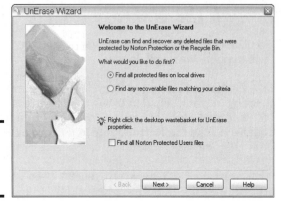

Figure 6-10:
The
UnErase
Wizard.

1. **From the wizard, choose from Find All Protected Files on Local Drives or Find Any Recoverable Files Matching Your Criteria.**

   Use the latter when you have some idea of what you're looking for. For example, if you want to find a Word document file, choose this and then specify any file that ends in *.doc.

2. **Click Next and then Next again.**

3. **Specify where the file was located, and click Next.**

   The UnErase search window opens. To cancel the search, click Stop Search.

4. **If you see the file you want to recover, select it in the list and then click Recover (see Figure 6-11).**

5. **Click Next and then click Finish.**

   The file(s) you selected are then restored. You should be able to find them on the drive or in the folder where they were originally stored.

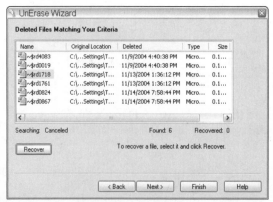

Figure 6-11:
Select the
file and click
Recover.

Book IV

Norton GoBack and Ghost

The 5th Wave   By Rich Tennant

Contents at a Glance

Chapter 1: Eliminating the Oops Factor with GoBack

In This Chapter

✔ Comparing Windows System Restore with Norton GoBack

✔ Turning off Windows System Restore before you use GoBack

✔ Understanding why you still need to back up

✔ Knowing where Norton GoBack can help you

"Gee, I wish I hadn't done that." Sound familiar? We all say it after making some bone-headed change where we didn't follow instructions, heed warnings, or didn't even bother to read the information to start with.

Norton GoBack lets you go back in time to the point before you made the blunder. If you've heard of doing something like this before, it's because Windows includes a tool called System Restore that lets you do the same thing. A number of different software publishers offer similar utilities, too, including shareware versions you can download and try for free from online file libraries like those at Download.com and Tucows.com.

Now if only Norton made a version of this that would take back dumb things we say or do in real life, eh? I bet we'd all buy that one and maybe give them to friends and family.

In this chapter, I introduce you to the life preserver Norton GoBack can toss you when your PC's running in uncharted and stormy waters. The more tools you have, the better your chances of getting your system back alive and well.

The Concept Behind GoBack-Style Programs

I'm throwing around terms like "going back in time," which may sound a little to you like H.G. Wells and the magic time machine. But it's not quite that nifty.

What programs like Windows System Restore and Norton GoBack do is make copies of your key files as they exist at a particular moment in time. This allows you to go back to that previous setup if catastrophe strikes (as it often does).

But these types of utilities don't make copies of everything, just the things necessary to make Windows run the way it ran last Tuesday or a month ago. If you messed up your big paper in your word processor yesterday, you're still on your own and that's why you'll see me do the mother-hen thing later in this chapter about backing up your files.

Comparing and Making Your Choices

If you have Norton GoBack, you now have at least two different ways you can roll back your PC to a point in time before you added or removed something or otherwise tweaked your setup to cause a fuss. The Windows System Restore tool does a similar — if slightly less robust — job as GoBack.

In the following sections, I compare these two utilities head-to-head so you can appreciate the differences. Then I show you why you want to use one tool or the other, but not both.

Weighing Windows System Restore against Norton GoBack

From your vantage point, the differences between the Windows restore tool and Norton GoBack may seem nonexistent. These tools are ones most people look at when they need them but happily ignore the rest of the time.

Both GoBack and System Restore are tools that:

✦ Record your setup as it exists at a particular moment in time (and that recording can be done automatically as well as manually)

✦ Allow you to restore that recording (called a *restore point* in both System Restore and GoBack) to try to overcome a problem caused by a change on your system

✦ Need to run all the time in order to be able to call upon a recording to restore

✦ Can be turned on and off at any time you choose

✦ May require a fair amount of available hard-drive space (perhaps as much as half a gigabyte or more) to store those recorded setups

But below the surface, there are some differences. On the plus side, Windows System Restore is free (at least in the fact that it comes packaged with Windows Me and later) and it's integrated right into the operating system, which usually means it plays well with the rest of your system.

Cleaning up your (drive's) act

Here's some smart advice too few people follow before using recovery tools like Windows System Restore, Norton GoBack, and Norton Ghost (discussed later in this book): Clean up your drives before you record recovery points. If you don't do this, you're apt to copy way too much junk into your recordings. This makes your recordings larger than they need to be with stuff you don't even want.

If you're using Norton SystemWorks or System-Works Premier, follow help found elsewhere in this book to perform a checkup on your system (through One Button Checkup or Norton WinDoctor), then use Norton Cleanup to remove unwanted temporary and Internet files from your PC and Norton Speed Disk (see the figure) to optimize the drive(s).

If you aren't using Norton SystemWorks, use Disk Cleanup and Disk Defragmenter, located under the System Tools section when you choose Start ⇨ All Programs ⇨ Accessories. Then turn on and use Norton GoBack or Ghost.

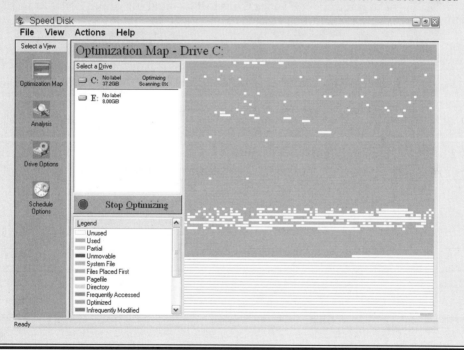

**Book IV
Chapter 1**

**Eliminating the
Oops Factor with
GoBack**

Norton GoBack, on the other hand, is a bit more customizable. It also features a "bail-out" tool to disable itself — with your help — if something goes wrong and your PC won't start normally after you've either installed and set up GoBack or made some change to it that makes the tool and your system unhappy.

Installing Norton GoBack

Unless you buy and install Norton GoBack directly, it's possible it was never actually installed on your PC. That was the case with mine when I got it as part of Norton SystemWorks Premier. Here's how you can tell if Norton GoBack is installed already on your PC: Choose Start ➪ All Programs then look for either Norton Ghost by itself or as part of Norton SystemWorks or SystemWorks Premier

If you discover that GoBack isn't yet installed on your PC, understand that installing Norton GoBack also turns on the feature. So don't install it if you don't plan to use it (you can always disable it later if you need to do so).

If you're using a PC on which you have more than one version of Windows installed, don't follow these steps for installing Norton GoBack. If you do, expect one very sour pickle of a dilemma where Windows won't load or you go into a nasty loop of `Operating system not found` error messages that make you wonder if your PC has lost its mind (or you're losing yours). I troubleshoot you through this in Chapter 2 of this book.

As long as you only have one version of Windows installed, go get your Norton GoBack or Norton SystemWorks CD. Then insert this into your CD or DVD drive, and follow these steps:

1. **Open Norton SystemWorks.**

2. **Click on Norton GoBack from the left-hand menu.**

3. **In the right-hand window, click Install Norton GoBack (see Figure 1-1).**

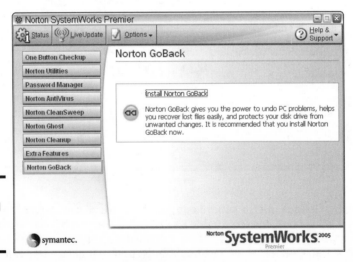

Figure 1-1:
Click Install
Norton
GoBack.

4. If prompted, point to your CD or DVD drive where your Norton disk is inserted, as shown in Figure 1-2, and click OK.

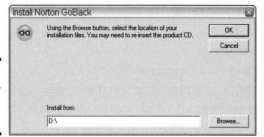

Figure 1-2:
Choose your
CD or DVD
drive letter.

Your Welcome to Norton GoBack Setup window (shown in Figure 1-3) should open. *Note:* If the Welcome to Norton GoBack Setup window doesn't open, you'll want to consult the next tip for details on how to proceed.

You can stop the installation at anytime if you click Cancel. However, if you do cancel, you may have to wait until you restart your PC before you can install Norton GoBack again. Without restarting, it's possible that the installation never quite does anything when you restart it.

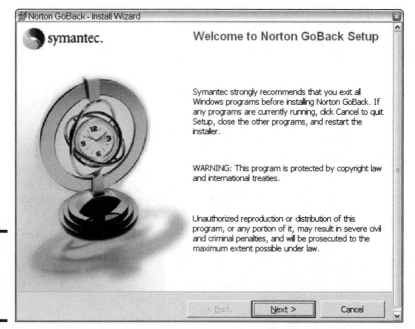

Figure 1-3:
Your
GoBack
setup
window.

**Book IV
Chapter 1**

**Eliminating the
Oops Factor with
GoBack**

5. **In the Welcome to Norton Setup window, click Next.**

6. **Read (really, you should) the license agreement, and then select I Accept the License Agreement, and click Next.**

7. **Choose your installation type (see Figure 1-4).**

   I recommend Custom Installation, because it gives you a bit more control over how the program is setup to work.

8. **Click Next and then click Next again.**

9. **Assuming you followed my recommendation in Step 7, you now choose the partition where GoBack will be installed (see Figure 1-5).**

   You can also click the up or down arrow to the right of How Much of the Space on This Drive Should Be Reserved for Norton GoBack History to increase (up arrow) or decrease (down arrow) the amount of hard-disk space devoted to your GoBack recordings.

10. **Click Next.**

11. **If you have a second drive, you then see the same screen shown in Step 9 again so you can opt to protect the second drive as well; select as desired and click Next.**

12. **From your Summary screen (see Figure 1-6), check to be sure the drives you selected have green check marks, and click Install.**

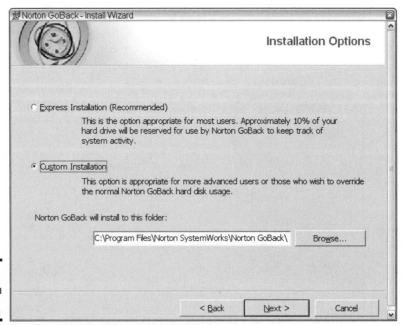

Figure 1-4:
Click Custom
Installation.

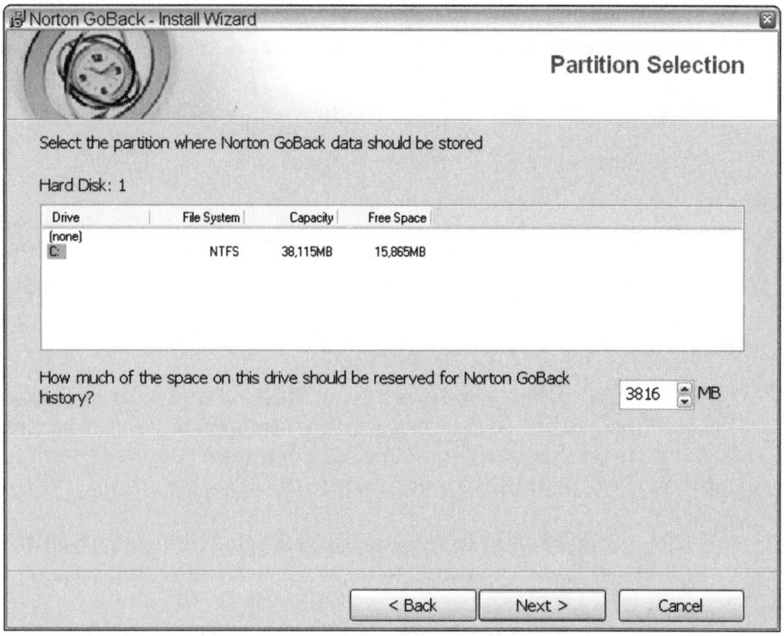

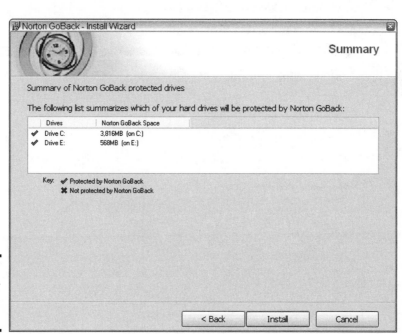

Figure 1-5:
Select the
partition
(drive) on
which to
install
Norton
GoBack.

Figure 1-6:
Review your
Summary
screen.

A status window opens showing you the installation progress. This process can take a while because Norton GoBack performs a full exam of the drive(s) selected to be sure they're in proper shape to accept GoBack.

13. **When the setup is done (finally!), click Finish.**

14. **Restart your PC to enable GoBack.**

Chapter 2 of this book takes you through your options for customizing this utility for your use. It also gives you a way around the obstacles and errors you may encounter.

Disabling System Restore

As I explain earlier, Windows System Restore and Norton GoBack do similar jobs. So you want to run one of them, not both. If you try to use both, you'll tie up system resources and use up a lot more room on your hard drive, because both utilities record restore or GoBack sessions.

If you definitely want to run Norton GoBack, you'll want to turn off — or disable — Windows System Restore. Follow these steps to do just that:

1. **Open the Windows Control Panel.**

2. **Double-click on the System icon.**

3. **Choose the System Restore tab.**

4. **Click to check Turn Off System Restore on all drives (see Figure 1-7).**

5. **Click Apply and then click OK.**

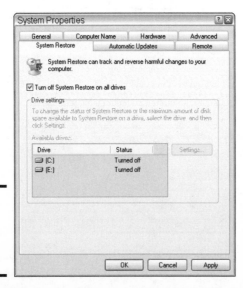

Figure 1-7:
Turn off
System
Restore on
all drives.

What about backups?

Don't think *either/or* when it comes to backups and using Norton GoBack. If you had to go into battle, would you only take one weapon? You'd want something to fall back on if your primary tool of choice fails. The same is true with GoBack and backups.

Start using Norton GoBack and record your setup as I show you in this book. But understand that GoBack won't rescue you from every situation, including a hard drive headed south for PC winter or a problem with your setup that got recorded in your GoBack you later restore.

Continue your backup routines even after you begin to use Norton GoBack. If you're not backing up, start doing so, using the information provided in Book I, Chapter 6.

Windows may ask you to restart your system to set the change in stone (or at least as much stone as a binary creature like a PC can pound). If not, you probably still want to restart your PC before you do anything else major on it, especially if you decided to turn off System Restore *before* installing Norton GoBack.

Evaluating Your Situation

Not convinced Norton GoBack is for you? Have questions about how or when you might put its setup recordings to use?

Hey, healthy skepticism is good. If you got Norton GoBack as part of Norton SystemWorks or SystemWorks Premier, you may not have chosen this package so much as it got bundled with other utilities you do want.

GoBack isn't perfect. Nor is it helpful in every situation you may run into (probably while you're doing 85 mph with your mouse).

Yet for Windows users of all types, programs like Norton GoBack can save you a long, arduous trip up the steep side of the learning curve when all you need to do is go back to that time before you added some crazy program or monkeyed with your setup in ways that send alarm bells ringing. More advanced users, on the other hand, may prefer to use a different program such as Norton Ghost combined with their system of regular backups to bring order again to an unruly PC.

**Book IV
Chapter 1**

**Eliminating the
Oops Factor with
GoBack**

Knowing your limitations

Norton GoBack allows you to determine how many recordings you can make based on a certain percentage of your hard-drive size — such as 10 percent of a 40GB hard disk, or 4GB — or a certain number of megabytes. You'll see how to configure GoBack in Chapter 2. But how large each of those recordings are, how many different recordings will be preserved for a possible restore at any given time, and how far they'll go back on your system varies for everybody.

As a general rule, don't assume that you can go back to a point many months or a year ago. In fact, you probably want to use the most recent recording you can when and if you do need to restore a recording from Norton GoBack. Don't worry about this just yet, however.

Of more immediate concern to you (besides the fact that you've run out of snacks at your desk) is when you can have Norton GoBack ride into your rescue. Although I'll give you specific examples of this as we move forward, right now, understand what GoBack likely can't help you with:

✦ **A hardware failure:** Norton GoBack really offers nothing that will help you if your PC problem is ailing hardware. If you think an issue may be drive-based, use Norton Disk Doctor to see what it reports (Book III, Chapter 3 introduces you to this specialist).

✦ **A very serious Windows problem:** If a problem is so serious that you can't get Windows to load, it may be nearly impossible — unless you have some advanced expertise — to get to the point where you can restore a Norton GoBack recording.

There are a few ways you can try to do this, but those could require a few chapters themselves, so let me offer an easier approach: If you have Norton SystemWorks or SystemWorks Premier, insert your recovery CD that came with SystemWorks to try to start the PC. Then you can use the Norton Utilities doctors like Norton WinDoctor and Norton Disk Doctor right from the CD to see if you can repair the system enough to get it running again.

✦ **A computer infection like a virus:** Although restoring a recording of your setup from Norton GoBack can temporarily help you to get Windows to load, it's probably no more than a short-term solution because the virus or other infection is still inside your PC and can reinfect the restored setup. Immediately run Norton AntiVirus and cure any infections before you run Norton GoBack again.

✦ **After you've reformatted or repartitioned your hard disk:** If you format your hard drive where Norton GoBack is installed and working, you're not only going to lose the software but any setup recordings that have been made. The same is true if you repartition that hard drive using disk-partition tools like FDISK and DISKPART (discussed in Book VIII, Chapter 1).

Even if you back up these files and restore them to the drive after formatting and/or partitioning, you may not be able to apply your GoBack recordings. In this case, you're usually better off applying a drive image such as you create using Norton Ghost or rely on your backups to restore your system to its former glory.

Trying other options

A good question to ask yourself either now or sometime before all hell breaks loose on your system is also an obvious one: What happens if you configure and use Norton GoBack, and then find that you can't get into Windows and GoBack to restore, or the restore you try doesn't help the situation?

If your PC won't load Windows on its own, use the Norton emergency recovery CD. This disc can be used to boot the system and let you run tools right from the CD, which may give you the ability to repair a problem to get you back to work. Run Norton WinDoctor, Norton Disk Doctor, and Norton AntiVirus.

If Windows will load, try to run these Norton Utilities (see Book III for more details) directly from Windows and follow through on any repair recommendations the doctors may offer you. You may be able to use a previous set of backups to restore your setup or read on later in this book to see what Norton Ghost can offer you.

Chapter 2: Configuring Norton GoBack

In This Chapter

✔ Knowing your choices for configuring Norton GoBack

✔ Protecting your GoBack setup with passwords and other security features

✔ Understanding how to disable or turn off GoBack as needed

✔ Overcoming problems with GoBack and your system

✔ Removing and reinstalling Norton GoBack

*O*ut of the box, Norton GoBack is all set to work in protecting your key system files and overall Windows setup in case something nasty happens to your PC at the operating system level.

Yet, as I hint in the previous chapter, you may have to do some tweaking to have GoBack work well for you. Through these adjustments, you can modify several different aspects of GoBack: You can change the overall security level and make it tough for others to fiddle with your GoBack setup, opt to clear your previous history under GoBack, and when or if to disable GoBack for short periods while you make changes to your system you don't want to have recorded in the history.

You also need to know how to remove the software. You may need to do so because you see a problem when running Norton GoBack, or because you need to make adjustments to it that you can't do through its options settings. In the latter case, you need to uninstall GoBack and then reinstall, but making more exacting choices as you set it up.

I end the chapter with some troubleshooting. When you consider the job GoBack does, you'll see why troubleshooting and tweaking is better than just throwing up your hands and disabling it — tempting as that may be. Turning GoBack off and leaving it off can leave you up Misery Creek with your paddles back at the base camp. If that sounds scary, it should.

Tweaking Your Configuration

The very process of installing Norton GoBack sets it up to work with a basic configuration, with very little required from you. Yet just because it's easy to use from that point on doesn't mean Norton GoBack is configured in the best way to work for you and the kind of PC setup you have.

In this section, I run through the options available to you for tweaking that configuration. Then in the next section, I dig just a little deeper (no shovel required, however) to make changes that can beef up your security so your 7-year-old child or ditzy, never-keeps-his-fingers-off-stuff coworker can't come along to fiddle with it in a way that results in a disaster. I mean, you wouldn't let these folks mess around with your household toolbox or rewire the toaster, would you?

When you install Norton GoBack, you're prompted to decide how much space to allot to each drive for storing your GoBack history; the GoBack history serves as the recordings I cover in the last chapter. In fact, that's about the only major decision GoBack asks you to make. If you installed using the Express Installation option, much of the process happens as though you're not even in the room.

One thing you can't configure with Norton GoBack is exactly which drives or partitions you want to include. The software automatically sets up a history on each hard disk or virtual drive (see Book VIII, Chapter 1 for details), so you can't pick and choose. (This can be a problem if you have a PC where you run different operating systems on different hard disks, as you'll see in the troubleshooting section of this chapter.)

Before you can tweak any of the GoBack settings, you need to get to the GoBack configuration window. Here's the fastest way to get there:

1. **Look for the Norton GoBack icon in your Windows System Tray.**

It's a yellow circle with two block arrows pointing to the left.

2. **Right-click on the icon and select Options.**

The Norton GoBack Options window, shown in Figure 2-1, opens.

When you're configuring other Norton tools, such as through Norton SystemWorks or SystemWorks Premier, you may prefer to get to the Option window by following these steps:

1. **Open Norton SystemWorks.**

2. **From the System Status screen (shown in Figure 2-2), select Norton GoBack.**

3. **Click the Configure button.**

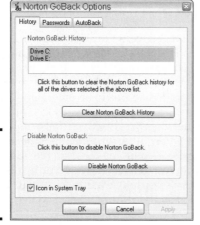

Figure 2-1:
Your Norton
GoBack
Options
window.

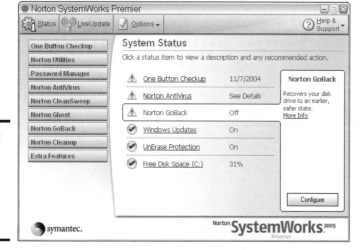

Figure 2-2:
Open
Norton
GoBack
from
System-
Works.

Each of the three tabs in the Norton GoBack Options window — History, Passwords, and AutoBack — focuses on a particular aspect of GoBack.

If Norton GoBack is disabled when you try to set options, you'll be asked if you want to enable GoBack. The tool must be on in order to change settings for it.

**Book IV
Chapter 2**

Configuring Norton
GoBack

Clearing Your GoBack History

Norton GoBack gives you the ability to wipe the slate clean, at least when it comes to the history it's recorded for you for later restoring and recovering. But, smart person that you are, you can probably imagine that clearing your history is an option you want to exercise carefully, because you lose the ability to go back to one of those recorded setups in an emergency.

Clearing your history is best done when you discover that you have problems on your system that are likely to have gotten written into your recorded history. When you correct these issues — perhaps by using one of the doctors available in Norton Utilities within Norton SystemWorks or by disinfecting a virus caught by Norton AntiVirus — you may want to wipe your history clean so you can make a fresh recording as the start of a new and improved history.

Follow these steps when you're absolutely, positively certain you want to purge your history.

1. **Right-click on your Norton GoBack icon and choose Options.**

2. **On the History tab, click Clear Norton GoBack History.**

3. **When asked to confirm, as shown in Figure 2-3, click Yes.**

Figure 2-3:
Confirm
your history
file purge.

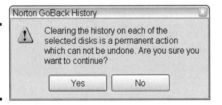

Norton GoBack History

Clearing the history on each of the selected disks is a permanent action which can not be undone. Are you sure you want to continue?

Yes   No

Make certain you begin your recordings soon after you purge the history to be sure you aren't caught short.

You wouldn't hit a writer wearing contact lenses, would you? I ask this because I have to tell you that, unfortunately, you can't adjust the percentage or exact amount of megabytes set aside on each hard disk or virtual drive from Norton GoBack after it's installed and enabled. To make this kind of change, you need to remove and then reinstall Norton GoBack, this time setting the exact drive space you want to reserve for your GoBack history. You can figure out how to do this later in this chapter in the "Troubleshooting Your GoBack Setup" section.

Protecting Your Work

Norton GoBack is designed as a protection mechanism for your PC. Use it to record your system when it's operating well, and you should be able to restore that previous setup from your GoBack history to get back to where you were. But in this section, I show you how to protect your protector from harm.

A really nasty reality about PCs is that probably one out of every four people who use — and abuse — them is best described as a tinkerer. Give someone just a couple of stolen moments at your keyboard, and he'll find a way to get into your system and make some bone-headed blunder with a setting that can make you and your PC miserable. If you're using basic, out-of-the-box Windows security, keep in mind that a talented 3-year-old can usually defeat the password screen (oops, there go the Christmas cookies from Bill Gates).

Thankfully, the good folks at Symantec know this, so they've given you two smart tools within Norton GoBack to help protect both you and your GoBack setup. The first involves password-protecting your GoBack and the second lets you restore your system to the same clean state each and every day.

But as with any protection mechanism — like a seatbelt or a building security system — you have to take some encumbrances with the safety.

Norton GoBack lets you set passwords that someone must enter correctly in order to perform certain jobs within this system snapshot tool. It also recognizes two kinds of PC user:

✦ Administrator

✦ User (also known as Mere Mortal)

An administrator can make any change, including turning GoBack on and off and clearing the history. A user, by comparison, may only be able to do certain things depending on how you've configured GoBack. By creating the two types of accounts, you can control who has the power and what others can — or more importantly, can't — do.

If you don't do anything with setting passwords, everyone who uses your PC is treated just like you, and everyone is assumed to be the administrator. To take advantage of password protection and to differentiate what a regular user can't do that an administrator can, you need to:

✦ Set a password for each of the administrator and user accounts already set up in GoBack (you don't have to create accounts yourself)

✦ Determine which features can be performed by which type of user

Here's how you do this:

1. **Right-click your Norton GoBack icon.**

2. **Choose Options.**

3. **Select the Passwords tab (shown in Figure 2-4).**

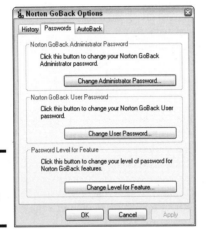

4. **Click Change Norton GoBack Administrator Password.**

5. **In the password window, click in the box next to New Password and type a password for the administrator (the longer and more random the password, the better — but you need to be able to remember it).**

6. **Type your password again in the Confirm New Password box and then click OK, as shown in Figure 2-5.**

7. **Click Change User Password.**

8. Type the new password into the box next to New Password, type it in again next to Confirm New Password, and click OK.

9. Click Change Level for Feature.

10. From the Password Level for Feature window, shown in Figure 2-6, adjust the options as desired.

Those featured checked User are available to anyone with the user password. Note that the administrator is considered a user as well, although an administrator also has access to features and functions a normal user would not. Any feature not checked in the user column needs the administrator's password to perform *except* where None is checked (no one can perform these functions, so be careful in choosing them).

Figure 2-6: Choose which feature each type of user can perform.

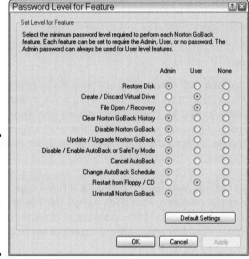

11. Click OK, and click OK again.

Don't make everyone who uses your PC an administrator in GoBack (or any other program or Windows itself, for that matter), or there's really no sense in applying the security option.

Taking Advantage of AutoBack Protection

AutoBack is the one feature here I think is truly cool. I can't tell you how many clients and customers have come to me over the years saying, "I want to start every day with the PC working as well as it does right now, without any fuss." This is just what the AutoBack tool does: It let's you start off with

Windows and your desktop exactly as it was the last time you used the PC — and the time before that and the time before that and . . . well, you get the idea.

This can be a big bonus for anyone who:

- ✦ Has to share a PC with others (especially kids who love to change settings even more than they enjoy fighting in the car when you're stuck in traffic)
- ✦ Likes to try new things but often gets stuck with dreadful results
- ✦ *Beta-tests* (checks hardware or software still in development and not yet on the market to see how well it runs on your system) programs or uses lots of different software that can make unwanted changes to your setup that you may live with long after the program is gone

Yet as good as AutoBack may sound, it's not for everyone.

Before you start

Before you turn on AutoBack and set it up to automatically revert your system to a previous state (the exact same condition your internal PC was when you first turned on AutoBack), there's something you should know: If you've made changes to any files on your system, these changes may be completely undone — they'll be back to the state they were in when AutoBack was enabled on your system.

Here's an example: I turned on AutoBack, opened a letter I was writing in Microsoft Word, made some changes, and then saved the file and closed it. Later, I ran AutoBack to restore my system to see how it worked. When I reopened the letter, bingo — all my most recent changes were gone.

Because you don't want to lose any changes to files, you need to practice good backups. If you create new files every day or have other files changed — even just the act of sending or receiving e-mail will make changes as new mail gets written into your virtual mailbox — you need to store these off your GoBack-protected hard drives.

Turning on AutoBack

In my experience, AutoBack isn't turned on by default. So if you want to use the feature, you need to switch it on. If you're convinced you want this tool — and you have backups in your future — here's how to turn on AutoBack:

1. **Right-click on the Norton GoBack icon in System Tray.**

Having his fun thanks to AutoBack

A friend of mine is the world's oldest kid when it comes to new software of any kind. The latest game, the newest version of Windows, or the earliest and most bug-ridden beta programs, and Andy is in pig heaven, grabbing a copy before anyone else. As a techie guru genius, he can fix almost anything that goes wrong with a PC.

But Andy also uses his many PCs for work in his ultra-busy home-based office. All too often, he'd be deep in a mess left behind by a new game struggling to recover from problems just as a client would call looking for a little 911 that required Andy's PC to provide. Telling a client who's looking for your technical expertise that you can't lend a hand because you just messed up your PC playing Doom 3 probably isn't good for business.

For Andy, however, the issue was time. He found himself wasting far too much time trying to reverse nasty changes or bad driver updates so he could get back to earning money to buy more games and other software.

He says AutoBack is his most-often-used Norton tool these days because he can easily install whatever he wants and rely on AutoBack to get his systems back up to snuff quickly. He then uses daily backups to restore files that have changed since that AutoBack history was recorded.

Andy says, "I used other methods to do it and still use them if AutoBack doesn't happen to help. But let me tell you, AutoBack is faster. I spend a lot less time troubleshooting. Yay!"

2. **Select AutoBack.**

3. **Select Enable AutoBack, as shown in Figure 2-7, and click OK.**

4. **Click OK when prompted to restart your system (AutoBack isn't ready for primetime until your PC restarts).**

Figure 2-7:
Turning on
AutoBack.

When AutoBack is enabled, you can determine exactly how and when the tool functions to revert your system back to the way it was. This can be done whenever you shut down and/or restart your PC. You can also tell it to pay attention and do something when AutoBack notices that you missed a time on your AutoBack schedule.

If you still have the Norton GoBack Options window open, you're ready to go. If not, open it again and then:

1. **From the AutoBack tab, click Change Options/Schedule.**

2. **Click to check the option you want to use for running AutoBack and/or adjust your listed schedule, as shown in Figure 2-8.**

3. **Click OK and then click Apply.**

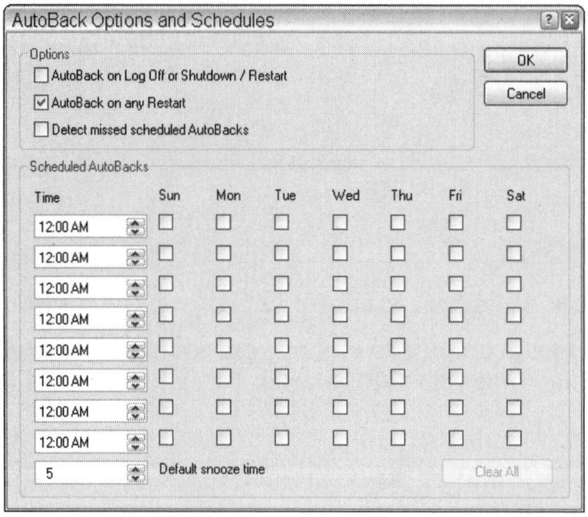

Figure 2-8:
Put
AutoBack
on a
schedule.

If you're in the middle of a Windows session and want to go back to that clean slate, you can do that. Just right-click on the Norton GoBack icon, choose AutoBack, and then click AutoBack Now.

Glance back at Figure 2-8 and notice that I selected AutoBack on Any Restart. This sets my system back to the way it was before, whenever my system is restarted. Any changes made to my desktop and other Windows settings during the session between being restarted get wiped clean.

I could also set this up to revert back to my "clean" setup every weekday morning at 7:00 a.m. If you want to use the schedule tool, just give a little thought (not too much — you don't want to tax yourself) to what time makes the most sense for you and your routine.

Going back with AutoBack

If you schedule AutoBack to automatically return your system to its previous state, you'll see a window pop up like that shown in Figure 2-9. This appears 60 seconds before AutoBack strikes. Ah, but this isn't any window — it's the annoying kind you can't close or get around unless you take action.

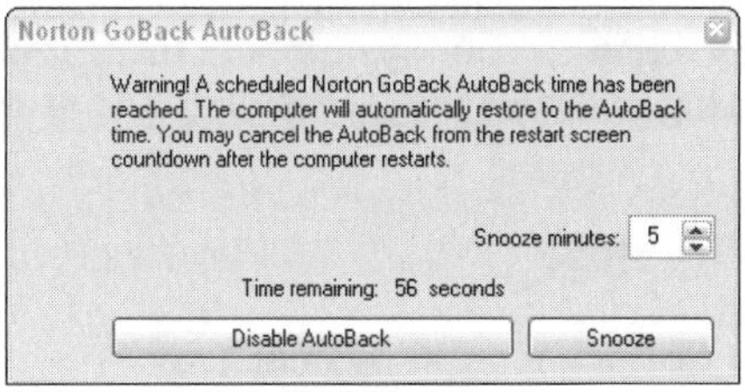

Figure 2-9:
Your
AutoBack
timer
warning.

Norton GoBack AutoBack

Warning! A scheduled Norton GoBack AutoBack time has been reached. The computer will automatically restore to the AutoBack time. You may cancel the AutoBack from the restart screen countdown after the computer restarts.

Snooze minutes: 5

Time remaining: 56 seconds

Disable AutoBack   Snooze

When it appears, you have these choices:

✦ Disable Norton GoBack.

✦ Snooze.

✦ Adjust your snooze time.

About Turning Off GoBack

You just got GoBack installed. Why am I telling you about turning it off?

There's a good reason. How well GoBack works on your system is often best determined after you've restarted your system again — after the restart during the install, that is. If everything's rosy and nice (read: you and the PC aren't screaming at one another), pretend you didn't even read this section.

But you may have problems. Norton GoBack isn't going to be compatible or live happily ever after on every PC. Drive-management software, other utilities you may run, or overall system problems could make your PC hiccup uncontrollably — or at least not run well — after GoBack is installed. The only way to get back in may be to turn off Norton GoBack. I get into that scenario more when we don our techie nerd clothes in the troubleshooting section, but there are other reasons you may want to turn off GoBack.

You may want to turn it off at least temporarily if you're performing some type of disk maintenance or you're installing some program that recommends you turn off all drive monitoring utilities first. In the latter type of situation, you probably have a wiser option than turning off GoBack. When it's disabled, all your recorded GoBack history gets purged. You can't go back if something happens (and you just know catastrophe will pick that vulnerable moment to strike). Consider instead using another option that lets you try out the effects of changes you make in a safe environment before you decide whether to keep them. This option is called SafeTry Mode.

Think of SafeTry Mode as operating your system with a safety net, just like the acrobats at the circus (except for the fact that the clowns aren't holding your net). This tool is ready to catch your system and bring it back without injury if things go awry during your tweaking session (as long as you remember to use it, that is).

Here's how to get into SafeTry Mode:

1. **Right-click the Norton GoBack icon in System Tray.**

2. **Select SafeTry Mode.**

Or try this instead:

1. **Open Norton System Works.**

2. **Click on Norton GoBack from the left-hand menu.**

3. **Select Disk Drive Protection, also from the left-sided menu.**

4. **Click SafeTry Mode, as shown in Figure 2-10.**

SafeTry steps you through the process to run it — and you can experiment while having a bit more protection.

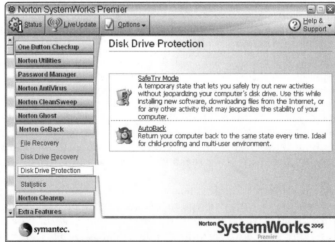

Figure 2-10:
Select
SafeTry
Mode within
Norton
GoBack.

There's one catch to using SafeTry Mode. You need to have at least 3GB of free disk space to use it, or you see a nagging message like the one shown in Figure 2-11.

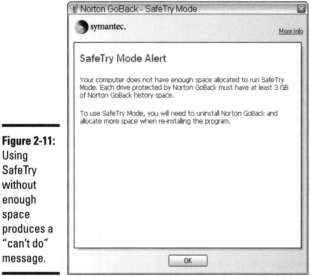

Figure 2-11: Using SafeTry without enough space produces a "can't do" message.

You can check your available disk space yourself right through Windows. Just open My Computer, right click on your GoBack-protected hard disk, and select Properties. Figure 2-12 shows you the information on my overloaded D: drive.

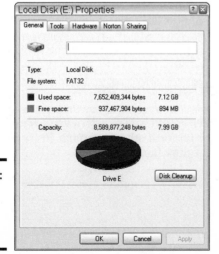

Figure 2-12: Checking your drive space available.

You may be able to clear up some space by eliminating unneeded temporary and leftover Internet files using Norton Cleanup or CleanSweep. This holds true for software installed on your drive that you just don't use. Yes, I'm sure you're planning someday to have enough time to try Mavis Beacon's typing tutor or 3D Chess, but it hasn't happened in two years, has it? So see if you can clear some room and try again with SafeTry Mode.

Troubleshooting Your GoBack Setup

Just as I warned you, any protective software like Norton GoBack can make it just a little tougher to troubleshoot problems. One big issue is the possibility that one or more of your hard drives won't respond correctly during startup and you're stuck with a PC that won't load Windows. But there are lesser problems, too.

This section offers some suggestions. But be sure to check with the experts by using the Symantec Web Site's technical support area. If you can't boot your PC to get on the Web, you may want to turn off GoBack (covered in this section) to get to the point where you can. Follow these steps to seek help from Symantec:

1. Go to www.symantec.com.

2. Click **Support.**

3. Click **Home and Home Office/Small Business.**

4. Click **Access Free Online Support.**

5. Click **Automated Support Assistant and let it guide you through the help process.**

You can also call Symantec's support lines. But if you check the booklet that came with Norton GoBack or Norton SystemWorks/SystemWorks Premier, you'll see this costs you, so you may want to check online for help first.

Using the Norton GoBack Boot menu

After Norton GoBack installs on your system, every time you start or restart your system you'll see a GoBack splash screen with a window telling you to press the spacebar to repair or perform other functions. Press the spacebar and you see the Norton GoBack Boot menu.

This menu — one you'll likely need to consult at some point — includes these options:

✦ **Restore Drive:** Choose this when you need to recover your system (more about this in Chapter 3 of this book).

✦ **Enable/Disable:** Allows you to disable Norton GoBack if you have a problem booting or enable GoBack if you have it turned off.

✦ **Enable AutoBack:** Turns on the feature already discussed.

✦ **Boot Floppy/CD:** Lets you start your system in emergency mode from either a Norton recovery CD or another tool with the drivers you need to try to troubleshoot your system.

Right now, focus on the Disable option. This is the one you want to use if your system won't start properly after you install Norton GoBack.

If you get into this jam and yet really want to use GoBack, this is a time to call on the experts. Go to Symantec's Web site to look for assistance.

Knowing what you can't do

I mentioned earlier that when you install Norton GoBack, it sets itself up on your hard disk(s). This is fine in most situations, but you hit some brick walls when you try to work around problems that may pop up out of nowhere.

For me, my test system has two hard disks, each running a different version of Windows. After I installed Norton GoBack on one Windows version, I couldn't boot up to my other Windows version. I got alarm bells, checksum errors when the PC first started up, and the dreaded `Operating system not found` message that means I'm going nowhere fast. I had to disable GoBack from the Norton GoBack Boot menu to get past this.

When you have multiple operating systems installed on one PC (and many people do this now), you usually have to install applications on each operating system, as if you had two separate PCs. But if I did this with Norton GoBack, I'd at best get an error message telling me I can't do that because GoBack's already running. At worst, I could have turned my system into a large paperweight because of the destruction I'd wreaked.

You know the old saying "In for a penny, in for a pound"? That applies in spades with Norton GoBack. You can't choose where it's installed and what drives it covers. You also can't try to get around GoBack by reinstalling it and then setting history space to 0 on one hard disk as a sly way of trying to prevent GoBack from working there. If you do — and believe me, I tried — you get an error message telling you that you can set no less than 10MB for history.

If you're using Norton GoBack on a system where you have two copies of Windows, or Windows and another operating system, GoBack just isn't a good choice. In this case, you're better off using System Restore from Windows.

Turning off Norton GoBack

Turning off GoBack gets rid of all your history recordings.

Norton gives you two primary ways to turn off Norton GoBack if the need or desire arises. The first method I show you works anytime you're in Windows, while the second technique can help you get into your system when a problem with GoBack is preventing you from getting that far.

Here's the normal way to turn off GoBack:

1. **Right-click on the Norton GoBack icon in Windows System Tray.**

2. **Select Options.**

3. **From the History tab, click to Disable Norton GoBack (see Figure 2-13), and click OK.**

You're asked to confirm your decision.

4. **Click Yes.**

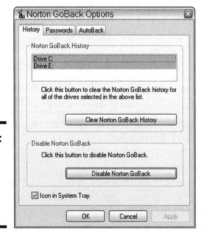

Figure 2-13: Click to disable Norton GoBack to turn it off.

If you can't get Windows to load because of error messages, you can try a second method. As your PC starts or restarts, you'll see a Norton GoBack screen with a small window telling you to press the spacebar to repair a problem. Follow these steps:

1. **Press your spacebar.**

2. **From the Norton GoBack boot menu, click Disable.**

3. **Click Yes to confirm your decision.**

4. **Just sit back and wait while Norton GoBack is turned off.**

You should then be able to get into Windows normally.

If you're running the AutoBack feature, you have to turn this off before you can disable GoBack. You'll see a nag screen telling you to do this if you haven't.

Every time your PC restarts with Norton GoBack disabled, you're prompted with a window asking if you want to re-enable the tool. Click Yes then to turn it back on at that time, or, if you want to do it midsession, use the steps in the following section.

Turning Norton GoBack on again

Want to turn back on Norton GoBack? You can do so at anytime, but if you do it when you first restart your PC, the tool is going to immediately want to reboot your system all over again. Frequent restarts are wise to avoid because they can shorten the life of the chips on your motherboard. So you may want to do this at a different time, such as just before you plan to shut your system down or restart it for another reason. Here's how to turn GoBack on during or at the end of a session:

1. **Right-click on your Norton GoBack icon.**

2. **Select Enable.**

3. **When prompted to restart your PC, click OK.**

The Norton GoBack Boot menu (covered earlier in the "Using the Norton GoBack Boot menu" section) also lets you turn on (enable) GoBack before Windows loads.

**Book IV
Chapter 2**

Configuring Norton
GoBack

Repairing Norton GoBack

What if Norton GoBack, your faithful protector, starts causing problems after you begin to use it? What if it presents you with error messages or other unwelcome treats?

Although removing Norton GoBack is an option, try to repair it first. Here's how:

1. **Insert your Norton GoBack or SystemWorks/SystemWorks Premier installation disc into your CD or DVD drive so it's ready and waiting in case you're prompted for the disc.**

2. **Open the Windows Control Panel and be sure you're in Classic view.**

3. **Double-click on Add or Remove Programs.**

4. **Locate and select Norton GoBack in the list and then click Change (see Figure 2-14).**

5. **Select Repair (see Figure 2-15), and click Next.**

6. **Click Repair.**

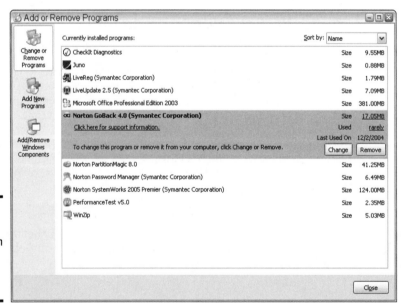

Figure 2-14:
Click Change from the Norton GoBack listing.

Figure 2-15:
Select
Repair.

Fresh copies of your Norton GoBack files are then transferred to your hard disk, overwriting existing files that may be corrupted or replace those that have gone missing. Now just sit back and evaluate whether your system and Norton GoBack are working better together.

Removing Norton GoBack

I've saved the most drastic solution for last: how to remove Norton GoBack. If you're having trouble with GoBack, you may want to try removing it and then reinstalling Norton GoBack to see if it works better with reinstallation.

Here's how to remove Norton GoBack:

1. **Open Windows Control Panel.**

2. **Double-click the Add or Remove Programs icon.**

3. **Select Norton GoBack from the list and click Remove (see Figure 2-16).**

4. **Click OK when you're asked to confirm your choice.**

**Book IV
Chapter 2**

Configuring Norton
GoBack

Figure 2-16:
Choose to
remove your
Norton
GoBack
setup.

If you want to keep GoBack off your system permanently, it's time to take the CD out of the CD or DVD drive, replace it in its package and shelve it. If you want to try reinstalling it to set up your system for GoBack a bit differently from the way you did before, refer to the installation instructions in Chapter 1 of this book for details on just how to do that.

Chapter 3: Rescuing Your System with GoBack

In This Chapter

✔ **Knowing when to use GoBack**

✔ **Understanding your rescue and recovery choices**

✔ **Trying different recovery types**

✔ **Catching mistakes and recovering additional files and folders**

✔ **Checking your GoBack statistics**

ongratulations! You've mastered some of the basics with preparing and using GoBack to protect the golden treasures contained on your PC's hard disk(s).

But protection is just part of the job. You also need to know how to use Norton GoBack to recover your system when havoc reigns or all that fancy protection is worth nothing. I definitely don't want to leave you alone in a crisis.

Yet your first step doesn't involve any software. First, you need to stay calm. Sure, thinking your disk has turned into a game of Scrabble isn't any fun, but your best chance is to keep panic at bay and proceed wisely. You also don't want to do much playing around with your system after you recognize you're in deep doo-doo — you can do further damage if you do.

Instead, you want to move toward a smart solution without a lot of intermediate — and desperate — steps. That smart solution is what I take you through here. This chapter should prepare you for just about anything — or at least anything related to misbehaving hard disks and the precious bounty they hold.

Knowing It's Time to GoBack

When your system has a major problem, in addition to staying calm, you need to be able to determine whether using GoBack is the right choice.

Use GoBack when:

✦ A newly installed program or *driver* (the software used to communicate with hardware devices like your PC's video card) fouls up your setup.

✦ You make a change to your setup that scrambles everything.

✦ You otherwise need a quick way back to the way your system was at some point before.

GoBack is *not* your best choice when:

✦ You think the hard disk is dying.

✦ You believe the problem is rooted in hardware.

✦ You're not sure whether the problem you currently have may have been recorded into recent GoBack System Safe Points.

✦ You stand to lose a lot of work created or modified since the last time GoBack recorded a System Safe Point.

If you suspect your hard disk is having problems because it's sounding a little like a car with a bad muffler or you're getting strange error messages, you want a solution that stores your files *off* that hard disk; GoBack records its System Safe Points directly *on* that disk, so you have no protection. Use something like Norton Ghost or another program that lets you back up files *off* that suspect drive.

Checking Your Options

Norton GoBack gives you five different tools to rescue your system. First, there are your three major choices:

✦ **Disk Drive Restore:** The one most used for recovering the contents of a drive to the way the drive existed before the trouble.

✦ **Advanced Disk Drive Restore:** A more powerful version of Disk Drive Restore that lets you specify which of your historical GoBack recordings — properly called System Safe Points — to use for drive rescue.

✦ **File and Version Rescue:** Rather than recover an entire disk, you can check through accidentally deleted or otherwise lost files so you can pick and choose what to restore.

Beyond these, you have two additional possibilities, the latter of which can be particularly important when you need to restore a drive yet not lose any work that has changed since the GoBack system snapshot was recorded and the time you need to restore your system with it.

✦ **Disk Drive Compare:** Use this tool to let GoBack create a virtual drive and then compare the files from your actual hard disk as it is right now against those in your virtual one, based on files and folders stored within a specific System Safe Point.

✦ **Post-Restore File Rescue:** Gives you a chance to restore those files lost to you during the disk-drive recovery process. Consider this option if you spot problems after recovering your hard disk using GoBack.

Taking the Right Steps

Roll up your sleeves and take a deep breath because you'll cover a lot of important ground quickly in recovering from a disaster. In this section, I take you through your main choices for restoring your drives to their former wonder. Then I show you how you can try to get back some files lost in the salvage operation.

Before you begin the recovery, stop and ask yourself whether there are any files on your drive that are just too important to lose. These files and programs *may* very well be there waiting for you after the restoration is complete — but you have no guarantee. So if you can get into Windows and copy really, really critical stuff onto a CD or another backup medium off the hard disk you're recovering, do so before you start using the tools.

Don't let this happen to you

Got a frustrating PC tale of woe to tell? Compare yours against this one, related by a fellow who contacted me asking for help.

Alex — his name has been changed to protect the guilty — bought Norton GoBack because misbehaving software kept trashing his system. He said he had been waiting for months for a chance to use Norton GoBack to see how well it would do. Yet, just as your aching tooth always starts to feel better right after you call the dentist, his system suddenly stopped throwing hissy fits.

Then one evening, while he was rushing to finish a report for work, a sudden power failure took down his system while he was doing a backup to his recordable DVD drive. When the power came back and he tried to restart the PC, Windows refused to load even in Safe Mode.

"Aha," Alex decided. "Finally I get to see how well Norton GoBack does!"

I'd love to tell you a wonderful, heartwarming story about how Alex's work and drive were saved beautifully by Norton GoBack — only I can't, because Alex discovered, much to his chagrin, that his teenage son had turned off GoBack the day before.

Instead of a nice clean disk restore, Alex had to piece things back together himself by the old-fashioned try-and-fail method. These days, he protects GoBack with a password (see Chapter 2 of this book) so he doesn't get into this situation again.

The good news: His son is finally no longer grounded.

Disk Drive Restore

Disk Drive Restore is the fastest way to recover a hard disk's contents when your system hits a snag. The big difference between this choice and Advanced Disk Drive Restore (covered in the following section) is that the latter gives you more options like choosing from multiple System Safe Points instead of simply your most recent ones (as Disk Drive Restore does).

Exactly how you start your Disk Drive Restore depends on whether or not Windows will load and run well enough for you to work.

✦ **If you *can't* get into Windows** or it won't run without system-halting errors, start or restart your PC, and when the Norton GoBack splash screen appears, click Restore Drive. After it's initiated, the restore process goes along automatically. You may or may not be prompted to restart your system afterward (I needed to restart once in restoring a drive, but not on my second try). After the recovery finishes, Windows will, you hope, be all happy again. Wow, you didn't even have to administer any Prozac to it. However, you may then want to use the Post-Restore File Rescue tool mentioned earlier in the "Checking Your Options" section to locate and recover files that have changed since you recorded the GoBack system snapshot used to restore your drive.

✦ **If you *can* get into Windows,** use the standard method for running GoBack recovery instead:

1. **Right-click on the Norton GoBack icon.**

2. **Select Disk Drive Restore.**

3. **From the Restore window, select the System Safe Point listed there (see Figure 3-1).**

Figure 3-1:
Select your System Safe Point and click Restore Now.

4. **Click Restore Now.**

5. **When prompted to restart your PC, click Yes.**

   As the PC restarts, you see the GoBack splash screen telling you that you can stop the disk restore if you press the spacebar.

6. **Don't press anything (unless you've changed your mind), and in a few seconds, GoBack begins the actual recovery process.**

   Be patient because this part can take anywhere from a few minutes to quite a bit longer. How long depends on the speed of your PC and the hard disk and how full the disk is you're restoring. Don't reboot your PC at this point or the salvage operation will probably fail.

   When your system finally comes back up (hallelujah!), you'll see a message like the one shown in Figure 3-2, telling you the patient was saved (also good news).

7. **Click OK.**

   The Post-Restore File Rescue window opens. I show you how to use this tool in the "Post-Restore File Rescue" section, later in this chapter.

Figure 3-2:
Your "success" message.

> **Post-Restore File Rescue**   More Info
>
> You have successfully restored your disk drive.
>
> Use this screen to locate and rescue files that you still want to keep.
>
> For additional help, click More Info from this screen.
>
> [OK]
>
> ☐ Don't show me this message again.

Advanced Disk Drive Restore

Advanced Disk Drive Restore works differently from the plain vanilla Disk Drive Restore in that you can choose which System Safe Point you use and it *must* be done from Windows; the Norton GoBack Boot menu doesn't give you this option.

Follow these steps to use the Advanced version:

1. **Right-click on the Norton GoBack icon.**

2. **Select Advanced Disk Drive Restore.**

   The recovery window opens. The large pane on the right lists important events like your system restarts, as well as your recorded System Safe Points, as shown in Figure 3-3.

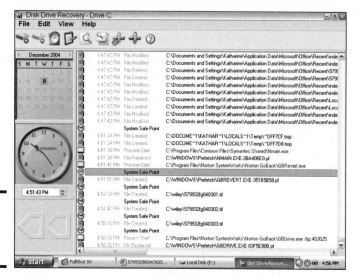

Notice that between the many System Safe Point listings are a number of other listings. These include files that have been created, modified, or deleted since each safe point was recorded. These are the files you stand to lose — at least in their current format — if you restore your drive to a safe point listed before them. This is my long-winded way of telling you to choose wisely. You may be able to recover these files later on using the File and Version Rescue option, but it's a crap shoot — and you could either win or lose.

3. **From the recovery window, review and select the System Safe Point you want to use to restore your hard disk.**

4. **Right-click on the selected System Safe Point and choose Restore Drive (or Restore Drive *x* to this Event, as shown in Figure 3-4).**

   You can also use the calendar and clock tools in the left-hand pane to choose a recovery point based on the time and date when your files and system worked well.

5. **When prompted to restart your PC, click OK.**

What happens now is basically the same thing that happens when you use the regular Disk Drive Restore: Your system restarts, the recovery process commences, you'll see a success message, and then the Post-Restore File Rescue window opens.

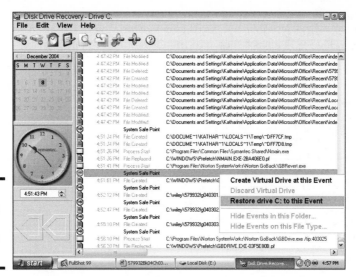

Figure 3-4:
Restore the
drive from
this System
Safe Point.

REMEMBER

Unlike GoBack's Disk Drive Restore, the Advanced version is *not* available
from the Norton GoBack Boot Menu. You must be able to get into Windows
to use the advanced version.

Catching Mistakes

With easy drive recovery now tucked safely into your tool belt, you can turn
to the nitty-gritty detail work: being sure you haven't lost any files and work
as a previous System Safe Point was restored. Post-Restore File Rescue is
probably the tool you'll use most often for this, but in the following sections,
I show you how to work with Disk Drive Compare and File and Version Rescue,
too. This way, you'll be prepared for anything. Let's go get 'em, tiger!

Post-Restore File Rescue

The Post-Restore File Rescue window opens after you recover a disk using
either Disk Drive Restore or Advanced Disk Drive Restore version. The only
time you *won't* see it pop up automatically is when you use the AutoBack
feature to recover (discussed in Chapter 2 of this book).

To open it manually (in case you haven't just performed the regular or
advanced Disk Drive Restore), right-click the GoBack icon in your System
Tray and select Post-Restore File Rescue.

You can also get to the Post-Restore File Rescue from the main Norton SystemWorks window, by clicking on Norton Go-Back in the left-hand menu, then clicking File Recovery, and then Post-Restore File Rescue from the right-hand screen, as shown in Figure 3-5.

Figure 3-5: Opening Post-Restore File Rescue through Norton System Works.

With the Post-Restore File Rescue window (shown in Figure 3-6) open, you should see listed every darned file that may have been created, modified, and even deleted from the time Norton GoBack created the System Safe Point until the time you start the recovery. Don't be too surprised if there are a slew of files in there — even if you don't create many files yourself, your system is always modifying and creating them as you check e-mail, use Windows, browse the Web, and play games.

Knowing which files to restore

How do you know which files you need to recover to your system? That's a really good question and the answer isn't simple. You may be able to spot ones you've made, such as word processing documents or spreadsheets or downloaded files. Look for those in the Post-Restore File Rescue window. As for your other files, one way to tell is simply by using your system a bit after your recovery. You may try to open a file and notice it's missing. Or Windows may complain with a pop-up message that it can't find something it needs. Jot down the filename (in case you forget) and then try the Post-Restore File Rescue tool.

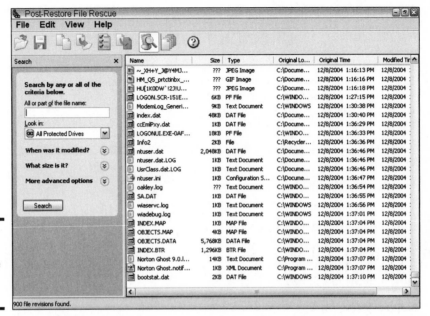

Figure 3-6:
The Post-
Restore File
Rescue
window.

Although I can't find any hard-and-fast rules listed in the GoBack documentation, I'd advise you to use the Post-Restore File Rescue tool as soon as possible after you've recovered a disk. This reduces your chance that a needed file could be lost.

Restoring files

Although the Post-Restore File Rescue window doesn't look especially friendly, it's pretty easy to use. The files placed in limbo between the time your System Safe Point was recorded and then applied and the way your disk was at the time of recovery are listed in the main windowpane. The name of the file is at the far left, and the type of file is listed in the Type column.

To open a file to view it:

1. **Select the file in the list.**

2. **Right-click on it and choose Open.**

The file opens using whatever program it needs (for example, Word documents will open in Word, PDFs will open in Adobe Acrobat, and so on).

**Book IV
Chapter 3**

**Rescuing Your
System with
GoBack**

Checking your statistics

Norton GoBack gives you a way to check your basic information about the size of your history store, how long GoBack has been protecting your system, and whether passwords have been set. Review this through the Statistics window.

To view this, open Norton GoBack or Norton SystemWorks/SystemWorks Premier, and select Statistics. The statistics summary shown in the figure appears.

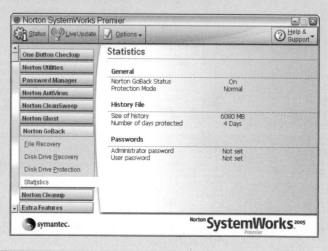

To save a file back to your disk, follow these steps:

1. **Select the file in the list.**

2. **Right-click and choose Save As.**

3. **Choose where to save the file and rename it as desired.**

4. **Click Open.**

You may also copy your rescued files or copy them to a specific folder on your disk, such as the folder where a file was originally located. To do a simple copy:

1. **Right-click on the desired file and select Copy.**

2. **Choose Start ➪ My Computer.**

3. **Click on the disk where you want to save the file, open the folder where you want to save it, then right-click and choose Paste.**

To copy a listed file to a specific folder directly:

1. **Right-click on the file to copy and select Copy to Folder.**
2. **From the Browse window, click the plus sign to expand the listings and then choose the location to copy the file.**
3. **Click OK.**

Not sure where a file was originally located? Look back at the Post-Restore File Rescue window and look under the Originally Located column. Can't find a file in your long rescue list? Use the search tool:

1. **In the left-hand Search pane, type in all or part of the name of the file you're trying to find.**

   If you don't know the whole filename, you can use wildcards. For example, if you know the file ends in the `.doc` file extension, type ***.doc**; if you know the filename starts with "budget", type **budget*.***.

2. **Click Search.**

   The Post-Restore File Rescue list changes to show all files that match the search criteria you set. If you don't find what you're seeking, try a different search.

Disk Drive Compare

What if you want to be able to go back to a System Safe Point and retrieve files that have changed or are otherwise missing from your current disk restoration? For this, you have the Disk Drive Compare tool.

Part of what you'll do is turn the files stored in a chosen System Safe Point into a virtual drive. Then you can compare your current drive to its virtual cousin and copy files from that virtual drive back to your active hard disk. Afterward, you'll want to purge the virtual disk so you're not storing an extra whole disk full of files right on your hard disk.

This is how you do it:

1. **Right-click on the Norton GoBack icon and select Disk Drive Compare.**
2. **From the Disk Drive Recovery window, locate a System Safe Point you want to compare against the current contents of a drive.**
3. **Right-click on that System Safe Point and select Create Virtual Drive at This Event.**
4. **Click OK when you see the confirmation window (shown in Figure 3-7).**

Book IV Chapter 3

Rescuing Your System with GoBack

Figure 3-7:
Wait for con-
firmation.

Okay, you have your virtual drive filled with the files from the System Safe
Point. Now what?

1. **Choose View ⇨ Edit Filters.**

Here, you can specify what files and file types to exclude from your
search (an example is shown in Figure 3-8), such as .TMP (temporary)
files you probably don't want or need.

Figure 3-8:
Use filters to
block those
files you
don't want
to list.

2. **Press Ctrl+F to bring up the file search window and type a filename
(wildcards are okay here, too), as shown in Figure 3-9.**

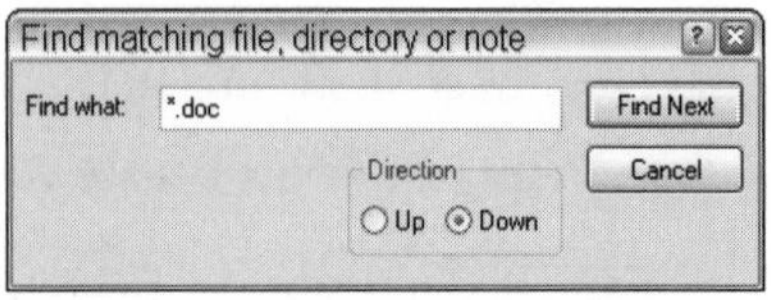

Figure 3-9:
Press Ctrl+F
to find files
by name or
wildcards.

3. **Click OK.**

Your cursor will highlight the first file in your right-pane window that matches that criteria.

4. **When you find a file you want to keep, right-click on it and follow the same steps provided in the "Post-Restore File Rescue" section to open and view, copy, or save a file from the virtual drive onto your hard disk proper.**

When you're done — and be sure you are — it's time to discard that virtual drive so it's not filling up your physical hard disk. This is a snap:

1. **Locate your virtual drive in the Post-Restore File Rescue.**

2. **Right-click and select Discard Virtual Drive *x* window.**

3. **Click OK when GoBack reports the drive has been removed.**

File and Version Rescue

File and Version Rescue is a tool that comes in handy when you either need to find files that have been lost or deleted or you've got an emergency where it would be helpful to access older versions of files or folders than you currently have on your system.

Choose this option either by right-clicking on your Norton GoBack icon and choosing File ⇨ Version Rescue or by opening Norton SystemWorks to drill down to File Recovery, where you can select this. The Post-Restore File Rescue window opens. Follow the instructions in "Post-Restore File Rescue," earlier in this chapter, to find, view, save, and copy these files.

Chapter 4: Snapping a Smart Drive Image

In This Chapter

- ✓ Understanding the benefits of Norton Ghost
- ✓ Knowing when another tool may be better
- ✓ Identifying what a Ghost image/backup contains and how it can be used
- ✓ Configuring Norton Ghost

*N*orton Ghost can make your work with a PC a whole lot less spooky by giving you a way to either restore a drive (similar to Norton GoBack, discussed earlier in this book) in an emergency or to copy the contents of a dying or too-full hard disk to a new hard disk.

Among many veteran PC users, Norton Ghost has a great reputation. In my experience, it's well-deserved. In the process of "creating" disasters to recover from, I often found myself with a hard disk that would no longer boot properly into Windows. For these situations, I called upon Ghost to restore my drive contents to the last backup I'd done to get back to writing this book.

In this chapter, I show you why you need this tool and how to configure it for use.

The Big Benefits of Norton Ghost

Norton Ghost lets you do three jobs very important to anyone with data and programs they want to protect — in other words, just about everybody. These jobs are

- ✦ Back up your hard disk(s) into a drive image
- ✦ Restore your entire backup or just select files or folders from it
- ✦ Copy the contents of one hard drive to another

Although all these functions can save your life (at least as it's lived at your keyboard), that final one — copying the contents of one hard drive to another — is a great bonus. When you buy a brand-new hard disk — and with high-capacity prices so good right now, you may as well take advantage of them — one of the most daunting tasks ahead of you is copying your setup from your existing drive to the blank new one. There are plenty of ways to do this, including other tools that work like Norton Ghost. But Ghost makes it so easy that it's a great way to get that job done fast.

You can get back to work or play quickly

Even if you run into a PC crisis that requires you going out to buy a new hard disk or — gulp! — a new computer, you can bring the new drive or system back up to its former working status through the use of Norton Ghost. So long as you have good copies of your backups, you can put the Restore Drive Wizard (shown in Figure 4-1) to work for you.

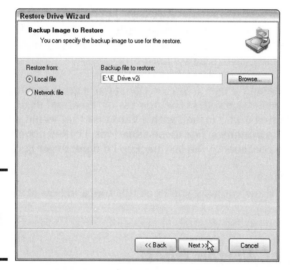

Figure 4-1:
Restore a drive using Norton Ghost.

Here's an example: Let's say you were wise enough to use Norton Ghost to create a full system backup last Monday. On Friday, you were doubly smart and performed an incremental backup to copy over any files that were added or changed since the full backup. Then first thing Monday morning, you turn on your PC and find your hard drive is dead, dead, and very dead.

If you're using a recovery tool like Windows System Restore or Norton GoBack, you can't even take any comfort because they're stored on the deceased drive.

The Department of Redundancy Department

Redundancy is a very big word with computers in more ways than character count. The term means different things in different areas of the industry, but it boils down to having more than one way to keep going if your normal route or device isn't available.

One very basic way for you to have redundancy on your home PC is to have access to more than one copy of your files and folders. Norton Ghost gives you that, but your best protection comes if you store your drive image and incremental backups off your main hard disk(s).

Sure, you can copy a backup of one hard disk to a second hard disk. Yet there's always the slim possibility that something could happen to your system like a power surge or a sudden flood that could fry your motherboard and take anything connected to it — which is just

about everything, including your hard disks — with it.

For best results, make sure you keep copies on a recordable CD or DVD or another location like the hard disk of another computer on your home or small-office network. Heck, I keep more than one copy of these disks and store them in different parts of my home and office. Better off being neurotic than spending hours redoing work or crying over split data.

If you've got one of those great new removable Universal Serial Bus (USB) or FireWire (IEEE 1394) external drives that connect through ports on the front or back of your PC, these can also be pressed into service as backup drives. I use one for that purpose and love it because I can connect/disconnect the drive any time I want and take it to a different system.

You could cry in your coffee and whine about the very bad week you've just started, or you could go get a fresh hard disk and put those backups to work for you in getting you back at the keyboard.

Here are the basic steps you should take to recover:

1. **Physically install the new hard disk and then partition and format it to prepare it for use (if you're using PartitionMagic, find out how to do this in Book VIII, Chapter 2).**

2. **Boot your PC using your Norton Ghost CD.**

3. **From Ghost, choose to restore a drive and then point to either the CD or other disk that contains your backup files.**

   As the backup gets applied, your new hard disk is set up very much like your other one, with the same programs, files, and preferences restored by applying the backup.

Should I use GoBack instead?

Many people will tell you it's not a matter of *either* using a backup program like Norton Ghost *or* a recovery tool like Windows System Restore or Norton GoBack. Safe backup procedures should include using both. Using them together gives you an additional way to get back up if you have a system meltdown. Not that you want to consider a PC version of Chernobyl, but the possibility is always there (minus all the messy radiation).

If your existing drive is fine but you want to be able to copy the setup and files from your present drive to a brand-spanking-new one, use Norton Ghost's Copy Drive feature to make it simple to duplicate your old hard disk onto your new one.

You can store copies off your hard disks

One area where Norton Ghost has a big plus over Windows System Restore or Norton GoBack is that you can store copies of your setup, files, and folders off your hard disks. GoBack records *only* to your hard disks.

Let System Restore or GoBack go it alone as the only chef in your PC health kitchen and you'll find you're only cooking on two burners. If that hard disk gets creamed by a virus, fried from a power surge, or pureed by a platter failure, your goose is juice because your data and backups are in the exact same place.

It keeps track of what you need to back up

All too often, when people perform backups (if they do it at all), they do so in a hit-or-miss fashion — when they remember, when they feel like it, when nothing better is happening. As you can guess, this way of backing up is fraught with the dangers of losing important files.

Norton Ghost provides a layer of *backup administration,* a fancy way of saying that it can keep track of what needs to be backed up because something has been created, downloaded, installed, changed, or removed since your last full backup. Although it isn't totally automated, it comes close and helps you with the detail work that can make the act of performing backups about as joyously anticipated as a trip to the dentist.

The Job of Norton Ghost

The *numero uno* job of any backup tool is to store a copy of your files to a second location, preferably off the hard disk where the files are originally kept and used.

Yet you can't just think in terms of huge Technicolor disasters when you consider a backup. Not every problem is so dramatic.

Some emergencies are smaller, like when you can't find the original or revised version of a document that may have been corrupted or accidentally deleted from your hard disk. I create hundreds of files in any given month just for my business, and when dealing with so many, I'm bound to lose track of one here or there. But even losing a single file can be a big deal — like when it's the IRS-requested copy of your 1999 tax return, the paper due at school today, or an Excel worksheet containing your vital budget numbers.

Norton Ghost lets you explore the contents of a backup file and grab important files from it individually. You don't have to apply the whole darned five-CD backup just to get at one or two files or a half-dozen folders. The Restore File and Folders Wizard (shown in Figure 4-2) helps you do just that.

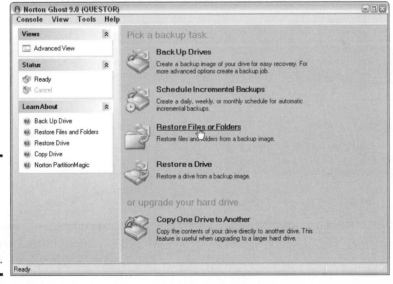

Figure 4-2: You can restore individual files and folders from your backup.

A full comprehensive backup with Norton Ghost is just that: a copy of everything on your hard disk. This includes

✦ Your Windows setup and all its programs, plus the Windows Registry

✦ Your stored preferences (ways you've customized programs to look and work)

✦ All your individual files and folders

Think of a backup as the world's largest ZIP file (ZIP is a format that lets you combine one or more large files into a smaller compressed file called an *archive*). That's not a bad way to think of the backup, because no matter how large the backup gets or how many recordable CD or DVD discs it takes to store, it's still a single file than spans multiple discs. Figure 4-3 shows the first disc in a five-CD backup set. Notice that just one file is listed there, and if I put in any of the other CDs used to record this, I'd see the same filename listed for each.

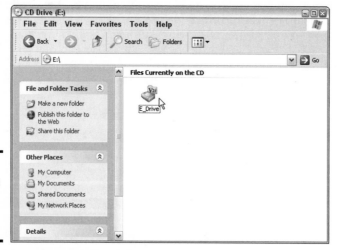

Figure 4-3:
Looking at a backup CD from My Computer.

If your backup takes two recordable DVDs or nine recordable CDs to store, you need to have *all* of those discs ready and available when you go to restore the drive. If one disc is damaged or missing, you're out of luck. So always have more than one backup available just in case.

Incremental backups are usually much smaller than a full backup because an incremental backup only copies those files that have been added or in some way changed since the time the full backup was recorded. When you restore your drive, you usually restore the *full* backup first and then restore your incremental backups.

Configuring Ghost for Your Needs

Norton Ghost makes things pretty easy for you. You really don't have to do anything but install it and use it. You don't have to adjust lots of settings or worry about much in the way of customization.

Yet there are a couple things you can do to make your job easier. One is to set a default location where you want your backups stored when you perform them. Follow these steps:

1. **Open Norton Ghost by double-clicking on its icon in the Windows System Tray.**

2. **Choose Tools ➪ Options.**

3. **On the Default Settings tab, click in the Default Location for Backup Files drop-down list (see Figure 4-4) and select the type of drive where you usually want to store your backups.**

4. **Click OK.**

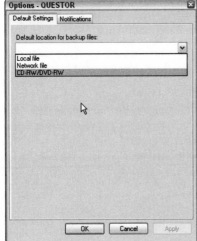

Figure 4-4:
Set a default
drive for
backups.

**Book IV
Chapter 4**

**Snapping a Smart
Drive Image**

You can also tell Norton Ghost to notify you by e-mail when certain events are performed or detected. To set this:

1. **Open Norton Ghost.**

2. **Choose Tools ⇨ Options.**

3. **Select the Notification tab.**

4. **Select Send Notification and type your e-mail address in the box provided.**

5. **Enter a name as a Send Name and then enter the address of your SMTP (e-mail box) server (check Outlook Express under Accounts or contact your Internet service provider for details).**

6. **Click OK.**

Performing System Maintenance

Unless you want your backups to take a lot of room to store and far longer to record than needed (and why the heck would you want that?), you should perform a wee bit of housekeeping on your hard disks before you run your backups, whether full or incremental.

Clean is good

Did you know that many types of PC hardware are manufactured in so-called *clean rooms,* where people wear dust-free clean suits and generally look like they're harvesting uranium on a distant planet? This is because cleanliness really counts with many PC components, where even a tiny amount of dust or debris can lead to big problems.

Now, you don't need to don a surgical mask and gown to work around your lil' ol' computer but try to avoid the slob routine, too. For example, don't use your Windows setup CD as a coaster for a sticky drink or as a temporary holding area for that triple-decker sandwich you just carried into your office.

The more you use your recordable CD or DVD drive, the more critical it is that you practice good PC housekeeping to keep the drive clean and in good working order. One of the best ways to do that is to keep all your CDs stored separately in a cool, dry, and clean location. If you notice dust or spots on a disc, use a soft, lint-free cloth to clean the CD. Don't use anything abrasive, which can scratch the disc and create problems when you try to read the disc or record to it.

Here's a checklist of some housekeeping you'll want to stay on top of:

✦ Uninstall any unneeded/unwanted programs

✦ Clean up temporary and Internet files left over from Web browsing

✦ Optimize/defragment your hard disks

✦ Check a problem drive using a disk analysis utility, such as Norton Disk Doctor (found in Norton Utilities packed into Norton SystemWorks or SystemWorks Premier)

✦ Browse through files and folders on your system to remove ones you no longer need to keep (including the hundreds of test shots showing the inside of your lens cap taken before you learned how to use that new digital camera)

Like many Norton products, Norton Ghost includes a LiveUpdate tool to automatically check for, download, and install security fixes and updates to your Ghost setup. Run this LiveUpdate occasionally to see if you need any updates. When you're connected to the Internet (required for LiveUpdate), open Norton Ghost, and choose Help ➪ LiveUpdate. When the LiveUpdate window (shown in Figure 4-5) opens, click Next and follow the on-screen prompts.

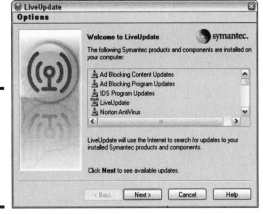

Figure 4-5:
Run
LiveUpdate
periodically
to make
sure you're
up to date.

**Book IV
Chapter 4**

Snapping a Smart
Drive Image

Chapter 5: Optimizing Your Image Results

In This Chapter

✔ **Understanding when it's a good time to back up**

✔ **Analyzing your system**

✔ **Knowing when to go another route**

Get ready — I'm about to hit you up with a choice.

You have got two options here:

✦ You can restore a backed up system that is filled with viruses, a gigabyte of leftover Internet files (taking up lots more space in the backup than you'd like), and programs you haven't run since you first unboxed the PC when new.

✦ You can choose a backup that is slim, trim, packed with everything you need and very little you don't. It doesn't take anywhere near as much space to store this backup as it does the first one and you'll be pretty pleased with the results.

Okay, time's up. Which do you want? Yeah, I thought you'd choose the second one — you're no dummy. In this chapter, I show you how you can make your backups fit that second description far better than the first.

Knowing the Best Times to Image Your Drive

Having a drive image like the kind Norton Ghost creates through its drive copy feature is obviously better than not having one. Yet certain times can be better than others to perform this copying routine. For example, you wouldn't necessarily want to image your hard disk right after you catch a killer virus.

Even when you're planning only to restore select files and folders from a backup because you've installed the operating system and your programs separately, you still don't want to carry all that undesirable weight and size of an unoptimized setup along into the backup. What if one of the files you restore introduces a virus into your virginal setup?

Clean it up for your base and then try to do another round of disk maintenance before it's time to run incremental backups (discussed in Chapter 7).

When your system is fresh

A fabulous time to back up your system for the first time is as soon as you unpack it from the box after you've brought it home from the store or delivered to you. At this time, the system is hopefully perfectly configured by the manufacturer before it was shipped and everything should work great.

The first thing you want to do with a new PC doesn't include having to sit there watching a backup. But maybe schedule the backup at the end of your first or second full day with the system, perhaps after you've started to customize Windows for your preferences and installed a few programs you can't live or work without.

Do a fresh backup again after you've upgraded your Windows version or made changes to your system that you want to be reflected in the images you make through Norton Ghost.

When the system works well

Ever have those wonderful days when you're just amazed at how well your PC is running and how well Windows is performing for you? If so, that's a superb time to make a full system backup.

If you need to take your PC into the shop or send it in for service and it comes back working perfectly, this is also an excellent time to back up.

Before making big changes

Probably one of the very best times to perform a full system backup is just before you plan to make some major change to your system. These changes may include (but aren't necessarily limited to):

✦ Upgrading your operating system

✦ Installing a Windows Service Pack to update your operating system (but it doesn't hurt to use this same smart practice before any type of update, just in case).

+ Installing a major new software package or a big upgrade to a current one (Microsoft Office is a good example of this)

+ Reformatting your hard disk to start fresh (the backup is there to restore files and folders but also to serve as a full solution if you can't get the system working properly again)

+ Changing out a major piece of hardware, such as your motherboard and/or CPU, your video setup, or another important component

Knowing When Not to Image

Obviously, any backup is better than none when you have to restore your system after some major foul-up or disaster. So if it comes down to a question of waiting forever until you get time to tidy up your system or snapping an image (what Norton Ghost calls its *backup*) while your drive's virtual bed is unmade, just go ahead and back up.

Fix problems; don't copy them

I'm not just telling you to take care of messes with your system before you start the way your mother told you to eat your vegetables. I speak from experience.

In preparing for this book, I created several scenarios to deliberately cause problems on my test system before I tried to fix them — or use programs like Norton GoBack and Norton Ghost to get back to work after chaos ensued. I also manufactured some disasters for the Norton doctors in Norton Utilities to diagnose. Most of the time, I was pretty successful.

But in one situation, I failed to notice a virus that Norton AntiVirus warned me it couldn't fix. Then I made a backup. The virus caused me some woe on the test system and I got rid of it.

Then came the moment when I applied my backup. Ouch! After getting over the first wave of problems from the virus, I found myself facing

them all over again because I'd copied the virus into my backup and, by applying the backup, I turned my Windows setup back into split pea soup — not the good kind either.

Yeah, I know better than to do what I did. But that's the point. Much of the mess people encounter with their PCs comes from issues they know better than to let go unfixed, but they're busy and they forget. Or they're not sure what's wrong so they ignore them until a bump turns into a grind.

Fix problems as you see them and before you back them up into Norton Ghost or store them in a backup with Norton Ghost. You won't remember issues later on. So when you have an issue come back to smack you in the head, you may not even recall having the difficulty before, let alone how you solved it.

Work clean, by all means.

But if you already have a full system backup or your base with incremental updates discussed in Chapter 7, keep those safe but handy while you try to get your system in better shape. When it is, you can run a fresh full backup or start a new base that you update through incremental backups.

Use the tools discussed in much of Book I to overcome problems with your system. Augment these with the Norton products you use that are designed to address certain problems, such as the following:

✦ Run Windows Disk Cleanup (shown in Figure 5-1) or Norton Cleanup or CleanSweep to remove unwanted files from your system.

✦ Use CheckIt Diagnostics from Norton Utilities to scan your system for problems with installed hardware and software.

✦ Consult with Norton WinDoctor and Norton Disk Doctor to identify and resolve issues these docs may spot.

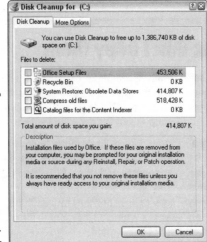

Figure 5-1:
Disk
Cleanup,
which
comes with
Windows, is
a great for
cleaning up
your system.

Chapter 6: Summoning Your Ghost

In This Chapter

✔ Considering backups as one part of a PC disaster recovery plan

✔ Knowing other tools to supplement your backups

✔ Getting comfortable with the Norton Ghost console

✔ Choosing your backup recording location and medium (and I'm not talking the psychic kind)

Making disk disasters, backups, and drive images sound funny or enticing is tough. However, you don't necessarily need to laugh or feel drawn in to get your spirits raised considerably when a Norton backup keeps your PC from turning into a ghost. A crisis averted is a beautiful thing! So is the sanity you save.

Before we get into the nuts-and-bolts of backups and Ghost in the next chapter, I need to cover a few details. One is the Ghost work window — you'll see why I call it two-faced. The other concerns how a backup should be just part of a total recovery plan.

The message here? Spend a few minutes developing a recovery plan and thinking about what you want to include — even though you'd like to forget, think also about past PC emergencies you've lived through. Then consider how you can use different tools to help.

Coming Up with a Backup Plan

Ever get nervous putting all your eggs into one basket? I do all the time. That's probably the reason I have spare car keys stashed just about everywhere I go.

Because of this, I don't want just one way I can try to get back to work or play when something really goes wrong on my system. As a pro, I know one solution doesn't fit all and that if you rely on just one method, you still run the risk that the method won't be the right one. Or even if it is the right one, some obstacle could prevent you from being able to use it.

Here's what I recommend you do if you're serious about protecting your files and folders:

✦ **Don't limit yourself to just one solution.** Use Windows System Restore or Norton GoBack, as well as a drive image or backup, in addition to spot copying really important files you can't bear to lose. The point isn't to have 100 copies, just two or three copies from different recovery tools.

✦ **Have a system.** Back up all your new or changed files at the end of the day. If you don't want to do it quite that frequently, back up at least once each week.

✦ **Get yourself an extra hard drive.** If you have a removable external hard drive on which you can store a large backup or drive copy without space problems, it can sit off your main hard disks and still be installed within the PC.

✦ **Don't take unnecessary risks without first performing a backup or drive copy.**

Knowing How a Ghost Backup Works for You

Norton Ghost actually gives you a couple of different backup methods all by itself. Use it and you can create

✦ A full system backup, which contains everything on your drive at the time you ran Norton Ghost to create it

✦ A base or starter backup to which you add incremental backups as files change

✦ A drive copy (a duplicate of your drive right now that you can apply to a new and hopefully larger hard disk)

Backup software like Ghost takes those thousands of files stored on the average PC and squeezes them into one humongous accordion-compressed file saved in a particular file format. That file then gets stored on a hard disk on your PC, on another computer on your home or small-office network, or on a removable disc like a CD-R or DVD-R.

When you need to try to recover from a disk problem, you load the backup software and then open the backup file to restore your files, folder, and setup to the hard disk. This gives you fresh copies of everything that was on the disk at the time it was backed up.

Norton Ghost stores backups in a few different formats. By default, these usually end with the `.v2i` file extension. A backup of your C: drive in Ghost would be saved as `C_Drive001.v2i`.

If you can avoid it, don't fiddle with your time/date clock in Windows (in the Windows System Tray). Norton Ghost calculates its actions based on your PC time, so if you set the time back or ahead, you'll start seeing error messages. Ghost won't understand what's happening and tells you it can't reconcile the changes based on the time. It should still operate, however.

Working with Norton Ghost

When you right-click on the Norton Ghost icon in your System Tray, you can perform many functions, check information, and even stop a Ghost operation without first opening the Norton Ghost console. Your options here include

✦ **Back Up Now:** Select this and you have more choices, such as Back Up Drives, Create Backup Job, and Back Up *Drive letter*.

✦ **Schedule Incremental Backups:** Choose this option to set a time to perform your next incremental backup to copy files added or changed since your base backup.

✦ **Restore a Drive:** Select this option to start a recovery process using a Ghost backup you've already done.

✦ **View Backup Jobs:** Click this to see what backup jobs are scheduled to run.

✦ **Run Norton Ghost:** Selecting this option opens the Norton Ghost console.

✦ **Restore Files or Folders:** Select this option to open the Backup Image Browser (discussed in more detail in Chapter 7) to let you recover individual files and folders from a backup image.

✦ **Cancel the Current Operation:** Choose this option to stop whatever Ghost operation you have running at the time.

✦ **About Norton Ghost:** This option allows you to check information about your Norton Ghost version and installation details.

Notice that an option missing here is to exit Norton Ghost. Ghost wants to run all the time, every session. This makes sense because if it's not running, it can't perform backups or launch a salvage operation.

Ghost's two views

Norton offers a two-faced Ghost. By that I mean that Norton Ghost has two very different views you can use to operate your backups and perform other tasks.

The default view of the Ghost console, called Basic view, is shown in Figure 6-1. It's simple to operate — you just point and click — giving you access to all the major features and tools Ghost offers. When you click on any of the options listed here, most will load a wizard that helps you even more, making it pretty difficult to take a wrong turn at Albuquerque.

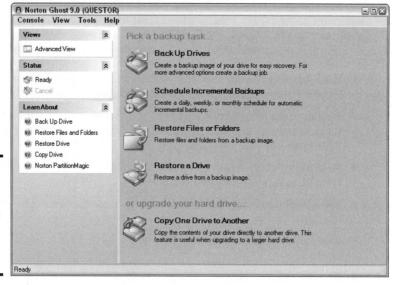

Figure 6-1: Ghost's Basic view, available by pressing F7 from within Ghost.

The other view — Advanced view — is the one I find the most useful because you can check information and configure a couple options there that basic operations don't give you. To open Advanced view, from Ghost Basic, press F8 or click Advanced View in the top of the left-hand task pane (see Figure 6-2).

Look at the left-hand task pane in Advanced View and you see your major tasks listed as well as Ghost's Status. Your Status should read "Ready" any-time it's not actually performing a backup. Toward the bottom of the task pane, find links to find out more about certain operations such as drive backup or copying.

To the right, you see four tabs listed, with the Drives tab open by default. Click a drive and you see basic information about it, including how full it is and when the disk was last backed up. This kind of at-a-glance view of things is a great reference. When you schedule a backup and want to check later to see if the backup was performed, just select the drive in Advanced View and find out.

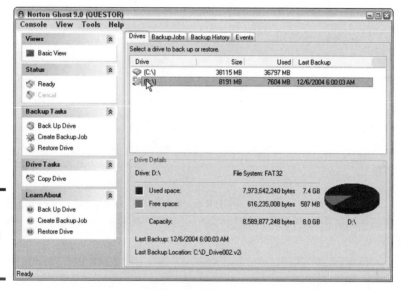

Figure 6-2:
Advanced
View offers
useful
options.

Click on other tabs as well, where you'll see:

✦ **Backup Jobs:** A list of your scheduled backups.

✦ **Backup History:** Find out when the drive was last backed up, to what location, and using what filename (see Figure 6-3).

✦ **Events:** This tab lists all significant events while Ghost is running, including when the program successfully loads after startup and what errors or problems it's encountered along the way (a good thing to check occasionally, especially if you question how well Ghost is running on your system); click on an event to get more details listed in the lower pane, as shown in Figure 6-4.

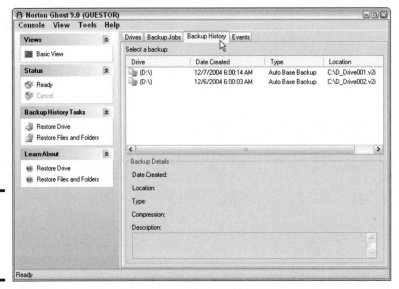

Figure 6-3:
View your
backup
history for
each drive.

To have Norton Ghost rescan your drive(s) at any time for changes, open
Norton Ghost and either press F5 or choose Tools ➪ Rescan Disk.

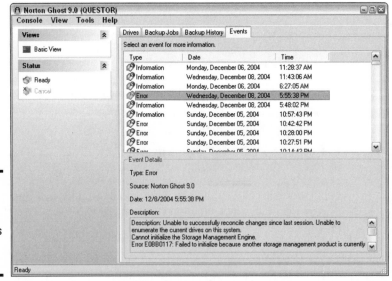

Figure 6-4:
Get
information
on warnings
and errors
with Ghost.

How to turn off Norton Ghost

There is no good way to turn Ghost off. Some people choose to load Task Manager and then locate Norton Ghost in the list of processes to try to force it to close — but that's not a very good idea. Any time you try to force a program closed in Task Manager it's likely the system will get cranky.

If you find yourself in a situation where you really would prefer not to run Norton Ghost for a single session, there's a way you can do this. But I'd recommend you use it rarely because you really want the protection and support Norton Ghost provides.

Here's how I recommend closing Ghost:

1. Choose Start ⇨ Run.

2. Click in the box and type MSCONFIG, **and click OK.**

3. When the System Configuration Utility opens, select the Startup tab.

4. Go down the list until you find the listing that begins: GHOST TRAY. Click to uncheck it as shown in the figure and then click OK.

When you restart your system, Ghost won't load in the background. However, you'll see the configuration utility window open. Click No, indicating that you don't want the utility to run again next time you restart.

Then just reverse the process when you're ready to turn Ghost back on full-time.

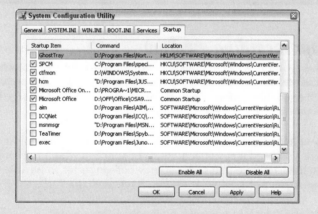

**Book IV
Chapter 6**

**Summoning Your
Ghost**

To wipe your backup history clean to start fresh, select the History tab in Advanced View, and then choose Tools ⇨ Clean Backup History. This removes any and all previous entries from your history listing in Ghost.

Keep your Symantec Recovery Disk handy

In the next chapter, you see both how to perform your backups as well as how to restore them. But for all of this, you'll want to have the extra CD that packs with Norton Ghost (or Norton SystemWorks/SystemWorks Premier) labeled *Symantec Recovery Disk.*

You need this disk if you find that you cannot boot Windows to run Norton Ghost to restore a drive. This CD is set up to allow your PC to boot and then permits you to run Norton tools like Norton Disk Doctor as well as launch drive recovery for Ghost.

Here's what you would do in this kind of emergency:

1. **Insert the Symantec Recovery Disk in your CD or DVD drive and restart your computer.**

2. **When prompted, press a key to boot from the CD.**

   Here, you'll need patience because it can sometimes take anywhere from one to several minutes before you see any action to screen.

3. **When a menu finally appears, you have the option to run utilities from the CD or choose Advanced Recovery Options and then choose to restore a drive.**

4. **Follow on-screen instructions to specify the location of your backup file and the drive you want to restore.**

   The restore process hums along on its own to apply your backup to the problematic drive.

Your recording medium

When you think about backups, you have to think about where you'll store these backups. Don't even think about a floppy disk, which has just a little over 1MB available. A floppy can store no more than a few large word-processing documents or a collection of small images.

If you have a very large hard disk with a slew of files, folders, and programs on it, you need a sizeable amount of space in which to store your backups. You have to have that room somewhere in order to be able to make the copies you need. So what do you have available?

Norton Ghost lets you save files one of three ways:

+ **To another hard drive on the PC (called a *local drive*):** I'm no fan of storing a backup on the same hard drive — even on a different partition on the same drive — as the original files. One disaster will wipe out both your originals and your only copies.

+ **To a hard drive located somewhere on another system that your PC is connected to through a home or small-office network (called a *network drive*):** If you choose this option, you'll need to know the ID of the other system to store files there.

✦ **To a CD/DVD recording drive.** You can't do unattended backups to CDs and DVDs, because you usually have to be present to swap discs during the process. Because you can usually only record about 650MB of data to any CD-R disc, you could need ten or more discs to store a backup of a 20GB hard drive, even though Ghost compresses your files as it backs them up. Back up frequently and you could go through a 100-disc bargain-priced spindle of CD-Rs in short order. By the time you've made just a few backups, you've got quite a disc library to manage.

Buying an external hard drive that connects to your PC's Universal Serial Bus (USB) or FireWire/1394 ports is a great idea. For less than $150, you can store copies for two full 60GB hard disks with room to spare. If you burn a lot of backups, you're spending a good chunk of change on recording media, even if it's the less expensive recordable CDs (CD-Rs). You'll get more use out of this drive than you will spending the same amount on an extended service policy.

Chapter 7: Exorcising Your Ghost CD/DVD

In This Chapter

✔ Making your Norton Ghost backup

✔ Doing incremental backups

✔ Scheduling backup jobs

✔ Reviewing your backup details

✔ Labeling and storing your discs

✔ Restoring a drive

✔ Getting back files and folders

Great Norton's Ghost, you just never know when you'll hit a dead system or an even deader hard disk. So it's time to create your first set of backups.

I'm not going to have you stop at just making that one backup set either. Nah, you're going to do the whole shebang — from incrementals and scheduling, right through to whole disk restoration and finding individual files and folders.

But just because the product's named Ghost doesn't mean you have to get spooked. This is a friendly spirit that doesn't require a Ouija board or a medium to help communicate. Instead, we scare up something good.

Making Your Ghost Backup

Now we're going to call up the Ghost to back up a drive. You probably have at least a CD recording drive if not a DVD/RW. Because recording to a CD or DVD drive is how Norton Ghost is frequently used, I show you how to make this type of image here. But you can also record your image or backup to a different hard drive, such as a second drive installed on your PC or located somewhere else on a network you're running at your home or office.

When you're copying to a recordable CD or DVD drive, as you are here, you're almost certainly going to require more than one disc. You also need to be sure you're using CD or DVD discs that are either recordable or rewriteable. Always have a bunch of them available. Trying to estimate ahead of time how many you'll need is difficult, but to give you an idea, the drive image for a 7GB drive took me six CD-R discs using high compression.

Just as you've seen with other Norton products, you have a few choices for exactly how you jump into performing a backup stored as a drive image. Any of these will get you into the Drive Backup Wizard, which steps you through the imaging process. To get into the Drive Backup Wizard, you can right-click on the Norton Ghost icon in the Windows System Tray, and then select Back Up Now. Or, from within Norton SystemWorks, you can click on Norton Ghost in the left-hand menu, select Basic, and then select Back Up Drives (see Figure 7-1).

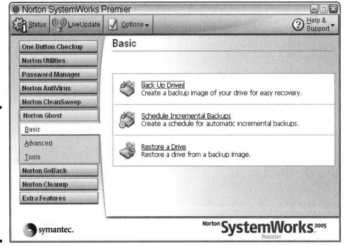

Figure 7-1: Getting to the Drive Backup Wizard from within System-Works.

When you have the Drive Backup Wizard open, follow these steps to create your backup:

1. **In the first window, click Next.**

2. **In the Drives to Backup window, choose the drive you want to back up into an image (see Figure 7-2), and click Next.**

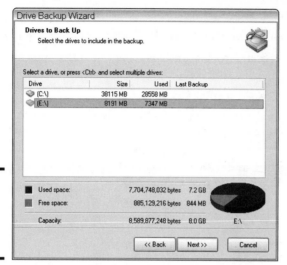

Figure 7-2:
Choose the drive you want to back up.

3. **In the Backup Location window, shown in Figure 7-3, choose the destination where your backup should be stored.**

   Here, I'm making a CD-based image so CD/RW-DVD/RW is checked.

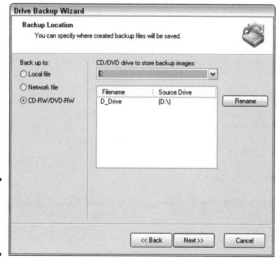

Figure 7-3:
Select your backup destination.

4. **Select the drive letter.**

5. **If you don't like the default name provided for the backup folder, select this and click Rename to type in a new name, then click Next.**

The Options window opens.

6. In the Compression drop-down list, select a compression level.

I recommend Standard, but for most space savings, you can choose High instead.

7. Select Verify Backup After Creation.

This is optional but selecting this is a really smart move to be sure the image you make is going to work for restoring the drive contents in an emergency.

8. Click in the box under Description and type some identifying information about this backup (see Figure 7-4).

9. Click Next.

Figure 7-4:
Choose your options and type a description.

A summary window appears giving you all the details about what you've selected in previous steps.

10. Make certain you have a blank CD/DVD-R or CD/DVD-RW disc inserted into your CD/DVD drive, and then click Next.

The Drive Backup Wizard status window (shown in Figure 7-5) appears. And you may be staring at it for a long time.

If you're the impatient type (like me), you may wonder if something has gone screwy because it may continuously report "Waiting." But here's how to tell what's going on: Run your mouse over the Norton Ghost icon in your Windows System Tray; it reports the progress percentage there.

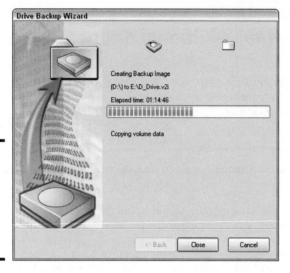

Figure 7-5:
Your progress window as the image is being created.

Drive Backup Wizard

Creating Backup Image

(D:\) to E:\D_Drive.v2i

Elapsed time: 01:14:46

Copying volume data

Back   Close   Cancel

During the process, you'll be prompted to insert a fresh disc whenever the current one gets filled up. You usually have at least a couple minutes in between the necessary disc swapping, so feel free to stretch your legs, get a drink or a snack, or take that all-important bathroom break. Just try not to forget Ghost in the meantime.

Need to stop a backup because you need to do something else? Some screens feature a Cancel button. There's a cancel option right on the left-hand menu in Norton Ghost's Advanced view. You can also right-click on the Norton Ghost icon and click on Cancel the Current Operation.

A recordable CD disk has a maximum 720MB available for storage (some of this space is used for details, so you may only have about 650 MB). A recordable DVD, by comparison, has close to 4.7GB available. Although recordable DVD discs are more expensive, DVD is usually your best bet because you'll need fewer discs and shave some time off disk swapping.

Exactly how long a drive image takes to make depends on a whole bunch of factors including the size of the drive you're backing up, the speed of that hard drive, and the speed of the source you're using as your backup location.

Creating a backup job

A backup job makes a copy of all your files and your basic system setup and stores them in one gigantic file (or a huge file split into smaller parts) that can later be restored if needed. There are, however, different types of backups, and I show you the difference between each in this section.

Setting additional options

In the Options window, you'll notice an Advanced button. Click this and you open a window where you can create a password needed to access or work with the drive image you're making.

You have two other options you can select. The first, Ignore Bad Sectors, allows you to skip over bad sectors on your hard disk during the recording process. This isn't a bad idea but it's not required. Your other choice — if you check it — disables Smart Sector copying, which you probably don't want to do. If you're not sure about this, leave it unchecked.

When you create a backup job, you set up all the details needed to tell Norton Ghost when, where, and how to perform your backup job.

Incremental backups aren't just interim backups done between full versions. A full drive backup copies the entire contents of the drive, and it's a free-standing, independent entity. Incrementals, on the other hand, are used to store those files that have changed or been created since the time you performed your first base backup on which each incremental backup is based. Your incremental backup is nothing without the backup on which it's based.

In between full system backups, you perform incremental ones to cover those files that have changed since the time of the last full version. In this section, I assume you've done your full backup, because there's no real sense in making an incremental copy unless you have the full one to support it.

Exactly how you decide when you perform a full backup and when you do the incremental backup is entirely up to you. Just be sure not to go too long between backups. If you depend on your files and their ability to run, and you tend to create lots of files, receive lots of e-mails, and download frequently, you probably want to perform a full backup every week or two. But if you use your system more recreationally, a base backup followed by monthly incremental backups may be adequate.

Performing your base backup

The first backup you perform here is the base backup. Then you perform incremental backups from there. The incremental backups are performed then on the schedule you designate (daily, weekly, monthly) as part of the base backup process. Here's an example: Let's say take the following steps to create your base backup; at that time, you also schedule how often Norton Ghost should go back and collect the files that have been added or changed since the base backup was recorded. These changes become the incremental backups. Follow these steps to start your base backup and schedule your incremental backups:

1. **Double-click on your Norton Ghost icon in Windows System Tray.**

2. **From Norton Ghost, click Create Backup Job.**

The Backup Job Wizard opens.

3. **Click Next.**

4. **Under What Type of Backup Would You Like This Job to Create? select Base with Incrementals, as shown in Figure 7-6, and click Next.**

Figure 7-6: Choose Base with Incrementals as the backup type.

5. **Choose the drive you want to backup, and click Next.**

The Backup Location window appears (see Figure 7-7).

6. **In the left-hand pane in the Backup Location window, select either Local Drive or Network Drive.**

7. **Select either a listed location or click the Browse button to select the Local or Network drive location where the backup should be stored, and click OK then Next.**

The Schedule Image window appears.

8. **Choose Weekly, Monthly, or No Schedule if you don't want to put yourself on a timetable, then click Next.**

Book IV Chapter 7

Exorcising Your Ghost CD/DVD

Backup Job Wizard

Backup Location
You can specify where created backup files will be saved.

Back up to:
○ Local file
⊙ Network file

Network folder to store backup images:

[   ] Browse...

Filename	Source Drive
D_Drive	(D:\)

Rename

<< Back   Next >>   Cancel

Figure 7-7:
Select your backup location.

If you select one of the schedule options, the right-side of the window displays your options to choose from, as shown in Figure 7-8. If you depend on your PC for work or school, I would recommend putting your incremental backups on a weekly schedule. If you use your PC far less frequently, setting this to monthly should do.

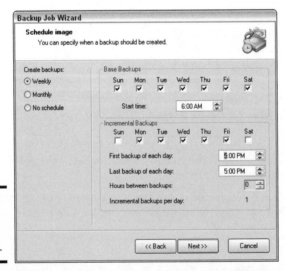

Backup Job Wizard

Schedule image
You can specify when a backup should be created.

Create backups:
⊙ Weekly
○ Monthly
○ No schedule

Base Backups

Sun	Mon	Tue	Wed	Thu	Fri	Sat
☑	☑	☑	☑	☑	☑	☑

Start time: 6:00 AM

Incremental Backups

Sun	Mon	Tue	Wed	Thu	Fri	Sat
☐	☑	☑	☑	☑	☑	☐

First backup of each day: 5:00 PM
Last backup of each day: 5:00 PM
Hours between backups: 0
Incremental backups per day: 1

<< Back   Next >>   Cancel

Figure 7-8:
Place your backup on a schedule.

9. **In the Options window, select any features you want to apply.**

I recommend you check Verify Backup Image. This tries to make certain that the file created by the backup process is good so it can be used to restore your PC if disaster strikes.

Also, if desired, you can break your one humongous backup file into smaller files that can then be copied or written to a CD or DVD disc if you have a DVD burner. Letting Ghost create these smaller files on a hard disk and then burning them to a CD or DVD drive is usually much faster than burning them to CD or DVD as you backup. To do this, you would select a hard drive to store the files in the short term, then from the Options page, select Divide the Backup Image and choose your size (no larger than 650MB for a recordable CD or 4.2GB for a recordable DVD).

10. **Type a description for the backup job if desired, and click Next.**

11. **Review the summary window, choosing whether you want to start the base backup now or wait until the first scheduled time. To start it now, select Create the First Backup Now.**

12. **Click Finish.**

If you choose to start the backup immediately, you'll see it begin. If not, the job goes into the pending list.

Want to consult your list of backup jobs? You can do this at any time by opening Norton Ghost in Advanced view and selecting the Backup Jobs tab (see Figure 7-9).

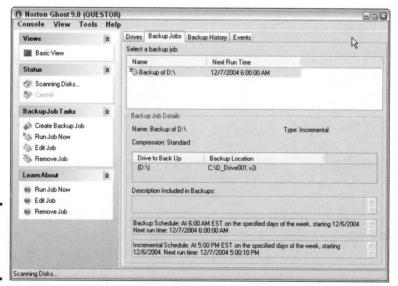

Figure 7-9:
See your
backup jobs
listed.

Acting on your backup job list

Look under the Backup Job Tasks listing in the left-hand pane in Norton Ghost (refer to Figure 7-9) and you see your choices for acting on backup jobs pending and listed:

✦ **Create Backup Job:** Loads the same routine covered in "Creating a backup job" section earlier in this chapter.

✦ **Run Job Now:** Starts the listed backup immediately, not waiting for the scheduled time.

✦ **Edit Backup Job:** Allows you to modify the backup location, schedule, or other details of your pending job.

✦ **Remove Job:** Deletes the listed job so it doesn't run.

You can also kill a scheduled backup job by selecting it in the list and pressing your Delete key.

Reviewing your backup facts

Don't happen to remember when you performed your last backup? Or perhaps you don't quite recall which of your hard disks was last backed up. To check your backup information, open Norton Ghost in Advanced view, and select the Backup History tab. When no backups have been performed yet — or when one you started got canceled or quit because of an error — your history will look quite blank. After you've performed backups, the history will reflect that, as it does in Figure 7-10.

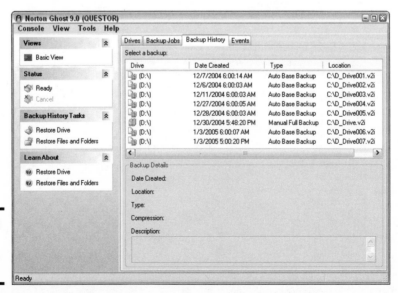

Figure 7-10: A virgin backup history.

Labeling and storing your backups

The last thing you want when you're faced with a hard disk emergency is to not be able to locate your Ghost image backup, find the image is damaged because the disc it's been recorded to hasn't been well cared for, or have to guess which disc is which in your backup set. Just a couple extra steps taken during the backup process can make all the difference here.

When you're working with CDs or DVDs for image storage, use a good permanent marker (I love fine or medium-point Sharpie markers for this) to record your details on each disc, such as:

✔ What the disc contains (for example, "Backup of my D: drive")

✔ The disc's order in the disc set (for example, "Disc 5 of 7")

✔ The date of the backup

Your discs should always be stored in a cool, clean, and dry place away from direct sunlight, magnets, and anything that may scratch them. Group them together, so you can easily locate them when you need them.

Check your Backup History tab whenever you open Norton Ghost to be sure backups you thought would run in fact did.

If you have to bail out on a backup in process or cancel a scheduled one, try to make time to perform the job as soon as possible thereafter. You don't want to get caught with your backup down.

Restoring a Backup

You know all the grousing you do about having to back up? Well, at the point you need to restore a backup, all that work (which really isn't much effort at all, especially with a program like Ghost) becomes well worth it because you have salvation — or at least a copy of your drive.

If your backup file is on CD or DVD, you need to get your disc set and make certain you have them all. This is where your good labeling and storage get appreciated because you can find and identify what you need.

Restoring a drive

Here you are at that magic moment when you get to put your hard work — the backup — back online by restoring the drive from which the backup was created.

Book IV Chapter 7

Exorcising Your Ghost CD/DVD

How much is too much?

I've had people come to me asking for good backup programs only to spill the beans that they frequently have to restore a drive they've backed up. First, I congratulate them for their good sense in performing those backups — because so many people don't — and then I ask them what the heck they're doing that requires them to restore so frequently.

Unless you're someone who tests hardware and software professionally or has some other unique situation where you need to get back to square one frequently (and for that, Norton GoBack's AutoBack tool may be a good choice), something's really wrong if you have to regularly restore your data.

If you've got a dying hard disk, save the money you pay in recordable disks or hard-disk space to buy a new hard disk. If the drive seems fine, but Windows fouls up frequently, try to get to the source of the problem and fix it. Some of the Norton Utilities physicians like Norton WinDoctor and Norton Disk Doctor, may be able to help diagnose problems.

Although backups work well, you're still putting your files and programs under great risk. You never know when your system may head south before your next incremental backup, and if you happen to get a bad backup, you may not get everything back.

To restore a drive, follow these steps:

1. **Open Norton Ghost.**

2. **From Basic view, click Restore a Drive (see Figure 7-11) or from Advanced view, choose Tools ⇨ Restore Drive.**

3. **Select the backup image you're restoring from, and click Next.**

   If it's on a disc, insert the first disc from the backup set into your CD or DVD drive).

4. **In the Restore Destination window, choose the drive where you want to restore the backup, and click Next.**

5. **Select the options you want to apply:**

   • **Verify image file before restore:** Assures that the restore doesn't fail in the middle.

   • **Check for file system errors:** Ensures data integrity when data is written to the drive being restored.

   • **Resize drive to fill unallocated space:** Lets Ghost adjust the drive size as needed to match the data being restored.

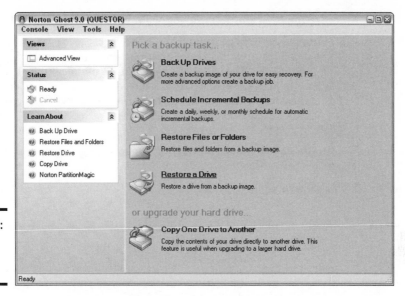

Figure 7-11:
Select
Restore a
Drive.

- **Set drive active:** Select this when the drive being restored is going to hold a bootable operating system. Normally, however, if you're restoring a bootable hard disk from your Ghost backup, this is handled for you automatically so you don't need to specify this.

- **Partition type:** Choose either primary or logical. Normally, you do not need to select this since Ghost knows what it's backed up.

- **Drive letter:** Select the drop-down list box to specify the drive letter for the drive being restored.

6. **Click Next and review your choices.**

7. **Click Next again to begin the actual restoration process.**

Restoring files and folders

What if you only need to get back a few files or a whole folder (or ten) from a full or incremental backup? You're much more likely to do this than you are to restore a whole drive — that is, unless you tend to race your PC in the Indianapolis 500.

When you're restoring files and folders, you use another tool to browse the individual files stored in the backup image: the Backup Image Browser. To open the Backup Image Browser, choose Start ➪ All Programs ➪ Norton Ghost ➪ Backup Image Browser. The browser opens and with it the Open window, to help you locate the backup image you want to check for files and folders.

**Book IV
Chapter 7**

**Exorcising Your
Ghost CD/DVD**

1. **Locate the files and folders you want to recover from the backup.**

To see the contents of a folder, click the plus sign next to it. To select a single file, click on it. To select multiple files and folders located next to each other in the list, press and hold your Shift key while you use your down or up arrow key to select the files and folders. To select multiple files and folders scattered throughout the list, press and hold your Ctrl key while you click on each file and folder you want. And to select all files and folders listed, press Ctrl+A.

2. **With the files/folders you want to restore selected, choose File ➪ Restore (or press Ctrl+R).**

3. **Click Restore.**

Mounting drives

Mounting drives has nothing to do with horse-back riding or working on the parallel bar in gymnastics. Here, *p* refers to treating a backup image like a true drive and bringing that drive "online" so that it can be worked with as if it were a physical drive.

You mount a drive temporarily, to do certain things, including the following:

✔ Run drive-scan utilities like Verify Backup Image, Windows ScanDisk, or Windows Chkdsk

✔ Export a backup image to another location

✔ Share the drive's contents on a home or small-office network

✔ Run programs from the drive

✔ Copy files and folders from the drive to another location

However, you don't need to mount a drive to restore files and folders contained within a drive's backup image.

Follow these steps if you want to mount a backup image as a drive:

1. **From the Backup Image Browser, select the image that contains the drive you want to mount.**

2. **Choose File ➪ Mount V2i Drive.**

3. **When the Mount V2i Drive window opens, click the drop-down list box to select the drive letter you want to assign (temporarily) to this mounted drive.**

4. **Click OK.**

When you're done working with the mounted drive, you dismount it by selecting the drive in the Backup Image Browser and choosing File ➪ Dismount Drive V2i.

Chapter 8: Getting Past the [Bleep] Factor in Starting Over with Ghost

In This Chapter

✔ Knowing the steps in starting over with a new or reformatted hard disk

✔ Creating a copy of your drive with Norton Ghost

✔ Partitioning and formatting

✔ Doing an emergency boot-up

✔ Knowing what else you may need to do

Most people approach the idea of trying to start fresh with a new system or a new hard drive with dread. "How will I ever get things just the way I had them before?" All those packages to reinstall, all those files to copy over, all those settings to get just right again. Some techs I know refer to this prospect as the [Bleep] Factor.

But with Norton Ghost, you have a tool that makes your job about as simple as it can be. You can copy your entire drive information (including your Windows setup, all the applications installed, the files and folders you currently have, and all your customized settings) right onto the new hard drive without losing one darned thing. This process is typically called *drive copying* or *cloning*.

In this chapter, I show you how to remove all the dread and just take the core data and setup from one hard drive and clone it to another. This chapter is all about fresh starts and how Norton Ghost can help them turn into happy reunions where your current programs and files get resurrected on the new hard disk. Won't it be glorious to get through a drive emergency without uttering a single curse word or having to re-create a single important letter, e-mail message, or spreadsheet? You better believe it.

Starting Over with Ghost

Too many people, when they get a new hard disk or feel obligated to repartition and reformat their existing hard disk, think they have to start over from scratch. This means they spend hours prepping the drive, setting up the operating system, installing numerous applications, updating their hardware drives, and making all those little tweaks to Windows to make it look the way they want.

But hey, you're not just anyone. You were smart enough to buy a helper in Norton Ghost. So how can you put Ghost to work for you in a way that saves time *and* frustration?

Earlier in this book, I show you how to use Norton GoBack and how to restore a drive using Ghost. Here, I focus on starting fresh with a new drive or system and your Norton Ghost drive copy.

Making a drive copy

Norton Ghost makes the job of copying the contents of a hard disk and transferring it to a fresh hard disk or system a piece of cake (really good cake, too).

You'll wish you'd always had the Norton Ghost.

Your only worry, when it comes to making a drive copy with Ghost, is having space for the drive copy, and that shouldn't be a problem in the most common scenario — copying an existing hard drive to a brand new drive. That new hard drive can be:

✦ One you install as a second drive only until you can copy the drive contents from the existing hard drive so you can retire the old one.

✦ A permanent backup hard drive you install mostly to hold files and backups.

✦ An external hard drive that may move between different PCs in your home or office.

When you have the space available (and trust me, Ghost will tell you early on in the drive-copy process if you don't have enough space — it carefully watches your available drive space and alerts you when there is not enough room), just follow these steps:

1. **Open Norton Ghost.**

2. **Choose Tools ➪ Copy Drive or click Copy Drive from Drive Tasks in the left task pane.**

The Copy Drive Wizard opens.

3. **Click Next.**

4. **Select the drive to copy (see Figure 8-1), and click Next.**

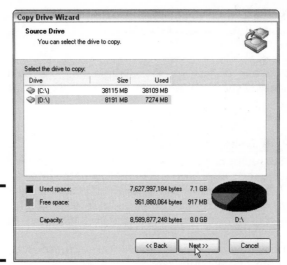

Figure 8-1:
Choose
the drive
to copy.

5. **Click on a drive to serve as the destination where your copy will be stored (see Figure 8-2), and click Next.**

6. **Confirm your choice and click Finish.**

Figure 8-2:
Pick the
drive to
store the
copy on.

Ghost tells you that you can save a single copy to multiple locations if you don't have enough room on one drive to hold it. Indeed you can. But should you? I don't think saving a single copy to more than one location is a particularly wise idea. When you do that, you're spreading out your risk along with the copy. If you encounter a problem with one of the locations you've used to store that single copy, you're sunk.

Write your copy to one location where the whole thing has room. If you're blessed with plenty of space elsewhere, make a second copy and store it there, too.

Reformatting your hard drive

When you have to reformat your hard drive, that's an excellent time to use a drive copy to store the setup, files, and folders from the drive as it is before the reformatting. You can temporarily store them in another location (such as a second hard drive), and then copy them back to the first hard drive after you reformat it, so you've got everything back in place.

Standard Ghost backups can also be used for this purpose. But you may find a simpler drive copy makes better sense.

If you're replacing an existing hard drive with a new one, your job is slightly easier if you leave the old hard drive in place to start. Then follow the directions to install the new hard drive.

Depending on the type of drive you buy and what other drives you have installed on your PC, you probably want to set this new hard drive up temporarily as what's called a *slave,* or a secondary drive to the existing hard disk. This usually involves connecting the new hard disk by ribbon cable to the existing hard disk and making a change to the jumper on the new drive. Your drive documentation should spell this all out. If it doesn't, visit the drive manufacturer's Web site (it should be listed in your drive documentation, too) where you can find complete directions for doing this.

After you've physically installed the new hard drive as a slave, you can use PartitionMagic (shown in Figure 8-3) to partition and format the new hard disk. Book VIII gives you details about using PartitionMagic for this purpose.

When the new drive is prepped and you've left the existing hard drive in place just long enough to copy your drive contents directly to the new hard drive using Norton Ghost, you can use Norton Ghost to create a copy of your existing hard disk and write it to the new hard disk. Then you can remove the old hard drive and reconfigure the new hard drive as the top job.

Every new hard drive, after it's been properly physically installed, must be partitioned and then formatted before it can be used. If you're using Norton PartitionMagic (covered in Book VIII) to create your partition, you can also format that newly-created partition right in PartitionMagic, as shown in Figure 8-4; no command line or boot disk is required.

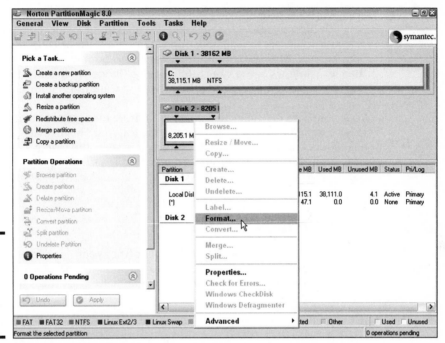

Figure 8-3:
A second
hard drive
installed
temporarily
as a slave.

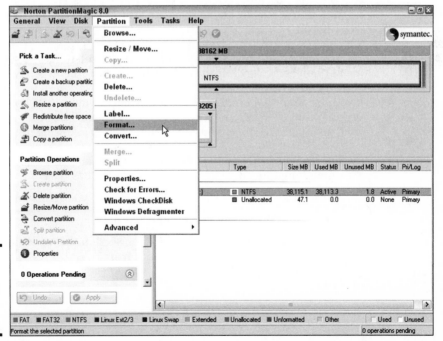

Figure 8-4:
Formatting
with Norton
Partition
Magic.

**Book IV
Chapter 8**

Getting Past the
[Bleep] Factor
with Ghost

Your Windows install CD, especially if it's a recent version (such as Windows XP), can both boot a PC and let you both partition and format a new hard drive for use. Insert the installation CD into your CD or DVD drive, restart your system, when prompted to type a key to boot from the CD do so, and then let Windows Setup run automatically. Choose to install a fresh setup and, when prompted, point to the drive you want to prep for use.

Your new hard disk may also come with drive-management software that takes care of partitioning and formatting for you. This management software also often aids in being sure the new disk is seen and works well with the programmable part of your motherboard called the BIOS, which acts as your hardware traffic manager on a PC.

Booting in an Emergency

Got an emergency that won't let you boot from your hard drive where Norton Ghost is installed? There's a way around this. Depending on how you got Norton Ghost, there's a CD that can help:

✦ Norton Ghost CD

✦ Recovery disk from Norton SystemWorks Premier

Just place the CD into your CD or DVD drive and restart your PC. When prompted to press any key to boot from the CD, do so. You can reach Ghost from there.

To use Norton Ghost in emergency mode, you need to have 256MB of memory on hand. Any less may produce an error when you try to run it.

If your PC won't boot from a CD, don't panic. Put down that bottle of Valium or Jim Beam! The likely culprit is that your PC hasn't been set up to boot from your CD/DVD drive. You can change that by following these steps:

1. **Restart your PC and look for the little message on screen that says something like** To enter Setup, press this key.

2. **Press whatever key or combination of keys you're instructed to press.**

    You'll be taken to your computer's Setup.

3. **When you get into Setup, look for the section that specifies which drive(s) your PC is designed to boot from.**

4. **Press the Page Down key or follow on-screen prompts to change your boot disk to the CD drive.**

5. **Then save your change and restart using one of the CDs I mention earlier.**

You can change your Setup back later, but it's really unnecessary. Just remember to take CDs out of the drive when you shut down or restart the PC and your PC will boot from the hard drive (after you get it recovered, that is).

What Else You Need to Do

After you copy the contents of one drive to another drive, you may need to do some other things. For example, if you're copying the contents of your old hard disk to a new hard disk in a brand-new system, that new PC may work a bit differently when you do so because you're copying over hardware settings and other details from a very different type of PC.

If you've had to make changes to your hardware beyond just replacing or reformatting a hard drive such as when you're starting with a wholly new system where you've copied your old drive, you may have to run Windows Setup again so it sees and works properly with your hardware additions. But this also may be necessary when you're copying an existing hard drive to a new hard drive or to a reformatted drive where you may have changed other parts of the system, such as installing a new motherboard or a CPU, for example.

If you're having problems running some applications or receive error messages about missing files or drivers, try to figure out which programs or drivers you need. Then reload them or see if you can locate specific files on your backup copy using the tools discussed in Chapter 7.

Visiting the Windows Update site almost immediately after recovering from an emergency to see if any changed hardware or settings require new updates or drivers is a good idea. If you don't have Windows Update set up to run and install updates automatically, be sure you're connected to the Internet, and then choose Start ➪ All Programs ➪ Windows Update. When Windows Update's site opens (see Figure 8-5), it scans your system and recommends any updates you need. Follow the site's recommendations — especially download any updates marked "critical" — and let the updates download and install.

**Book IV
Chapter 8**

**Getting Past the
[Bleep] Factor
with Ghost**

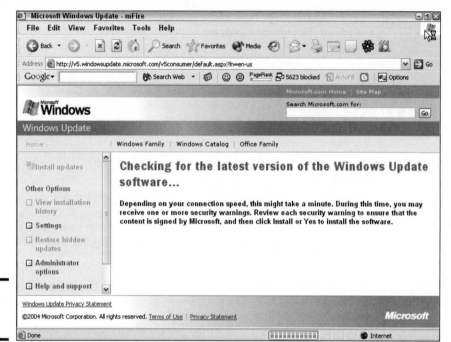

Book V

Norton AntiSpam

The 5th Wave   By Rich Tennant

Contents at a Glance

Chapter 1: Getting the Skinny on Spam

In This Chapter

✔ Getting a handle on what spam is

✔ Identifying the evils

✔ Making sure you don't contribute to the mess

*R*emember the good old days when you just complained about the junk mail that arrived in your snail-mail box? At least back then, the limitations of printing costs kept some mail out.

Unfortunately, e-mail ads cost advertisers almost nothing to send, making it a great way to sell a product without huge up-front promotional fees. Anybody can set himself up as an entrepreneur with just some item to hawk and a list of valid e-mail addresses. Even the federal CAN-SPAM act of 2003 has done almost nothing to slow the tsunami of ads.

Only unwanted e-mail isn't just an annoyance. As you're about to find out, you don't just get hit by an overflowing mailbox. Everyone who uses e-mail bears the direct or indirect cost of moving tens or even hundreds of millions of ads around every day. You pay the cost in higher Internet service provider (ISP) fees, longer sessions just to retrieve all your mail, and e-mails lost in a blizzard of ads or wrongly screened out as spam.

Spam also costs you time: You may get so many ads in a single mail session that you get lost trying to find the e-mail you *want* to read. Accidentally open some of these ads, and you're shocked by what they're advertising. Yet with all that, you probably have no idea of just how many thousands — yeah, thousands — of spam messages you get in a year.

In this chapter, I give you a sense of the scope of the problem known as spam.

Understanding the Sheer Volume of the Problem

Before the debut of e-mail, Spam was either a Hormel meat product or a really funny Monty Python song.

Unfortunately, that's no longer the case. Today, people angrily snarl the word *spam* as they sit weeding through all the strange messages that arrive in their virtual mailboxes (take a gander at my inbox in Figure 1-1).

The antispam company Brightmail (www.brightmail.com), which is now part of Symantec, estimates that at least one piece of unsolicited advertising is sent for each and every piece of legitimate communication. Check your e-mail and you'd swear the figure is much higher. With mine — and I get dozens of legit messages every day — the ratio is more like 20:1. Those odds may peak your interest in Vegas, but who wants a mailbox filled with this stuff?

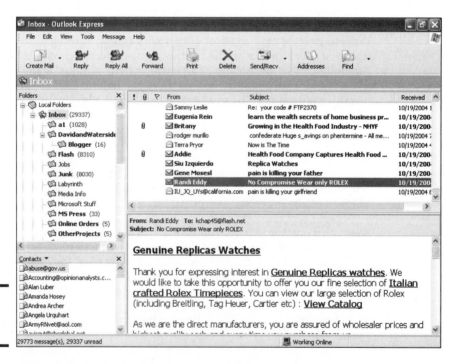

Figure 1-1:
Just a bit
of spam.

Although hard-and-fast figures are hard to find, it's estimated that companies just within the U.S. are spending *millions* each year in trying to trap ads before they get distributed to their workers, distracting them from business and tying up the network resources. Globally, spam is said to account for *billions* in man hours and equipment to keep systems running under the weight of the ad burden. Some companies report that they lose between $500 and $1,500 or per person per year in overall worker productivity just related to spam.

This estimate is backed up by *Information Week,* a major computer services publication, which reported in May 2003 that about 200 minutes are lost per person for every 1,000 spam messages that person receives. If you get 4,500 to 5,000 pieces of spam a year on average, you lose up to 1,000 minutes a year, or 1 percent of an average work year. This translates into more than 16 hours, or two full 8-hour workdays. Ouch!

Like most other costs in life, when spam happens in the workplace, a lot of this loss in productivity gets passed along to you as a consumer. Spam may add cents or dollars onto every month's Internet service bill and contribute to higher member-only site registration prices. Indirectly, you can see prices for non-related products inch up, because more money is being spent in computer services.

Spam is also a pretty common way for viruses and worms to get passed around the Internet. Spammers often send little files along with their ads and some of these contain infections or malicious code. People open them even though they know better — and then they have the added cost of time and money in combating the infections and any damage they've done.

But not all the costs can be tied to dollars-and-cents. One price paid is not being able to use e-mail as a very effective communications tool. Every time you send out a résumé, a proposal, or some other important communication through e-mail, you run the risk that your e-mail will never reach its destination. Your e-mail may get lost on an overworked mail server or get marked as spam by security software before it gets where it's going.

Spam isn't a local or an American problem. In the last decade, the world really has become a global marketplace. People from all over the world can reach each other easily both through Web sites and through e-mail. For free-enterprise enthusiasts, this is great.

However, lots of the unsolicited ads you can get may be from overseas, with some offering products that don't meet U.S. safety standards. Buy them and you usually won't enjoy the protection of American consumer laws. In some cases, you may even break local, state, and/or federal laws by buying them. This is frequently the case with some of the prescription medication you can buy over the Internet.

About those dirty pictures you found on your drive . . .

Three items commonly hawked in unsolicited e-mail ads are "prescription pills without a doctor" (boy, now there's a great idea!), bogus mortgage approvals (people who lie to you deserve your business?), and sexually oriented material. But it's the last one that can present a strange problem for some people.

If you're a legal buff or frequent watcher of Court TV, you're always hearing about "computer forensics" or the way so-called experts can look at your drive and determine what you've been doing, even long after you delete key files. All too often, what you hear about is pornography found on a drive. Almost without fail, someone will say, "Well, he must have been downloading all that dirty stuff because nobody accidentally gets hundreds of naked pictures on his PC." Although a true expert in computer forensics can tell the difference between "accidental" downloads and those deliberately procured and stored, many others cannot.

The problem is, you can. Pop-up ads, Web sites, images attached to newsgroups you read online, and pictures sent as part of the ads you get in e-mail can all leave behind files on your system that you don't want and probably won't know are there. That's not to say that people don't *choose* to download racy stuff — but occasionally, these sexy snaps can make their way onto a PC only being used for online bingo games and doing schoolwork.

I ran into this with a new PC. A week after I started using it, I happened to look in a folder I didn't recognize and found all these pictures of buck-naked people. What bothered me most was that I knew I was the only one with access to my new system and that I certainly didn't download them. It took time to track down that they had all been stored from images sent in e-mail ads.

Sure, you can just cross your fingers and hope that the PC police never arrive at your door and seize your hard drive, but trying to limit what comes into your system in the first place is a better idea. Both Norton AntiSpam and Norton AntiVirus can help zap these before they settle, while the Web cleanup tools offered in SystemWorks and CleanSweep can remove the dust and debris left behind by your earlier exploits (intentional or not). Find out more about how Norton products help in Chapter 2 of this book.

Netiquette: E-Mailing Responsibly

Not all spam is your fault. There will always be people out there who will try to find a way to contact you either by phone, e-mail, or snail mail to target you for some product you don't want.

Yet everyone who uses e-mail bears a little responsibility in this global issue. Certain things you do — or don't do — when you're using the Internet can add more e-mail to the burden, pass infections onto others, or encourage spammers to strike by buying their products.

In Chapter 2, I show you how Norton AntiSpam and other products can help and exactly what steps you can take to reduce your spam quotient beyond just blocking. But even before you know the preventive steps, you probably want to identify and stop any behavior that may add more unwanted mail to your mailbox or to others.

Here's a list of some of the worst things many e-mail users do on a daily basis:

✦ **Sending out mass e-mails to friends and coworkers:** What *you* may consider a great joke that you just *have* to share, may be seen by someone else — even your best friends — as spam.

✦ **Sharing your personal information in public areas such as an Internet chat room or message board:** Whenever you share your e-mail address in these areas, it can be picked up by spammers and added to spam lists.

✦ **Signing friends up for offers:** Web sites are always asking you to share e-mail addresses of the people you know. The problem: The people you know may not appreciate your giving them your e-mail address, because it can add them to the spam cycle.

✦ **Failing to monitor what the kids are doing:** Kids have the tendency to reveal a lot of private information, and some of their behavior online isn't any better than it is in real life. Without controls on their Internet time, they also may visit and sign up for services you may not like.

✦ **Not using a virus scanner or antispam software:** Some spam may have viruses, worms, or spyware attached that can do evil things to your system and even send itself out to all the people in your contact lists.

✦ **Not scanning for adware or spyware:** As you'll discover in Book VI, adware and spyware contribute to computer insecurity and can seriously overload you with spam from marketers who watch where you go online.

✦ **Buying products from spam:** One of the reasons spammers send out this junk is that people buy what they're selling.

Chapter 2: Canning the Spam

In This Chapter

✔ Identifying some of the common ways spammers get your e-mail address

✔ Understanding how Norton products like AntiSpam can stem the tidal wave

✔ Knowing what other steps you can take to reduce your spam volume

You know how easy it is for little ole you to get 4,000 to 6,000 unsolicited e-mail ads every year — and how much time you may take processing all that junk. And I bet you want to take action.

Sure, you may fantasize about sending spammers on a one-way vacation to the Bermuda Triangle or waking them up at night to deliver truckloads of spam into their homes, but you probably need a better solution than that. Yes, you can write your congressperson, but even though antispam laws are on the books, your electronic mailbox is still full of the stuff.

In this chapter, I not only show you how to put the spam back in the can, but how to keep it from ever getting to you in the first place. Just a few common-sense measures — combined with a spam-fighting tool like Norton AntiSpam — can give you a powerful line of defense against those miracle wrinkle creams, "genuine" jewelry fakes, buy-a-mansion-with-no-money-down offers, and racy ads.

Knowing How Your E-Mail Address Gets onto Spam Lists

Ever wonder how some of these spammers find your address? The answer is simple: Spammers get it any and every way they can. They use special programs to look for e-mail addresses posted on the Internet (including in places like message boards and chat rooms), they buy lists of e-mail addresses, and they entice you to send your address to them by offering some helpful service.

Your e-mail address is very valuable to an advertiser and the people who handle ad campaigns for them. Every e-mail address represents a potential customer — some percentage of every ad sent generates sales, even when the product is really bogus. A couple years ago, someone marketed a special aerosol spray that was supposed to give you better cellphone reception. It didn't work, of course, but just one week of blitzing everyone with ads gave the people behind the product a very lucrative payday.

For all the talk of targeted ad campaigns and customizing the right product to the right shopper, women's mailboxes are chock-full of ads for Viagra and sports cars, while men often get ads for cookware, dress sales, and cosmetics. Marketers want to get their products seen by as many people as possible — and many of them are willing to intrude, misdirect, and otherwise force them upon you whether you're an ideal candidate or not.

But not all spam just flies at you from thin air. You do certain things on the Internet that help contribute to the volume you receive, including the following:

✦ Signing up for free news alerts, newsletters, and tips

✦ Downloading free or trial software

✦ Having friends, family members, and enemies who sign you up for endless free offers (tell them to stop!)

✦ Patronizing Web sites that sell their customer and membership information or share the information with third parties

✦ Posting your e-mail address in a public place

✦ Responding to spam

Getting what you ask for

Many Web sites and even brick-and-mortar stores give you the option to leave your e-mail address to sign up for special services like a free newsletter, tips, or news and sales alerts. Now, these services can be great. Every week, one of my local restaurants delivers a list of its weekly menu specials to me, and my favorite cable news show sends mail each morning telling me what's coming up on the show that night.

But some sites get pretty slick about this. They know you don't always bother to read the fine print. So when you go to sign up for a newsletter, you probably fail to notice that the form has all these boxes checked agreeing to let the site share your address with other companies.

Technically speaking, when you sign up for a free e-mail–based service, the e-mail you get from that service isn't spam. But if you're like most people, you forget you've signed up for all this stuff and then get annoyed when you start to receive it.

Falling for the bait-and-spam approach

People love free software. They usually don't even demand that the software be particularly good, as long as the price is right.

Knowing this, spammers and others who see the value in having your e-mail address on file may set up a special download — or even a whole library packed with games, utilities, or images. You don't have to pay a cent, but you have to supply your e-mail address. It may not occur to you that there's anything wrong in providing your e-mail address — at least not until you notice that your spam volume has jumped threefold.

You also sometimes see this with catalog orders or when you request a brochure. Even though the free item is supposed to come via snail mail or delivery service, the site asks for your e-mail address.

Getting sold out

You may see your private information as just that: private and yours. But that's not how everyone sees it.

With the Internet, e-mail addresses are treated like a commodity. People and organizations keep large lists of addresses and then sell them either en masse or to the highest bidder. The buyers can be anyone from charitable and political organizations to religious groups, marketing firms, or other commercial groups.

The source for your e-mail address is all too often companies you do business with, those that — to augment their sales — sell or share information about their customers or clients to marketing services, to parent companies, and to other vendors. The result is that, although you signed up for one free weekly e-mail alert, you get 30 to 40 extra pieces of e-mail from all the other folks who got your address from the first guy.

Another wrinkle appears with today's big business where mega corporations buy up littler fish all the time. One day, you sign up for electronic sales circulars from a mom-and-pop store online. The next day, Mom and Pop have been bought out by Acme Global Monopoly, Inc., which shares your e-mail address with all 10,000 of its other companies.

Here's a suggestion that may help. Most Web sites have a privacy statement — usually listed as a link called Privacy or Privacy Policy, in very fine print at the bottom of the page — that spells out how the company uses any details about you that you share with them. Clicking this link and reading the page before you enter any details like your phone number, your credit-card number, or your e-mail address, is a good idea. If you don't like what you read there, don't give the company your business — or your e-mail address.

Broadcasting your address

Do you run a Web site or are you involved with one? Do you sometimes post messages or ask questions on Internet newsgroups or message boards? If so, you probably post your e-mail address so people can contact you. Posting your e-mail address on public sites is one of the fastest ways to get popular — and not in a good way — with spam artists.

In the real world, unfortunately, some spammers also borrow your e-mail address to use as their return address. Just like you can print any return address on an envelope you're sending out in snail mail, e-mail software can be set to someone else's name. You may have gotten spam in your inbox that says it's from *you*.

In "What Else You Can Do," later in this chapter, I show you some tricks for posting publicly without inviting a flood of unwanted messages or imposters.

Responding to spam

Ever get an ad or other unwanted message and feel compelled to fire back a flaming reply? So have I.

Ask questions, make a fuss

If you find something in a site's privacy statement that really upsets or confuses you — and some can make it sound like they own anything you happen to post on the site — let them know or ask what they mean.

Most sites list contact information where you can call a toll-free number or send e-mail. Even if they don't, most Web sites can be reached by sending a message to webmaster@*the sitename.com*.

I've seen sites completely rethink their approach to sharing or securing your details after they've been hit by a ton of customer complaints. But they won't know and can't change if you don't tell them.

Also, be prepared to complain loudly if you suspect a company you've done business with has shared your private information. Unfortunately, even some sites that promise complete privacy and insist they won't sell your data do so.

Do this and I won't buy your product!

One of the reasons spam is such a problem for everyone is that it's so darned successful. For relatively little money (at least, little cost to spammers), they can send out hundreds, thousands, or even tens of thousands of messages with the knowledge that between 1 and 10 percent of the people who see it will buy what's being hawked — it doesn't even seem to matter how bogus or overpriced the product is.

I don't know about you, but I hate rewarding rotten behavior. I won't do it with kids or pets, so why should I do it with advertisers? If spammers don't see a profit, they're probably much less likely to deluge your mailbox.

So what do you do if you hate spam but an ad comes in that really tempts you? Try this: Use a Web search engine to find the toll-free number, the snail-mail address, or the e-mail address for the company who makes the tempting product. Then contact the company and let them know that, although you'd love to buy their product, they invaded your privacy to sell it to you. Tell them that if they'd stop the spamming, you'd become a happy customer.

In real experience, I've had several companies respond positively to this. A few have dropped e-mail marketing campaigns or killed contracts with advertising agencies that engaged in bad selling practices. Sometimes, they'll even offer you a discount on the product to boot.

The problem here is that, when you respond, you've basically confirmed for the spammer that he's reached a live person (a spammer's favorite target audience). Also, many spammers are smart enough to use a fake address to contact you, so when you try to reply or send their ads back, you find a dead address instead.

Beware of unsolicited messages that feature a link in their e-mail to "unsubscribe." Although some sites do, indeed, take your request to be removed from their mailings seriously, many actually use those tools to verify that the address they have on file is a "live one" so they can spam you more frequently.

Seeing How Norton Products Can Help

The main job of Norton AntiSpam (shown in Figure 2-1) is to separate out the unsolicited ads and other unwanted e-mail from the messages you *want* to get. However, that doesn't necessarily cut down on the number of spams you receive — it just acts on the number you see in your inbox. (You have to deal with it somewhere — by emptying your Norton Antispam folder, for example.)

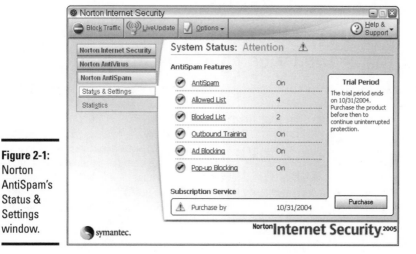

Figure 2-1:
Norton AntiSpam's Status & Settings window.

Norton Internet Security with AntiSpam adds the ability to block the transmission of cookies from a Web site into your PC. Chapter 3 shows you how to configure this, but you can also click the down arrow next to the Norton globe icon in your Web browser and select Block Cookies (as shown in Figure 2-2).

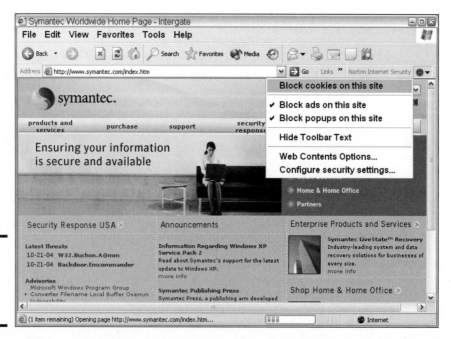

Figure 2-2:
Block cookies from Web sites.

By blocking ads, you may be able to reduce your overall volume of spam, because some of the ads can transfer adware or spyware to you, which can then be used to target you for more advertising or intrusions. Norton AntiVirus — or any good, regularly updated virus scanner that can check your e-mail and file attachments — can help spot and remove infections and adware or spyware before they strike. (See Book VI, Chapter 1 for more information on PC infections and intrusive software.)

Norton Personal Firewall — either as a stand-alone or as part of Norton Internet Security — can block unwanted connections to your PC that can pass files to you without your knowledge or try to scan your system for private information like your e-mail address.

Norton Password Manager lets you keep track of passwords you need for Web sites so you don't have to rely on cookies and other files Web sites pass to you to help you use their services. Because cookies and other files can be used to track where you go online and grab your e-mail address or other data, anything that helps cut down on your need to use them can reduce your spam volume.

What Else You Can Do

Norton AntiSpam can definitely help you take back control of your virtual mailbox. But as I mention earlier in this chapter, Norton AntiSpam helps *after* you receive the spam — it doesn't keep you from getting the ads in the first place.

Beyond using Norton AntiSpam or other spam-fighting tools, you want to act smartly to reduce your exposure. In the following sections, I fill you in on some of the ways you can do just that.

Don't leave your e-mail address on the bathroom wall

Treat your e-mail address as though it's valuable — because it is. Just as you wouldn't hand your telephone number out to everyone you meet, you certainly don't want to leave your e-mail address everywhere online.

Get a spare

Many people have access to more than one e-mail address. Many Internet service providers (ISPs) give you a certain number of accounts and mailboxes with your monthly service. If you're an AOL user, for example, you can have up to five different screen names on one account, each with its own e-mail address.

Parents keeping the mailbox key

If you want to be able to give your kids some access to e-mail, but you don't want to risk their seeing racy ads or sharing lots of private information with strangers, consider this: Set up a separate e-mail address as a family mailbox. Ask your children to be selective. You, as the adult, should be the primary person to check for e-mail.

You can set up separate folders in your mail software and move each child's personal e-mail there when you're sure none of the messages contains anything offensive. (Chapter 4 shows you how to add folders and move messages.)

Consider creating or using one e-mail address strictly as the one you share for any type of site or service where you need to supply your e-mail address. This address should be separate from a private e-mail address that you offer only to friends, family, colleagues, and others you truly want to hear from.

Although you'll still get spam on this "public" address, you give yourself one other e-mail address where your spam volume should be far less.

If you don't have access to a second e-mail account, you can sign up for a free one through Yahoo! (www.yahoo.com). However, beware of all the extra stuff they offer to send you as part of your free account — or you'll wind up with even more ads. Also, if asked to provide an alternative e-mail address when you sign up for a secondary one, don't feel obligated to provide one. Any additional e-mail addresses you provide may increase the possibility of spam being sent to you.

Tricking the spam artists

Another way to approach the situation is to con the con artists, so to speak. For this, you type a slightly adulterated address and then force a person who wants to send you e-mail to edit the address before he can successfully send mail.

For example, say you want to post your e-mail to a message board so those seeing your note can reply to you privately. Anyone who clicks on your name on the post will have an e-mail window open up for them to make it easy for them to contact you. You don't have to worry as much about these individual people — spammers aren't finding your e-mail address that way. They're finding it by using special Web programs that *spider* the Web, searching for bits of information like your e-mail address. These programs know what an e-mail address looks like (it has an @ sign, a period, and an extension like com or net).

If your e-mail address is IHart@smidgetwidget.biz, that's normally what you have listed in your e-mail software and the address you give out. However, you don't want the spider to find you, so you creatively nip-and-tuck your e-mail address to read IHart@smidgetwidget-dot-biz.

Before anyone can reach you at this address, that person needs to change the last part of your e-mail address from -dot-biz to .biz. One of the automatic e-mail–address-gathering programs probably won't be able to figure this out — and if a spammer getting your address tries to send mail, the spam will get bounced back to them. The downside is that others, including those you want to reach you, may not catch on either. One way to handle this is to include a note in your post or on your Web site telling people what to do (as I do on my Web site, shown in Figure 2-3).

Figure 2-3:
Disguising
your e-mail
address is
one way to
outwit the
spammers.

Contact me at katejchase-at-intergate.com

(Please note: you need to edit the address so it looks like a standard address like johndoe@smith.us)

Chapter 3: Configuring Norton AntiSpam

In This Chapter

✔ Creating a Blocked List

✔ Knowing what LiveUpdate does for AntiSpam

✔ Using ad blocking

✔ Changing settings to make AntiSpam work better

✔ Taking additional precautions

*J*ust how effectively Norton AntiSpam works for you in combating unsolicited advertising and other gruesomes in your virtual mailbox depends in large part on how you set it to work.

If you leave Norton AntiSpam the way it is when it first installs, it will still help you. But if you look at your individual situation and the kinds of unwanted material you get, and tweak the settings a bit, you could make AntiSpam do a much better job of trapping the junk while letting the important messages get through.

This chapter is all about control. In these pages, you tell Norton AntiSpam how to respond, what to allow through, what to block, and how carefully you want to avoid messages containing obscene language. You can even set AntiSpam to catch all those messages with claims to "make money fast." After all, if the sender were making so much money, he'd probably be vacationing in the Caribbean rather than sending you e-mail.

Norton AntiSpam — or any software similar to it — can only do so much without your help. To do your part, you have to reduce your unwanted mail overall. If you don't, you can wind up with a situation where AntiSpam is working furiously every time you download another batch of 100 to 200 messages (with only one real communication in the bunch). Why download all that nonsense onto your hard drive?

Setting Up Norton AntiSpam

Whether you install Norton AntiSpam all by itself or through Norton Internet Security, you can decide how exactly you want it to run and what it should catch. You can let it run very automatically, as it will do by default, or you can customize settings to try to get better results by creating a Blocked List and an Allowed List and other options.

To open Norton AntiSpam:

1. **Click on the Norton AntiSpam icon (or the Norton Internet Security icon if you're using the Internet suite) in the System Tray.**

2. **Select Open Norton AntiSpam (or Open Norton Internet Security).**

   Note: Older versions may just list the product title without saying Open.

3. **If you're using Norton Internet Security, click Norton AntiSpam after the main Norton Internet Security window opens.**

Or:

1. **Choose Start⇨All Programs.**

2. **Select Norton from the list (the exact name you'll see varies depending on which Norton products you have installed), and then choose Norton AntiSpam.**

However you open Norton AntiSpam, the main window, shown in Figure 3-1 appears. (The version in Figure 3-1 is with AntiSpam bundled in Norton Internet Security.) Look a little closer and you'll spot the fact that AntiSpam has two listings; the Status & Settings window shown in the figure, and the Statistics window. (For more on the Statistics window, check out Chapter 5.)

Near the top of the Status & Settings window, you see a triangle with an exclamation point, the universal symbol for "Hey, look!" This tells you there's an important message. Look again for the symbol near the bottom of the window and you see that, in this case, it's just warning me about a trial version close to expiring.

There may be some differences between what you see here in figures and what you have if you're using an earlier version of Norton Internet Security or Norton AntiSpam. Figures here are shot using Norton AntiSpam 2005.

Identifying the settings you can change

When you click an option in the Status & Settings window, a menu of choices usually opens at the right of the window, allowing you to toggle the feature on or off or to get more information. Figure 3-2 shows you an example of the screen you see after clicking on Ad Blocking — the little menu on the right tells you more about the feature you've chosen (click More Info to get additional details).

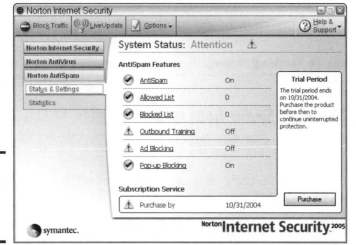

Figure 3-1:
AntiSpam's
Status &
Settings
window.

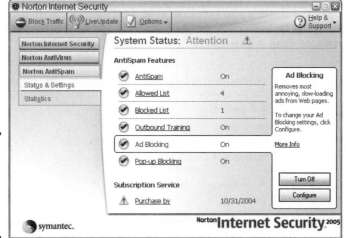

Figure 3-2:
Use buttons
to toggle
features on/
off or to
configure.

Your options include the following:

✦ **AntiSpam:** The main power switch; if it's set to Off, Norton AntiSpam won't do anything.

✦ **Allowed List:** The e-mail addresses of those people whose messages you want to see.

✦ **Blocked List:** The e-mail addresses of anybody whose messages you don't want to deal with (junk or other unwanted messages).

✦ **Outbound Training:** A tool to train Norton AntiSpam to differentiate between gems and coal by analyzing details about the e-mail you send out.

✦ **Ad Blocking:** Stops ads in your mailbox; can strip many of those slow-loading ads from the Web sites you visit.

✦ **Pop-up Blocking:** Stops pop-up ads from opening on the Web pages you visit.

Telling AntiSpam how to work

To turn AntiSpam off completely, just choose it from the Status & Settings window and then click Turn Off).

But there's more to AntiSpam than simply on and off. You can adjust your overall security level. Just follow these steps:

1. **Click AntiSpam in the Status & Settings window.**

2. **Click Configure.**

The General window (shown in Figure 3-3) opens.

3. **Drag the slider up to increase your AntiSpam security level (and how thoroughly AntiSpam checks your mail and blocks unwanted material), or drag it down to reduce your security level.**

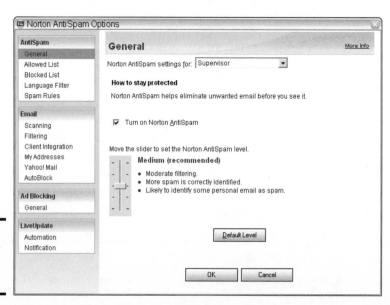

Figure 3-3:
Adjust your security level.

Using Important AntiSpam Features

Even without Norton AntiSpam, most e-mail software lets you designate whose e-mail can and can't make it into your inbox. But you have to get the e-mail addresses just right, or these tools (called *filters*) won't work. One of the most common tricks perpetrated by spam scam artists is to change their e-mail address — just a one-letter difference can throw off antispam filters, so you constantly have to update your Allowed and Blocked lists to keep the junk out.

Norton AntiSpam makes it slightly easier than some e-mail software to set up these lists. Extra features like Norton AntiSpam's mail analysis try to make an educated guess about which message is legit and which you shouldn't bother with.

Because most people use Norton AntiSpam as part of Norton Internet Security, I show you how to work with it from the suite. However, if you bought AntiSpam separately, don't worry. Just click your AntiSpam icon to load the program and make the changes suggested. The same basic options are available from the stand-alone version as are available when you select AntiSpam from Norton Internet Security.

Setting up an Allowed List

Instead of having all your e-mail messages dump into one central location like your inbox, you can set up an Allowed List that should only allow mail from specific senders to make it in. In everyday use, however, other mail will occasionally make it in, so AntiSpam's Blocked/Allowed lists aren't perfect.

You can add names to the Allowed List by typing each one in or by telling Norton AntiSpam to start your list from all the names stored in your address book (available in whatever software you run for e-mail). The latter method works well if you're careful about whose name makes it into your address book. I show you both ways, just in case.

After you add addresses to your Allowed List — either manually or by importing — you can edit it or delete it. Just click the Edit or Delete button in the Allowed List window.

Adding addresses manually

Follow these steps to add a name to your Allowed List manually:

1. **Open Norton AntiSpam.**

2. **In Status & Settings, click Allowed List and then click Configure.**

The Allowed List window opens.

3. **Click Add.**

4. **Enter the first and last name of the person (optional) and then type in the person's e-mail address (required), as shown in Figure 3-4, then click OK.**

Figure 3-4:
You can
add people
to your
Allowed List
manually.

The name and address is then placed into your list. You can continue on to create additional entries.

Importing your address book

To save time, you can import every listing in your address book instead of entering addresses manually (if you want, you can always delete your arch-enemies from your Allowed List later):

1. **In the Norton AntiSpam Status & Settings window, click Allowed List and then click Configure.**

2. **Click Import Address Book (see Figure 3-5).**

When Norton AntiSpam is done, you see your address book entries added to your list, as shown in Figure 3-6.

Creating a Blocked List

A Blocked List is the opposite of the Allowed List: It lets you assign addresses for senders you don't want to hear from and whose undesired messages will be dumped into the virtual bit bucket — depending on your AntiSpam version, these messages get moved into your Norton AntiSpam folder or into your Deleted folder.

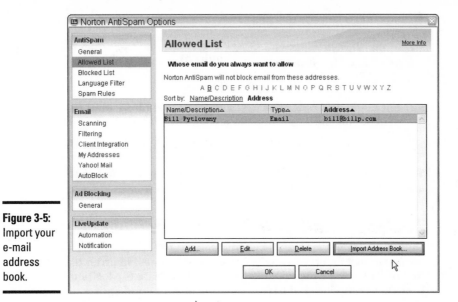

Figure 3-5:
Import your
e-mail
address
book.

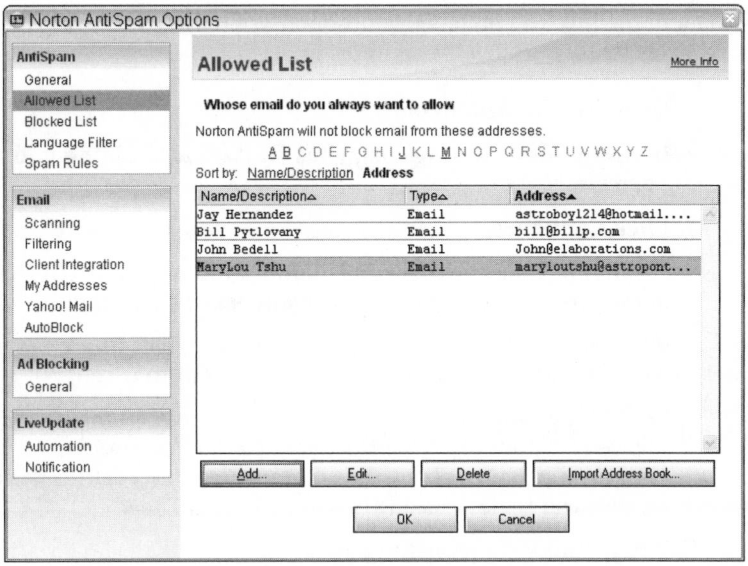

Figure 3-6:
Your
Allowed List
entries,
imported
from your
address
book.

To add entries to your Blocked List:

1. **In the Norton AntiSpam Status & Settings window, click Blocked List and then click Configure.**

The Blocked List window appears.

2. **Click Add and enter the first and last name plus e-mail address for the person you want to block, then click OK.**

3. **When you're done adding entries, click OK to close the Blocked List.**

You can also edit and delete entries the same way you do for Allowed List addresses.

Analyzing mail with Outbound Training

Outbound Training is the $64 name attached to the feature in Norton AntiSpam that can try to analyze your outgoing mail in order to improve Norton AntiSpam's judgment in how to differentiate the legitimate messages from the spam. The goal here is that less of your good stuff winds up in your Norton AntiSpam folder, and less of the junk ends up in your inbox.

Out of the box and installed, Outbound Training is set to Off. If you want to try this feature, follow these steps:

1. **Open Norton AntiSpam.**

2. **In the Status & Settings list, click Outbound Training and click Turn On.**

3. **Click Configure.**

In the How to Improve Spam Filtering window (shown in Figure 3-7), notice that some items are already checked (turned on).

4. **Make any desired changes (for example, select Block Email from Anyone Not in the Allowed List if you want to do so).**

Note though that if you choose this, any e-mail from anyone not on your Allowed list goes into your Norton AntiSpam (or, sometimes, your Deleted) folder; you want to check these folders regularly (at least once a day) to be sure you're not missing e-mail you should see.

5. **When you're done making changes, click OK.**

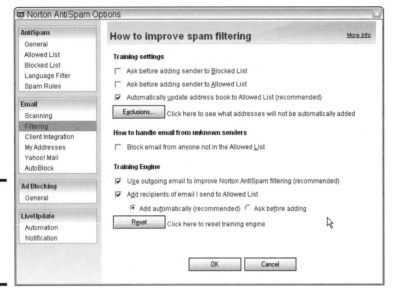

Figure 3-7:
Teach
AntiSpam
using
Outbound
Training.

Watching the language

Spam comes from anywhere and everywhere. Sometimes, foreign advertisers are so eager to get their message out to consumers that they don't bother to make sure that the recipient can read the language in which the ad is sent.

Out of the box, Norton AntiSpam is configured to handle a host of languages, including Swahili, Tonga, and Azerbaijani. If you want, you can limit your inbox to those messages in just the languages you understand. Here's how:

1. **Open Norton AntiSpam.**

2. **In Status & Settings, click AntiSpam.**

3. **Click Language Filter from the left-hand menu.**

   Notice that when the list of languages loads, everything is checked/ selected.

4. **Instead of unchecking each one that isn't a language you speak, click to check the Allow box and then click it again to uncheck it.**

   Now all the entries have a red x mark rather than a check.

5. **Go down the list and click to recheck the languages you want to allow, as shown in Figure 3-8.**

6. **Click OK.**

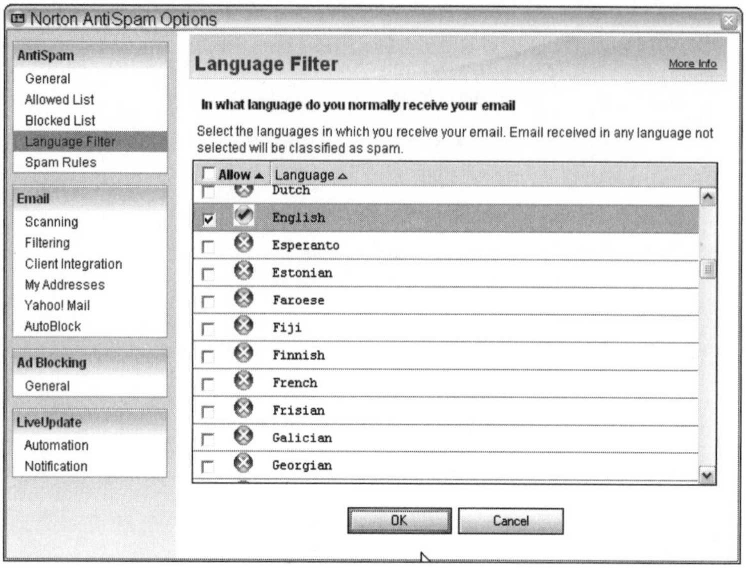

Figure 3-8:
You can block all messages that don't come to you in a language you understand.

Laying down the spam laws

You have to live by a system of rules — why shouldn't your e-mail?

Norton AntiSpam follows rules when checking for any messages that meet a particular condition. When AntiSpam finds messages that match the rules you've set up, it acts upon that message according to your rule. For example, you can tell Norton AntiSpam to dump any message with the word *sex* in it into your Deleted folder or another folder. However, by blocking "sex" you also block messages from someone with an address in a city or town such as Middlesex or Essex. So you have to exercise care and be prepared to make changes as needed. Again, check your Deleted folder (where these messages should go once trapped) or the Norton AntiSpam folder to be sure you aren't missing e-mail you need to read.

You can also tell Norton AntiSpam that whenever you receive e-mail from a special person — say your boss or your kid — it gets moved to a folder where you store important messages.

To create a rule to treat all messages using a specific phrase as unwanted e-mail, follow these steps:

1. **Open Norton AntiSpam.**

2. **Click on AntiSpam in the list.**

3. **Choose Spam Rules from the left-hand menu.**

4. **Click New.**

5. **In the Custom Spam Rule window, type** your loan application **(as shown in Figure 3-9), and click Next.**

6. **When asked which part of the e-mail message to check for this word or phrase, click Entire Email, then click Next.**

7. **Choose Spam.**

8. **Click Next, and then click Finish.**

Figure 3-9:
Set a
custom
spam rule.

The rules are added to your list of rules, as shown in Figure 3-10. Now every time you receive e-mail with the words "your loan application," Norton AntiSpam will treat it like a piece of spam and send it either to your Deleted or Norton AntiSpam folder (depending on your version).

To change a rule, select it from the list and click Edit. If you want to remove a rule altogether, just choose it and click Delete.

Using LiveUpdate

Norton AntiSpam turns on the LiveUpdate feature without any further assistance from you. You can, however, turn it off or stop it from running automatically whenever you want it. Although you might have reason to temporarily stop LiveUpdate (for example, your Internet connection is down), you don't want to turn this tool off and keep it off because you won't receive the updates you need. This could leave Norton AntiSpam operating less effectively, and you don't want that.

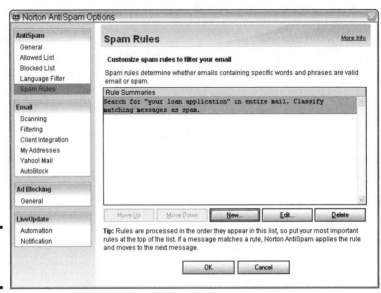

Figure 3-10:
A list of
spam rules.

Follow these steps to change LiveUpdate settings:

1. **In Norton AntiSpam, double-click AntiSpam.**

2. **Select Automation under LiveUpdate.**

3. **If you want to disable LiveUpdate, click to uncheck it, then click OK.**

4. **Click Notification from the LiveUpdate menu.**

5. **To stop LiveUpdate from running automatically, click to check Notify Me When Updates Are Available, and click OK.**

Blocking ads

To cut down on the number of ads that show up as you browse Web pages, you want to enable Ad Blocking. Select Ad Blocking from the Status & Settings window, then click the Turn On button.

With Ad Blocking enabled, you can add individual Web sites — ones with annoying ads you'd like to lose — to your Ad Blocking list to try to keep the ad from displaying. Even better, you can add a site to the list, but then choose to permit certain ads on the site. This is great because some of what gets blocked on a Web site may be *required reading,* meaning the page may not be able to load properly if the ad — or something that AntiSpam thinks is an ad — doesn't run. You may want to try this if you use ad blocking then find you can no longer load a specific Web page properly.

Here I walk you through an example where you can add a site (in this case, CNN) and then specify a part of the site where you permit the ad to run. For example, I want to add CNN to the Ad Blocking list, but I know that if a pop-up window doesn't appear, I can't use the online voting feature at the site. Here's how to do this:

1. **Select Ad Blocking from Norton AntiSpam.**

2. **Click Configure.**

3. **Click Advanced.**

4. **Click Add Site and then type in** www.cnn.com **(see Figure 3-11), and click OK.**

This adds CNN to your Ad Blocking list on the left.

5. **Select CNN in your Add list. Click the Add button to the right which opens the Add New HTML String window.**

6. **Click Permit and then type** /adpopup **(as shown in Figure 3-12).**

7. **Click OK, and then click OK again.**

Pop-up ads are treated just like the ads you just configured to block in the Ad Blocking section. You can add sites, allow or block specific ads from a site, or remove or change a site you've already added, using the same instructions given under Ad Blocking.

When spam multiplies faster than bunnies

As I write this, in fact, my editor was shocked to learn I receive hundreds of spam mails a day at one of my several e-mail addresses. That's the price I pay as a public person who has to give out her e-mail address routinely.

Even though I recognize that, it's still hard to scan through all that spam looking for actual mail from friends, bosses, and colleagues regardless of how much Norton AntiSpam helps. I've had to retire perfectly good e-mail addresses simply because they became over-run by unsolicited ads, electronic chain mails,

and file attachments I won't open from people I don't know.

But I don't make all my e-mail addresses public. Where I limit who knows these e-mail addresses, the amount of spam I receive drops sharply to as low as 1 piece of spam for every 30 spam messages I receive at my publicized e-mail address. You can get results like that too by being very selective about when, where, and how you leave your contact info online.

Figure 3-11:
Add a site
to your Ad
Blocking
list.

Figure 3-12:
Specify that
a pop-up ad
can load
while
blocking
everything
else.

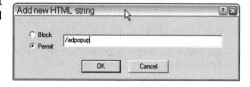

Chapter 4: Controlling Your E-Mail

In This Chapter

✔ Integrating Norton AntiSpam to work with your e-mail software

✔ Tweaking changes to both AntiSpam and your e-mail

✔ Using the spam-fighting toolbar

✔ Running AntiSpam with Outlook Express

In the preceding chapters, I guide you through choosing basic Norton AntiSpam settings and help you decide which features to turn on or off. In this chapter, it's time to see how your spam-fighting tool works with your e-mail. You'll be amazed how much faster it is to tweak your AntiSpam settings than it is to sit there deleting junk mail after junk mail.

I also show you how to use Norton AntiSpam through the most popular e-mail software, Outlook Express, which comes bundled with the Microsoft Internet Explorer Web browser. Unfortunately, only Microsoft Outlook Express as well as Microsoft Outlook are directly supported for use with Norton AntiSpam. I focus on Outlook Express here because it's the most popular e-mail software.

Have We Met? Introducing AntiSpam to Your E-Mail Software

Because Norton AntiSpam's main job is to combat the torrent of unwanted solicitations that flood your e-mail inbox, it has to join forces with your e-mail software to do this. The two of them have to work together.

After you install Norton AntiSpam, either by itself or through Norton Internet Security, you're asked if you want to integrate AntiSpam with your mail client (which just means have it work with whatever software you use to check your e-mail, such as Microsoft Outlook Express or Microsoft Outlook), as shown in Figure 4-1. Click Yes.

Next you see the First Run window (shown in Figure 4-2), which spells out what AntiSpam will do: add buttons to its spam-fighting toolbar. Click OK to close this window.

Figure 4-1:
Integrate
AntiSpam
with your
e-mail
software.

Figure 4-2:
AntiSpam
adds
buttons
to help.

Norton AntiSpam goes ahead and handles the basic configuration for you, then notifies you that it needs to restart your mail client. When you get the message, click OK. After your e-mail software reloads, notice that the Norton AntiSpam icon has been added to your client's toolbar, as shown in Figure 4-3 for Outlook Express. Click the down-arrow next to the icon, and you see a short menu with your Norton AntiSpam choices.

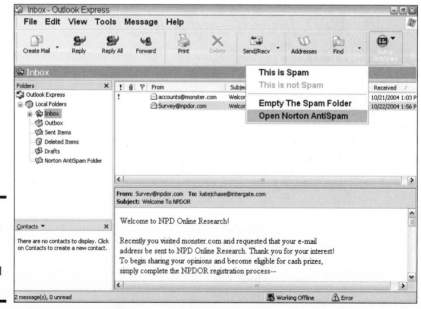

Figure 4-3:
The Norton
AntiSpam
icon added
to your mail
software.

You can open Norton AntiSpam at any time by clicking on the down-arrow next to the Norton AntiSpam icon in Outlook Express and choosing Open Norton AntiSpam.

Setting E-Mail Options

In Chapter 3 of this book, I walk you through setting up basic options for AntiSpam. But you can make some additional changes to your product, tied specifically to how that product interacts with your mail software.

Start by going into Norton AntiSpam to see your additional choices for setting up how this product — and others, like Norton Internet Security and Norton AntiVirus — interacts with your e-mail:

1. **Open Norton AntiSpam.**

2. **Double-click AntiSpam from the Status & Settings window.**

3. **Look at the left-side task menu under Email (see Figure 4-4).**

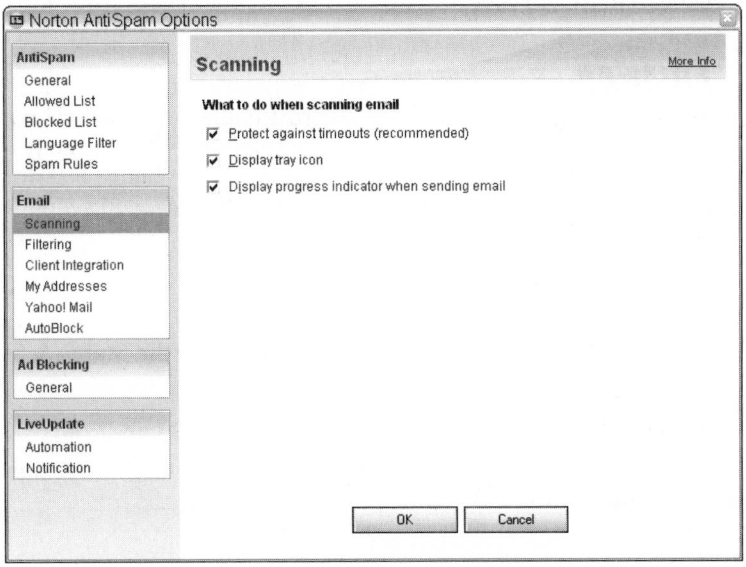

Figure 4-4:
Your e-mail
options in
Norton
AntiSpam.

> **Norton AntiSpam Options**
>
> **AntiSpam**
> General
> Allowed List
> Blocked List
> Language Filter
> Spam Rules
>
> **Email**
> Scanning
> Filtering
> Client Integration
> My Addresses
> Yahoo! Mail
> AutoBlock
>
> **Ad Blocking**
> General
>
> **LiveUpdate**
> Automation
> Notification
>
> **Scanning**   More Info
>
> **What to do when scanning email**
>
> ☑ Protect against timeouts (recommended)
> ☑ Display tray icon
> ☑ Display progress indicator when sending email
>
> [OK]   [Cancel]

You see six categories — Scanning, Filtering, Client Integration, My Addresses, Yahoo! Mail, and AutoBlock — each of which I tell you about in the following sections.

4. **When you're done changing your settings, click OK and close the Norton AntiSpam window.**

Scanning

This window (refer to Figure 4-4) and Norton AntiSpam as a whole are designed to work with Norton AntiVirus's e-mail scanning capabilities. See Book VI to find out how to configure Norton AntiVirus to scan your e-mail for problems and infections.

Your options in this window (all checked by default), include:

+ **Protect Against Timeouts:** This feature helps your e-mail sessions to stay active when there's a delay caused by Norton AntiSpam and/or AntiVirus scanning your e-mail.

+ **Display Tray Icon:** This places an envelope icon in your Windows System Tray that shows you when mail is being received and checked.

+ **Display Progress Indicator:** This animates the envelope icon to show the processing of your e-mail.

You definitely want to keep Protect Against Timeouts selected, otherwise you may end up with interrupted or prematurely terminated e-mail sessions. But the tray icon and progress indicator are extras that you don't necessarily need to leave checked.

Filtering

In the Filtering window, you can configure how Norton AntiSpam handles the Allowed and Blocked sender lists (see Chapter 3). If you really want to limit whom you get e-mail from, for example, you can change filtering in Norton AntiSpam to treat mail from anyone not on the Allowed sender list as a spammer.

To see your options:

1. **In Norton AntiSpam, select AntiSpam from the Status & Settings window, and click Configure.**

2. **In the left-hand menu, under Email, choose Filtering.**

   Your configuration options open in the How to Improve Spam Filtering window, shown in Figure 4-5.

3. **Make any desired changes.**

   For example, to really lock down your mailbox, select Block Email from Anyone Not in the Allowed List. To have Norton AntiSpam ask you before it automatically adds an e-mail address to either the Blocked List or the Allowed List, select one or both applicable check boxes.

4. **When you're satisfied with your settings, click OK.**

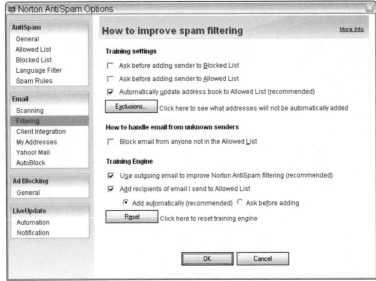

Figure 4-5:
Handling the
Blocked and
Allowed
sender lists.

Client Integration

Client integration is a fancy way of saying "your compatible e-mail software options." Normally, you don't have to worry about making or changing options here, because Norton AntiSpam checks to see what e-mail software is available on your PC during its own setup process. So if it finds Outlook Express or Microsoft Outlook — or both — Norton AntiSpam automatically checks these and makes sure the settings are correct.

To see what's listed on your system:

1. **In Norton AntiSpam, select AntiSpam from the Status & Settings window.**

2. **In the left-hand menu, under Email, click Client Integration.**

   If you're using Microsoft Outlook Express or Outlook, be sure that the appropriate option is checked.

   In the lower part of the window, you'll see two additional options checked that specify from which address books (the lists e-mail software keeps to manage those you communicate with by e-mail) Norton AntiSpam should import names and addresses. Both options are checked by default and there's really no reason to change this.

3. **When you're done, click OK to close this window.**

Notice too that the Client Integration window specifies what address books can be used to import e-mail addresses for use with the Allowed List.

My Addresses

One nasty little trick spammers often use to get you to pay attention to their stuff is to send you e-mail faked to look like it came from you or one of the other people who share your computer. This method helps such ads get around your spam filters and does get your attention along with your irritation.

The My Addresses section of Norton AntiSpam lets you designate all the e-mail addresses you and those who share your PC have so these can be set up as exemptions to the e-mail addresses listed in your Allowed List. This means that incoming messages that "look" like they come from you will be treated as spam, which they most likely are.

Notice, however, that by filtering out your own e-mail addresses to defeat the tireless spammers, copies of e-mail messages you may accidentally send yourself when you click Reply to All in response to a message will also get trapped.

Norton AntiSpam automatically adds any e-mail addresses for you found in your e-mail software. But if you're like some of us, you may have multiple e-mail addresses, not all of which may have found their way into your address book and then into Norton AntiSpam's My Addresses list. So you'll want to check which of your e-mail addresses have been listed.

1. **In Norton AntiSpam, double-click AntiSpam.**

2. **In the left-hand menu, under Email, click My Addresses.**

   You should see your currently recognized e-mail addresses listed.

3. **If any address shown is not entered correctly, select it in the list, click Modify, and edit the address, then click OK to save the address with its change.**

4. **To add an additional address, click Add, then type the e-mail address into the window (see Figure 4-6) and press OK.**

5. **Repeat Step 4 as needed to add more addresses; then click OK and close Norton AntiSpam.**

Yahoo! Mail

You only need to worry about this option if you use Yahoo! Mail, the search engine company's free Web-based e-mail service. This is the only Web-based e-mail that is fully compatible with Norton AntiSpam.

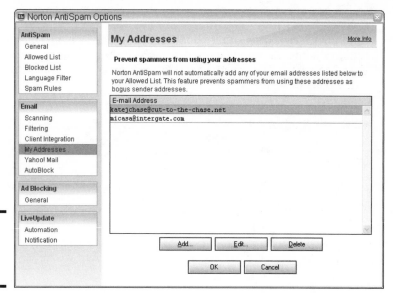

Figure 4-6:
Add your
e-mail
addresses.

To configure Yahoo! Mail, follow these steps:

1. **Open Norton AntiSpam.**

2. **From the Status & Settings window, select Norton AntiSpam and click Configure.**

3. **Click Yahoo! Email from the left-sided menu.**

4. **From the Yahoo! Email window, click to check Enable Yahoo! Email filtering.**

   Doing so pops up a window in which you need to type your Yahoo! ID, password, and connection details (refer to your Yahoo! E-mail account for details).

5. **Click OK.**

   The account information you added in Step 4 then gets added to the listing at the bottom of the Yahoo! Mail window.

6. **Click Scan Now to scan your Yahoo! Mail for spam.**

7. **When done, click OK.**

If you need to add support for additional Yahoo! Mail addresses you or someone who shares your PC, click Add after completing Step 5 and provide the information for the second account (just as you did for the first) before you take Step 6.

AutoBlock

AutoBlock lets you set other conditions for blocking mail. Open the configuration window, shown in Figure 4-7, and you see that most options are already enabled. These settings tell AntiSpam to block from your ready view any e-mail in which:

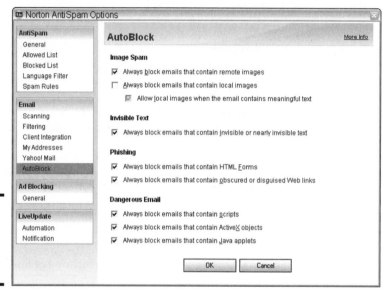

Figure 4-7:
Your spam-fighting AutoBlock settings.

+ Remote images are offered (where your PC must connect to a third-party server to open the files to see them)

+ Invisible or nearly invisible text is included

+ The Web page address is obscured or disguised

+ Scripts, ActiveX controls, and Java applets that can run and do damage to your system are included

Using AntiSpam with Outlook Express

Because nearly everyone gets Outlook Express installed automatically with the Microsoft Internet Explorer Web browser, Outlook Express is the most frequently used mail client. So in this section, I show you how to work with Norton AntiSpam from Outlook Express.

Marking messages

Depending on how you've set up Norton AntiSpam, the spam fighter makes certain assumptions about what's legit and what simply isn't. Yet you can still end up with messages in your inbox that you don't want. So Norton AntiSpam works its way into Outlook Express, putting an icon on the toolbar, so you can mark the messages that find their way into your inbox as spam or not spam.

Follow these steps to mark your messages:

1. **Open Outlook Express.**

2. **Click on your Norton AntiSpam folder to open it.**

3. **Select the first message in your list that you want to mark.**

4. **Click the down-arrow next to the Norton AntiSpam icon on your Outlook Express toolbar and select This Is Spam or This Is Not Spam.**

You can also right-click on a message, select Norton AntiSpam, and then This Is/Is Not Spam (see Figure 4-8).

5. **Proceed down your list to mark other messages as spam or not.**

When you mark a message as spam, it's automatically moved to your Norton AntiSpam folder, in the left-hand task pane.

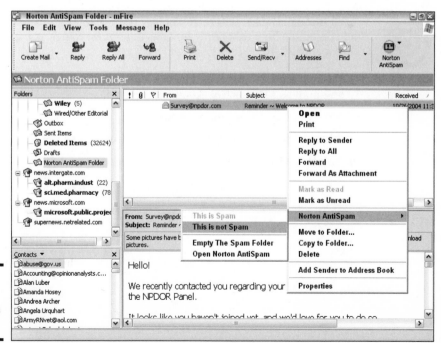

Figure 4-8:
Mark a
message as
not spam.

Coping with less-than-perfect results

Over the years, I've used a drive-full of anti-spam tools to see which work best with fighting unwanted messages while still allowing all the right mail through. All that effort shows results that are often less than perfect. I always end up plowing through the junk-mail folder to be sure I'm not missing something I need. You probably will, too. Don't think of this as a failure of Norton AntiSpam. You'll see this with any spam-fighting software.

The best way to deal with this is to go through your Norton AntiSpam or other junk folders before you empty them. Then consider tweaking your configuration — by setting up the spam rules discussed in Chapter 3 of this book — to help direct your "good" mail where it needs to go and to catch the "bad" stuff.

Moving messages

All the spam that Norton AntiSpam catches as well as the messages you mark as spam become outcasts in the no-man's-land of the Norton AntiSpam folder. But sometimes, legitimate messages you really want can get consigned there, too.

Check through the list before you empty the Norton AntiSpam folder. If you find something here that really belongs in another folder, you can move it there manually. To do this:

1. **First, follow the directions in the "Marking messages" section to mark the mail as "This Is Not Spam."**

2. **Select the message you want to move.**

3. **Right-click and select Move to Folder (see Figure 4-9).**

4. **Select the folder from the folder list (see Figure 4-10) and click OK.**

You can also drag a message from one folder and drop it into another.

Emptying the trash

Remember: Before you get rid of those messages in the Norton AntiSpam folder, review them to be sure nothing important is there by mistake.

Ah, but there's an important point to note here: When you empty your AntiSpam folder, you're just sending the messages there to your Deleted Items folder. To remove them completely, you need to empty the Deleted Items folder (open the Edit menu in Outlook Express and select Empty Deleted Items folder) after you've purged messages from the Norton AntiSpam folder.

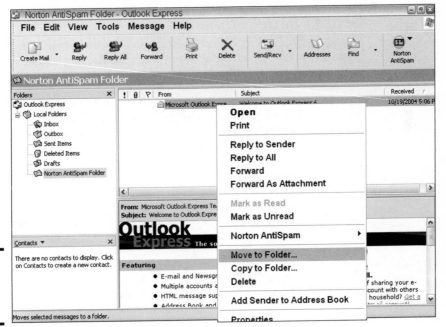

Figure 4-9:
Select a message to move.

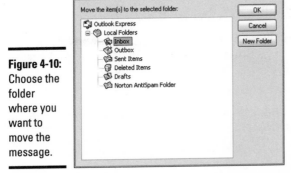

Figure 4-10:
Choose the folder where you want to move the message.

When you're sure you want to get rid of all the contents of the folder, click the down-arrow next to the Norton AntiSpam icon and select Empty the Spam Folder.

Glance back in your spam folder and you'll notice it's lonely in there. But don't worry. More spam will arrive — it's almost as guaranteed as death and taxes.

Getting better organized

As you find yourself trying to wrest control of your e-mail away from the loud and obnoxious advertisers and scam artists, you may be hit by the urge to clean and organize, too.

Is your inbox like the virtual equivalent of Grand Central Station or LAX, with stuff flying in from a number of different people and places for a host of different purposes? If so, you may want to organize Outlook Express to reflect your needs.

A common way to do this is to add folders where you can store messages you want to keep outside your busy inbox where all your new mail flows in. If you were to see my main mailbox, you'd see a dozen folders all labeled for the different people I work with and the various projects I'm involved in.

You can add one or more folders, rename them to help you identify them, move existing messages to these folders (just as you move non-spam out of your Norton AntiSpam folder), and even set up spam rules (covered in Chapter 3) to direct new messages into these special folders and out of your inbox.

For tips on moving messages, see the "Moving messages" section, earlier in this chapter, and to make spam rules, turn to Chapter 3.

To add a folder and to name it, follow these steps:

1. **Click in your left-hand Outlook Express mail task pane where you want the new folder to go (for example, click the inbox to add a subfolder beneath it).**

2. **Right-click and choose New Folder (see Figure 4-11).**

3. **Type a name for the folder in the Create Folder window, as shown in Figure 4-12, and click OK.**

   You can also choose File➪New Folder, and then click on the "New Folder" label added to change its name.

Figure 4-11:
Create a
new folder.

Figure 4-12:
Label your
new folder.

When you're done, you see a new folder added where you want, with the label you want. You can then move messages here and add spam rules to direct appropriate e-mail into it.

Chapter 5: Evaluating Your Results

In This Chapter

✔ **Knowing what to do when the wrong e-mail gets blocked**

✔ **Reducing the amount of spam that makes it through**

✔ **Using LiveUpdate**

✔ **Adding the products included in the package**

✔ **Changing your ad blocking settings**

*E*quipped with your new knowledge of the pervasiveness and impact of spam on your life and your wallet and fresh from configuring Norton AntiSpam to wrest control of your Inbox away from the spam artists, you're ready to step back and evaluate how well all this is working.

The information I cover in this chapter isn't just busy work. When many people first set up anti-spamming software, they realize they can tweak it so it catches most of the bad stuff. But you know that spammers change their MO (*modus operandi* or method of operation in the world of crime) regularly to try to get their ads and worse past your best line of defense. So over time, you may start to see more spam make it through unless you evaluate and tweak your software somewhat regularly. The techniques I describe in this chapter will help you stay at least a half-click ahead of the problem.

Identifying Problems or Weaknesses

Norton AntiSpam works pretty automatically. If all you ever do is look in your mail software's Inbox, you may not realize what the spam-fighting tool is doing for you in terms of the volume of unsolicited ads it intercepts.

What you're apt to notice instead are the times when spam slips through security and lands in your Inbox or when you have to go looking in the Norton AntiSpam folder trying to track a message someone says she sent but which you don't find.

Instead of getting angry when AntiSpam catches what it shouldn't or doesn't catch what it should, focus on tweaking your settings.

Consulting your statistics

Norton AntiSpam keeps records and information about the number of messages it's scanned, statistics on how many of these are valid e-mails and how many are spam, and details about its own accuracy in correctly identifying spam. Consulting these statistics can be a good way to see how hard Norton Anti Spam is working for you and whether it has a good track record in identifying spam without your help.

To view your statistics for Norton AntiSpam, just follow these steps:

1. **Open Norton AntiSpam (or open Norton Internet Security 2005 and choose Norton AntiSpam from the left-hand menu).**

2. **Then click Norton AntiSpam (see Figure 5-1).**

3. **Click Statistics.**

The Statistics window (shown in Figure 5-2) opens.

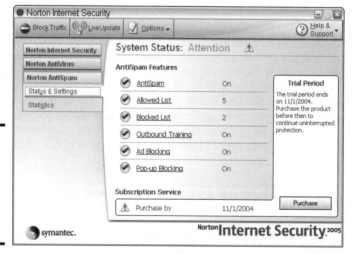

Figure 5-1:
Click to
expand the
left-side
Norton
AntiSpam
menu.

The Statistics window offers you information about:

✦ How many e-mails have been scanned since Norton AntiSpam was installed (or since the last time your statistics were reset, which you can do by pressing the Reset button at the bottom of the Statistics window.

✦ How many e-mails have been sent that Norton AntiSpam used to train itself to recognize spam (see Chapter 3 for more details).

✦ How many valid versus spam e-mails have been received and how many were correctly identified.

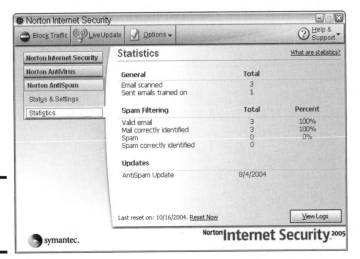

Figure 5-2:
Your spam-
fighting
statistics.

Look again and you see too that it reports when Norton AntiSpam was last updated. This date changes whenever the LiveUpdate tool runs, finds, and applies updates to your software.

There is also a button labeled View Logs. Click this and you see a breakdown of your spam catching and ad blocking activity through AntiSpam by category, as shown in Figure 5-3. To find out more about using Log Viewer, check out Book II, Chapter 3.

Figuring out what to do when the wrong e-mail gets blocked

Of all problems related to spam, having your important messages blocked can be one of the most vexing, because you worry that something you truly need to see — a job offer, a love note, or a potential client asking for your help — winds up in the junk pile in the Norton AntiSpam folder rather than in your Inbox. Emptying the spam folder without checking it first is too easy — and unless the person writes you again ("Hey, you never answered my e-mail"), how would you even know what was lost?

One way to pretty much eliminate the possibility a specific person's e-mail ending up in your Norton AntiSpam folder rather than in your Inbox is to place this person on your Allowed List (see Chapter 3). Likewise, to always route messages from a particular person (your arch enemy, for example) into the junk pile, you can add him to your Blocked List.

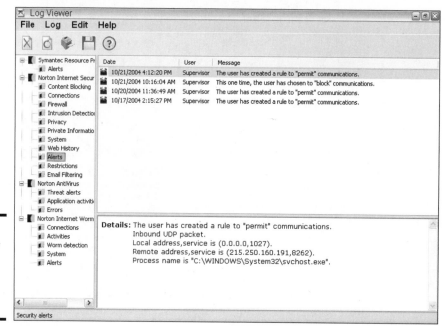

Figure 5-3:
Check your recorded anti-spam scanning activity.

If a certain word often gets used in the subject line of important messages, you can create a rule so that any messages with that word (and it needs to be fairly unique) get placed in your Inbox or another folder you choose.

Handling an increase in the amount of spam

Unfortunately, these days the number of unwanted ads and other such messages you get is likely to rise rather than fall. Norton AntiSpam, after all, is designed to sort the good from the bad rather than keep the spam from reaching your system at all.

Be more concerned if the number of spams that make it through AntiSpam rises. The bottom line: You can't blame Norton AntiSpam if you're getting more and more spam messages in your Norton AntiSpam folder. However, if you're finding more and more spam messages in your Inbox (instead of being filtered into the AntiSpam folder), it usually means you need to re-examine your configuration. Consider:

✦ Whether you need to set up more or broader rules to trap them

✦ Whether to add e-mail addresses of recurring offenders to your Blocked List

✦ Whether to reset your AntiSpam configuration so that any mail not from someone on your Allowed List is automatically treated as spam

Use the recommendations provided in Chapter 2 to help reduce your risk of getting onto spam lists. You can also check with your Internet service provider — most of them have their own Web sites with tips on how to reduce spam — to see what they recommend to broaden your spam-fighting.

The more spam you see with file attachments, the more important it is that you follow warnings provided in Book VII covering Norton AntiVirus. Specifically, you want to be sure not to open these attachments and to scan your e-mail using a program like Norton AntiVirus, which is designed to check for possible threats within e-mail attachments.

If you're not using Norton AntiVirus, you can still check e-mail attachments by using another virus scanner, including the online drive and e-mail scanner available at the Panda Software site at `www.pandasoftware.com/ activescan/com/activescan_principal.htm`. Perform these scans regularly.

Be just as careful with file attachments from people you know. They may unwittingly pass you a computer virus or spyware along with a free tool or game they share with you.

Revising the Blocked List

The Blocked List you set up in Chapter 3 should be the start — rather than the absolute finish — of your blocking process. As long as you receive spam (and unless we start charging spammers by the piece, spam will be with us for a while), you can always add new e-mail addresses to the Blocked List.

Using LiveUpdate

Use the LiveUpdate tool regularly to keep Norton AntiSpam or the suite it's installed with absolutely up-to-date. Although LiveUpdate monitors for new files all by itself, you may not notice the little alert that appears telling you that updates are available. You may close the window just to get it out of the way or you make a mental note to update later only to forget.

Follow these steps to run LiveUpdate manually:

1. **Connect to the Internet (if you aren't already).**

2. **Open Norton AntiSpam.**

3. **Click LiveUpdate and then click Next (see Figure 5-4) as the wizard walks you through the download-and-apply process.**

Figure 5-4:
Upgrading your Norton files through LiveUpdate.

If you rarely or never see the LiveUpdate tool launch, you probably want to check to see how you have it set up under AntiSpam. To do this:

1. **From Norton AntiSpam, click Options.**

2. **Select the LiveUpdate tab.**

3. **Be sure Enable LiveUpdate is checked.**

If you aren't receiving notifications, your options should be set to let LiveUpdate run automatically.

4. **Click OK.**

Changing the Way AntiSpam Blocks Ads

Are you seeing more ads make it through your defenses when Web browsing than they did when you first set up Norton AntiSpam? Or do you find that it blocks ads so ferociously, it's making it tough to open ads you do want to see? If the answer to either of these questions is yes, think about checking your settings for how Norton AntiSpam blocks, then tweak them as needed.

To review and change your Ad blocking options:

1. **Open Norton AntiSpam (if using Norton Internet Security, open it).**

2. **Click to expand the AntiSpam menu at the left side of the window.**

3. **Click Ad Blocking and press the Configure button.**

   If ad blocking is not turned on, click Turn On and then click Configure.

4. **From the Ad Blocking window (see Figure 5-5), be sure both Turn on Ad Blocking and Turn on Pop-up Window Blocking are checked.**

5. **Click the Advanced button to view your extended settings (as shown in Figure 5-6).**

   You can add specific sites and configure them here (see Chapter 3 for more information).

6. **Click OK twice to close.**

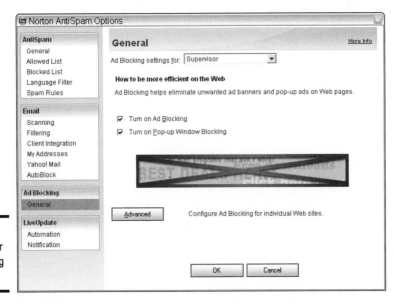

Figure 5-5:
Check your
ad blocking
settings.

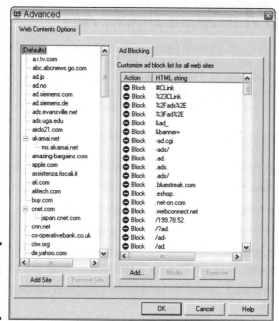

Figure 5-6:
Review your
advanced
settings.

Updates to Ad Blocking files are among the many file upgrades available
from the LiveUpdate tool.

Book VI

Norton AntiVirus

The 5th Wave
By Rich Tennant

"You should check that box so they can't profile your listening and viewing habits. I didn't do it and I'm still getting spam about hearing loss, anger management and psychological counseling."

Contents at a Glance

Chapter 1: Arming the Repel Shields on Viruses and Trojans

In This Chapter

✓ Finding out what you need to know about computer viruses, worms, and Trojans

✓ Using Norton AntiVirus to find out even more

✓ Being careful about opening e-mail file attachments

✓ Watching what you download

✓ Leaving some sites alone

✓ Knowing the problems of sharing disks and drives with others

✓ Reducing your risks of catching something

*E*very day, somewhere in the world, a new computer infection is released. Then there are all the variations that have been created by tweaking what a formerly released virus does. This tweaking is done for two basic reasons: to change what the infection does or to get past virus scanners that are looking for its predecessor.

Today, everyone has to be prepared to do battle against the ever-changing flood of computer infections. If you aren't prepared, your much-needed PC may turn into a large and expensive paperweight.

Before I jump into virus scanning and problem solving with Norton AntiVirus, I fill you in on the risks out there, how they change, and what you may be doing to expose yourself to them, as well as how Norton AntiVirus addresses and tries to fix them when they arrive on your PC.

Viruses, Worms, and Trojans — Oh My!

Battling the winter cold or the summer flu is bad enough. But at least with them, you know that rest, some aspirin, and some orange juice will eventually get you back on your feet. However, administering orange juice and TLC to a computer when it picks up one of the tens of thousands of infections out there is awfully hard. This is why you have antivirus software — the flu shot of the computer world.

Although all these different terms tend to be used interchangeably when discussing computer infections, there are actually key differences between viruses, worms, and Trojans. So I want to begin with a brief primer on what each means and how it behaves.

Not all virus warnings are real. People with way too much time on their hands start rumors about new viruses that are nothing more than fairy tales. Most of these feature really extreme symptoms like, "It makes your hard drive begin to belch smoke." By the time the hoax is discovered, the tale may have spread far and wide. Use resources in this chapter to weed out the fact from fiction. But you also may want to check out some virus hoax sites that help you separate fact from twisted fantasy, such as these:

✦ www.hoaxbusters.ciac.org

✦ www.symantec.com/avcenter/hoax.html

✦ www.vmy.ths.com

Vindictive viruses

A *virus* is special computer code, often embedded in a program. When that program is run, the virus attaches itself to certain files on your computer, such as core files needed to run Windows. But what happens from that moment forward really differs from one virus to the next. Some viruses immediately execute their nasty actions, which can range from displaying an annoying message to making Windows slow down, all the way to destroying the contents of your hard drive or messing up your BIOS (turn to Book I, Chapter 3 for more info on BIOS), so your hardware is no longer detected or no longer works properly.

Other viruses can sit on your PC for weeks or months before they actually inflict their damage. For example, the Michelangelo virus you may have heard about only activates itself on the famed artist's birthday, while the Chernobyl virus (also known as CIH) attacks your BIOS on the anniversary of Russia's great nuclear disaster.

Yet others play mean games with you. One virus out there plays its own version of Russian roulette. It pops up a message telling you that if you guess the correct number, it won't destroy the contents of your hard drive. Variations on this virus, however, erase your hard drive regardless of whether you guess right or not. Maybe it's too much to ask for a virus author to be ethical, eh?

The first recorded computer virus was discovered in 1987 by ARPANET, the military-based information network on which the Internet is based. Since then, we've seen more than 100,000 more.

What about macro viruses?

You may use macros everyday and not even know it. Macros are used in a number of different ways. Some of them allow you to record a series of keystrokes so that you can later type in that same information but by just pressing a few keys. For example, if you write a lot of letters, you may set Microsoft Word so that, when you press Ctrl+Shift+S, your signature and address appear where the cursor is, so you don't have to type it out every time.

But one of the primary kinds of macros uses a special file that runs a programming routine. For example, businesses and organizations often store these kinds of macros in a template that they hand out to employees to help them create new documents. These macros may apply formatting to a document or automatically print a file a certain way. Microsoft Office products such as Word and Excel make extensive use of this feature. The figure shows the option in Word (available under the Security tab after you choose Tools⇨Options) for changing your macro security to protect yourself against these viruses.

Knowing how often macros are shared with a large number of people through the use of these templates, authors began to use macros as a medium to spread their viruses. In response to this, products like Norton AntiVirus are designed to check documents for the presence of macro viruses so that you can detect and repair an infection before you pass it along.

**Book VI
Chapter 1**

**Arming the Repel
Shields on Viruses
and Trojans**

The diabolical worm

Unlike a virus, which can make a big splash immediately, a worm can be far more insidious. A worm usually makes copies of itself — called *replicating* — and begins distributing these copies everywhere.

A popular way for worms to replicate is through e-mail, where you open a file attachment that begins the infection. After you open the attachment, the worm immediately sends copies of itself, under your e-mail address, to the names of other people stored in your e-mail software's address book. This is almost diabolical, because people who know you are much more willing to open file attachments you send than attachments they get from strangers.

Eventually, enough copies of that worm are out there that *mail servers* (special computers and software used to pass e-mail around the globe) begin to go down all over the place. Their resources (hard drive space, memory, and CPU) are completely eaten up by trying to deal with all the worm copies.

To be fair, special worms, called *ethical worms,* also exist. Ethical worms are specifically designed to sit on a system or network to monitor activities for diagnostic purposes. However, those aren't the kind you're apt to see arrive in your e-mail.

Beware of Trojans bearing gifts

Trojans, also called Trojan horses and Trojan viruses, get their name from the old story of Helen of Troy and the great wooden horse sent into the enemy's camp as a gift. While the enemy slept off its night of partying, warriors emerged from the horse and slew them.

Just like their historical namesake, Trojans can appear to be normal or even beneficial programs or tools, making you far more inclined to give them a try. For example, one Trojan was created and sent out to members of a particular online service, promising users the ability to get into areas online they couldn't access otherwise.

After you execute a Trojan by running such a program or tool, the Trojan does its real work, which may be to steal your passwords or log your keystrokes (a way to find privileged information such as your credit card number or account information). Some also create a *back door,* or hole in your PC security, so that a hacker or a program can get access to your system either now or later.

Using Norton and Other Resources to Find Out More

You may not want to become a PC virus specialist, but you may want to find out more about new viruses, worms, and Trojans to get a handle on the kinds of threats you face. You can use Norton AntiVirus and other resources to aid you in that pursuit.

First, open your Web browser after installing Norton AntiVirus, and you see that a Norton Antivirus icon has been added to your browser toolbar, as shown in Figure 1-1. This not only lets you check files you're downloading from the Internet (find out how to configure this option in Chapter 5), it also gives you easy access to Norton AntiVirus tools.

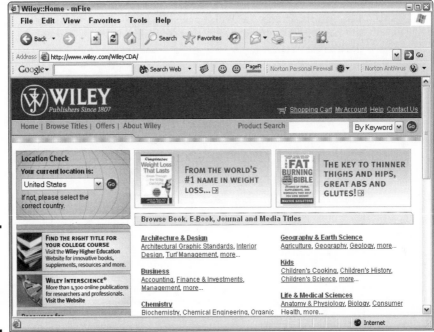

Book VI
Chapter 1

Arming the Repel
Shields on Viruses
and Trojans

Figure 1-1:
The Norton
AntiVirus
icon added
to your Web
browser.

If you click the icon, the tool allows you to scan selected files. Notice that there's a down-pointing arrow next to the icon. Click this, and a menu appears, as shown in Figure 1-2. There, you'll see the following choices:

✦ **View Status:** Opens the Norton AntiVirus Status window (see Figure 1-3) which gives you an at-a-glance summary of what's enabled and when your last scan was run.

✦ **View Quarantine:** Displays the list of suspicious files identified and isolated on your PC by Norton AntiVirus.

✦ **View Activity Log:** Shows you a summary of the Norton AntiVirus threats identified and the actions taken (see Figure 1-4).

✦ **View Virus Encyclopedia:** Allows you to look up a particular virus name and what it does.

✦ **Launch Scan Menu:** Brings up your list of scans so you can run them.

Here's an example. Starting in the next chapter, I show you how to perform your virus scans. But you probably noticed that Norton Antivirus ran a first scan when you installed the software. Let's say that, after your first scan, you use the View Activity Log (see Figure 1-4) or View Quarantine (see Figure 1-5) options from your Web browser's Norton AntiVirus menu. In it, you see the name of a suspicious file that Norton AntiVirus believes is infected with a particular virus.

Figure 1-2:
The Norton AntiVirus menu from your Web browser.

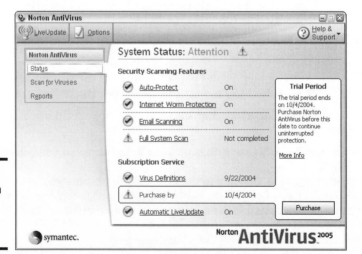

Figure 1-3:
The Norton AntiVirus Status window.

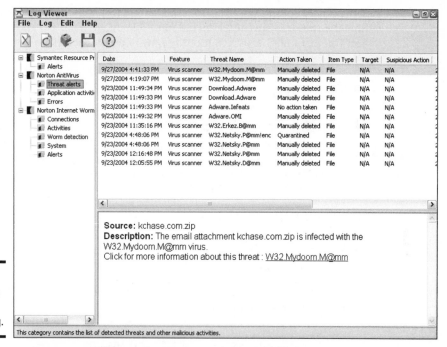

Figure 1-4:
The Norton
AntiVirus
Activity Log.

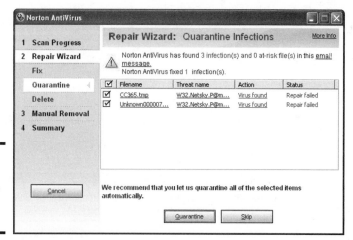

Figure 1-5:
View a
list of quar-
antined
files.

If you double-click on the underlined threat name in the Quarantine window
(you need your Internet connection live to do this), your Web browser
launches to a page at Symantec that gives you a profile of the threat Norton

AntiVirus encountered, as shown in Figure 1-6. There, you can read about how the threat is spread and what kind of damage it's been known to do — and you just may be able to identify how you contracted it.

Note: The Activity Log and the Log Viewer get additional treatment in Book I, Chapter 7.

Using the Virus Encyclopedia

Now that you know how you can look up threats, let's see how you can use the Virus Encyclopedia made available from Symantec to look up viruses you haven't yet seen. You can also view a list of the most recently identified threats.

To open the Virus Encyclopedia:

1. **Connect to the Internet.**

2. **Open your Web browser.**

3. **Click the down-arrow to the right of the Norton AntiVirus icon, and select View Virus Encyclopedia.**

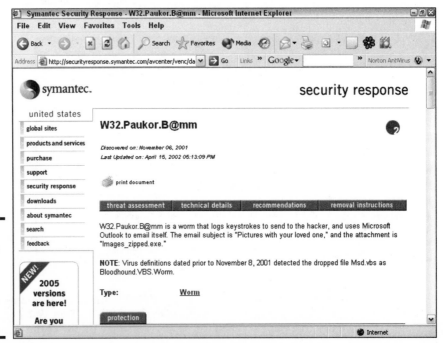

Figure 1-6: Information about a threat Norton AntiVirus found.

The Virus Encyclopedia opens, as shown in Figure 1-7. Notice that you can search for virus names alphabetically or use the search tool at the top of the screen.

As an example, let's use it to look up the "I Love You" virus (here, I'll type the quotation marks). This is a common one you may have heard about through the media; the virus transmits as a file attachment through e-mail (it's called a virus although it's behavior can be more like a worm). The subject line of infected e-mails usually reads, "I love you."

To search:

1. **Type** I Love You **into the search window.**

2. **Click Search.**

Wow! Look at your search results (shown in Figure 1-8), and you see a lot of variations on this one little virus. To find out more, click on the blue underlined hyperlink for a particular threat name to open the details about it.

**Book VI
Chapter 1**

**Arming the Repel
Shields on Viruses
and Trojans**

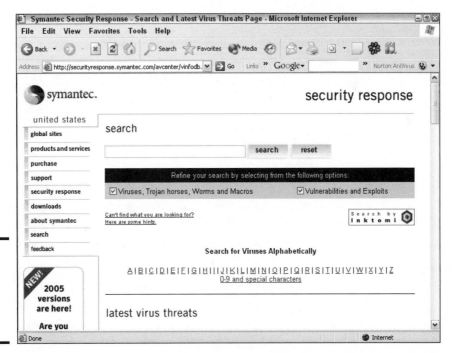

Figure 1-7:
The Virus encyclo-pedia's opening page.

If you're not quite sure how to spell a name but think you know the first few letters, you can also try an alphabetical search. Here's how to do this from the Virus Encyclopedia:

1. **Click the down-arrow to the right of the Norton AntiVirus icon, and select View Virus Encyclopedia.**

2. **Under Search for Viruses Alphabetically, click the letter that corresponds to the first letter of the virus name (in this example, the letter *I*).**

3. **When you get your results, let's say you're specifically interested in the virus threat listed as Iraq War or Iraq War Hoax. Click the hyperlink for it and the virus detail opens, as shown in Figure 1-9.**

Being aware of current threats

With new viruses and old virus variations appearing virtually every day, the names of these threats change frequently as well. One day, the news warns you about the Melissa worm, and the next you're told to guard against the Moo Shoo Pork virus (okay, I made that one up, but some of the names get pretty silly).

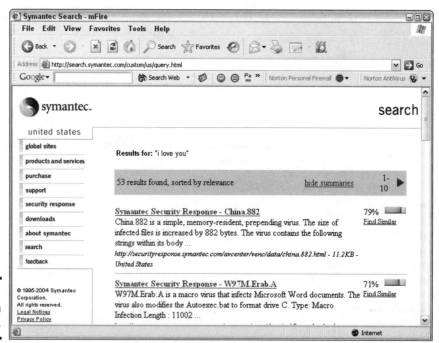

Figure 1-8:
Results from
your search.

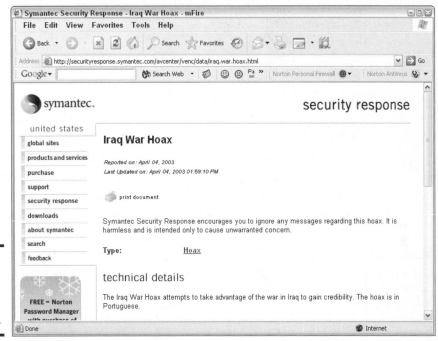

Book VI
Chapter 1

Arming the Repel Shields on Viruses and Trojans

Figure 1-9:
Details about a particular threat hoax.

Because Norton AntiVirus and other virus scanners give you a way to update them on a regular basis to protect against new threats, you don't necessarily need to spend lots of time researching these yourself. But occasionally checking the details of the threats you're hearing a buzz about is a good idea.

To check a list of the most current threats:

1. **Go to your Web browser and click the down-arrow next to the Norton AntiVirus icon on the browser toolbar.**

2. **Click View Virus Encyclopedia.**

3. **From the Virus Encyclopedia page, scroll down until you see a section similar to that shown in Figure 1-10.**

Other resources

In addition to the Norton AntiVirus and Symantec site, a number of other online resources are available, where you can both educate yourself about viruses in general and identify the most-recently-released infections.

Figure 1-10:
Symantec's
list of new
threats.

The following list provides just a few of the sites you may want to visit along with the Symantec resources discussed in the previous sections:

✦ **Security Advisor:** www3.ca.com/securityadviser/virusinfo/
default.aspx

✦ **CERT's Virus resource:** www.cert.org/other_sources/viruses.html

✦ **The Disaster Center:** www.disastercenter.com/virus.htm

✦ **F-Secure's Virus Center:** www.f-secure.com/virus-info/

✦ **McAfee's Virus center:** www.mcafee.com/anti-virus/default.asp

✦ **Microsoft Security virus information:** www.microsoft.com/security/
viruses/virus101.mspx

✦ **Sophos's virus information:** www.sophos.com/virusinfo/

✦ **Timberwolf's virus center:** www.timberwolfsoftware.com/avic/
index.asp

✦ **The Virus Bulletin:** www.virusbtn.com

Threats versus real infections

Take the time to notice that Norton AntiVirus — in Scan summaries, the Activity Log, and the View Quarantine option — uses the word *threat* more often than *active infection*. There's a reason, and the difference is very much like referring to someone in the commission of a crime as "a person of interest" rather than calling him "the probable criminal."

Norton makes its best educated guess in determining whether a particular file represents a legitimate threat. But it may not always be 100 percent sure — or right — that a virus is indeed present. Just because you have a file that

contains a virus doesn't mean you're infected yet. Often, the infection occurs after you open the file. If you run Norton AntiVirus before you do that, and your scan includes the location of the file, you usually won't get infected. There are exceptions, of course.

So the term *threat* gives you a sense that it's an assumption rather than an absolute fact. But it's important to realize that any antivirus scanner may report both *false positives* (where it assumes a file has an infection when it doesn't) and *false negatives* (where it reports no infection where one is actually present).

How You Get Infected

They say "Forewarned is forearmed." That old phrase applies well to the subject of computer viruses and how you end up being exposed to them.

Even though Norton AntiVirus and other products like it are constantly updated to detect and repair the most-recently-released viruses, they can't spot and neutralize everything. Also, at least a few days may pass from the time a virus or variation is first distributed until a virus specialist can identify what it does and how to identify and counteract it. This means there may be a delay before your virus software publisher makes an update available to check for it.

So it falls to you to exercise some care in the way you use your PC and share or receive files to reduce your risk of infection. In fact, that's the major topic of Chapter 7 of this book. For now, I want to identify the major sources of risk you face.

Opening e-mail

How many times have you heard, "Don't open file attachments from people you don't know"? You probably see an Open Attachment Warning every time you try to open a file attachment (see Figure 1-11), yet most people don't heed that warning.

Even if you do, there's no guarantee that the files you receive from your mom or your best friend or your boss aren't infected. **Remember:** Not all viruses wreak havoc and, among those that do, not every virus does so immediately upon receipt.

Figure 1-11: The Microsoft Open Attachment Warning.

Downloading files

Most people love to download. Who wouldn't when the Internet is brimming over with free programs, *shareware* (try-before-you-buy) demos, trial versions of commercial software, and thousands of neat screensavers, movies, songs, and games?

However, just because a Web site or online service posts a file that you can download doesn't mean it's safe. In fact, every once in a great while, you hear some horror story about a big-name software company accidentally including a virus on its commercial releases, unwittingly infecting its trusting customers. I could name more than a dozen such companies, but my lawyer wouldn't like that.

I'm not trying to scare you, but stop and think: If a commercial company that knows better sometimes makes mistakes, and you couple that with the knowledge that not all viruses can be detected when they first come out, what about all those I've-never-heard-of-them-before-but-they've-got-cool-files Web sites?

Most Web sites do, indeed, check their files before they make them available for download. But they may miss one, or the virus they've included may not yet be detectable. Other sites may never check their files before they release them to the public.

Browsing the Web

I hate to tell you this, but you could scrupulously avoid downloading any files, refuse all file attachments, never share files with others, and *still* face a problem.

When virus scanners don't always agree

Ever have a pain or some other medical complaint and find that if you talk to two different doctors, you get two very different opinions? You start to wonder, "Okay, I trust them both. So who's right?"

The same thing can happen with different antivirus utilities (and besides Norton, there are others, including McAfee VirusScan and Panda ActiveScan to name but two).

Some people take their viruses and the threat of them so seriously that they use more than one virus scanner to check their files. These people may use Norton AntiVirus plus use the free "while you're online" Panda ActiveScan available at www.pandasoftware.com/active scan/ (see the nearby figure).

I used to help check uploaded files for America Online before they became part of the library

collections online. As part of this work, I frequently used three or more virus checkers to be sure an infection didn't make it through to the members. One thing I discovered in my work is that different virus checkers are both better and worse about detecting possible infections. Some of the discrepancy in reporting may have a lot to do with how recently each virus scanner has been updated to catch the most recent viruses. But differences in how these programs are written and how sensitive they are in their work also play a role.

How do you know which to believe? Oh boy. I was afraid you'd ask that, because it's a real coin toss sometimes. Trust the one that has been updated most recently. Repeating the scan doesn't hurt either. Better safe than sorry. Now where's that lucky (fake) rabbit's foot?

Book VI Chapter 1

Arming the Repel Shields on Viruses and Trojans

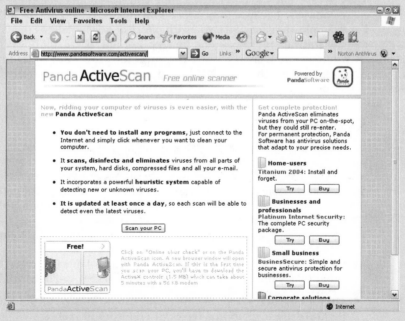

Many Web sites today run special *applets* (mini applications) that add new features to the browser that is trying to view these sites. They go by different names, including Java applets and ActiveX controls. In some respects, they can function much like programs you install on your computer. However, these applications, even though you don't have to install them, may be downloaded into your browser when you open the site. Some leave remnants behind even after you leave the site.

Unfortunately, rogue applets (though written for malicious rather than useful purposes) can be a means of spreading computer infections. Most Web sites and the people who run them try very carefully to be sure they aren't passing something along to you that could damage or otherwise affect your system. But it happens.

Disgruntled employees or contractors could add such an application to the Web site, or someone else like a hacker could break through security and change the Web site to include such a rogue applet. These are often spotted and fixed rapidly, but considering the fact that some big sites get more than a million visitors a day, many people can be affected before the problem is caught.

You also need to be aware that some Web sites exist just to try to spy on information contained on your PC or to pass along an infection to you. They're rare, but you find them. Often, you have a hint that these sites aren't quite copasetic because they offer some much-coveted but illegal feature. For example, they may lure you with offers of downloading copies of commercial software for free — and believe it or not, Microsoft does *charge* for its Windows and Office software (as do all the other companies that are in business). If something sounds too good to be true, it most likely is — and you're better off leaving that site for safer waters.

Sharing disks

One of the great things about using computers today is that sharing files with other people is so easy. Sharing files is a must when you're at work, where you may need to collaborate with others or have them review your documents. People tend to do a fair amount of file sharing out of the office, too — they swap photos, music, and other files among friends and family.

You can share files in a bunch of different ways, including the following:

✦ By writing these files to a floppy disk, a recordable CD or DVD disc, or other removable media (Zip drives, external USB, or Firewire/1394 drives)

✦ Over a network, where the main files can be located on your drive or a central drive such as you have with network file servers

+ By uploading them to and downloading them from a Web site or *intranet* (a private, member-only form of the Internet used in many corporate and office settings to allow people to work collaboratively on files and documents)

+ By swapping files back and forth in an Internet chat room (America Online and many other services have chat rooms that allow people to share files while they converse)

+ By sending them through e-mail

+ By sharing them during an online meeting, through features in products such as Microsoft Office's collaborative features, in Microsoft NetMeeting and in Windows/MSN Messenger

Can you guess what each of these methods has in common besides file sharing? Each and every one is a way you can spread or receive a computer infection.

Reducing Your Overall Risk

Now that I've left you gasping in horror with how easy it is to obtain a computer infection, let me add that full-blown virus infection with terrible consequences is still a relatively rare occurrence. In fact, people tend to suspect viruses far more frequently than they actually turn out to have one. Usually, aging hardware or an otherwise fouled-up PC is the cause of their problems.

However, you have to think about this issue as you tend to think about terrorists these days. Maybe you have a new prison in your area that boasts all the security measures to make sure no one gets loose. You take comfort in the fact that authorities tell you no thief or mastermind can escape. But you can't afford to assume that it *can't* happen. You still want to lock the doors and make it tough for the wrong people to get in to reduce your overall risk that they will.

Likewise, you need to do what you can to reduce your overall exposure to computer infections. Norton AntiVirus will help you in that, but you want to protect against the possibility that you'll come up against an infection for which there is no current cure. In the following sections, I show you how to do that. Turn to Chapter 7 of this book for even more recommendations.

Watching what you do and where you go

Just like a strange city, the Internet offers great attractions, inviting places to feast and shop, and lots of interesting things to see. It also boasts a fair number of dimly-lit back alleys and shady characters.

Be discriminating about where you go on the Internet and what you do when you get there. This little bit of common sense — the very kind you probably use when you visit a strange city — goes a long way toward reducing your risk potential.

Using authorized sites for downloads

When you absolutely need or lust for a new file, try to limit your downloads to authorized or well-known sites. For example, use the Windows Update tool in recent versions of Windows to locate and download updates, instead of going to "Sam's House of Windows Files."

After you receive your download, don't run it until you've run your virus scanner to check it. After an infected file gets executed, the infection can pass into your system. By then, it could be too late to undo the damage. Some viruses are smart enough to disable your antivirus software before they do anything else (see Chapter 2 for more details).

Trusting no one!

Yes, even nice people spread computer viruses. People who should know better accidentally spread them, too.

My very first virus infection ever was not only a real beaut (it attacked my BIOS and its settings so my hard drives were no longer detected), but it came from a trusted friend and someone who knows almost as much about PCs as I do (*read:* we both know better than to do what we did). That one mistake ruined my 15-year perfect record — along with my BIOS settings. The virus was easier to fix than my ego.

Assume nothing. Check all your files for infection before you open them. Encourage others with whom you share files to do the same. Extend this care to files that are shared over a network at work or at home, given to you on a floppy or other disk, or received through e-mail.

Keeping Fear from Ruining Your PC Experience

You now know that new viruses, worms, and Trojans are created and distributed on a daily basis around the world. That's a startling realization because it means you must prepare to handle them so you either (a) avoid the risk or (b) prepare to handle them if they appear.

Ah, but you're not alone. You have Norton AntiVirus and this book to show you how to use it effectively. Keep Norton AntiVirus updated (you'll see how to do that in Chapter 5), and perform your scans regularly. If you do, you won't have to curtail your zestful exuberance for the Internet or sharing files among friends, family, and co-workers in order to stay safe.

Chapter 2: Are You Infected?

In This Chapter

✔ **Knowing the symptoms of virus infection**

✔ **Taking the right steps when you suspect an infection**

✔ **Running your first Norton AntiVirus scan**

✔ **Troubleshooting with Norton AntiVirus**

✔ **Figuring out what to do when a virus "kills" your antivirus software**

The media talks about killer PC viruses and worms so frequently that it's easy to assume that, whenever something goes wrong on your PC, it must be a virus. As you use Norton AntiVirus and see all the stuff it picks up, the media's hysteria may only be reinforced in your mind.

I've got some good news for you: The statistical chance that your PC will be turned into a smoldering, oversized paperweight by a virus is pretty low, even with the vast number of infections in circulation today. The amount of hardware that has to be replaced in the aftermath of a virus is minimal.

Now consider this: One of the reasons the infection-damage rate is low is because people have gotten smarter about using antivirus software and exercising precautions. You can't rest on the hope that nothing will happen. You need to be prepared.

This chapter helps you identify some of the signs of possible infection, then offers you a game plan for what to do when you believe you are infected.

Recognizing Common Symptoms of Infection

Different infections can display a wide range of symptoms:

✦ You notice a sudden change in performance or operation when you've made no modifications to your system.

✦ Your antivirus software won't load even when other programs do.

✦ You discover you can't restart your system when there's little reason to suspect a hard-drive failure.

✦ Trying to run simple tasks on the desktop produces strange error messages like "Cannot find command interpreter" or "Cannot locate the program." If you restart your system, the same problem continues.

✦ Strange messages appear on the screen that don't look like they were generated by Windows or your programs. Often-used themes with these messages is "Legalize cannabis" or "End government prosecution of hackers" (both of which are generally a good sign the error messages are from a virus).

✦ If you go into your CMOS Setup (the "Setup" you see referenced when your PC first boots, where you can change system settings before Windows loads), you notice settings have been changed, or now show defaults (like a day and date of January 1, 1980).

The same virus infecting two different PCs can make those PCs respond differently. Sound tough yet? Add to this the fact that many of the symptoms a virus may demonstrate could also be explained by many non-virus problems. So just because your computer is displaying some of the symptoms listed here doesn't mean you have a virus. That's where the information in the following section comes in handy.

Knowing What to Do When You Suspect an Infection

If you notice one or more of the symptoms in the preceding section, it's probably not the time to open a bottle of champagne, that's for sure. Instead, you want to try to take steps to get the situation back under your control before you jump to desperate measures.

If you suspect a virus, follow these steps:

1. **Don't panic.**

That sounds too obvious, but people do all sorts of goofy things when they're desperate. If you must, step away from the PC for a short while, and return when you feel ready to deal with the problem.

2. **If you have a second PC available, keep it handy with an Internet connection open.**

You may be able to find the meaning of error messages by going online.

3. **Remove any floppy disks from your floppy drive.**

Some viruses — called *boot sector viruses* — copy themselves to the *boot sector* (the section at the beginning of a drive that is specially configured to allow it to boot the system) of disks and can spread through the use of infected floppy disks.

4. **Close all applications on your desktop.**

If you have any unsaved work, save it to a special location (such as a separate folder) away from your other files.

5. **If Norton AntiVirus will run, immediately perform a full system scan.**

If it won't run, jump to the section, "Dealing with Viruses that Disable Norton AntiVirus," later in this chapter.

Don't send files to anyone until you're able to perform a full scan of your system. If, after you run the virus check, you determine you *do* have a virus, let others to whom you've recently sent files know, so they can check their own systems.

6. **After you run a virus scan and it either repairs your files or finds no virus, copy important files to a location off your main hard drive or create a backup.**

   Do not make a drive copy or record a Norton GoBack setup or a Windows System Restore point at this time. You don't want to take the chance that you'll store the infection with it.

7. **If you use Windows System Restore or Norton GoBack, try loading a previously recorded setup.**

   If you have multiple recorded versions (also called *restore points*), try to go back to a point before you first noticed the problem.

8. **Know where your emergency disks (like the ones you create later in this chapter) and/or Norton AntiVirus installation CD are so you can use them if needed to scan.**

Book VI
Chapter 2

Are You Infected?

Storing a virus in the restore points created by Windows System Restore and the saved configuration files stored by Norton GoBack is possible. That's why you should *not* use these tools when you have an active problem, until you can rule out an infection.

Dealing with Viruses That Disable Norton AntiVirus

The people who develop computer viruses may not be particularly ethical, but some of them sure are smart. A successfully written virus doesn't just require a certain amount of programming skills. It also demands knowledge about how most users will try to respond when they suspect they've been hit with infection.

In the later 1990s, when the public became a bit more savvy about the whole virus phenomenon, many began to obtain antivirus software — like Norton AntiVirus — to try to limit their risk of getting a killer infection. That's the good news.

However, this shift required a change in how PC germ doctors operate. No longer could they just put out a virus or other type of infection hoping to strike those who hadn't bought antivirus software. They also had to rearrange their *code* (the commands and settings used in software development of any kind) to attack antivirus software.

Using AntiVirus as a PC troubleshooting tool

A great deal of my work involves showing people how to get past PC emergencies. I've worked with tens of thousands of people desperate for help. When someone comes to me saying her PC is acting very strangely, I always ask the same two questions:

✔ **What was the last thing you did with your PC before the strangeness appeared?** Perhaps as much as 60 percent of the major problems people see with their PCs occurs shortly after they make some change to them. That change can be anything from adding or removing hardware or software, to running a new kind of utility, to tweaking the Windows Registry. Often enough, you can get the system back to normal if you identify and undo that change.

✔ **When did you last run a virus scan?** Statistically speaking, the incidence of

damage from a serious virus is pretty low compared to failed hardware, grunged Windows installations, or wacky programs. But by running the scanner first, you may me able to immediately eliminate a virus as a suspect. After the scan finishes, you have distinct results — "Yes, there's a virus" or "No, there isn't a virus." You've removed your doubt and you can move on to the next stage of troubleshooting.

What you do next depends on what you're experiencing. You may want to use other utilities, such as Norton System Doctor from Norton Utilities or the One-Button Checkup from Norton SystemWorks to see if they can spot a problem. You can also consult with Device Manager and CMOS Setup (discussed in Book I, Chapter 3) to eyeball listings to see if they've changed.

Now, many so-called "smart" viruses are designed to go after the antivirus software first, making the tool unable to load. With the software disabled, the virus can then do its thing. That's the bad news.

But don't despair — at least, not yet. There are two ways you can run your virus scanner, even if it won't load normally:

✦ From emergency disks

✦ From the Norton AntiVirus installation CD

See the following sections for information on how to prepare yourself for these emergencies. See "Using your disks" for information on how to run your virus scanner from either of these two options.

You can also try online virus scanners as well, like Panda ActiveScan at www.pandasoftware.com/activescan.

Preparing for Emergencies: Creating the Basic Rescue and Emergency Boot Disk Set

When Norton AntiVirus installs, it recommends you create a special disk called the Basic Rescue and Emergency Boot Disk. This disk can be used to scan your system for viruses even when your computer won't start otherwise.

If you have a floppy drive (not all new PCs do) and blank floppies (you need three), create the Basic Rescue and Emergency Boot Disk now. It gives you a safety buffer just in case.

Book VI
Chapter 2

Are You Infected?

Getting the file you need

In order to create the Basic Rescue and Emergency Boot Disk, you need a particular file called NED.exe. The good news: If you don't already have this file on your computer, you can get it from your Norton AntiVirus installation CD or you can easily download it from the Web.

Looking for the file on your hard drive

To check for the file on your system:

1. **Choose Start⇨Search.**

2. **Click All Files and Folders.**

3. **Click inside the box below All or Part of the File Name and type** ned.exe **(see Figure 2-1).**

4. **Click Search.**

   Search should find your file (as shown in Figure 2-2). If it does, proceed to the section "Creating your disks." If it doesn't find the file, go to the following section, "Looking for the file on your installation CD."

Looking for the file on your installation CD

To find the file on your Norton AntiVirus installation CD:

1. **Place the Norton AntiVirus installation CD in your CD or DVD drive.**

2. **Click Browse CD.**

3. **Double-click the SUPPORT folder.**

4. **Double-click the EDISK folder.**

   The NED.exe file should be there. If it is, proceed to the section "Creating your disks." If for some reason the file isn't there, go to the following section, "Finding the file online." If the file is there, select it and then click OK.

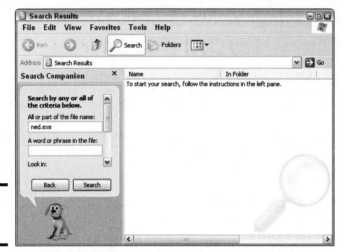

Figure 2-1:
Search for
NED.exe.

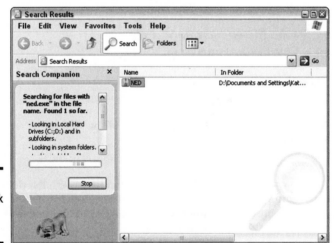

Figure 2-2:
Double-click
on the file
to launch.

Finding the file online

If you can't find the file on your PC or you don't have the installation CDs, you can download it from Symantec at `www.symantec.com/techsupp/ebd.html`. When you're asked "Do you want to run or save this file?", click Save, and save it to your desktop.

Then proceed to the section "Creating your disks."

Creating your disks

Be sure you've located the ned.exe file (on your hard drive, your installation CDs or online). Then follow these steps to create your emergency disk:

1. **Double-click on the** ned.exe **file.**

NED launches (see Figure 2-3).

Figure 2-3:
Creating
your
emergency
disks.

**Book VI
Chapter 2**

Are You Infected?

2. **Click OK to start the disk-creation process.**

3. **When prompted, insert your first blank floppy into your floppy drive.**

4. **Follow the steps necessary to finish creating the emergency disks.**

Label and date your emergency disk set, as instructed. Then put them in a very safe place.

In your CMOS Setup (refer to Book I, Chapter 3 for more information), there's an option called Drive Boot Sequence or something very similar. This setting specifies which drive the PC should check first to try to boot the computer. Most people use their C: or primary hard drive to boot their PCs. When the PC boots, it looks to see if it can boot from the first drive listed, then to the next drive, and so on. You may need to go into CMOS Setup, locate this setting, and temporarily change the boot sequence order to the drive where your emergency disk is located (the A: or floppy disk if you make the floppies, or the letter for your CD or DVD drive if you use the Norton AntiVirus CD). After you've run the scan, you can go back to CMOS Setup and change back to your regular boot sequence.

Using your disks

If your PC won't start on its own, or if you don't want to risk running it out of fear that a possible virus may do damage, you need to either use the emergency boot disks you created (see "Creating your disks" earlier in this chapter) or insert the Norton AntiVirus installation CD.

To boot the PC using the rescue disks you created:

1. **Place Emergency Disk 1 into the A: drive, and then restart your computer.**

   The PC launches in DOS, a command-line environment that looks similar to the Command Prompt window you may have seen in Windows. If you need help, press your F1 key.

2. **Select the option you want to run.**

3. **Follow the onscreen instructions for inserting and removing the Emergency Disks.**

4. **When the Emergency program is done, remove the Emergency Disk from drive A:, and then restart your computer.**

To run your Norton AntiVirus installation CD to start your PC long enough to scan for viruses, follow these steps:

1. **Insert your Norton AntiVirus installation CD into your CD or DVD drive.**

2. **Restart your PC.**

   If your PC is up and running when you want to do this, make certain you shut down and restart.

Be sure that your PC can boot from CD. If it can't, you need to use the Emergency Disk floppies or change your boot sequence. To change your boot sequence, you need to restart your system, then look on the initial screen and follow directions to press a specific key or series of keys to enter Setup. When you're in, look for the section (each Setup can be a bit different) that shows which drive(s) can be used to try to boot your PC. Be sure your CD or DVD drive letter is listed there. If not, select it and follow onscreen directions to enable this as a boot drive.

Performing a Scan

Now — finally! — let's get to that first scan. (This may not be your actual first scan — Norton AntiVirus, when it installs, tries to get you to perform one practically before it fully loads on your desktop, so you may have done it then.)

To start a scan:

1. **Double-click the Norton AntiVirus icon on your desktop or in the System Tray.**

   If your Norton AntiVirus is part of a suite, click on Norton AntiVirus after your suite opens.

2. **From the Status window (shown in Figure 2-4), click Scan for Viruses.**

A list of scans appears (see Figure 2-5):

- **Scan my computer:** Use this to perform a full system scan.

- **Scan all removable drives:** This checks your removable media drives, like your CD and/or DVD drives and Zip drives.

- **Scan all floppy disks:** Use this to check a floppy disk currently inserted in your floppy disk drive.

- **Scan drives:** Lets you scan all the drives attached to your PC, including your hard drives. All drives are selected by default, but you can click to uncheck a drive you don't want to include (see Figure 2-6).

Book VI
Chapter 2

Are You Infected?

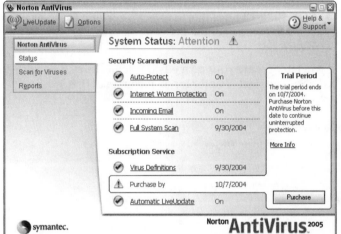

Figure 2-4:
The Norton AntiVirus Status window.

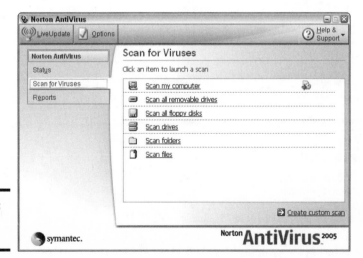

Figure 2-5:
Choose a scan.

Figure 2-6:
Selecting
drives to
scan.

- **Scan folders:** Choose this if you want to click to check folders to include in the scan (see Figure 2-7).

- **Scan files:** Choose this to select a specific file to examine. From the File window, select the file you want to scan and click Scan (see Figure 2-8).

If you later create your own custom scans, they'll be added to the scan list. (See the next chapter for an example of this.)

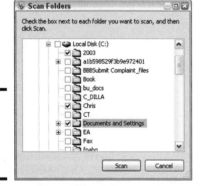

Figure 2-7:
Click to
choose
folders to
scan.

Figure 2-8:
Point and
click the file
to scan.

3. **Choose the scan you want to start.**

   Whichever scan you choose, it launches and displays the Scan Progress window, shown in Figure 2-9.

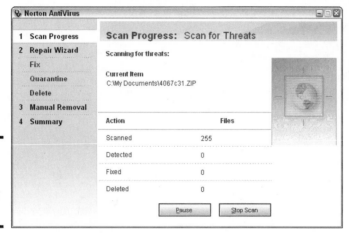

Figure 2-9:
Chart your progress through the scan.

4. **If you need to stop or pause the scan, just click the appropriate button.**

   A stopped scan will close altogether, while a paused one will wait for you to click Resume.

   Exactly how long the scan takes depends on how comprehensive a scan you're doing (scanning a file is much, much faster than a whole drive, which is faster than scanning the entire PC).

   After the scan is complete, you'll see a Scan Summary window that reports what the scanner located, as shown in Figure 2-10.

If no viruses or spyware or adware are spotted, you're home free, at least in terms of having a virus. But if Norton AntiVirus found something, it will automatically try to repair the file(s) affected through its Repair Wizard (unless you configured Norton AntiVirus to ask you what to do first — find out more about configuring in Chapter 3 of this book).

Unfortunately — cue threatening-sounding music — Norton AntiVirus may not be able to repair or remove everything it finds automatically. This is where words like *quarantine* and *manual removal* come in, and I take you through both of these processes in Chapter 4 of this book.

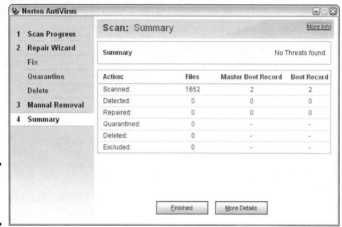

Figure 2-10:
Your scan
results.

Chapter 3: Quarantining, Repairing, and Deleting Infections

In This Chapter

✔ **Understanding your scan results**

✔ **Determining what Norton repairs or eliminates**

✔ **Knowing the steps to take for anything Norton couldn't remove**

✔ **Researching your threats**

*O*kay, you've run your first major scan. Now comes the moment of truth. It's time to look at what Norton tells you it uncovered.

Are you or aren't you the not-so-proud recipient of an infection, or two (or ten)? Just as important, is Norton AntiVirus telling you it successfully eliminated them?

There are some big differences between how Norton handles infections found under older versions of Windows (98 and Me) and how it does this in Windows 2000 and Windows XP. So if you happen to run Norton AntiVirus on two different PCs at home — one running Me and one running XP, for example — you have to change your steps slightly. In this chapter, I let you know how.

Coping With the Bad News

"Don't get mad or scared — get protected," a PC virus specialist once told me, and she's right. Don't take personally word that you've been infected. Just find a way to deal with it so you don't have to worry about it.

You need to understand a bit about how Norton AntiVirus works and how it comes up with its results. Exactly what steps it takes depends on how you set Norton AntiVirus to respond when it thinks it's found a feverish file. To figure out what you've told Norton to do, follow these steps:

1. **Open Norton AntiVirus.**

2. **Click Options.**

3. **From the Auto-Protect screen, look under How to Respond When a Virus Is Found (see Figure 3-1).**

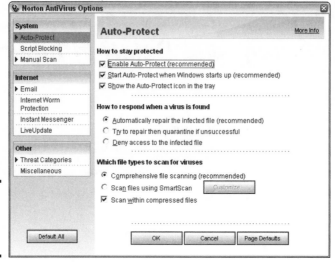

Figure 3-1:
Telling
Norton how
to respond.

Here are your three options:

✦ **Automatically Repair the Infected File (Recommended):** This means Norton AntiVirus will do its best to neutralize the file and if it can't, it will usually remove it or quarantine it. (This is the setting that's usually selected.)

✦ **Try to Repair the File Then Quarantine if Unsuccessful:** If Norton AntiVirus can't repair the problem, it tries to quarantine it (you'll find out all about this shortly in the "Understanding Quarantines" section) to reduce your chance of infection.

✦ **Deny Access to the Infected File:** This stops Windows and you from trying to run or open the file, which could then spread any infection to other parts of your PC; it's like the file got sentenced to eternal solitary confinement and is used for files you can't seem to get rid of.

Another choice is available when you do some but not all scans: Ask Me What to Do. This forces Norton to stop and ask how you want to handle the action on this file. This way, you can deny access to one file while opting to repair or delete others.

Getting the results of your scan

If you're using Windows 98/Me and you have Norton running on autopilot, Norton AntiVirus identifies the file then tries to repair it. If the file won't let Norton AntiVirus work on it, the virus checker either tries to quarantine the file or deletes it. Your Scan: Summary window shows you what actions were taken (see Figure 3-2).

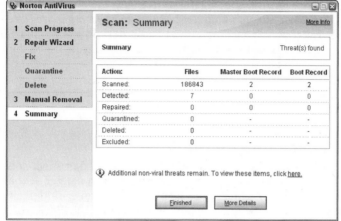

Figure 3-2:
The Scan:
Summary
window lists
results.

Your summary tells you how many:

✦ Files were scanned in that session, including boot and master boot
   records

✦ Threats were detected and, if any involved your boot or master boot
   records, how many for each

✦ Threats were repaired, quarantined, deleted, or excluded (the last one
   refers to threats you tell Norton AntiVirus to ignore (more about that in
   "Figuring Out What to Do if AntiVirus Can't Repair an Infected File")

Click More Details to see exactly what Norton found or click Finished to
close the Scan: Summary window.

Under Windows 2000 and XP, Norton AntiVirus also tries to repair files, but if
it fails to do so, it usually doesn't let you quarantine or delete them. Instead,
it denies access to the file. The downside to this, besides not having as many
choices, is that you may not be able to delete the file either through Norton
AntiVirus or through other tools like My Computer or Disk Cleanup utilities.
It's sort of like having a villain move into your home, but you keep him
locked up in the basement — you don't want to let him in and you can't
seem to get him out.

Norton AntiVirus does one more important job under Windows 2000 and XP
that it won't under earlier versions: It automatically looks inside compressed
files like the .cab (cabinet) files squeezed together into one smaller file on a
Windows CD or in your Windows backup folder or in .zip files (files you zip
together using a tool like WinZip [www.winzip.com]).

With your new knowledge about what the Scan: Summary window tells you,
you can see what Norton picked up during its checks.

If you have everything in Norton AntiVirus set to automatic and you're using Windows 98 or Me, you may not have to do anything more here except click Finish. But if you're using Windows XP or 2000 or you've changed the way Norton AntiVirus is to respond to a scan, you may be asked if you want to quarantine, delete, or deny access to a file.

In the following sections, I take you through what these options mean and what you should do.

Understanding quarantines

A *quarantine* is a way to keep an infection-exposed or suspicious file from being run or otherwise putting your other files in danger. Just as you might place a sick visitor who arrives by plane from a fever-ridden city into quarantine (you don't know that the person will spread the illness, but you don't want to take that chance), Norton places files it considers risky into a virtual holding pen, away from interaction with your system.

In some cases, Norton AntiVirus's Repair Wizard will either automatically quarantine some of the files it can't repair or ask if you want to do this. Here, you'll want to review what files Norton AntiVirus has found. (Turn to Chapter 1 of this book, for more information on viruses, Trojans, and worms.) Figure 3-3 shows a report where two problems were found and one was successfully repaired, leaving one to be dealt with.

You can choose to quarantine all that Norton AntiVirus suggests, or you can click to remove the checkmark from one or more files before you click Quarantine.

Figure 3-3:
A file to
quarantine.

If the quarantine isn't successful, you may be asked if you want to delete the file(s). You may not even get the choice to quarantine one, more, or all files Repair Wizard couldn't fix. (See the following section for more information.)

Letting Norton AntiVirus remove the file

When all else fails, Norton AntiVirus may give you the chance to delete the file altogether, to just get it off your system. Figure 3-4 shows a situation in which a file couldn't be repaired or quarantined, so I'm left with doing away with the problem file.

Book VI
Chapter 3

Figure 3-4: Delete problem files.

Click Delete to remove all the files or click to remove marks from those you don't want to remove before you click Delete. To keep the files — but why would you want to do that? — click Skip.

Before you delete, you may want to see if you can figure out what the file is and where it came from. Look at Figure 3-5 and you see a situation where problems were spotted in an e-mail message. Click the blue underlined e-mail message link to see who the file was from (but don't open the attachment). Also check for the name of the file. If this file came from someone you know, you can ask the person to resend it *after* he's done a virus scan. To compare, Figure 3-6 shows an infected file attachment in e-mail that Norton AntiVirus was able to fix.

After you do press delete, you'll see a window like that shown in Figure 3-7, alerting you to the fact that the file is being removed. It also informs you that the deleted file will be stored temporarily in the Quarantine folder, just in case you made a mistake and need to restore it. Click Yes to continue to remove the file(s).

Figure 3-5:
Seeing
where the
infection
came from.

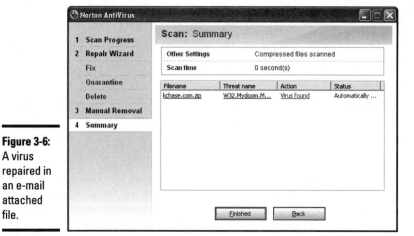

Figure 3-6:
A virus
repaired in
an e-mail
attached
file.

Figure 3-7:
Confirming
the kill.

Working with quarantined and deleted files

Where do all those quarantined and deleted files go and what are you supposed to do with them? You've come to the right place.

Follow these steps:

1. **In Norton AntiVirus, click Reports in the left-hand task pane.**

2. **Click View Report next to Quarantined Items (see Figure 3-8).**

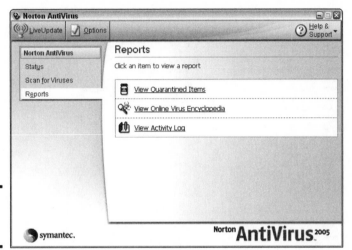

Figure 3-8:
The Reports
list.

When the list opens, you see the files that have been either quarantined or deleted, as shown in Figure 3-9.

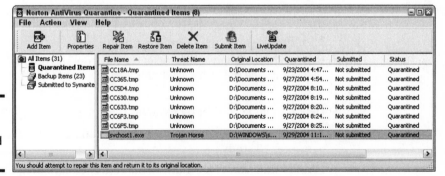

Figure 3-9:
The
quarantined
Items list.

3. **Select a file from the list, and then look at the toolbar near the top of the window.**

4. **Click the toolbar icon that fits what you want to do.**

Here are your options:

- **Add Item:** Adds a file to the quarantine list (it doesn't have to be one Norton AntiVirus has already identified). When you click this, a window opens letting you browse to the location where the file is stored and then select it (see Figure 3-10).

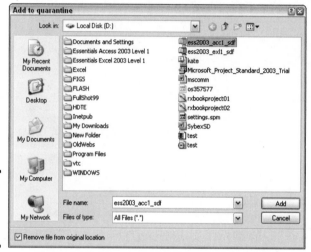

Figure 3-10: Add a new file to quarantine.

- **Properties:** Provides details about the selected file.

- **Repair Item:** Lets you select a file and run Repair Wizard again to see it if can be repaired. You may want to try the LiveUpdate feature first to see if an upgrade to your virus definitions list will repair the file now.

- **Restore Item:** Removes the selected file from the quarantine list to recover it (see the "Uh . . . I didn't mean to delete that" sidebar for details).

- **Delete Item:** Permanently removes the file from your system.

- **Submit Item:** Sends this file and a report about it along to the folks at Symantec to study.

- **LiveUpdate:** Launches your Norton AntiVirus updating tool (see Chapter 5).

5. **After you're done, click the X at the top-right corner of the window to shut it.**

TECHNICAL STUFF

About backed up items and submitted items

In the Quarantined Items window, you may notice two more options on the left besides Quarantined Items: Backup Items and Submitted Items. Backup Items refers to copies of files Norton AntiVirus stores before it tried to repair them. These files can be deleted, restored, or in some cases, reported to Symantec. Submitted items are the files, if any, you've chosen to send to Symantec to help them learn from it and, hopefully, update Norton AntiVirus so it can catch and repair these types of files in the future.

Here's something else you need to know. Sometimes when you go to look at your quarantined files, a window pops up like that shown in Figure 3-11, asking if want to recheck your quarantine files against newer virus definitions. Clicking Yes is usually smart, just in case you can salvage a file otherwise headed toward the chopping block.

Setting up exclusions

Exclusions are a way of telling Norton to leave a file or service on your system alone and not to treat it like a bad guy. On some screens, you will see an Exclude button. If you click to check an item on the list and then click Exclude, Norton AntiVirus takes that one item off your suspect list. Normally, you'd only do that if Norton AntiVirus reported as a threat a file you know is a good tool.

Here's a hypothetical example of a situation that pops up from time to time: Let's say you run a special tool called IWin (there are several programs called "IWin," but this is fictional in this situation) from an online auction site that runs in the background all the time to notify you when your bid on a killer stereo has been trumped by somebody else. When Norton AntiVirus scans, it may pick up IWin as either a virus or a non-virus threat. When you first see IWin show up on a Norton hit list, you can select it and exclude it so that NAV doesn't target it again.

Figure 3-11:
Check
quarantines
against
Norton
AntiVirus
updates.

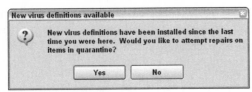

"Uh . . . I didn't mean to delete that"

You may later discover that a problem file you deleted either isn't really infected or you've been able to find a different tool to repair it (see the "Figuring Out What to Do if AntiVirus Can't Repair an Infected File" section). When you want to restore a file you've deleted or quarantined, use the Quarantined Items window. Select the file from the list (see the figure), and then click Restore Item from the toolbar.

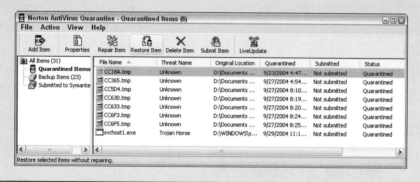

Figuring Out What to Do if AntiVirus Can't Repair an Infected File

Assume for a minute that the worst has happened: Norton AntiVirus finds something it really believes is a virus, but it doesn't seem to be able to act upon the file to repair, quarantine, or delete it. If this happens, one of two things is true: The file is a virus, or it's not.

Not all files can be repaired, because not all the files Norton AntiVirus suspects are actually viruses. *Adware* (a program usually transferred to your system to push pop-ups and other ads to you based on the places you go) is a great example of this — because if you repaired an adware program, it wouldn't be an adware program, would it? Its only purpose is to try to track you and feed you ads.

Look at Figure 3-12 and you see a Scan: Summary where seven non-viral (usually adware) viruses were found, but none of them has been acted on. To view these items, click as directed in the window (or click More Details — it does the same thing). This opens an info window about these non-viral threats, as shown in Figure 3-13. Check the Status column, and you'll see they're all listed as *at risk,* which is Norton AntiVirus's less-than-direct way of telling you it hasn't done anything with them except to point them out to you.

Figure 3-12:
Scan:
Summary
shows non-
viral threats.

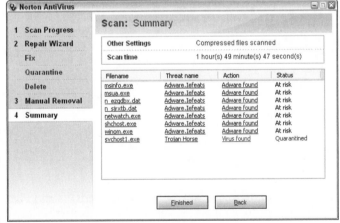

Figure 3-13:
Adware files
marked
but not
removed.

In Chapter 6 of this book, I show you some alternative programs you can try that may be able to remove adware (and with some programs, other types of risky files) that Norton doesn't.

You can try to delete the file yourself using one of the Windows file manage-ment tools like My Computer or Windows Explorer. But what if it's a file you really need? Some of the files that can be infected may be needed by Windows to run. Deleting the wrong thing could send Windows into a tizzy and make it unable to load.

The first thing you want to do is to run LiveUpdate to see if there are updates available that may be able to repair the file.

If running LiveUpdate doesn't help you repair the file you need, follow the same basic steps in Chapter 1 to find out more about different viruses, Trojans, and worms, in order to get the gritty little details about a file Norton AntiVirus spots and reports to you.

As an example, I'll use one of the problems Norton AntiVirus reports as it begins to do the cleanup work after a scan. Figure 3-14 shows Norton AntiVirus pausing in a scan to tell you that, while running Repair Wizard, it located two files it can't fix.

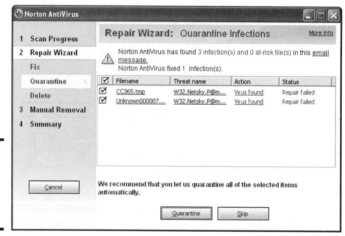

Figure 3-14: Repair Wizard reports problems.

You probably want to follow Norton AntiVirus's advice and quarantine these files, but you want to get a better idea of what exactly they are. Click one of the blue hyperlinked names under Threat Name. If you're connected to the Internet, that click launches your Web browser, opens the Symantec Security Response site, and lets you read through the details (sort of like a rap sheet) currently available about the file Norton AntiVirus discovered, as shown in Figure 3-15, which shows the details for another nasty program, Netsky. This one turns out to be a pesky little worm, which, if left on your system, could start sending itself out to people in your e-mail address book. Look back at the Norton AntiVirus window you saw in Figure 3-14 and click Quarantine.

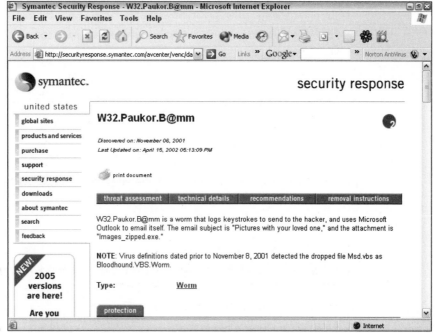

**Book VI
Chapter 3**

**Quarantining,
Repairing, and
Deleting Infections**

Figure 3-15:
A virus's
rap sheet.

Preventing Reinfection

What you can do to prevent similar files or threats from reaching you depends on what Norton reports to you. If the infected files are several files you downloaded from the same Web site, you may want to avoid getting new files from there. You may also want notify the person who runs the site (usually available through e-mail at webmaster@whateversiteitis.com to check these files before someone else without antivirus software gets hit.

When you look up the details about a threat through Norton AntiVirus, you may see some of the ways this file is spread. This may give you an idea about mail you want to avoid, for example. The information you get under details may be able to help you understand what you need to do in other situations, too.

When you get an infection or threat through e-mail, go back and see who sent you the mail (but certainly don't try to open the file attachment until you've quarantined or eliminated it altogether). If it's someone you know, you want to alert that person to the fact that he passed an infection along so he can scan his own system. But if the mail was sent by someone you don't know, you may want to add that e-mail address to a blocked sender list.

To do this for Outlook Express:

1. **Select the message in the right-hand pane of your Inbox.**

2. **Choose Message⇨Block Sender.**

A window pops up (see Figure 3-16) telling you that the sender of that e-mail has been added to your blocked list and asks if you want to remove all messages from that person.

3. **Click Yes.**

A final window tells you all messages are now deleted.

If you later need to remove someone you've erroneously added to your Blocked Sender's list, here's how:

1. **Choose Tools ⇨ Message Rules.**

2. **Select Blocked Senders List.**

3. **Locate and select the e-mail address for the person you want to delete from your blocked list, and click Remove.**

4. **Click OK to confirm this.**

5. **Click OK until you close the menus.**

Here's something to notice if you look at Figure 3-16, which shows a preview of your e-mail in the bottom of the right-hand message window in Inbox. While Outlook Express usually turns on the preview option by default, you may want to turn the preview off because it can place you at greater risk (because you're essentially opening the contents of the message by previewing it).

To turn off the preview:

1. **In Outlook Express, choose View⇨Layout.**

2. **Uncheck Show Preview Pane.**

If you're using software other than Outlook Express, check the program's help file under the Help menu to find out how to block a person's e-mail address.

Figure 3-16:
Remove all messages from this sender.

Outlook Express

(i) 'MAILER-DAEMON@sokol.lm.pl' has been added to your blocked senders list. Subsequent messages from this sender will be blocked.

Would you like to remove all messages from this sender from the current folder now?

[Yes]   [No]

Chapter 4: Choosing Your Scanning Options

In This Chapter

✔ Telling Norton AntiVirus how you want it to work

✔ Specifying how the scanner works with messaging services and e-mail

✔ Customizing your scans

✔ Scanning on the spot

✔ Understanding why automation can slow things down

*L*ike most products, Norton Antivirus has two basic ways in which it can perform its job of keeping your PC safe from infection. Which one you decide to use is entirely up to you.

Norton AntiVirus can go ahead and proceed using the way it's been set up to operate by its developers (often called the *default mode*). Or you can change the program's settings to make it run more in the way *you* would prefer to use it, based on your unique style of working with your PC.

Understanding the Pros and Cons of Automation

Let's deal with a nasty truth up front: The more Norton AntiVirus scans and the more you let it operate in an automated fashion, the more some PCs seem to transform from speed machines into slugs. To some degree, this is true with many antivirus utilities, but in my experience, Norton beats the rest in this department.

How much you notice this really depends on the speed of your PC and the type of work you do. If you're the kind of person who runs a very fast PC with not much loaded or tends to use a PC more for recreation than work, you may not be bothered. But if you're like me and you depend on your PC to move lots of files and e-mails around quickly, you probably will.

Also, if you're as patient as I am (translation: not very), and you experience this slowness, you may be tempted to disable the antivirus software altogether (or just to curse frequently). But going to that extreme isn't necessary. After all, scanning can save you from problems you can't spot yourself.

You can deal with this in two ways that involve less fussing and more satisfaction. One method is to take advantage of the customization methods covered in this chapter to adjust Norton AntiVirus to your needs. Run the scanner manually, for example, but make sure you:

✦ Do it at least once a week.

✦ Perform a full system scan when you do.

The other method beckons back to the first two chapters of this book, where you can find important tips for limiting your risk of infection. Limiting your risks doesn't mean you can turn off and forget about Norton AntiVirus. Instead, by practicing good PC safety — sort of the virtual equivalent of washing your hands extra carefully during flu season — you may be able to safely limit the amount of time it has to run.

The bottom line is that if you choose when to use Norton AntiVirus rather than letting it ride herd over your desktop all the time, you can limit some of the bottlenecks.

Chapter 7 shows you how to analyze your Norton AntiVirus activity history to see if it's safe to turn off some of the automation.

Besides these two common ways to limit slowness, you can do other things to try to improve performance, even if you choose the most automated options. People who watch virus trends for a living say that many infected files are passed through unsolicited e-mail, the scourge we call *spam*. Thus, do what you can to reduce the amount of spam you receive. The idea is less spam, less files. If you have Norton AntiSpam, use it. Other programs are also available — as commercial products, as shareware that you can try before you buy, or as freeware you can use for your personal system.

Telling Norton What to Do

When Norton AntiVirus first installs, it's set to AutoProtect mode, a fancy way of saying it's signed you up for continuous monitoring with all the major features turned on for the most comprehensive scanning. Although Chapter 7 of this book gives you more in-depth coverage of tweaking your settings, here I show you what Norton AntiVirus sets up automatically, how to turn it off, and how to tweak it a bit.

Viewing your current setup

To view your current setup:

1. **Launch Norton AntiVirus.**

2. **Click Options near the top-left corner of the Norton Antivirus window.**

3. **Look at the checked (turned on) features listed in the AutoProtect window (see Figure 4-1).**

**Book VI
Chapter 4**

Choosing Your
Scanning Options

Figure 4-1:
The
AutoProtect
features
running.

The first three items checked make sure AutoProtect is on continuously or at least until you turn it off. If you click to remove the check from one or more of these check boxes, you begin to diminish AutoProtect's constant coverage. Turn off all three, and AutoProtect is completed shut down.

Temporarily disabling AutoProtect

If you just need to turn off AutoProtect once in a while, here's a less drastic method:

1. **Right-click the Norton AntiVirus icon in your System Tray.**

2. **Click Disable AutoProtect.**

   The Protection Alert window appears.

3. **Click on the down-arrow next to 15 minutes, and choose the length of time you want to disable AutoProtect (see Figure 4-2).**

4. **Click OK.**

My recommendation is to leave AutoProtect on until Norton AntiVirus has a few days to run on your PC. If running the program all the time in the background — what all programs with icons sitting in the System Tray, in the lower-right corner of the desktop, do — doesn't interfere with your work or slow down your PC, you don't have to change any of the settings.

Figure 4-2:
Temporarily
turn off
AutoProtect.

Chapter 4 tells you about how Norton determines what to do with the threats it identifies.

Enabling SmartScan

When you're looking at the AutoProtect window in Norton AntiVirus, you may be wondering about the SmartScan option under Which File Types to Scan for Viruses. SmartScan is an alternative to the already enabled continuous scanning that tells Norton to scan only for files of a particular type, like executable files (ending in .exe or .com), which is the file extension used for most programs.

So far, not every type of file has been successfully hacked to carry a virus. Just on your hard drive alone, maybe the majority of the files stored there can't be infected. What SmartScan does is let the scanner concentrate only on those files that are at risk.

Norton has already programmed AntiVirus's SmartScan to look through most important file types. If you want to add more file types to watch because you think you may have a problem with a specific file type, or you want to remove certain file types from the list because these get checked through some other means, you can change what SmartScan checks. To do so, follow these steps:

1. **Select Scan Files Using SmartScan (see Figure 4-3).**

Notice this turns off the top (recommended) option.

2. **To view and customize the file type list, click Customize.**

3. **From the Program File Extension window (see Figure 4-4), you do one of three things:**

- Just view the file types listed.

- Click New to add a file extension type (the three-character suffix at the end of a filename (for example, .exe or .doc).

- Remove a listed file type by pointing to it, and then click Remove.

4. Click OK, and then OK again to close AutoProtect.

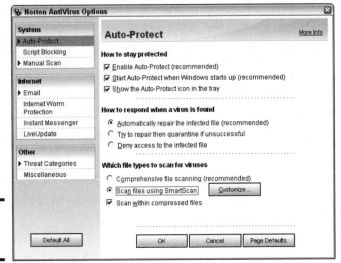

Figure 4-3:
Choosing
SmartScan.

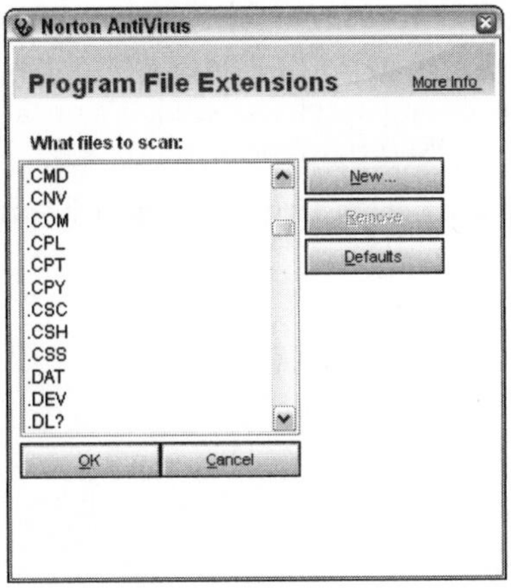

Figure 4-4:
Viewing
scan-
worthy file
types.

Configuring for Instant Messaging and E-Mail

Norton AntiVirus does more than just check files already stored on your drive(s) for virus infection. It can also check both incoming and outgoing e-mail, as well as files traded through popular Internet messaging programs including:

✦ AOL Instant Messenger (AIM)

✦ MSN/Windows Messenger

✦ Yahoo Messenger (version 5.0 and later)

When you first install Norton AntiVirus, it's already configured to check these messaging services, as well as the e-mail you send and receive. You can change these settings as needed or desired. For example, you may not use messaging services at all or you may not use them to transfer files (the result: reduced risk and probably no need to scan).

Instant messages

To view your current configuration to scan messaging files, follow these steps:

1. **Open Norton AntiVirus.**

2. **Click the Options button near the top-left corner of the Norton AntiVirus window.**

The AutoProtect screen opens.

3. **Click Email or Instant Messenger from the left-hand task pane.**

4. **The Instant Messenger screen opens, as shown in Figure 4-5.**

Before you even reach the Instant Messenger screen, Norton AntiVirus has checked to see which instant messaging programs you have installed. If you don't see all your messaging services listed, it's because Norton AntiVirus supports only a few IM programs currently.

5. **Click to remove the checkmark from any features you want to turn off.**

6. **Click OK.**

E-mails

Now let's view your options for configuring how Norton AntiVirus works with your e-mail. To do this:

1. **Open Norton AntiVirus.**

2. **Click the Options button near the top-left corner of the Norton AntiVirus window.**

The Options window opens to the AutoProtect screen.

3. **Click Email in the left-hand task pane.**

The Email Scanning screen appears. Note that any option checked means that the option is currently set.

Book VI
Chapter 4

Choosing Your
Scanning Options

Figure 4-5:
Protected
services are
checked.

You see that several options are marked as recommended. Normally, you want to leave any recommended configuration alone. However, you can choose to experiment slightly, then modify Norton AntiVirus settings based on your results.

Here's an example. Let's say that you use Norton AntiVirus's default settings so that it regularly checks files on your system. If that's the case, then you don't need to scan all over again when you send e-mail with previously scanned files attached to it.

To tell Norton AntiVirus to stop scanning e-mail messages you send:

1. **Click to uncheck the option labeled Scan Outgoing Email.**

2. **Click OK.**

Don't change this setting unless you really do scan regularly. You won't win friends or impress the boss if you unintentionally pass a virus along.

You can also set some advanced e-mail options. To view these:

1. **Open Norton AntiVirus.**

2. **Click the Options button near the top-left corner of the Norton AntiVirus window.**

The Options window opens to the AutoProtect screen.

3. **Click Email in the left-hand task pane.**

An Advanced option appears below Email.

4. **Click Advanced to open the Advanced Email Options screen (see Figure 4-6).**

   Three choices are listed, each checked automatically:

   - **Protect against timeouts:** If you have dial-up or fussier broadband Internet access, this option tries to prevent the connection from being dropped due to the increased time needed to scan files sent or received through e-mail.

   - **Display tray icon:** This shows an active envelope icon in the Windows System Tray (the bottom-right corner of your window at the far end of the task bar) while scanning e-mail messages.

   - **Display progress indicator when sending email:** Does just that with a small window at the bottom-right of your desktop window, just above the taskbar.

5. **To disable one or more of these options, click to uncheck them; then click OK.**

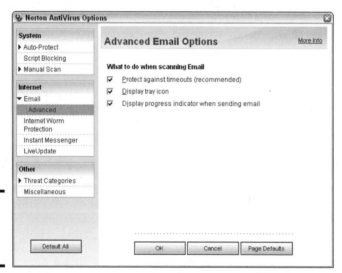

Figure 4-6: More choices for e-mail.

Protecting Yourself from Internet Worms

Among the fastest growing categories of computer-spread infections is the Internet e-mail worm. Mail worms are a little like ants in your kitchen: One isn't so bad, but by the time an army has moved in, you're in trouble.

One of the toughest parts about dealing with worms is that they *replicate* themselves, meaning they send countless copies of themselves out again and again through often innocent-looking mail messages. As the volume of worm copies builds, everything slows to a crawl trying to handle them.

In fact, these mail worms aren't just annoyances. A single widespread worm can

✦ Bring companies' network operations to a stand-still

✦ Take whole parts of the Internet down

✦ Lose untold numbers of e-mail (always the important stuff, never the ads)

✦ Account for millions of dollars of time spent globally trying to halt them

Norton AntiVirus already has protection against such worms set and ready to go when you install it. To see your settings to defeat these worms:

1. **Open Norton AntiVirus, and click Options.**

2. **Click Internet Worm Protection in the left-hand task pane.**

This opens the Worm Setting screen as shown in Figure 4-7 (*Note:* If you're using an earlier version of Norton AntiVirus than 2005, Worm Protection won't be listed.

**Book VI
Chapter 4**

**Choosing Your
Scanning Options**

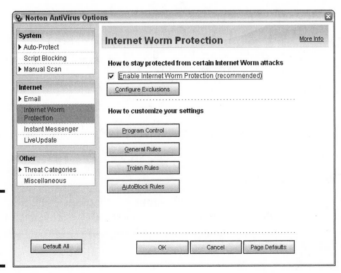

Figure 4-7:
Worm
protection
turned on.

One thing to note about the options available from the buttons on this page is that you probably don't want to change settings unless you:

✦ Have a very good reason

✦ Have some idea what you're doing (and I could fill a book with these specifics alone)

Make a bad choice and you could let worms in or deny your regular Internet programs (such as instant messaging and other software that runs when you're online) from getting and keeping a connection.

Right now, let's look without touching, moving down from the top:

1. Click Configure Exclusions.

You see a list of Internet signatures (a type of ID verification) that Norton AntiVirus says it won't monitor.

2. Click OK.

3. Click Program Control.

A list of programs Norton AntiVirus lets access the Internet (see Figure 4-8) appears. You can add more programs to the list through the Add button, change settings for the selected program if you click Modify, and take a program off the list if you select it and click Remove.

4. Click OK.

5. Click General Rules.

A list of "weak" spots or ports of entry that have been blocked off to keep a worm from getting in appears. Like with program control, you can add or remove choices here, or modify a setting.

6. Click OK.

7. Click Trojan Rules.

The different ways Trojan infections are kept out appears.

8. Click OK.

9. Click AutoBlock Rules.

This displays a list of specific computer addresses (a PC's ID number on the Internet) that Norton AntiVirus excludes because it's picked up suspicious behavior from that address. If yours is blank, no computer addresses are blocked.

10. Click OK.

11. Click OK to go back to the main Norton AntiVirus window.

If you make lots of changes to your Norton AntiVirus setup, you may reach a point where you just want to return everything to the default settings, or the way Norton AntiVirus was set to work when it was first installed. To do this, just right-click the Norton AntiVirus icon in your System Tray and choose

Norton AntiVirus Options. When the Options window opens, click the Page Defaults button at the bottom of the window.

**Book VI
Chapter 4**

**Choosing Your
Scanning Options**

Figure 4-8:
The OK'ed programs list.

Customizing Your Scans

Look at the Scan for Viruses window (see Figure 4-9) and you see several different types of scan types available. But what if you want to mix and match exactly what Norton AntiVirus checks without running two or more smaller scans or having to run a full scan. That's when you want to consider creating a custom scan just to check exactly what you want but not a thing more.

If you want, you can even schedule these custom scans to run in between full scans. This is useful if you store incoming files in the same folder or group of folders and you'd like to check them for viruses more frequently than the once a week or so you perform your exhaustive, system-wide check.

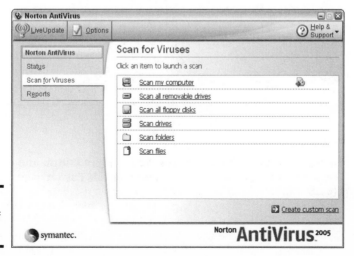

Figure 4-9:
Selection of scan types.

Creating custom scans

Do you have certain folders and/or files that you want to scan more frequently than you perform a full system scan? For example, you may have a folder of documents in which you copy files from your office to work on at home. You want to scan this folder before you open any of the transferred files. However, you don't want to perform a full scan to do this or have to go through the steps to specify this same folder again and again for spot searches.

Norton AntiVirus allows you to create a custom scan where you select the files and folders you want to include in this pick-your-own scan session, which you can run again and again, as needed.

To start this process when you're in your Web browser, follow these steps:

1. **Click the down-arrow next to the Norton AntiVirus icon on your browser toolbar.**

2. **Select Launch Scan Menu.**

3. **From the Scan for Viruses window, click Create Custom Scan.**

The Norton AntiVirus Scan Wizard opens.

4. **Click Next.**

The window shown in Figure 4-10 appears.

Figure 4-10: The Norton AntiVirus Scan Wizard helps you create your own scans.

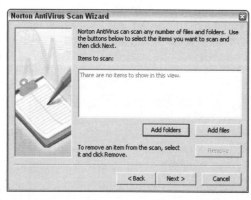

5. **To add specific folders, click the Add Folders button and click to check the folders you want to include in this custom search (see Figure 4-11).**

Figure 4-11:
Add folders
to your
custom
scan.

6. **To add specific files within a folder, click the Add Files button and click to check the files you want to include (see Figure 4-12).**

7. **When you've chosen all desired files and folders, click Next.**

8. **Type a name for your custom search.**

9. **Click Finish.**

   Norton AntiVirus automatically adds the name of your custom scan(s) to its list of scans you can perform.

Figure 4-12:
Add files to
your custom
scan.

You can repeat these steps as many times as needed to create additional custom scans. I have four or more custom scans set up at any one time. I use these to do separate scans through different folders where I store files sent to me for work as well as ones where I store files from friends. By keeping the files separate, I can quickly identify which client sent me the tainted file, so I can alert him.

In Chapter 7 of this book, I show you why it's good to contact the source of a virus (when you know the source) when you find out you've gotten an infection through that person. More about what you should do when you discover a virus in Chapter 4.

Running a custom scan

Now that you've established a custom scan, you can run it as easily as you execute any of the other types of Norton AntiVirus scans. *Remember:* It's been added to your scan list.

To perform your custom scan:

1. **Open Norton AntiVirus.**

2. **Click Scan for Viruses.**

3. **Locate your custom scan in the list and click on it (see Figure 4-13, where "Job" is the name of the custom scan created).**

Norton AntiVirus starts the scan and returns its results, just as with any other scan.

Want to run your custom or other scans when you're not sitting at the keyboard? Chapter 5 shows you how to set them up.

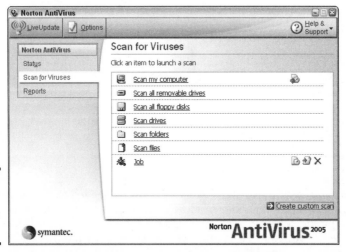

Figure 4-13: Running your custom scan.

Editing your custom scan settings

What if you discover that you forgot to include a file or folder you wanted as part of this custom scan, or what if you want to remove a file or folder from it? You edit it, that's what:

1. **Go to the Scan for Viruses window and look again for your custom scan in the list.**

2. **To its right, click Edit.**

This reopens the Norton Antivirus Scan Wizard.

3. **Click Add Folders or Add Files to add additional folders or files. To delete folders or files, select the item you want to delete from the list shown (see Figure 4-14), and click Remove.**

Figure 4-14:
Edit your
custom
scan
selections.

4. **Click Next.**

5. **To save the custom scan with the same name, click Finish.**

If you want to change the scan's name, click in the box containing the current custom scan name and type a different name; then click Finish.

Next time you run this scan, it will use your modified settings.

Deleting a custom scan

You can remove a custom scan you no longer use. To delete it, simply return to the Scan for Viruses window, look for the custom scan to remove, and click Delete. You'll be asked to confirm its removal. Click Yes.

Chapter 5: Automating and Updating Your Scanner

In This Chapter

✔ **Putting your scanner on a schedule**

✔ **Setting up a schedule for custom scans**

✔ **Knowing why you need LiveUpdate**

✔ **Downloading and installing Norton updates**

*W*ith so many new viruses and other computer infections arriving on the scene every month, the virus scanner you purchase and install this week may not be ready to fight next week's selection of new infections. This is even faster than a teenager changes his taste in music.

Considering how much risk potential is out there, you can't afford to be caught short. But who has the time to keep on top of this? You may barely have time to grab lunch or play a quick hand of Windows Solitaire as it is.

Yet, as you're about to see, Norton AntiVirus makes your job quite a bit easier by giving you the tools necessary to perform your virus scanning without your needing to remember to do so. Norton AntiVirus also provides a way to keep your scanner up-to-date to cover the most recent threats.

Scheduling Your Virus Checking

We live in an automated world where our coffeemakers can turn on at the right hour and start the morning brew just as our eyes flutter open, while another device can turn our cars on remotely to let them warm on a chilly morning.

You may already have a little experience with PC-based automation. Maybe you use it with other Norton products or directly through Windows, which includes a Task Scheduler utility to let you run maintenance tasks on a set schedule.

When you schedule your virus checking, you take the worry out of wondering if you remembered to do it. That's a big issue with any utility but incredibly important with virus checking where you increase your risk the longer you go between scans.

Picking a good time

Just as with most maintenance routines related to your PC, schedule your virus checking for times when you're not sitting, working at the desktop. If you leave your PC on when you depart the office or after you go to bed, you can have the scan run anywhere between late at night and early in the morning.

Here's another point to consider: If you have other automated system checks, like Windows Disk Defragmenter or Norton SpeedDisk, try not to set all of them up for the exact same time. For example, if you have Disk Defragmenter

scheduled for 3 a.m. on Wednesday, stagger running your virus scan for 3:30 or 4 a.m.

To see a list of tasks scheduled on your PC outside your Norton products, consult the Windows Task Scheduler. Choose Start ⇨ Control Panel, and then double-click on Scheduled Tasks from Classic view (click Classic view from the left-hand task pane). Everything currently scheduled for the PC, including the Norton tools scheduled through Norton products like Norton AntiVirus, is displayed (see the nearby figure).

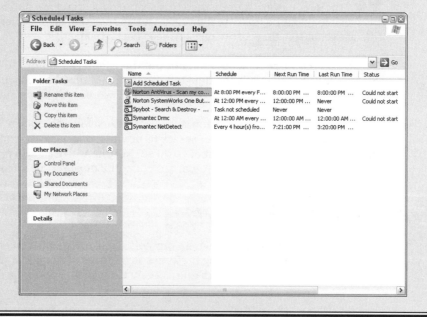

 Automating your virus checking has another big advantage: Scanning when you're not in the middle of other work or play is usually best. It's about more than the distraction of having another window open — it's about performance. Run Norton AntiVirus with lots of files open, and the desktop slows considerably. This is especially true if you have Norton AntiVirus set to check through everything from e-mail to file downloads to instant messaging.

Scheduling your scan

When you decide you want to automate your scans (good choice), you want to set its schedule. You can tell Norton AntiVirus to run daily, weekly, or on a unique schedule of your own design.

You can start by creating an initial schedule. Just follow these steps:

1. **Open Norton AntiVirus.**

2. **From the System Status window (shown in Figure 5-1), click Scan for Viruses from the left-hand menu.**

   The Scan for Viruses screen appears.

3. **Locate Scan My Computer at the top of the list; move along this row to the right, and click the Schedule icon.**

   The Schedule tab appears, as shown in Figure 5-2.

**Book VI
Chapter 5**

**Automating and
Updating Your
Scanner**

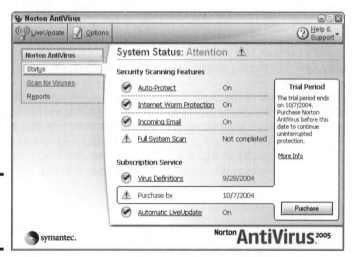

Figure 5-1:
The System
Scan
window.

4. **Click New.**

5. **Click the Schedule Task drop-down list to choose the frequency with which to perform this scan.**

6. **Use the Start Time up and down arrows to select the time you want the scan to run.**

7. **Under Schedule Task Weekly, use the arrows to choose what day of the week to perform the scan.**

8. **When you're done, click OK.**

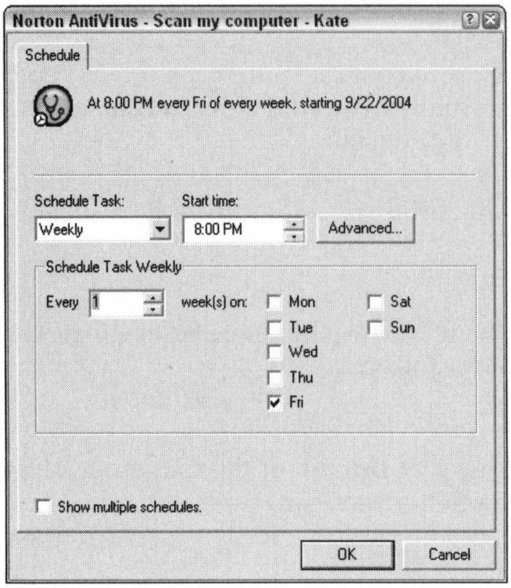

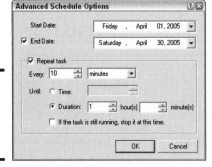

Figure 5-2:
Set your
scanning
schedule
in the
Schedule
window.

Refer to Figure 5-2 and you notice a couple of things not mentioned in the steps. First, you have an Advanced button. Click this, and you open a window, shown in Figure 5-3, where you can set a specific range of dates (example: April 1 through April 30) during which to keep this schedule. Click OK to close it.

Next, at the bottom of the main Schedule window, you see a check box (unchecked) marked Show Multiple Schedules. This is available because you can actually put your scanner on more than one schedule. For example, you can set up a full scan to occur every Friday at 5 p.m., as well as set up one that occurs Wednesday at 6 a.m. If you check this check box, you can see your multiple schedules when you have more than one set.

Figure 5-3:
Specify
advanced
scheduling
options.

Modifying the schedule

When you need to modify your schedule, just repeat the steps you took for setting your initial schedule. However, instead of clicking New in Step 4, click in the drop-down list at the top of the window and select the scan number to modify. If you have just one scan scheduled, you don't need to select one. After you've made your change, click OK.

Deleting a scan schedule

If you decide you want to delete one or more scan schedules so that you can run them manually, you need to go back into the scheduler. To do this, follow these steps:

1. **Open Norton AntiVirus.**

2. **From the System Status window, click Scan for Viruses.**

3. **Click the Schedule button to the right of Scan My Computer.**

The Schedule window opens. If you have just one scan scheduled, it will automatically be selected in the top drop-down list.

4. **If you have more than one scan, click within the drop-down list (see Figure 5-4), select the scan you want to delete, and then press your Delete key.**

5. **Click OK to close the Schedule window.**

When you delete your automated scan(s), you have to remember to run the scanner yourself.

Book VI
Chapter 5

Automating and
Updating Your
Scanner

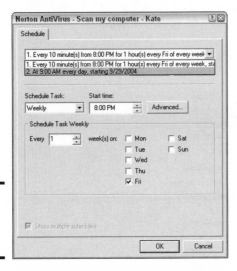

Figure 5-4: Delete a scan schedule.

Scheduling your custom scan

In Chapter 2 of this book, I show you how to create custom scans. Would it help if you could run your custom scan automatically, at a time you set, every day or every week? This way, you wouldn't have to remember to execute it yourself. Also, if you create more than one custom scan, you can set up schedules for each so that all of them get run around the same basic time.

Here's how you place your scans on a schedule:

1. **Open Norton AntiVirus.**

2. **Click Scan for Viruses in the left-hand menu.**

The Scan for Viruses window appears.

3. **Locate your custom scan in the list; then, at the right, click the first of the three icons at the right of your custom scan name, as shown in Figure 5-5.**

A window opens named for your custom scan.

4. **To add a task to the schedule, click New.**

5. **Click the drop-down list under Schedule Task and choose the frequency with which you want this scan to occur.**

6. **Use the Start Time up and down arrows to select the time you want the scan to run.**

7. **Under Schedule Task Weekly, click to check the day on which the scan should run.**

Figure 5-6 shows you an example schedule.

8. **Repeat Steps 3 through 8 to establish schedules for any additional custom scans.**

9. **When you're done, click OK.**

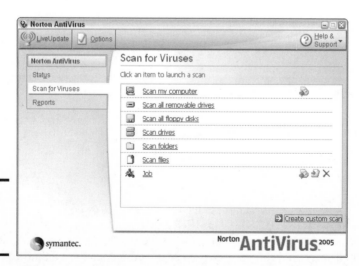

Figure 5-5:
Click the
Schedule
icon.

Figure 5-6:
Select the
frequency
and time.

If later, you decide you want to adjust the schedule for your scan, you can re-select the custom scan and click the Schedule icon again to modify the given schedule.

Using LiveUpdate

Don't you love it when a feature's name makes it crystal clear what it does? If only all would be so simple.

LiveUpdate is the feature within certain Norton products like Norton AntiVirus that allows you to keep your software up-to-date. For Norton AntiVirus specifically, this means downloading the latest virus definitions, also called *virus signatures,* to update your scanner so it can detect and defeat the most recently released threats.

However, you'll find that besides the virus definitions, LiveUpdate may also provide updates to files within your antivirus package.

Knowing what you face

LiveUpdate requires an open connection to the Internet. If you're using Norton AntiVirus on a PC where you have no means of connecting to the Internet, it's going to be impossible to take advantage of this option.

You may use a broadband connection, like cable or DSL, which is always on. But if you use a dial-up connection over a phone line, you'll want to connect manually before you launch LiveUpdate.

Some people — especially those using a slower-speed dial-up Internet connection rather than higher-speed broadband like cable and DSL service — avoid using the LiveUpdate tool because they mistakenly believe it's a very long download. Yet you aren't downloading the whole Norton AntiVirus program, just relatively small packets of updates. Even on a dial-up connection, this rarely takes more than a few minutes.

LiveUpdate does all the work for you. Although you can make selections ("I'll take this but not that"), simply accepting all the files LiveUpdate offers and following the onscreen prompts to finish is normally smart. When the update is done, the changes downloaded are automatically applied to Norton AntiVirus without your assistance.

Performing a LiveUpdate

Before you perform your first update, you need to know how often to do it. To some degree, that's entirely up to you. Symantec reports that it provides an update to its virus definitions at least once a month and, usually, more frequently than that. Some choose to check once a week; others wait out the month. I'd recommend you check at least every few weeks and make a point of doing so if you hear about a hot new infection going around.

Follow these steps to run LiveUpdate:

1. **Launch Norton AntiVirus.**

2. **From the System Status window, click LiveUpdate.**

The first window you see is a list of the LiveUpdate-compatible Norton components installed on your PC, as shown in Figure 5-7.

3. **Click Next.**

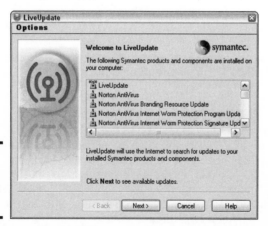

Figure 5-7:
Norton
products on
your PC.

A window appears telling you LiveUpdate is connecting to Symantec and searching for updates to your installed components. Don't press anything while it searches. If it finds none, it will report this to you. You can then close LiveUpdate. Otherwise, LiveUpdate displays a list of updates it's located for you (see Figure 5-8). By default, all are checked (meaning they're selected for download).

4. **If you absolutely don't want something, click to uncheck it.**

   Think before you deselect something — if you deselect it, your computer won't be armed with all the latest protection.

**Book VI
Chapter 5**

Automating and
Updating Your
Scanner

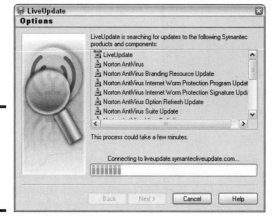

Figure 5-8:
LiveUpdate reports list of updates to your software.

5. **Click Next.**

   Once the updates are downloaded, a new window tells you that it's in the process of installing your updates. When complete, it notifies you (see Figure 5-9).

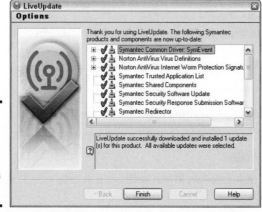

Figure 5-9:
After installation, Live Update's job is done.

6. **Click Finish.**

Note that, occasionally, after performing a LiveUpdate and clicking Finish, you'll see an additional screen, like the one shown in Figure 5-10. This window tells you that in order to finish the LiveUpdate installation, your PC needs to be restarted. You can restart immediately, or you can opt to wait to let the final installation occur the next time you restart your PC. Which you do normally doesn't matter. However, many updates won't require a restart.

Figure 5-10:
You may
need to
restart
your PC.

> **Restart Needed to Finish Installation**
>
> We recommend that you restart your computer to finish installing the new updates. Do you want to:
>
> ⦿ Restart your computer now.
> ○ Continue working with Windows.
>
> If you decide to restart your computer now, please save all your unsaved work before pressing the OK button.
>
> [OK]

If you don't restart your system often, you may want to restart as soon as possible after a LiveUpdate. This way, days don't go by in between the update and the final installation. You don't want to take the risk that an update to your virus scanner prevents it from catching a fresh-off-the-virus-press infection.

Using LiveUpdate Express Mode

You can modify LiveUpdate so that it doesn't require you to step through the process (called Interactive Mode). This way, called Express Mode, an update can be performed without your sitting there pressing the Next button.

Change to Express Mode when you want to automate the process and don't feel a need to pick and choose which files LiveUpdate provides you. However, if you prefer to know what you're getting, stay with Interactive Mode.

To switch to Express Mode operation:

1. **In Norton AntiVirus, click LiveUpdate.**

2. **From the LiveUpdate window, choose Options⇨Configure.**

The LiveUpdate configuration window opens to the General tab.

3. **Click Express Mode.**

You're notified that Express Mode settings will take effect next time LiveUpdate runs.

4. **Under Express Mode settings, click to check both or either options, if desired (see Figure 5-11).**

5. **Click OK to finish.**

You can also run LiveUpdate from the Windows Control Panel. Just double-click the Symantec LiveUpdate icon to launch it.

Book VI Chapter 5

Automating and Updating Your Scanner

Figure 5-11: Select Express Mode settings.

Figuring out what to do when LiveUpdate doesn't work

Depending on your type of Internet connection, you may find that using the LiveUpdate feature either doesn't work well for you or often fails to connect.

If you experience this problem, don't stop updating Norton AntiVirus. Instead, use an available Internet connection to visit the Symantec Web site at http://securityresponse.symantec.com/avcenter/download.html.

If you're using a PC that isn't connected to the Internet, you may want to download the updates on a computer where you have access. Then you could store these updates on a recordable CD or DVD, which you can then insert in your non-connected PC and install. To do this, you may want to create a folder you name "Norton Updates" or something similar. Go to the aforementioned Symantec site and download the files to this folder. Then use Windows XP or your CD/DVD burner software to copy these files to a recordable CD/DVD.

Chapter 6: Snooping on the Snoopers: Spyware and Adware

In This Chapter

✓ Understanding what spyware and adware is

✓ Identifying how it gets on your PC

✓ Knowing how Norton AntiVirus scans for spyware and adware

✓ Finding out about alternatives

Don't look around right now, but someone's watching you.

Who? That's a very good question. The problem with answering the question of who is that there may be more than one person or company and they may be monitoring you in such a way as to slip in completely under your radar. Even when you discover these monitoring programs it's tough to find out who sent them and even harder to get these snoopers to leave.

No, don't turn around. You won't see them over there. They're in your PC, hiding, watching, and waiting. If you think you're alone at the keyboard, think again.

This chapter looks at secretive snoopers called spyware and adware that are designed to transfer to your system to track information about you. What I tell you here isn't meant to make you paranoid, just motivated to get rid of them.

You'll find out how Norton AntiVirus can help identify and remove some of these snoopers. I also share some additional utilities you can try if you're using Norton products other than Norton AntiVirus or want to see what Norton AntiVirus could miss.

Knowing Who's Watching You

Just about anyone who wants to watch you also has access to your PC. All those great ways you can interact with others, download a wealth of cool files, and visit various Web sites online conspire to make you fairly susceptible.

Don't think only sleazy Web sites pass snooping software along to you. Some of the biggest, most prestigious companies in the U.S. and the world either produce — or contract with specialists to create — tools to mine information about you, from you. This practice is often referred to by the more socially acceptable term, *data mining*.

Plus, don't forget that anyone who can come along and sit down at your keyboard for just a few seconds to a few minutes could leave something unwanted behind. In any given week, I must see a dozen products offered that give everyday people a way to spy on their co-workers and loved ones, online and off. In the following sections, I tell you about some of the PC-based snoopers.

Spyware, adware, and snoopware defined

Terms like *spyware, adware, snoopware, scumware,* and *parasite software* get used pretty much interchangeably, but these terms don't always mean the very same thing. Some of these programs log information about you but don't look for details any more specific than what you're interesting in buying. Others aggressively record everything you type and do on your PC. Here's the skinny on these various menaces:

✦ **Spyware** is frequently used to identify the major form of *adware,* although it can also mean snoopware defined later in this list. Adware is a type of program that monitors your Web browsing habits and then tries to feed back to you ads — delivered in e-mail or as pop-up ads — that either increase the likelihood you'll buy the product you're looking at or tempt you with the alternatives offered by a competitor. This is advertising in the Internet age.

✦ **Adware** can refer to two different types of software. One is spyware and the other refers to software offered for free or at a reduced cost in exchange for showing you lots of advertisements. This second type is also called ad-sponsored freeware or marketing ware.

✦ Then there's true **snoopware.** Almost since the very minute PCs began rolling off the assembly lines, people have produced special tools whose only purpose is to watch how people use their PCs. A certain amount of this is legitimate: Some snoopware just checks to see what resources you use most often so some decision-maker can tell what's most needed so they can chuck the rest.

Snoopware and keyboard tracking software are also grouped into spyware, but their purpose can be quite a bit more malicious or intrusive than adware also called spyware. I've separated them in this chapter to reduce the confusion.

Norton products define spyware strictly as the snooper-style programs.

Ads that go pop

Pop-up ads are small ads that appear in their own separate window when you visit a Web site in your Web browser. You may notice some pop-ups are getting pretty aggressive. Some do their very best to keep you from closing them. They trick you by moving the "X" mark to close them from its usual place at the top-right corner of the window. Or they require you to say Yes or No to the ad offer, only for you to learn that if you click Yes to close or No you don't want the ad, you get transported to the Web site sponsoring the ad against your will.

Among the worst of them are those pop-ups that offer you help (like the one shown in the figure).

If you don't take the time to look at it fully, you might think it's a message from Windows itself. But it's not. Click Yes or No, and you go to their Web site. Me? I don't usually seek help from or do business with people whose first contact with me is to lie or manipulate. If you can't trust someone's greeting, what can you trust?

Remember: Not all pop-ups are bad. Some alert you to information you really do want and many non-sales sites use them to provide details not available from the page itself or to provide a form for you to type in details you freely offer to give.

What spyware and adware does

Meet spyware and adware. Whether you know it or not, you've probably already been introduced.

One day you go to a Web site that offers the latest and greatest Panasonic cameras. While you browse through the selections, you suddenly notice pop-up ads appear offering Nikon or Fujifilm cameras featured by a totally different sales site. You might think, "That's strange," but it doesn't occur to you something's up until these pop-ups seem to be targeting you for the exact type of camera you're shopping for. As you look for specific features on a Panasonic, the pop-ups respond by giving you competing cameras with those same features.

Is this intrusion or help? That judgment lies in the eye of the beholder. You may really appreciate the help or it might just make you curse.

To best monitor your Web habits, these programs need to reside on your PC so they get passed to you in different ways, such as:

✦ Through a Web site application that downloads and runs in your browser

✦ Through free software you choose to download

✦ As file attachments in e-mail sent to you when you register at a Web site or otherwise expose your e-mail address to sites you visit

✦ Attached to legitimate software you install on your PC

Not all of this happens secretly. There are Web sites that offer you software and when you accept it, they present a license or user agreement that may spell out the fact that spyware/adware is part of the package. You must agree to this before you can start the download. The problem is that most people don't read these agreements. They're long and filled with legalese while you just want the software. So you click, giving your virtual signatures in agreement and then get more than you bargained for.

Looking over your shoulder for snoopware

Not all spies wear a trench coat or dark glasses. And it's no urban myth: There are programs out there whose sole purpose is to record everything you type or click.

Think about that! How many times do you type in your passwords, your account names, and your address? How would you feel if someone eavesdropped on your e-mail, your instant messages, and your chat-room conversation? Are you sure it isn't happening to you right now?

Almost since the very minute PCs began rolling off the assembly lines, people have produced special tools whose only purpose is to watch how people use their PCs. A certain amount of this is legitimate: Some snoopware just checks to see what resources you use most often so some decision-maker — like your boss or network administrator at work — can tell what's most needed so he can chuck the rest.

Snoopware, which is also called spyware, tracks some or all of your PC activities. These can be as simple as tools that help someone know when you go online (so he can find you to chat). Others are sophisticated enough to record every little thing and quietly report the results back to a spy.

True snoopware, unlike the spyware-adware, is much more apt to be employed by someone who wants to find out information from you specifically. They may want your name and address so they can send you traditional junk mail. Some want your financial details like bank and credit-card account numbers. Then there are those who just want to know everything about you.

Today, some bosses take advantage of these snoopers to tell which of their employees is visiting Web sites they shouldn't during the workday or to spy on what's being said over network or Internet chat rooms or messaging services like ICQ and AIM.

Is this legal?

Laws differ all around the nation related to computers. But in many areas, there's nothing on the law books that strictly *and* effectively prevents advertisers or the people who do marketing research or anyone else from sending you one of these files, secretly or not. The Internet is a global beast and even when a community enacts anti-ad laws, they usually don't apply outside the city limits.

Data mining is a highly profitable industry today just as advertising has always been. The folks behind these programs argue that they aren't doing anything wrong because they aren't spying on you specifically, just trying to target you intelligently with the kinds of products and services you seem to want.

Many insist they don't try to obtain any data that uniquely identifies you. They also say they're helping reduce the amount of unsolicited ads they send to your e-mailbox because they can deliver it as pop-up ads you can close.

Yet some send you spam as well, although they say it's also targeted to offer you only those things for which you've already expressed an interest. Considering how chock-full your virtual mailbox is and how many ads you probably get for products you would never buy, it's hard to imagine anybody trying to reduce your spam.

These snooping tools — often called *keyboard recorders* — are seen much less often than spyware and adware. Also, it's much more likely that the keyboard trackers will be installed purposely by someone with access to your PC rather than downloaded unwittingly over the Internet.

What keyboard recorders record can be sent back to the "spy" in different ways:

+ Automatically through e-mail
+ Through a Web browser when you visit a particular site
+ While you're connected to instant messaging or a chat room
+ As a hidden file on your PC where a person can retrieve it later

Some people install keyboard snoopers as a practical joke. A friend's teenager installed a keyboard snooper on his mom's PC, admitting later he thought it was like being able to read her diary. Yet you have to assume that most people who install this stuff really want to snoop on you. These days, you hear about them being used by a spouse in a nasty divorce case, a boss trying to get the goods on an employee, or parents who feel the need to know *everything* their child is doing. You'll even see online stores that specialize in spying products (hidden cameras and secret microphones) hawking such software.

But there's one more thing to understand: Not all keyboard trackers run as software. Visit www.keyghost.com and you'll see a keyboard tracker that leaves no program behind to be detected by Norton AntiVirus or another threat checker.

With some, a small device installs between your PC and keyboard that stores a certain amount of data. If you don't know much about PC hardware or rarely look behind your PC where the keyboard connects (see Figure 6-1 with no snooper connected), you might never know you're being watched.

Yet even if you decide to pull the PC out to look behind it, you have to know what you're looking for — and it could be tough to tell a "snooper" from a normal piece of hardware.

Follow the keyboard cable down from the connection shown in Figure 6-1 and you might see a strange connector, like that in Figure 6-2. If you know that *most* keyboards have a solid cable that runs between the keyboard and PC (wireless keyboards don't have the cable), you might get suspicious.

But what you're seeing is an adapter that switches my USB keyboard into one that can attach through my keyboard port. No spies here. Still, a piece of spy hardware is probably going to look like just another piece of equipment. There won't be any large sign attached alerting you that they're spying on you.

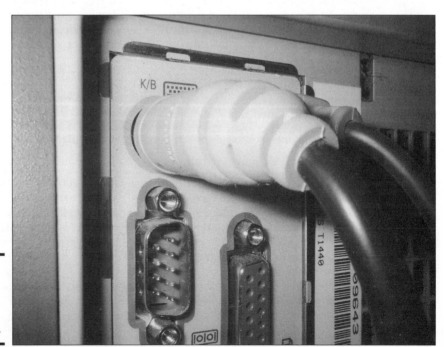

Figure 6-1:
The keyboard port with connection.

Figure 6-2:
Is this a
spy?

Studies show people either don't believe they're being spied on so they don't watch for it, or they see spies everywhere. Reality probably lies somewhere in between.

The difficulty in removing spyware, adware, and snoopware

If you're expecting your Web browser or Windows to protect you against all these intrusions, think again. Web browsers are designed to give you easy access to the entire Internet rather than to keep intruders out. All browsers allow you to set some degree of security and parental controls, but they still won't address the issue of unwanted file transfers.

For example, here's how to look at your advanced options for configuring the Microsoft Internet Explorer Web browser:

1. **Launch Internet Explorer.**

2. **Select Tools⇨Internet Options.**

3. **From the Internet Options window, select the Advanced tab (see Figure 6-3).**

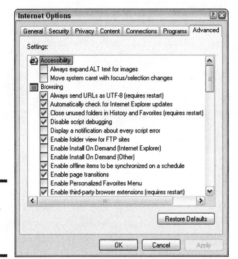

Figure 6-3:
No help for blocking adware.

Don't assume you're safe

I got interested in the subject of defeating spyware and snoopware when I happened to run my first spyware checker and discovered I had 127 of these little blood-suckers on my system. Can you imagine?

I'm a PC pro. I know what to avoid and I take lots of precautions (firewall, advanced security through Windows XP Professional, and special network tools, to name just a few). So if I can pick up more than 100 in just a few months, I wondered what was happening to people who didn't know as much about PC security and even less about how the industry can use your own tools against you.

What I found in my research was astounding. No one spyware checker seems to catch and neutralize everything. In one day, I ran five different checkers with each one discovering at least a few trackers that the ones I ran before it did not. Not every checker could disable or eliminate every piece of spyware.

That's not entirely the fault of the checkers. Just as hackers learn how to exploit security flaws, the people who want to monitor your Web habits or PC activities learn to work around the common things such spyware checkers look for so they can escape detection.

The software constantly evolves so it can stay viable even though savvy consumers like you know they exist. In turn, the folks who write spyware checkers continuously update their programs to try to catch more of their workarounds, which means the spyware producers change theirs again, and so on. It's a vicious and speedy cycle.

Or I can save you the trip and tell you there's really nothing there to help. You can't block pop-up windows or make any changes that can cut these intruder-ware packages off at the pass.

For this assistance, you need to look outside your browser and Windows to programs that can reduce your potential for receiving them. Norton AntiVirus is one of them, and there are many others available, including some that are free to use. I take you through Norton AntiVirus first, then show you some other options you can try.

But if you noticed I said "reduce" rather than "eliminate," there's a reason. There's a lot of variation in these checkers and they don't spot, block, or kill everything. Read the "Don't assume you're safe" sidebar to find out more.

Configuring Norton AntiVirus to Scan

Norton AntiVirus treats any kind of possible intrusion or annoyance like those we've discussed as a threat. The threats it can recognize include the following:

+ Viruses and worms.

+ Spyware and adware.

+ Remote-access programs (these can allow someone to take control of your PC remotely); however, not all remote-access programs are bad — technical-support people often use remote-access programs to look at your system while you're on the phone to them so they can see what you have and how it's configured.

+ Hacker tools (utilities hackers may try to pass you that will give them access to all or part of your PC or Internet connection).

+ Dialers (programs that can sit in the background, using your phone line to dial out to others like a giant speed dialer; you might see strange long-distance charges appear on your phone bill).

+ Prankware (practical joke–style software that either changes the way your keyboard or programs behave or make it seem like a virus or hacker has attacked you).

+ Other security risks (identified problem programs that may not necessarily do damage but are known to be passed around).

Just by the way it works, Norton AntiVirus will try to block pop-up windows and adware or spyware that attempts to pass onto your desktop. This way, you don't have to turn on the checking in Norton AntiVirus because it's already there. Instead, you configure which threats you want Norton AntiVirus to take most seriously.

Understanding the limitations

Spyware and adware change regularly to try to avoid detection. The result is that no one program seems to do a perfect job of eliminating all the threats that are available at any given moment.

Because Norton AntiVirus's catch capabilities get boosted regularly through LiveUpdate, there's a good possibility the spyware it doesn't spot and kill in its first pass may get taken care of on the next. Yet you also may want to give Norton AntiVirus some backup by using at least one other spy and ad checker. This may increase your odds of keeping your system clean.

The pop-up ad I show you in the "Ads that go pop" sidebar came through right after I activated Norton AntiVirus to cover pop-up ad blocking. I also had another very good pop-up ad blocker running. It's not that they fail to block ads; they just don't block them all.

Setting your options

Without your changing anything, Norton AntiVirus is already set up to try to catch and block all the threat types we've already discussed. But it doesn't hurt to check these settings to be sure that no one else with access to your PC has changed them.

Follow these steps to check your settings:

1. **Open Norton AntiVirus.**

2. **Click Options.**

3. **From the AutoProtect window (see Figure 6-4), click Threat Categories from the left-hand task pane.**

4. **In the categories list shown in Figure 6-5, look to make sure that all threats you want covered are checked (turned on). Click to check those you want handled that aren't (or click to uncheck any you don't want to block).**

5. **Click OK.**

Watching your threats

With Norton AntiVirus configured to check for adware and other spyware, it will look for these as part of the scans you run. If it locates one or more of these during the search, you'll see the numbers tally up in the scan progress window.

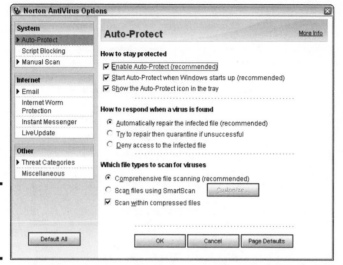

Figure 6-4:
Choose
Threat
Categories.

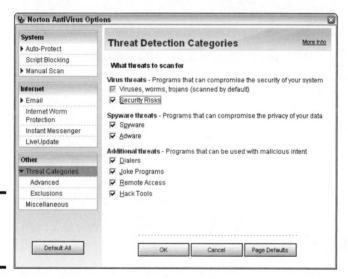

Figure 6-5:
Checked
threats are
monitored.

It will report these in the Scan: Summary (see Figure 6-6) you see when a scan finishes. Yet you're more likely to see them come up in the Repair Wizard window (see Figure 6-7) because they can't be "fixed" like viruses and other types of threats.

When you see a screen like this, follow directions to delete these threats to remove them from your computer.

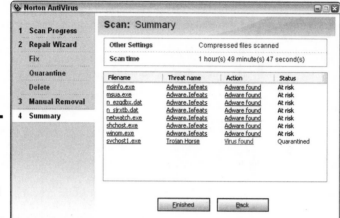

Figure 6-6:
Scan:
Summary
gets both
adware and
Trojan.

Figure 6-7:
Norton
AntiVirus
reports
adware
found.

Trying Other Options

The search for the best snooper eliminator can be elusive. Finding just one program that can spot everything is difficult. But who wants to run a dozen of these programs at once?

If you're not too bothered by ad-based spyware, just run Norton AntiVirus or a similar program (if you don't have Norton AntiVirus among your Norton software) to pick up what it can. But if you're inclined to shut the gates and bar the door, you may want to try some of the other utilities available.

My favorites are the following:

✦ **BillP Studio's WinPatrol** (www.winpatrol.com): This software offers comprehensive coverage to defeat all types of spyware, viruses, unwanted browser add-ons, and browser hijack tools; people like the cute watchdog icon in the System Tray and that WinPatrol gives you details about processes that could and/or should be running on your system.

✦ **LavaSoft Ad-Aware** (www.lavasoftusa.com): This is an often-recommended and highly aggressive adware/spyware eliminator; it's good at differentiating Windows Registry changes from spyware.

✦ **SpyBot Search and Destroyer** (http://security.kolla.de): This is an award-winning anti-adware and spyware tool that also blocks pop-up ads (see Figure 6-8).

Figure 6-8:
SpyBot blocks a browser pop-up.

Running multiple virus or spyware and adware checkers simultaneously isn't a good idea. Instead of giving you super protection, they can compete with each other for resources. They can even mistake one another for adware!

Here's a better idea. Run Norton AntiVirus, SpyBot, or WinPatrol for regular or continuous monitoring, but turn them off once or twice a week so you can perform a full-system check with a second tool. It allows you to spot-check and get rid of more invaders. You also get an idea of which works best for you so you can make it your default checker.

Chapter 7: Threat Monitoring and Tweaking Norton AntiVirus

In This Chapter

✔ Using Log Viewer to review connection and threat activities

✔ Assessing your situation

✔ Knowing when to increase or reduce the amount of time Norton AntiVirus scans

There's one last important subject to tackle. For this step, your PC needs your eyes in addition to Norton AntiVirus.

Here we can put to use the information Norton AntiVirus collects for you during its scans, analyze them, and see what you can discover from it to reduce your overall risk of infection or intrusion. When you know how often you see problems and where they come from, you may want to adjust your Norton AntiVirus setup to either run more or less frequently.

Using Log Viewer to Investigate Your Threats

Every time Norton AntiVirus encounters something suspicious and every time it repairs, quarantines, deletes, or marks a file at risk — with or without your help —an entry is recorded in the Activity Log. Norton AntiVirus keeps all these details so you can go back to look them over from time to time to see what's been happening. The Log Viewer tool takes all those entries and organizes them into categories to give you a better idea of what you're looking at.

How often you review your log really depends on you and how you use Norton AntiVirus. If Norton AntiVirus runs pretty much on its own with little interaction from you, you can miss a lot of the juicy and scary details unless you consult your Log regularly (say, once a week or so).

Viewing your Log

There are two major ways you can open your Log Viewer:

♦ In Norton AntiVirus, simply click Reports in the left-hand menu and then select View Activity Log from the Reports window (in earlier versions, you may need to choose View Report next to the Activity Log).

✦ If you're using your Web browser, click the down-arrow next to the Norton AntiVirus icon and select View Activity Log.

Whichever way you open the Log Viewer, the same window opens, as shown in Figure 7-1.

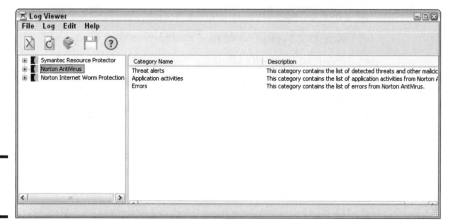

Figure 7-1:
Your Log
Viewer.

Near the top of the viewer you see a menu bar with the following choices, which you can click to view separate drop-down menus:

✦ **File:** Lets you set viewer options or exit the viewer

✦ **Log:** Allows you to refresh (update) or clear all categories or to disable logging altogether (not recommended)

✦ **Edit:** Lets you copy entries or select all entries in a category

✦ **Help:** Opens Norton AntiVirus Help to get more information

Below the menu bar you see a short and simple toolbar (shown in Figure 7-2) with just a few options. These include, moving left to right:

Figure 7-2:
The Log
Viewer
toolbar.

✦ Delete entries in the selected category

✦ Display new log entries in a chosen category

✦ Print a hard copy of log entries in the current category

✦ Save a list of entries for the selected category as a text file

✦ Get help for the specified category

Now look at the three categories shown on the left side of the viewer window. Click the plus sign next to each to expand them to show subcategories in the larger pane to the right (see Figure 7-3). Then you can click on a subcategory to see the entries in the larger pane. Each category has a specific focus.

Note, too, that you may or may not see three entries here. Different versions or packages may change these listings slightly.

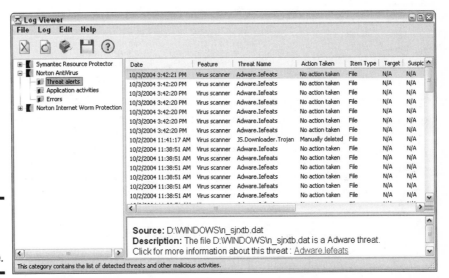

Figure 7-3:
Expand the
categories
to see more.

Using Symantec Resource Protector

This category logs any and all attempts by a connection or program to make some unauthorized change to the operation of Norton AntiVirus. You see entries for this when a site or an individual is trying to do something that could disable Norton AntiVirus or otherwise give an Internet worm or a hack attack entry. As you can see in Figure 7-4, someone tried very hard to do that on the two days listed here.

Click Alerts and then select one of the entries from the right-hand list. Now look down at the bottom of the pane and it will explain what culprit (referred to as *actor*) tried to access which file (called *target*).

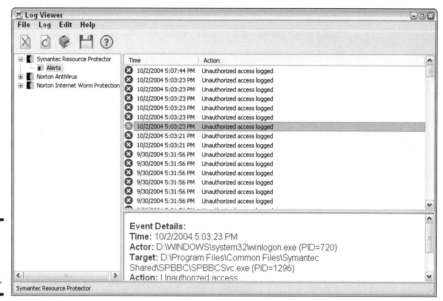

Figure 7-4:
Logging
unauthor-
ized access.

Besides the real troubles reported through the Alerts section here, you also see entries for normal, nonsuspicious activity. For example, if Norton AntiVirus crashes on your desktop and you press Ctrl+Alt+Delete to bring up Task Manager to try to force-close it so you can continue working, this will show up under Alerts because Windows is trying to shut the non-responding window.

Looking at categories from Norton AntiVirus

Check this category when you want information about your non-worm Norton AntiVirus problems and events. Click to expand this option from Log Viewer's left-hand pane and you open three subcategories:

✦ **Threat Alerts:** Click here for a record of all suspicious files and activities that Norton AntiVirus intercepted (successfully or unsuccessfully) with columns covering the name of the threat, when it happened, and what action was taken (as shown in Figure 7-5); look at the bottom of the right window to see more information and to click on a link to get details about the threat.

✦ **Application Activities:** Look here for a record of when scans were run and when Norton AntiVirus was loaded or disabled.

✦ **Errors:** Check these entries for any errors Norton AntiVirus recorded.

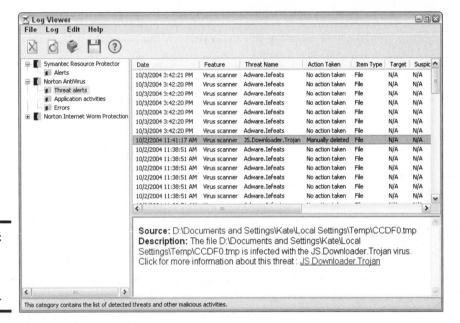

Figure 7-5:
All your
detected
threats in
plain view.

Some of it's going to be Greek to you

When you explore entries in your Log, not everything is going to make sense.

Here's something I find works well for me. When I face a new collection of information with Log Viewer and I'm just not sure what I'm looking at, I try to slow down and think of it like a jigsaw puzzle. The big picture you're trying to fit together is a sum total of

✔ The many connections you have everyday both to the Internet (and along your network if you use one at home or the office)

✔ All the files that flow into and out of your system during these connections (you're going to find you have connections you didn't know you had — and I don't mean your rich uncle)

✔ Everything else Norton has been designed and tweaked to watch

Look for patterns, because that can be the key to solving any kind of puzzle. If you recognize program names, this can tell you what's using a suspicious connection. If you're looking at a dated entry, and you happen to remember you were online at that particular time doing some exact thing, you may be able to see a pattern in what kind of entries are tied to very normal things you do.

The more frequently you use Log Viewer, at least at first, the sooner these patterns help you distinguish the normal from the unusual. Patience helps (as if you have time for that).

Checking data from Norton Internet Worm Protection

This final category gives you some of the best detail. It breaks down the huge volume of data into several subcategories, each offering specifics. Click each subcategory to see all entries for that section.

Here's a look at each and the kind of information you can find there:

✦ **Connections:** Each time your Internet or network connection contacts or is contacted by some external party (another Web user, a Web site, a hacker, or a person you're chatting with online), an entry gets stored here, as shown in Figure 7-6.

✦ **Activities:** This is a diary of your Norton AntiVirus *events* (anything Norton AntiVirus does on your system, such as performing a scan, quarantining a possible virus, or repairing one).

✦ **Worm Detection:** This reports the number of possible Internet worms Norton AntiVirus is monitoring at any time (see Figure 7-7).

✦ **System:** Most of the entries here tell you about connecting or disconnecting from the Internet (when it mentions a network adapter, it's referring to either a modem or network card address used by your Internet connection).

✦ **Alerts:** Check here to see what communications were blocked using special rules Norton AntiVirus uses to try to identify potential invaders like worms and hacker attacks (see Figure 7-8).

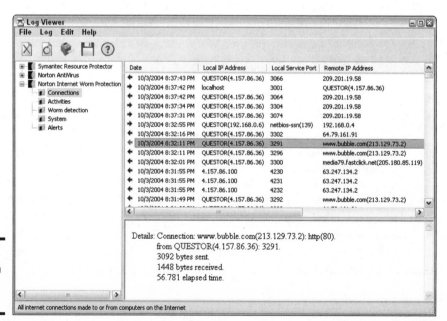

Figure 7-6:
Who's been contacting you?

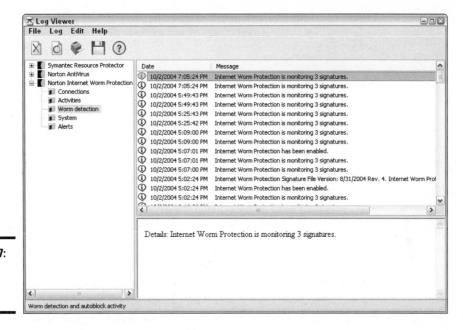

Figure 7-7:
Possible
worm
attacks.

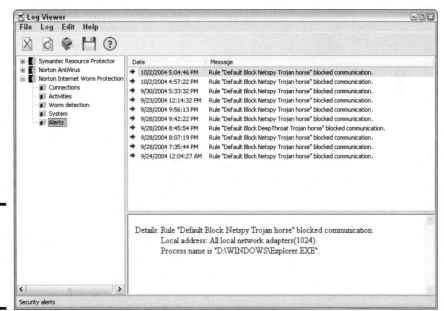

Figure 7-8:
View alerts
about
blocked
connec-
tions.

If you want to delete all existing entries in a category of your Log so you can start the Log entries fresh, select the category and then either press the

Delete Log Entries icon on the toolbar or open the Log menu and select Clear Category. You may want to export your entries to a text file or print them out before you do this.

Exporting your Log

If you get very serious about watching your Norton AntiVirus Log and you want to keep a comprehensive record of what happens, you may want to export entries from the Log Viewer into text files you can store elsewhere. If you export entries, you don't have to worry that the Log will grow too large or that entries you want to keep will be lost. After the entries are exported, you can clear a category and start over.

You may want to create a special folder where you can keep these logs together for later reference.

Follow these steps to export a category's listings to a text file:

1. **Select the category you want to export from Log Viewer.**

2. **Click to open the Log menu and choose Export Category As or click the Export icon on the toolbar (if you don't see this icon, you may have an earlier version than Norton AntiVirus 2005).**

3. **From the Save As window, click the drop-down list box to the right of Save In near the top of the window, and locate the folder where you want to store the Log.**

4. **Click in the box next to File Type and name the Log you're saving.**

5. **Click Save.**

These files get saved automatically as simple text files so you can open them by double-clicking on them from My Computer or Windows Explorer where they'll open in Windows Notepad. You could also import them into other programs like Microsoft Word or Microsoft Excel or Microsoft Access which accept text files and can automatically convert them into tables.

Analyzing Your Scan Summaries

Your Norton AntiVirus logs can give you great historical background on all the things Norton AntiVirus does, all the communications it blocks, and all the threats you receive. If you follow my advice about checking them occasionally and trying to see patterns, you may be able to tell whether Norton AntiVirus as you're running it now has you well protected.

But don't forget about the scan summaries you get at the end of each scan which can offer you the scoop on anything just identified. Here's an example: Let's say your scan just finishes and you see that you just got a whole batch of unwanted ads, many of them with file attachments containing one particular type of infection. That tells you now may not be the right time to disable Norton AntiVirus for the evening.

Tweaking Norton AntiVirus

Knowing whether monitoring software like Norton AntiVirus should run all the time, as it wants to, or more selectively, which you may like a lot better is always difficult. By now, you may have run enough scans that you have a good idea of how it impacts on using other programs on the desktop. If your Windows session really slows down when an e-mail or other scan takes off, you may want to pull back on the reins.

One of the reasons I combined using your monitoring tools with this section on tweaking is that what you glean from your Norton AntiVirus Log may give you a better idea on how protected you are. That's a bit better than a coin toss when deciding how to tweak your settings.

It's a really tough balancing act when you're trying to prevent a situation where the PC scans more than it works while also doing your best not to get caught with your system unprotected. Some people get irritated and disable Norton AntiVirus altogether, which makes no sense if they're receiving adware and viruses. Turning off Norton AntiVirus completely is sort of like choosing to stop locking your doors because you hate having to fumble with your keys.

Knowing when to throttle back

If you're like most people who install Norton AntiVirus, you tend to let it run as much as it wants. Unfortunately, your PC can take a performance hit when you do that.

When you review your current scan summary and look back at recent entries in the Log Viewer, you may — to your extreme pleasure — discover that you're not seeing much of anything being caught. That could mean some of the suggestions you've taken about reducing your risk are working, with Norton AntiVirus's able assist.

If so, you may be able to scan much more selectively. You could disable Norton AntiVirus for an hour or five or until the next restart as you saw how to do in Chapter 3. Or, if you feel confident you can resist the temptation to open files you've just downloaded or e-mail with attachments you just got *before* you scan them, you don't have to keep Norton running in the background every minute of the day.

To turn off constant monitoring with Norton AntiVirus loaded every time the PC (re)starts:

1. **In Norton AntiVirus, click Options.**

2. **Under How to Stay Protected, uncheck Start Auto-Protect when Windows starts up (see Figure 7-9).**

3. **Click OK.**

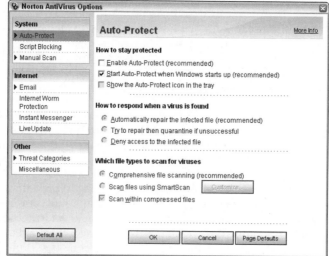

Figure 7-9:
Turn off
Norton
AntiVirus
auto startup.

You can also create and use custom scans to check your most at-risk files and folders rather than performing as many comprehensive scans that look at everything. Yet you also want to run those big scans at least once a week unless you honestly have a history of never seeing any threat.

Other ways to reduce your amount of scanning include removing scans from instant messaging (you configure that in Chapter 5) if you absolutely never accept files through your Net communications programs like AIM or MSN/Windows Messenger. Be selective.

Knowing when to let Norton scan more

Just as you may choose to scale back Norton AntiVirus's scans when the coast appears to be pretty clear, evidence in your Scan: Summary or Log may make you change your mind.

About installing programs

Running background programs like Norton AntiVirus can interfere with certain other things you do. A great example of this happens when you're installing a new program.

Here's what happens: When Norton AntiVirus detects something's happening on the system, like during the copying of files from a CD to your hard drive as you do when you install a program,

Norton AntiVirus flies into action. It's checking everything. That's what it's supposed to do.

But the delay created by that scanning can slow down the installation process or even halt it altogether. In extreme cases, your system can lock up, forcing you to push the panic, er, hit the power button.

I don't always have Norton AntiVirus running in the background. When I know someone else will be visiting my office or home and that person may want to use one of my PCs, however, I turn back on Auto-Protect mode. I can't necessary prevent a friend or family member from doing something stupid online, like downloading a questionable file, but I can use AutoProtect to reduce my risk.

To return to full comprehensive checking with Auto-Protect, follow these steps:

1. **From Norton AntiVirus, click Options.**

2. **Under How to Stay Protected, click to check all three items.**

You can choose just one or two if you want — just be sure your risk is covered.

3. **Click OK.**

If you have kids or others who use your PC, double-check your Norton AntiVirus Options page regularly to be sure someone hasn't turned off features you want to keep running.

Book VII

Norton Internet Control Tools

The 5th Wave   By Rich Tennant

© RICHTENNANT

"Amy surfs the web a lot, so for protection we installed several filtering programs that allow only approved sites through. Which of those nine sites are you looking at now, Amy?"

Contents at a Glance

Chapter 1: Barricading Yourself with Norton Personal Firewall

In This Chapter

✔ **Defining a firewall's job**

✔ **Knowing the difference between Norton Personal Firewall and the Windows firewall**

✔ **Recognizing known side effects**

✔ **Installing and configuring the firewall**

✔ **Testing your connections and security**

✔ **Temporarily disabling the firewall**

Some experts try to scare you by telling you the only way to be safe on the Internet is to completely disconnect your PC from it. Even though we live in a time where hackers, viruses, spyware, and adware, plus Net-based fraud including identify theft, abound, that's pretty silly — and impractical — advice.

Yet it would be nice if you could put the equivalent of a bulletproof vest over your modem to try to shield you, your Internet connection, and the files on your PC from harm when you're online. Maybe you'd like something that could tell you when any program on your system starts communicating with some unknown party over the Internet so you can try to figure out what's up.

A firewall isn't quite like a Kevlar vest or body armor, but it does behave like a cyber sentry for your system, guarding you against intrusions and other nasties that come through your online connection. In this chapter, I show you more of what a firewall does, why you should have one, and how to configure Norton Personal Firewall to work effectively for you.

Taking the Fear out of Being Close

The news media — especially the TV news shows — love to scare people with extreme stories of the dangers that wait for them online. What you may not notice is that the TV folks might have a vested interest in telling you how scary the Internet is — after all, TV viewing is *way* down since people began using the Net on a regular basis.

Even so, there are legitimate worries. If you have an Internet connection that's available all the time — for example, you're using a cable or DSL modems — other people, outside your home or office, can "borrow" your account without you knowing it. You may have a disagreement with somebody in an online chat room and notice that, afterwards, every time you go online, your connection acts strange and slow (possibly because your archenemy is attacking your Internet connection). Other miscreants may be trying to peak into your PC to see what you have stored there, or they may be sending you little files that, when opened, gather details from your system and deliver it back to the snoops.

These are the very reasons you may want to install a firewall. First, you need to know exactly what a firewall is, how Norton Personal Firewall differs from other firewalls, and what kind of results (good and bad) you'll see by using a firewall.

The job of a firewall

In a building, a physical firewall is used to try to stop the spread of a blaze. On a PC, a firewall's job is to make spending time on the Internet safer. As a virtual sentry or gatekeeper, a firewall controls who gets into your PC from the outside and what programs on your system connect to the Internet from the inside.

A good firewall has to work around a whole avalanche of programs you use while you're online or programs that need to connect to the Internet while you're using them. You'd be surprised how many of your programs now use the Net as part of how they work. For example, if you're reading a document in Microsoft Word and click on a link, the word processor opens your Web browser and goes to the Web site listed in the link. Likewise, you may have games that allow you to play with other people online or to go online to check for updates. Windows itself is filled with programs and tools that directly connect online.

The firewall also has to stand guard against outside intrusions — if you install Norton Personal Firewall, you can be notified when someone tries to get into your system. And you may be alarmed at how frequently that happens.

How Norton Personal Firewall is different from the Windows firewall

Windows includes its own firewall called the Internet Connection Firewall (in Windows 98/98SE/Me and original Windows XP, or Windows Firewall in Windows XP with Service Pack 2 installed). Differences between the Windows and Norton firewall won't be very conspicuous to you. In fact, they do the same basic job. The main difference between the programs is that Norton Personal Firewall is designed with these two specific changes in mind:

✦ It lets you modify some of the settings that the Windows firewall doesn't let you modify (at least, unless you know some advanced tricks and tweaks).

✦ It works effectively with other Norton products.

Under most circumstances, you should only run one firewall at a time. So if you're running the Windows firewall (or you're not sure), you need to check this and turn the Windows firewall off before you use Norton's. Here's how:

1. **Choose Start ➪ Connect To ➪ Show All Connections.**

If you're using Windows XP with Service Pack 2 installed, choose Start ➪ Settings ➪ Network Connections.

2. **Click on your Internet connection, and then click Change Settings of this connection (see Figure 1-1).**

3. **Select the Advanced tab, and remove the checkmark next to Protect My Computer and Network by Limiting or Preventing Access to This Computer from the Internet, as shown in Figure 1-2.**

If you're using Windows XP with Service Pack 2 installed, double-click the Windows Firewall icon in Control Panel, and then select to turn off the firewall.

4. **Click OK to close all windows.**

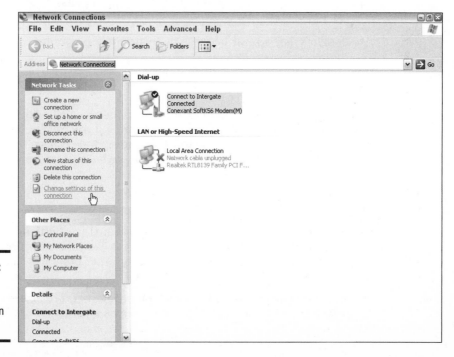

Figure 1-1:
Change
your
connection
settings.

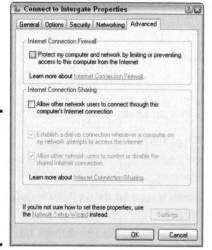

Figure 1-2:
Turn off the Windows firewall when using Norton Personal Firewall.

If you try to use a different firewall program when you install and begin using Norton Personal Firewall, you may see at least three major problems crop up:

✦ Your system and your Internet connections may slow down or get difficult to use.

✦ You may run out of available desktop memory to handle the programs you have open.

✦ Conflicts may appear between the two similar programs, where one may "tattle" on the other.

Potential side effects

Your firewall has to achieve a perfect balance between allowing you to do what you want on the Internet and still protecting you from outside intrusions or from information being tracked from spyware dialing out to deliver your private details to someone else. When the balance isn't perfect, you see problems.

Side effects of using a firewall include

✦ Getting hit by too many screens asking what you want to do when you try to load and use your Internet programs like your Web browser, instant messaging and e-mail software, or other programs that directly connect to the Internet

✦ A new slowness to moving around on the Internet, because the firewall is being careful about what it allows to open and run

✦ An inability to connect to the Internet as you did before or, after you do connect, an inability to reach one, more, or all Web sites or Net-based services like instant messaging or your e-mail servers

✦ An inability to send or receive files through chat rooms and instant messaging

Most of these side effects can usually be fixed by adjusting your firewall settings or setting up specific conditions on how you want an Internet tool or service to work separate from how the firewall works with programs the rest of the time.

Here are some of the ways you can work around them right now, because these issues can halt your connections or deny you the ability to use tools such as some instant messaging services. First off, whenever Norton Personal Firewall encounters a new "connected" program it doesn't know how to operate with, it pops up a window telling you that either:

✦ A program on your computer is trying to access the Internet

✦ A remote service is trying to access something on your PC

In the window that pops up, it gives you a drop-down menu with several options, including

✦ **Permit Once:** This lets the connection occur once only, after which you'll see the pop-up window again if the same program or remote service tries to connect.

✦ **Permit Always:** This gives the program or connection a blank check, so to speak, to allow communication whenever.

✦ **Block once:** This stops the program/connection immediately and one time only.

✦ **Block Always:** This prevents the program/connection from access permanently.

✦ **Automatically Configure Access:** This lets Norton Personal Firewall automatically set up conditions for the program/remote access.

✦ **Manually Configure Access:** This lets you specify the conditions for access (for example, some instant messaging programs provide a help file that tells you how to manually configure your firewall to work with them).

How you respond depends on whether you can identify the program/remote access involved. For example, if you have software to allow you to make phone calls over the Internet and the firewall window pops up asking how you want to handle it and specifies the program's name so you recognize it, you'll want to choose Automatically Configure from the drop-down list. This option is usually the best for any program or remote access that you do recognize.

Book VII
Chapter 1

Barricading
Yourself with Norton
Personal Firewall

But if you're unsure what program or remote party is trying to get through, use Block Once and then click on the More Information link in the window to try to determine what exactly is going on.

Avoid using Block Always or Permit Always unless you're sure this is a program or remote party you definitely want to allow or refuse.

 If you have trouble setting up a program or remote party using the Automatically Configure option — meaning that the connection doesn't work well — try to find out more about the program or remote party to then manually configure it within the firewall. Here's an example: You're using ICQ and you can't seem to get a connection. You visit the ICQ.com site, look under help to find out what settings you need to use to allow ICQ to operate around your firewall, then choose the Manually Configure Access option to apply the settings ICQ's help provides you.

The $64 techie terms used

The deeper you drill into your firewall setup and the more you try to figure out what it's doing or has already done, the more you're apt to see some confusing terms. Most of the alphabet soup acronyms like TCP and IP refer to the way communications occur between you and the mother ship, er, your Internet service provider or a Web site's host server.

Here's a list of some of these terms so you can follow along even if you forgot to do that four-year degree at MIT:

✔ **ICMP:** Short for Internet Control Message Protocol, ICMP provides background support for passing data (messages and files) around on a network or the Internet.

✔ **Inbound:** Any data being sent into your PC from a network or Internet connection.

✔ **IP address:** The actual Internet Protocol (IP) network address that identifies an Internet connection (for example, 201.177.99.124); each one is unique and yours can be *static* (it stays the same with each Internet connection — this is what you generally have

with high-speed access from cable and DSL modems) or *dynamic* (it changes each time you connect to the Internet — this is often what you have with dial-up Internet connections).

✔ **Outbound:** Any data being sent out from your PC.

✔ **Protocol:** A communications standard for how information is transferred from one PC to another.

✔ **TCP:** Short for Transmission Control Protocol (TCP), TCP is part of TCP/IP, the protocol that helps you get connected to the Internet or to other computers on your home or office network. FTP or file transfer protocol sites used for uploading and downloading files are an example of TCP.

✔ **UDP:** Short for User Datagram Protocol, UDP is a type of connectionless protocol normally sent over a home or office network. For example, when you do a Domain Name Service (DNS) query to try to identify a PC on the network, this is a form of UDP.

Raising Your Shields

The minute Norton Personal Firewall finishes installing and restarts your PC, your basic firewall setup is configured. Norton has preset it to a medium level of security where it alerts you to particular problems but handles everything else pretty much on its own. You may not need to do much if anything to your firewall to have it do a reasonably good job.

Many of the PC security pros I know recommend non-experts follow this simple security fitness regime when working with their first firewall:

1. **Install your firewall using recommended or default settings.**

2. **Test the heck out of the firewall by trying out every Internet program you use before you make any adjustments.**

   Carefully note what doesn't work anymore.

3. **Test your firewall settings using online or downloadable PC security test software to make sure you're adequately protected.**

   One great test site for trying this out is Gibson Research (www.grc.com). PC Pitshop (www.pcpitstop.com) also has a security-checking tool, along with virus checkers and other online helpers.

4. **If you do need to tweak, make one change at a time and retest your connections with each change.**

   The one-change-at-a-time rule allows you to see whether your change helps or hurts — and if it hurts, reverse your change.

5. **When your firewall and your connections are working, keep observing good security practices because a firewall can't safeguard you from everything.**

Following this advice is a really good idea — certainly wiser than installing the firewall, hitting a snag, and then just removing the firewall again. Step 3 alone can turn you from PC novice into a grizzled vet: Pros know you can create new problems when you try to tweak too many settings at once.

Testing your connectivity

Personal firewalls have been around for several years now and most of them, Norton included, are designed to recognize and work with all the most popular programs and tools you use on the Internet.

Whenever I install a firewall or other Internet protection software, I immediately test all the programs I use to make sure everything still connects as it should. This way, I can figure out if I need to make any adjustments to the firewall while the installation is fresh in my mind. You may want to do the same thing.

Don't forget to run:

+ Every one of your Internet connection types (choose Start ⇨ Connect To ⇨ Show All Connections)

+ All your e-mail software

+ Al Web browsers

+ Messaging programs like AOL Instant Messenger (AIM), MSN or Windows Messenger, Yahoo! Messenger, and ICQ

+ Any software you use for Web publishing, like Microsoft FrontPage or Macromedia DreamWeaver

+ FTP software used to upload and download files

+ Chat software and Web sites with built-in chat

+ Online games or games that install on your system but need to connect online

If absolutely nothing will connect, you probably want to stop and adjust your firewall security level now. However, if only one or two programs won't connect or run properly, just jot a quick note of the programs and your experience. You can finish testing other programs before you go back to tweak.

Testing your overall security

Norton Personal Firewall includes a helpful tool called Security Check that analyzes your security setup and alerts you to potential problems or weaknesses that the Net bad guys can exploit. Before you take the steps to run Security Check, make sure you're connected to the Internet because the tool actually operates from the Symantec Web site.

Then follow these steps:

1. **Open Norton Personal Firewall.**

2. **From the Status & Settings window, click Security and then click Check Security (see Figure 1-3).**

The Symantec Web site opens.

3. **Click Go.**

4. **Under Security Scan, press the Go button (see Figure 1-4).**

The Symantec scan begins, stopping first to download a special ActiveX control needed to do the job. You'll be prompted to accept the download.

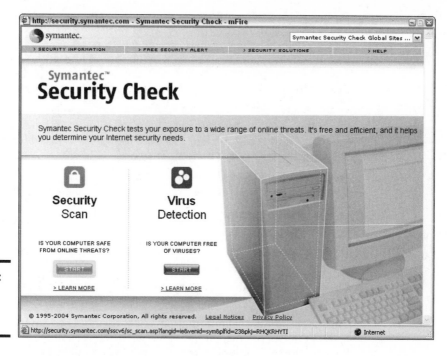

Figure 1-3:
Choose
Security
Check.

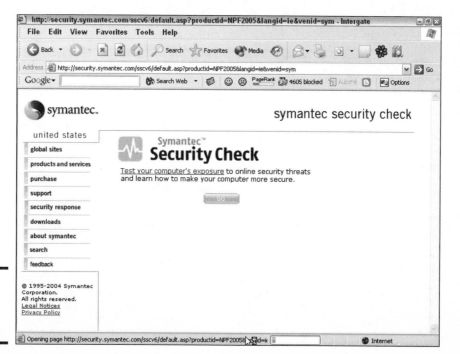

Figure 1-4:
Start the
security
scan.

5. Click Yes.

Figure 1-5 shows the progress screen, which notes your IP address and the city where your connection is being routed into at the top of the screen. Press Stop at any time to halt the scan. How long the scan takes really depends on the speed of your Internet connection and how well your PC is configured for security.

When the scan finishes, you get a page detailing exactly what the scan found. Look at Figure 1-6 and you note the symbols listed for the different aspects of security checked. They are

- **Green checkmarks:** Indicate that section passed muster, but you can click Show Details to see exactly what was examined in the scan.

- **Exclamation marks in yield signs:** Indicate items presenting possible risk.

- **Red X marks:** Identify definite risks (in Figure 1-6, the red X tells you that Norton AntiVirus isn't installed).

6. Check the information here by clicking the Show Details link (see Figure 1-7).

This opens additional information below the checked categories. Details listed here can help you understand what else you may need to install besides Norton Personal Firewall or settings you need to adjust in the firewall to increase your security safety.

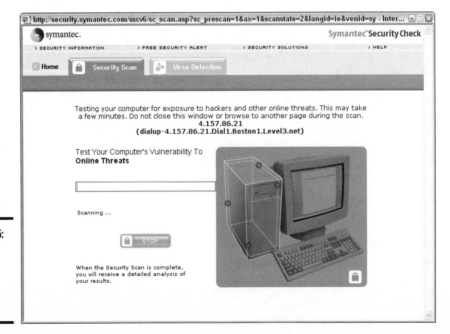

Figure 1-5:
Charting your security scan progress.

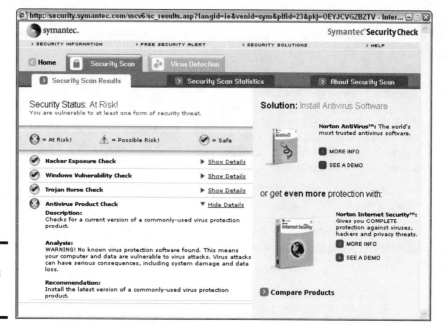

Figure 1-6:
The results
of your
scan.

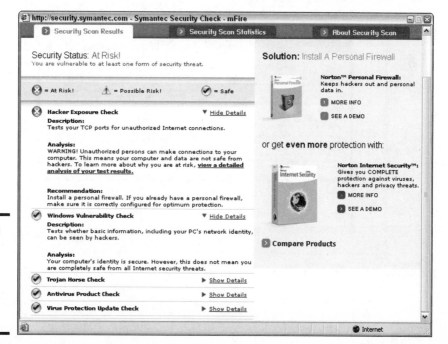

Figure 1-7:
Check the
details to
find out
what else
you need
to do.

Other ways to test

Symentec's Security Check tool is useful because it gives you a way to test your setup. However, you also have to take into account that it's run by the publisher of your security tool, which also offers a number of other tools they would love for you to buy.

Thus, you may want some independent verification your system is properly protected. Different system checkup sites around the Internet allow you to test certain aspects of your security — although many of them, like the Symantec site, are run by people who have security products to sell.

Ask friends and coworkers for recommendations for a good online PC security checking site. Some of my favorites are

✔ **Gibson Research's ShieldsUP!:** `https://www.grc.com/x/ne.dll?bh0bkyd2` (see the figure)

✔ **Audit My PC:** `www.auditmypc.com`

✔ **Hacker Whacker:** `www.hackerwhacker.com`

After you make any necessary changes, rerun Security Check to see if you pass with flying colors now. In fact, you should retake this and other security tests whenever you make a change to your PC security. See the "Other ways to test" sidebar for some suggestions for other security tests besides Symantec's that you can try.

Tweaking it just right

After you've tested your software to see how well it runs and connects, and after you've checked your overall security, you can start digging around under the firewall's access cover to see what settings are currently in place and which you can tweak. To reach that access panel:

1. **Open Norton Personal Firewall.**

2. **In the Status & Settings window, click Personal Firewall and then click Configure (see Figure 1-8).**

The Norton Personal Firewall window opens (see Figure 1-9).

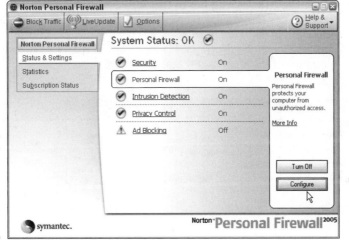

Book VII Chapter 1

Barricading Yourself with Norton Personal Firewall

Figure 1-8
Select Configure to tweak your firewall.

If you're using Norton Internet Security, you adjust the firewall settings a little differently. Follow these steps instead:

1. **Open Norton Personal Firewall or Norton Internet Security.**

2. **In the Status & Settings window, click Personal Firewall, and then click Configure.**

Let's go back to the firewall configuration screen you first saw in Figure 1-9. Starting here, this is what you need to do to tweak key settings to resolve common problems:

✦ **Select the Firewall tab and move the slider switch to increase or decrease your firewall security level.** Click OK when you're finished.

✦ **Select the Programs tab (shown in Figure 1-10) to view, add, or remove programs that can access the Internet through your firewall.** To adjust settings for an existing program, select the program and then click the down arrow to the right to choose from the following:

- **Automatic:** Lets Norton Personal Firewall automatically adjust itself to work around the program.

- **Permit All:** Tells the firewall to allow this program to do whatever it chooses to do.

- **Block All:** Tells the firewall to block any aspect of this program from connecting directly to the Internet.

- **Custom:** Use this to set custom options for this specific program.

✦ **Select the Networking tab to block or allow other PCs on your home or small office network from accessing your PC directly.** Click Add to add a PC by its name or IP address (click the Wizard button to help, or choose Start ➪ My Network Places to find other PCs on your network, along with their names and addresses).

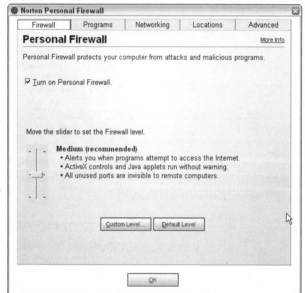

Figure 1-9:
Your firewall security level and feature settings.

Adding or tweaking specific programs

Because Norton Personal Firewall looks for popular Net-based programs as it's being set up for use, the firewall catches and tries to configure those programs it finds. But you may need to change the setting for a listed program or add a program to the list that the firewall did not pick up on its own.

Figure 1-10:
Choose
program
access
level.

In this example, I noticed my firewall didn't pick up another messaging tool called Trillian (available at www.ceruleanstudios.com) that I use, so I'm going to find and add it before I play with its settings. Here's what to do:

1. **Open Norton Personal Firewall or Norton Internet Security.**

2. **From Status & Settings, click Personal Firewall and then click Configure.**

3. **Select the Programs tab.**

4. **Under Programs Control, click the Add button.**

The Select a Program window appears.

5. **Locate and select the software you want to add and then click Open.**

6. **Click in the What Do You Want to Do? drop-down list box and choose how this program should run, such as Permit.**

Checking your statistics and logs

Beyond the kind of tweaks you may want to make on the spot after installing the firewall to help you get your "wired" programs their access to the Internet again, you should also check some of the information Norton Personal Firewall collects in its work as well as the results of the security checks I show you how to perform earlier in this chapter. This kind of feedback can tell you:

✦ If your security is set too high (you're seeing very few attempts to intrude upon you and you feel a bit restricted by the firewall)

✦ If it's set too low (you're seeing lots of threats and some problems still manage to make it through)

✦ Whether it's too automatic or not automatic enough (if everything is on autopilot, you may have no idea of what's going on; if it's not automatic enough, you may be pestered by too many pop-up alerts)

Within Norton Personal Firewall — or Norton Internet Security if you're using Personal Firewall within it — the way to find this information is through the Statistics window, as well as by viewing logs of your firewall-protected connection activity.

To understand how to use the Log Viewer, refer to Book II, Chapter 3. The firewall and connection information is the same between Norton Personal Firewall and Norton Internet Security.

Here, I want to show you how to view statistics. Follow these steps:

1. **Open Norton Personal Firewall or Norton Internet Security.**

2. **In the Status & Settings window, click Statistics from the left-hand menu.**

The main Statistics window (shown in Figure 1-11) opens.

In Figure 1-11, you can see information on when I was last attacked and how many intrusion attempts have been made on me. Figure 1-11 tells you I've had 303 attempts. I only had the software installed for about 24 hours at the time that humungous number was reported.

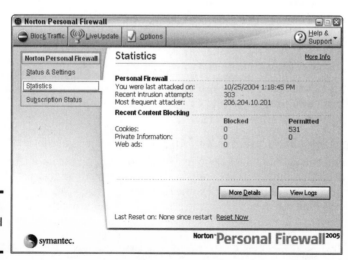

Figure 1-11:
Your firewall
statistics.

3. **Click the More Details button to see a more exhaustive breakdown of different parts of your Internet connection activity, as shown in Figure 1-12.**

   Refer to the sidebar "The $64 techie terms used" to make sense of any alphabet soup you don't quite understand.

If you start seeing lots of attempted intrusions, do *not* lower your security level.

Disabling or turning off the firewall

The difference between disabling and turning off the firewall, at least through Norton, is that disabling is temporary and done for a period of time such as 5 or 10 minutes, a few hours, or until your system restarts. To keep the firewall from restarting automatically when you start your computer, you need to turn it off.

Follow these steps to temporarily disable the firewall if you're using Norton Personal Firewall:

1. **Click the Norton Personal Firewall icon in the System Tray.**

2. **Select Disable Norton Personal Firewall.**

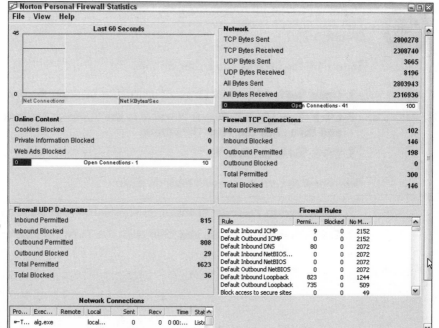

Figure 1-12: A summary of your most important connection details.

3. **In the Disable window, select how long you want to keep the firewall turned off (see Figure 1-13), and click OK.**

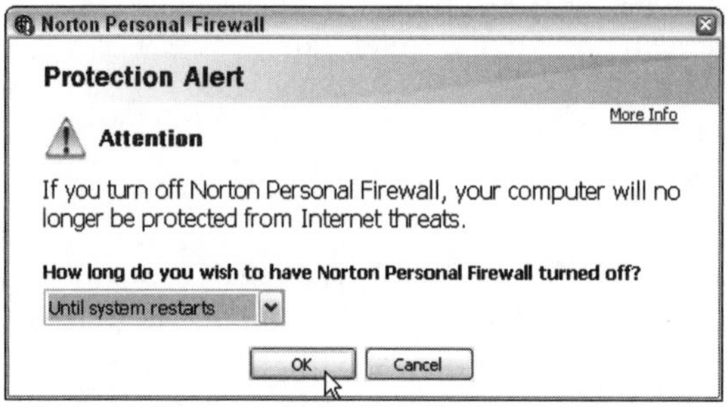

Norton Personal Firewall

Protection Alert

More Info

⚠ **Attention**

If you turn off Norton Personal Firewall, your computer will no longer be protected from Internet threats.

How long do you wish to have Norton Personal Firewall turned off?

Until system restarts ▾

OK   Cancel

Figure 1-13: Temporarily shutting down your firewall.

If you're using Norton Internet Security, disabling the entire suite for a short period is usually easier than just disabling the firewall. Just follow these steps.

1. **Right-click the Norton Internet Security icon in the System Tray.**

2. **Select Disable Internet Security.**

3. **Select your time period and click OK.**

To reenable your firewall at any time, right-click the icon in your System Tray and choose Enable Norton Personal Firewall (or Enable Norton Internet Security).

To turn off the firewall altogether, do this:

1. **Open Norton Personal Firewall or Norton Internet Security.**

2. **Click Firewall or Personal Firewall in the Status & Settings window, and then click the Turn Off button.**

3. **Click Yes to confirm it.**

Here's how to turn the firewall back on again:

1. **Open Norton Personal Firewall or Norton Internet Security.**

2. **Click Personal Firewall, and then click the Turn On button.**

Chapter 2: Quarantining Yourself with Privacy Control

In This Chapter

✔ **Knowing what Privacy Control offers you**

✔ **Configuring how much information gets revealed online**

✔ **Adding, modifying, or removing specific personal information**

✔ **Toggling Privacy Control features on and off**

Think of Norton Privacy Control as you would putting a really good sturdy set of blinds on the windows at the front of your house. Although you may love letting the light shine in, you don't necessarily want everyone who walks by to see what you're doing in there. Without blinds and locks for your doors, you'd be too embarrassed to wear those silly bunny slippers or that funky old college sweatshirt.

Blinds are a great analogy because Privacy Control lets you decide what information about yourself is shared while you're online. You control whether the blinds are open and what others can see.

Establishing Privacy Control through Norton

Privacy Control has two main parts. One part blocks details from being passed without your consent, and the other part allows you to store private information (such as account numbers and your address), and then choose when and where to provide that information online (without having to type it in again each time).

Options available under Privacy Control include the following:

✦ **Security Level:** This is how much security you want to set (Low, Medium, or High — but no DefCon1)

✦ **Add Private Information:** Here you can set up all the details you want — exactly as you want them to appear — when you choose to send your particulars to a site.

✦ **Browser Privacy:** This controls how much overall secrecy your browser should exercise when a site wants your private details.

What you don't know can hurt you

How much can people find out about you through your Internet connection and the kinds of programs you use? Way too much! You can get an idea for yourself by taking the Privacy Test at www.pdaconsulting.com/security.htm.

I've run lively Internet chat rooms on various online services. Part of my job was to keep hackers and crackers and other problem children out. With just a few tools and even before I had much experience, I used to be able to spot a lot of details about a person the minute he joined the chat.

From the IP address (see Chapter 1 for more info), I could tell what ISP a person used and the city or region where he was connecting from. If I used another tool, I could better pinpoint his exact location. I could use his IP address, if I needed, to find out exactly who the person was (name, address, phone number). Another simple

tool often let me determine his e-mail address. Seeing what software a person used to join the chat gave me a good idea of their overall experience level.

None of this information came to me through hacking a person's PC. All I needed to do was use a variety of tools freely available on the Internet to check details that these people had added to their Internet connection setup. Without thinking, lots of people willingly fill in their address, phone number(s), date of birth, employer information, and sometimes even credit-card details and store it in software used when they access the Net.

Privacy Control and Norton Personal Firewall, both part of Norton Internet Security, allow you to set up a gate — and lock it — between you and this potential privacy leak.

+ **Enable Secure Connections:** This tool is incredibly helpful when you're online shopping or doing other tasks where you really want to have a secure tunnel between you and your keyboard and the Web site's server without anyone else listening in.

Certain options, like browser privacy and secure connections, are turned on for you automatically when Privacy Controls installs as part of Norton Internet Security. Other options, including your private information, are available but you need to set them up.

Configuring the Basics

Privacy Control, along with Parental Controls covered in Chapter 3, is only available through Norton Internet Security Suite. Out of the box, Privacy Control is turned on when you install and load Norton Internet Security. You're free to turn it off or tweak it to allow only some security features to run.

Follow these steps to open your Privacy Control window:

1. **Open Norton Internet Security by right-clicking on the icon in the System Tray and choosing Open Norton Internet Security.**

2. **From the Status & Settings window, click Privacy Control and then click Configure (see Figure 2-1).**

   The Privacy Control window (shown in Figure 2-2) opens.

Figure 2-1: Select Privacy Control and then Configure to open the Privacy Control window.

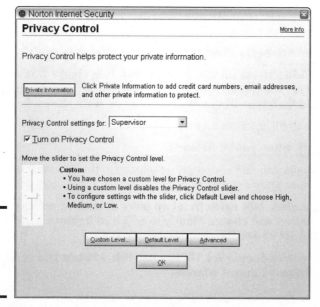

Figure 2-2: Choose options for Privacy Control.

Note the slider switch at the bottom left of the window. Use your mouse to push this up to increase your privacy level, or down to decrease it. Stay right here on this screen because there's more to customizing your privacy than meets the eye.

By default, privacy is set to Medium, which is a good workable security level. The higher you set your security level, the more apt you are to see problems with some sites that demand details from you that Privacy Control will block. If you turn Privacy Control off (by deselecting the Turn On Privacy Control check box) or set a low security level on the slider switch, you're probably going to leak more details than you want. You can also go back and adjust your privacy level at any time.

Setting your privacy security level too high may interfere with the proper opening or running of some Web sites you may visit.

Adding your private information

Privacy Control lets you specify bits of data you may want or need to share on a Web site by typing them in ahead of time and storing them in Norton. This tool is helpful if you install Privacy Control and block cookies, only to find you suddenly have to type all the details in again that your browser used to remember for you. You may encounter this if you use an online banking or a brokerage site, for example.

To set up your private information:

1. **From the Privacy Control window, click Private Information.**

   When you start off, nothing will be listed in the Private Information window.

2. **Click Add to begin to set up your private details.**

3. **In the Add Private Information window (see Figure 2-3), choose the type of personal information you want to add from the drop-down list box and then type in the information you want shown here.**

   Be sure to fill any field marked Required.

4. **Click OK when you're finished.**

   The details you just added are now listed in the Private Information window, as shown in Figure 2-4.

5. **You can click Add again to set up more details, or select your existing information and choose Modify to edit it or Remove to delete the selected set of details.**

6. **When you're done, click OK to close this window and return to the main Privacy Control window.**

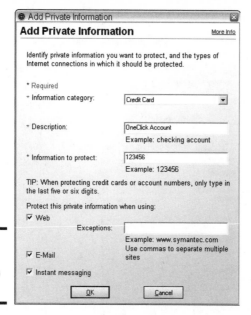

Figure 2-3:
Add your
private info
details.

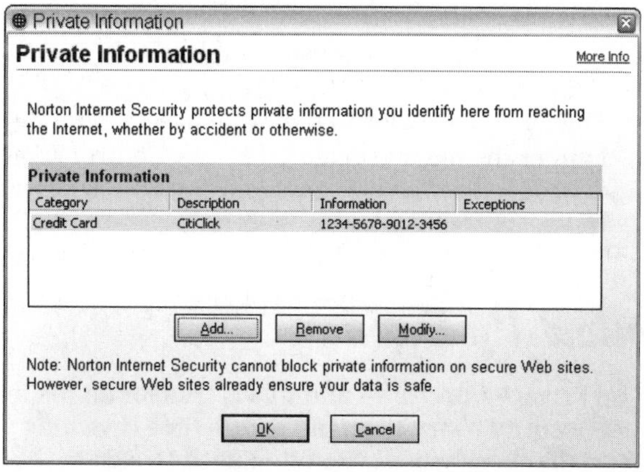

Figure 2-4:
Add, modify,
or delete
details
you've
already
set up.

Tweaking advanced options

To take a look at your more advanced choices for configuring Privacy
Control, click the Advanced button in the Privacy Control window. The
Advanced window, shown in Figure 2-5, appears.

Here, you can permit or block different features from Web sites either already
on the list or that you use the Add button to place on the watched site list. You
can then configure different aspects of that Web site — so you can change a
feature currently blocked to one marked Permit.

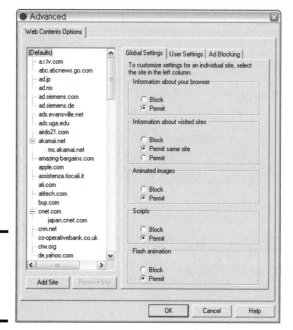

Figure 2-5:
Your
advanced
setting
choices.

You probably don't need to make changes to these advanced settings unless you notice problems between the Privacy Control you've set up and Web sites you visit. Then you may want to either go back and modify your level of security, shown under the main Configure Privacy Control screen (refer to Figure 2-2) or add a specific Web site here and tweak how private you want to be on that site.

Performing a Follow-Up Exam

After you set up Privacy Control — and this is true for all the features in Norton Internet Security — try to spend a little time revisiting your favorite Web sites, especially those where you often need to sign in (like an online store where you have an account or your banking site or membership-only Web sites). As you do, notice anything that seems different. For example, look for sites where you now have to sign in every single time just like you're a new rather than a returning customer.

Little blips like this can indicate something about your Privacy Control settings: They may be set too high, for example, or demand a custom tweak so you can work around problems on one or two sites. The first thing you can do is adjust your Privacy Control security system from High to Medium by pushing the slider switch in the main Privacy Control screen down. You may not want to do this, however, when just one or two sites are being cranky.

Instead, you may want to set up conditions for specific sites. Here's an example: Let's say your Privacy Control works great except for one Web site where you suddenly can't easily use the shopping cart option to make purchases. You can add the site into Privacy Control and then allow it to use a different privacy setting from that used for all other sites you visit.

To set up conditions for a site, follow these steps:

1. **Open Norton Internet Security.**

2. **Click Privacy Control in the Status & Settings window, and click Configure.**

3. **Click the Advanced button.**

4. **Under Web Content Options, click Add Site.**

5. **Type in the address for the Web site you want to custom-configure here (see Figure 2-6), and click OK.**

Figure 2-6:
Add a Web
site to your
custom list.

**Book VII
Chapter 2**

Quarantining
Yourself with
Privacy Control

6. **From the Web Content Options window (see Figure 2-7), select your newly added Web site from the left-hand list.**

    Now look at the right side of the window which is open to the Global settings tab.

7. **To change from default settings for anything listed here, such as Information about visited sites, click to uncheck it, then choose Block or Permit (use Permit when you're trying to cure a blocked site).**

8. **Select each of the other tabs — User Settings and Ad Blocking — to see if you want to make any additional changes.**

9. **When you're done, click OK.**

After you make changes here to add a site, you'll want to revisit that site to see if it works better now that you've done some tweaking. If it does, you're all set. If the problem persists, you may want to try a few different tweaks and keep revisiting the site after you make each tweak, to see if some adjustment is still needed.

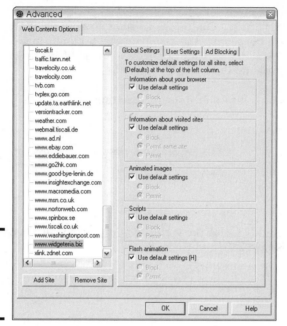

Figure 2-7:
Customize
settings for
your added
site.

You can also set Privacy Control to use a custom security level other than those offered by default from the slider switch. Remember I mentioned you can set Browser Privacy and take advantage of Secure Connections in Privacy Control? These can be set — or turned off — from the same screen.

To set a custom security level:

1. **Open Norton Internet Security.**

2. **Click Privacy Control in the Status & Settings window, and click Configure.**

3. **Below the slider switch, click Custom Level.**

The Customize Privacy Settings window, shown in Figure 2-8, appears.

4. **In the Private Information drop-down list, select your desired security level.**

5. **In the Cookie Blocking drop-down list, select the anti-cookie security you want.**

Look at Figure 2-8 and you see the checked (enabled) options Enable Browser Privacy and Enable Secure Connections (https). Normally, you want to leave these completely alone, because the whole idea of Privacy Control is to limit your risks in transferring details over the Internet.

Figure 2-8:
You can customize your privacy levels.

However, if you absolutely can't open or access a feature on a Web site any other way, you can try unchecking Enable Browser Privacy here (click OK when done) to see if this repairs your ability to access the site. If it does, that's great but you don't want to run all the time without full browser security. Instead, you may want to add that site to your custom list as you did in the first set of steps in this section, then set custom options for that site.

Snoops and snoopers

People can spy on your Internet activities, no matter what you happen to do online, in numerous ways. Don't make the mistake of thinking that if you don't do anything interesting online, you won't provoke someone's interest. Some people find and use tools to snoop because they're bored themselves, some do it because they just want to know more about you specifically, and others do it primarily because they may be able to grab your account names, passwords, and other unique information like credit-card numbers and expiration dates they can use to their advantage later.

Unfortunately, tools are available online to make it possible for even non-techie wizards to perform this kind of James Bond–like spying. Ironically enough, some of the spam you receive (see Book V) is likely from people trying to sell you software to watch your friends, family, employees, and workmates.

Browser privacy and secure connections are incredibly important, because you don't want someone eavesdropping on the details you pass to a Web site when you order products online or check your bank-account information.

Chapter 3: Taking Advantage of Parental Control

In This Chapter

✔ **Understanding what Parental Control does for you**

✔ **Turning on Parental Control**

✔ **Setting up separate accounts for the kids and adults who use your PC**

✔ **Customizing what programs or Web sites can be used for each account**

✔ **Testing what your kids can see**

Child safety is a big issue anywhere. But the online world presents special challenges in the form of virtual bogeymen, pitfalls, and the kind of Web sites that can fluster or enrage a mature adult.

Another challenge is that kids sometimes sit at the keyboard for hours at a time, given the opportunity. Knowing what they're doing each and every minute is tough — and you can't assume they're always just doing their homework. Yet even when kids are being good, they can still stumble across a Web site you'd prefer they didn't.

Parental Control in Norton Internet Security is a way for you to define the boundaries of your kid's online world, choosing which programs he can run and what types of Web sites he can browse and open. In this chapter, I show you how to turn it on, configure it, and test your results.

Controlling What Your Kids and Strangers See

If you've tried the Content Advisor feature or the AOL Parental Control in America Online software, Norton Parental Control works very much like these. Parental Control establishes a safety zone to restrict which Web sites or Internet software, like instant messaging, kids can access while they're online. Controls like this work by breaking the Internet down into low- to high-risk areas based on the type of content or features a particular Web site or program offers. Then you set which zones or categories or programs you think are acceptable for your kids. You can turn on Parental Control (which is turned off when Norton Internet Security first installs) and use it as is, or you can customize it as much as you feel necessary.

Nothing replaces a parent's watchful eye

Programs like Norton Parental Control can help you as a parent or caregiver for a child or teenager reduce a kid's access to sites that discuss adult subject matter. But don't think of Parental Control as the total solution. You still need to monitor your child's online experience just as you'd want to keep track of where he is when he's traveling through an unfamiliar neighborhood or city.

Having the main family computer set up in a common room in the house where adults are often present can help a lot. When kids have PCs in their own rooms, you have to figure out a way to keep an eye on what they're doing — and that's not always easy.

Also, each child can have his own account, each with its own custom settings. This way you can adjust the access based on the maturity level or interests of each of your children. Parental Control, unlike some cyber-nanny software, also lets you differentiate between a child and a teenager to give the older child slightly more access than a younger one.

How well Parental Control will work for you depends on four basic building blocks:

+ How you configure settings for your kids

+ How strong your password is for your Supervisor account (make it easy and the kids will figure it out when you don't remember it)

+ How careful you are not to leave the Supervisor account logged in so your kids can't come along and undo your work

+ How frequently and thoroughly you test your kids' accounts to see what they can and can't access

Kids have a knack for playing with computer settings and guessing easy passwords that can defeat your best attempts to control what they do and where they go online.

The same user accounts you'll set up here for Parental Control can also be used for the Privacy Control feature discussed in the previous chapter. This means you can adjust specific privacy settings for each person with his own account.

Beyond what Privacy Control and Parental Control offer, you may also want to have a regular discussion with your kids about the need to maintain privacy online. You probably don't want them sharing their phone number or address or other particulars with strangers. Spell out what they absolutely should not disclose to others and ask them to let you know if they have problems online (for example, someone keeps contacting them or asking for private information).

Setting Up Parental Control

You've got a number of steps to get through in turning on and setting up the Parental Control. Try to follow along in order, because some parts — like the Supervisor login — need to be done before you can do other parts of the setup.

Logging on as Supervisor

Right out of the package, Norton Parental Control and Norton Internet Security recognize just one account, called a Supervisor account because it allows the person using it to make master changes to how Internet Security and kid-safe control settings are configured. However, by default, no password is assigned to this account. You'll want to add one. I show you how to do that after you log in, in the "Running the Parental Control Wizard" section.

You must be logged in as the Supervisor in order to turn on the Parental Control feature and then create accounts and set up controls for the kids.

Follow these steps to log in:

1. **Right-click the Norton Internet Security icon in System Tray and choose Account Login.**

2. **In the Log On window (see Figure 3-1), click OK.**

**Book VII
Chapter 3**

**Taking Advantage of
Parental Control**

Figure 3-1:
Type your
password to
log on.

You can also log on directly from Norton Internet Security:

1. **From the Norton Internet Security window, click User Accounts in the left-side menu.**

2. **Press the Log On button (see Figure 3-2).**

3. **Type your password, and click OK.**

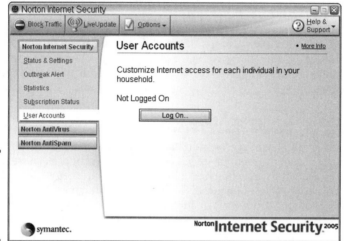

If you try to use the Parental Control feature without logging on as Supervisor, you'll receive an error message telling you that you don't have sufficient privileges to do that. Unfortunately, the error message doesn't actually suggest you log on to cure that problem, so it's something to keep in mind.

Running the Parental Control Wizard

Initial setup of the Parental Control tool is managed from a wizard helping you with bits of information each step of the way. Be sure you've already logged on as the Supervisor before you start. Then follow these steps:

1. **In Norton Internet Security, click User Accounts in the left-hand menu.**

   The screen should look like that in Figure 3-3.

2. **Click Parental Control Wizard link from the top right-hand portion of the window.**

3. **Select whether to use existing Windows accounts (if your kids have their own separate accounts for use on the PC) or Norton Internet Security Accounts (if you don't have accounts set up under Windows), then click Next.**

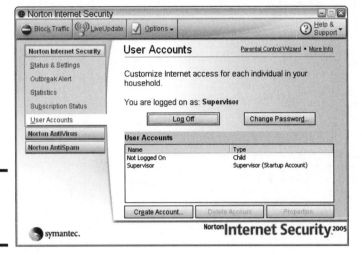

Figure 3-3:
The User
Accounts
screen.

4. **Type a password to apply to the currently unprotected Supervisor account, then type it again to confirm it (see Figure 3-4), and click Next.**

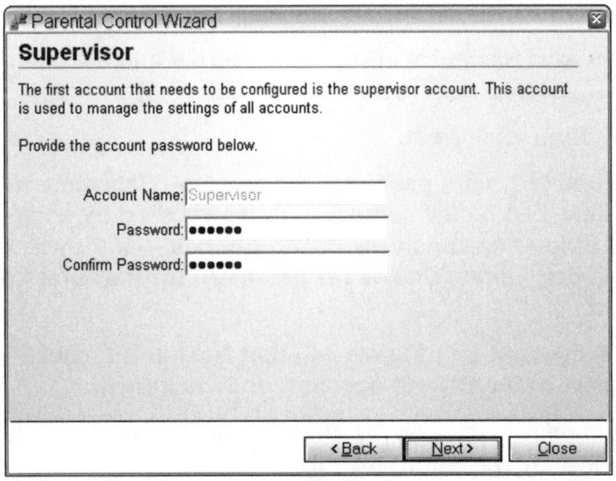

Figure 3-4:
Give a
password to
the
Supervisor
account for
better
security.

5. **In the Create Accounts window, shown in Figure 3-5, use the blank boxes to type in the names of the people who will share the same PC, then click in the drop-down list box next to the names to specify whether that person should be treated as a:**

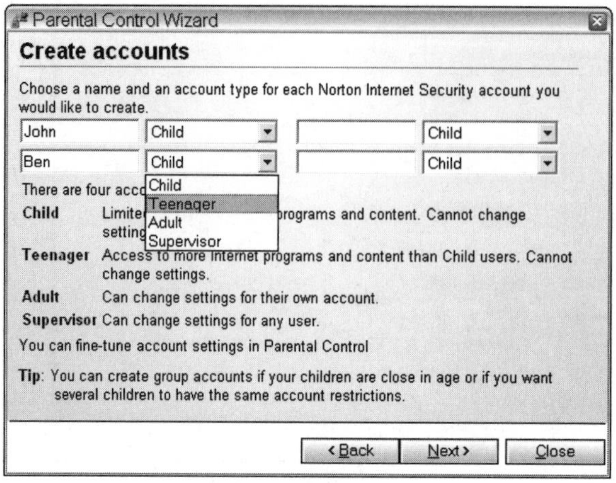

Parental Control Wizard

Create accounts

Choose a name and an account type for each Norton Internet Security account you would like to create.

| John | Child ▾ | | Child ▾ |
| Ben | Child ▾ | | Child ▾ |

There are four acc

		Child
Child	Limite	Teenager	rograms and content. Cannot change
	setting	Adult
		Supervisor
Teenager	Access to more Internet programs and content than Child users. Cannot change settings.
Adult	Can change settings for their own account.
Supervisor	Can change settings for any user.

You can fine-tune account settings in Parental Control

Tip: You can create group accounts if your children are close in age or if you want several children to have the same account restrictions.

[< <u>B</u>ack] [<u>N</u>ext >] [<u>C</u>lose]

Figure 3-5:
Set up accounts for everyone using this PC.

- **Child:** Has limited access to the Internet but can't change account settings.

- **Teenager:** Has access to more content than the child status but can't change his own settings.

- **Adult:** Has full access to the Internet and can change settings for his own account but not for anyone else.

- **Supervisor:** Has full access to the Internet and the ability to change others' settings and turn Parental Control off and on.

6. **Click OK, then click Next.**

7. **When prompted, set a password for each user/account you set up in Step 5 (these can be the same as passwords used by each person to access Windows on the PC or different ones — if they're different, be sure that each person knows his password for Parental Control), and click Next.**

8. **Select the account (see Figure 3-6) that Norton Internet Security should treat as the default account, and click Next.**

   Note: Not Logged On or an Adult account is better than a Supervisor account or a Child account for this purpose.

9. **Click Finish.**

Passwords you set in the preceding list are case-sensitive. If you use a mix of uppercase and lowercase letters in setting the password, the person logging in to the account must use the exact same mix.

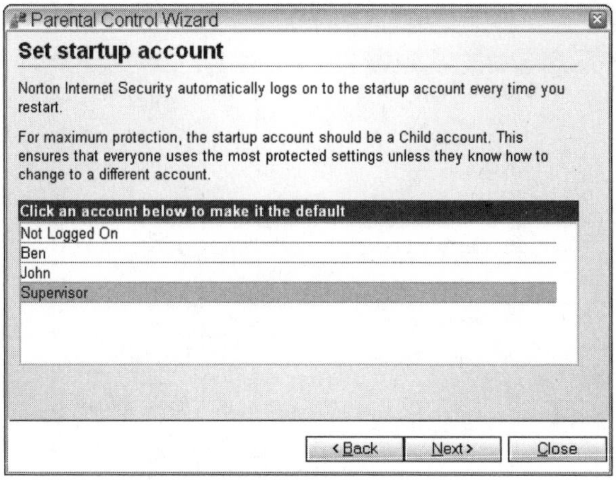

Parental Control Wizard

Set startup account

Norton Internet Security automatically logs on to the startup account every time you restart.

For maximum protection, the startup account should be a Child account. This ensures that everyone uses the most protected settings unless they know how to change to a different account.

Click an account below to make it the default

Not Logged On

Ben

John

Supervisor

< Back   Next >   Close

Figure 3-6:
Choose a
default
account.

Turning on Parental Control

After you've done the setup to use Parental Control, you still need to enable it so it's ready and running ahead of your kids. Remember to log on as a Supervisor for this if you've already logged off.

Take these steps to enable Parental Control:

1. **In Norton Internet Security, click to open the Norton Internet Security menu at the left side of the screen.**

2. **Choose Status & Settings.**

3. **Select Parental Control and then click Turn On.**

Tweaking your Parental Control settings

Parental Control comes preset to try to keep children out of Web sites with content most parents would find inappropriate. Yet you can also customize settings to make allowances when you need more — or less — flexibility for your kids.

You may want to test your accounts and how loose or restrictive the Web access is for Child and Teenager accounts before you make adjustments.

Follow these steps to view your setting options:

1. **Log on as a Supervisor and open Norton Internet Security.**

2. **From the Status & Settings window, click Parental Control, and then press the Configure button (see Figure 3-7).**

The Parental Control window, shown in Figure 3-8, opens.

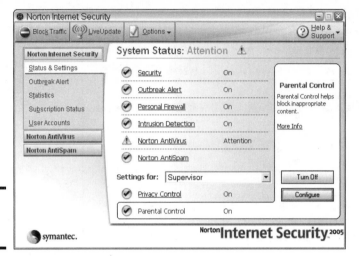

Figure 3-7:
Press
Configure.

Figure 3-8:
The
Parental
Control
window.

3. **In the Parental Control window:**

- To select the account name you're adjusting settings for, select the Parental Control Settings For drop-down list and choose an account.

- To block or permit full categories of sites (such as Humor or Sex Education), click Sites and then choose your categories and settings from the window shown in Figure 3-9, and click OK.

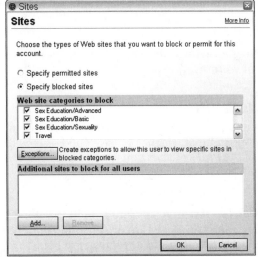

Figure 3-9:
Block or
permit
whole Web-
site
categories.

- To add specific sites to a blocked or allowed list, follow the steps in the previous bullet but click Add Site, type in the Web address (for example, **www.nakeddogs.org**) and click OK.

- To specify which types of software can be used to access the Internet, press the Programs button, and make sure checkmarks appear next to all allowed programs and that all programs you don't want to permit are unchecked (see Figure 3-10), and click OK.

- To allow or block access to Internet newsgroups, press the Newsgroups button, specify the newsgroups or newsgroup types to show or hide, and click OK.

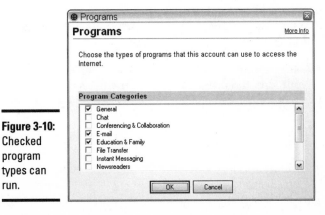

Figure 3-10:
Checked
program
types can
run.

- To go back to the default, out-of-the-box settings for Parental Control, which erases all your changes, click the Defaults button and click Yes to confirm your choice.

4. **When you're satisfied with your changes, click OK to close the Parental Control window.**

Testing your accounts

Before you give out accounts and passwords to your kids, you want to make sure the accounts work and that, when you use a child or teenager's account, he can't get access to the types of sites you want to keep out of his reach.

Follow these steps:

1. **Right-click the Norton Internet Security icon in the Windows System Tray and choose Logoff (if logged in) or select Account Login and then sign in with the first of your child or teenager accounts, and click OK.**

   Click the down arrow next to the account name to select a different user than the one listed (see Figure 3-11). When prompted, type the password for that user's Parental Control account.

2. **Open your Web browser (connect to the Internet if you haven't already).**

3. **Use a search engine to locate a racy Web site, and then click to open it.**

4. **Repeat Step 3 and try a number of other sites.**

5. **Jot down any notes about what kinds of content gets through.**

6. **Run your Internet programs such as chat software or messaging to see how well they continue to work while you're still logged in as a child.**

7. **Repeat Steps 1–6 for other Child/Teenager accounts you created.**

8. **If necessary, go back and customize the settings for your child or teenager again to increase or decrease the restrictions or to block specific sites and programs.**

After you've tested their accounts and made any needed changes for access, you can then supply your kids and other adults with their passwords. Remind them to log in using their own account.

Figure 3-11:
Log in as a
child to test.

Overcoming password insecurity

Passwords are essential to any type of computer security. Perhaps even before you grew accustomed to using passwords to get into Windows or to check e-mail, you may have used them to play games, to get into restricted-access events, or to withdraw money from your bank's ATM (the PIN used by bank cards is a type of password).

The biggest problem with passwords is that humans use them. And humans often find it difficult to remember a difficult password, so they tend to make their passwords very easy to remember. In fact, we make them so easy to remember that people who may barely know us can guess them. Would you believe one of the most frequently used passwords is the word *password?* This is followed by birth dates, pets' or children's names, and just random simple words like *flower* or *computer.* Sad but true.

To make matters worse, we then write these passwords down to make them easy for others to find. You don't want to know how many people jot their account passwords on a sticky note they attach to the sides of their monitors!

But for passwords to work best and to help keep your kids out of your Supervisor account in Parental Control, you need to get tough about your passwords. Follow these recommendations:

- Make it a mix of letters and numbers.

- Mix uppercase and lowercase letters.

- Create a password that is at least seven or eight characters long.

- Try to come up with a system to remember a tough password.

- Change your password regularly.

Visit http://www-csr.bessy.de/comput/ a_good_password.html to see a good guideline document for setting up strong passwords.

Chapter 4: Using Password Manager to Keep Your Password Under Wraps

In This Chapter

✔ **Knowing the basics of password protection**

✔ **Practicing real-time safeguards**

✔ **Choosing hard-to-guess passwords**

✔ **Creating a profile**

✔ **Storing your user info in Norton Password Manager**

✔ **Editing your entries**

*L*isten to the news, and you may be scared to death. The media makes the Internet sound like one part Great Library of Alexandria, two parts lots of fun, and three parts con artists, stalkers, and serious criminals all just waiting in the shadows to pounce upon you.

In truth, the Internet is neither as dangerous as it sounds nor anywhere near as secure as you'd like. The key to safety online is often as simple as guarding your personal details, and Norton Password Manager attempts to handle that job for you. In this chapter, you discover how to set up your very private personal data and then let Norton Password Manager handle much of the rest. The program does more than simply store your passwords as you'll see in the following chapter. You can also associate profiles with your passwords that allow you to specify a name separate from a business name.

Shh! Can You Keep Your Passwords a Secret?

Want to know the main reason bank accounts get pilfered of precious cash? It's not because of ingenious hackers or armed bank robbers. Instead, it's because people write their access codes on the backs of their ATM cards and then leave those cards in ATM machines or somewhere else they can be swiped (in both senses of the word).

The same low-tech thievery happens every day with computer security. That's bad, especially because you're *the* first line of defense in keeping no-goodniks out of your system and your accounts. Although Norton Password Manager provides you with help, only you can be sure your passwords are strong and that you don't make them easy to steal.

In the following sections, I show you what you need to do — in addition to using Norton Password Manager — to keep your private details from prying eyes.

Creating smart passwords

The best passwords are the hardest to guess. To keep your information secure, get in the habit of making your passwords strong and smart rather than short and simple.

When you're trying to come up with a password, follow these guru guidelines:

✦ **Use passwords that are a minimum of seven or eight characters.** The more characters, the harder it is to guess.

✦ **Make the characters a combination of letters and numbers.** For example, you could use dqy78r0x.

✦ **Where possible, use at least one symbol, like !, #, $, %, ^, &, or *.** For example, you could use r!93xo3P.

✦ **Have a unique password for each account.**

✦ **Avoid whole words, especially familiar names.** The more random, the better.

Don't let them watch every move you make

You may have heard about special programs that can be installed to run "in the background" on a computer, out of normal sight, that then track every keystroke you press. By storing your sensitive numbers so you don't have to type them in each time, Norton Password Manager reduces the chance that such programs, if present on your PC, can capture your details. Other Norton tools, like spyware and adware checking in addition to Norton AntiVirus, can reduce your risk of getting infected or implanted with one of these nasties and then having your information sent back to the cretin who originated it.

Keep in mind, too, that some passwords are *case-sensitive,* which means that it matters whether you match upper- and lowercase letters when you type. For instance, if you're on such a site, where your password is something like K3C^4UV and you type in k3c^4uv, you get an error telling you the user name and password don't match the site's records. Don't worry: Norton keeps track of this for you, so the case will match. However, beware of the Caps Lock key being on because this can give you different results than you want.

When creating a password for use on case-sensitive sites and in programs, remember that you can use a mix of upper- and lowercase letters in a smart password. A mix of cases gives you an edge, because most people use exclusively lower- or uppercase letters. Make a password-cracker cry with your cleverness.

Protecting your password

Passwords are as vital as the key to your car or the access code to your office or home. Basic security involves at least two parts: a unique user name and a password.

No software — not even Norton Password Manager — can protect you if you use a really easy-to-guess password, you never change it, and you leave it printed on a sticky note on your monitor or taped to your keyboard so you don't have to remember it.

Likewise, don't respond to e-mail requests that seem to come from your bank, credit-card company, or other party asking you to verify your password by typing it in. Some 99 times out of every 100, these e-mails are sent by scammers just trying to get your user name and password. If they get it, they can use your account to look up your credit-card information, which may give them your home address, your social security number, and a lot of other information you don't want anyone else to have.

Avoiding password detection

Today, your personal information is a product. Some people are willing to steal to get it — just as some people are willing to steal TVs or car stereos. Ever been to an Internet chat room? Check around, and you'll find whole discussion rooms devoted to people — often kids — trading stolen credit-card and account passwords with others. You don't want the data they trade to be yours.

One of the best ways to avoid detection is to choose a good password — one that isn't easy to guess. Of course, if you spend time trying to come up with a password that's a little more difficult to guess, you may forget the password if it's for an account you don't use frequently. For this reason, you may decide to jot down the password somewhere where you can refer to it. Although that may *seem* like a great idea, it's very poor security. People who want to find your password know the best places to look, like taped under a keyboard, just inside the center desk drawer, or written in the front of a date book.

Norton Password Manager makes your job easier because it can store your passwords so you don't have to remember a dozen or more different ones for all the places and files that demand a password for access. (The "Storing your passwords" section later in this chapter tells you how Norton Password Manager goes about storing your passwords.) Beyond storing it — so you can get rid of all your reminder notes — Password Manager also *encrypts,* or scrambles, your password so it can't be easily detected by others.

Here are some other tips to keep in mind to avoid detection:

✦ **Don't choose to have other programs store your passwords.** Doing so means others can sit down at your PC and sign in when you aren't around.

✦ **Don't let others watch you as you type in your password.**

✦ **Change each password you use at least every 60 days.**

✦ **If you feel you must jot down passwords on paper (for example, so you have a written backup in case Norton Password Manager crashes), place this information in a secure place where others can't find it.** For example, if you have a locking file cabinet, file your passwords in it and make sure to keep it locked.

Managing Your Private Information

Norton Password Manager not only tracks and retrieves passwords you need online, but also stores a host of different details, from your full name to user account names, to work addresses, and credit card numbers.

Think of a profile as the sum total of the necessary information you want to keep in Norton Password Manager for yourself. By storing specifics within a profile, you won't need to type the same details again and again when you visit Web sites, fill out forms on the Web, order products, and other procedures requiring your private data.

Creating your profile

To use Norton Password Manager, you must create a profile. If the same computer with the software will be used by more than one person, you can set up a profile for each individual.

When Norton Password Manager first installs, you see a prompt to create your profile immediately. Many people wait until they look at the program itself before doing so. Here I assume you haven't established your profile yet:

1. **Double-click the Norton Password Manager icon in the Windows System Tray.**

2. **Click Create New User Profile.**

3. **Type a unique name for this profile and choose your country/region.**

4. **Click Next.**

5. **Type or choose the desired information for each window, starting with Identity through Credit Cards.**

Press Next when done with each screen to proceed.

6. **After you've added details for one credit card, click Add Another Credit Card (see Figure 4-1, which shows the Credit Card profile entry screen) to provide details for a second one, or select Next to finish data entry.**

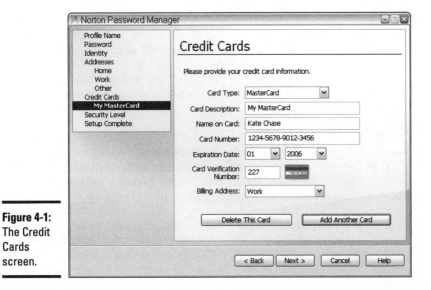

Figure 4-1:
The Credit
Cards
screen.

7. From Security Level, click to choose High (best), Medium, or Low, as shown in Figure 4-2.

8. Click Next.

Figure 4-2:
Set your
level of
security.

You can choose how much or how little detail you want to keep in the manager. Obviously, however, the more you add, the less likely you'll have to type in information on individual sites and in programs.

Whenever you use your desktop or portable PC in a public area, always change the security level to High if you normally use a lower security level.

Setting a default profile

When you first set up Norton Password Manager and your profile, you're asked if you want to set this profile as the *default profile,* which means the one that loads automatically. If only one person uses the software and only has one profile set up, this acts as the default profile anyway.

But when you create more than one profile, it's probably useful to designate one as the default profile — chosen from the person most likely to use the program and the PC most frequently. The default account will then load, with those needing another profile able to use the Switch Between Profiles option to sign into their own accounts.

Editing your profile

Change your address or credit-card details whenever needed, such as when you move, switch phone numbers, or add a new credit card. To do this:

1. **Right-click on the Norton Password Manager (keys) icon in Windows System Tray.**

2. **Select Open Norton Password Manager.**

3. **Choose Edit a Profile.**

4. **Go through the screens and make your necessary changes.**

5. **Click OK and then close Norton Password Manager.**

Notice that, before modifying your account, you see two buttons on your screen (see Figure 4-3): one to back up your profile data and the other to restore previously saved profile data. Choose Backup Data. After you've done this, you can use the other option to restore your data. This is useful if your Norton Password Manager information becomes corrupted and you want to copy back previously saved information.

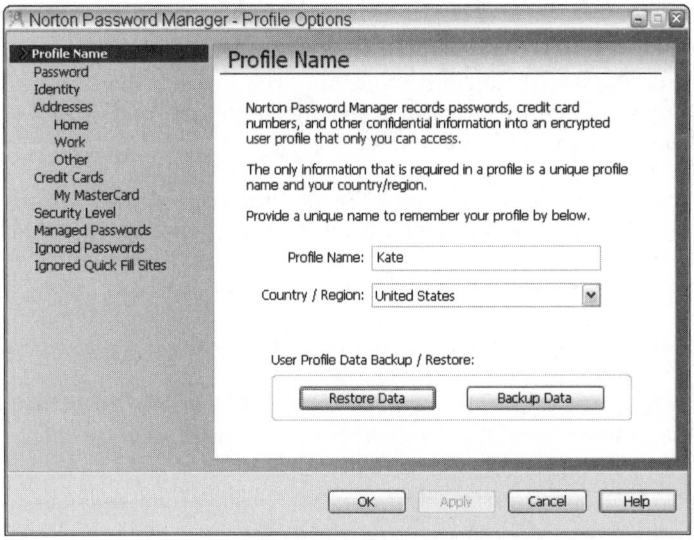

Figure 4-3: Protect your stored data.

Convenience versus security

The easier you make it to use Norton Password Manager or any other program on your system without having to stop and supply a password, the less secure it will be from unwanted visitors. It's one of life's guarantees, along with death and taxes.

Password Manager's Low security level means you just have to sign into the program once using your password. After that, you can use the program — and all the details it contains — without being hassled, right up through the time you restart your system or close Password Manager. But it also means that anyone who sits down at your keyboard can do the exact same thing.

Although you may be tempted by this ease, the Medium setting is better (prompting you to supply the password again after a period of time), and the High setting is the best (asking you for the password each time you — or anyone else — tries to use it).

To change your security level, double-click the Norton Password Manager icon in the Windows System Tray, choose Security Level, and select High.

Signing into your profile

Norton Password Manager is meant to run in the background all the time after it's installed, and it will automatically reload itself into the System Tray, from which you can summon it forth.

With your profile set, sign into Norton Password Manager. You may see the sign-in screen appear automatically when Windows loads. Otherwise, double-click the manager icon in Windows System Tray or right-click and choose Sign In User Profile.

Your profile name should already appear. Type in your password and click OK.

If more than one profile has been set up, click on the down arrow to the right of the profile name in the sign in box, and select your specific profile name before you type your password, then click OK.

Switching between profiles

You don't have to restart your system or restart Norton Password Manager to switch users and their profiles in the middle of a Windows session.

For example, maybe you've been using your PC to visit a news site where you need to sign in. While you're reading, someone else in your home or office needs to borrow your PC to order a great shirt from L.L. Bean. Assuming you each have a profile set up, just follow these steps:

1. **Right-click on the Norton Password Manager icon in the Windows System Tray.**

2. **Select Switch User Profiles**

3. **Choose the proper profile and sign in with the second person's information.**

When the second person is done, the first person can return to his keyboard, right-click on Password Manager, and click Switch User Profiles again, and then choose the original profile again.

Changing Password Manager options

Perhaps you'd like to run Norton Password Manager a bit differently from how it's already set up. For example, let's say you don't want Norton Password Manager to load automatically with every Windows session, and you'd rather launch it when you need it.

To modify general options in Norton Password Manager:

1. **Right-click on the Norton Password Manager icon and select Open Norton Password Manager.**

2. **When the window opens, click Options.**

3. **Uncheck any option you don't want, such as Norton Password Manager running at startup or the automatic loading and running of LiveUpdate (see Figure 4-4).**

4. **Click OK.**

**Book VII
Chapter 4**

Using Password
Manager

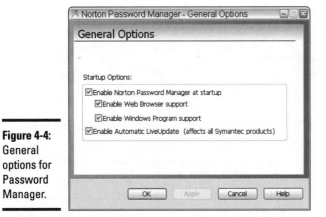

Figure 4-4:
General
options for
Password
Manager.

Adding additional profiles

Sharing a PC is pretty common today. Because of this, you can opt to create more than one Norton Password Manager profile to accommodate multiple people, each with their own address, phone number, managed passwords, and credit-card specifics. To do this:

1. **Double-click on the Norton Password Manager icon in the Windows System Tray or right-click it and select Open Norton Password Manager.**

2. **Click Create a Profile or Add a New Profile.**

3. **Fill out the information as covered in "Creating your profile," earlier in this chapter.**

Using your account

With your profile set up and your Password Manager account signed into, you're ready to begin using Norton Password Manager. Understand, however, that most of the time, the program will sit minimized in your Windows System Tray until it perceives it's needed. This occurs when you visit a Web site or open a program where you need to provide your user name and password or encounter a Web or program form that needs to be filled out.

There's just this one little problem

Although Norton Password Manager will work well for you in many aspects of security and filling in all those pesky forms, there are some limitations. A big one is that it doesn't work with all programs or automatically provide your details on all Web site forms.

You won't be able to use Norton Password Manager to provide user names and passwords for the following programs:

- ✔ America Online
- ✔ CompuServe
- ✔ EarthLink Total Access
- ✔ Microsoft Money 2003 and 2004

That's not all. You also probably won't be able to use it to supply passwords to work with the following types of files:

- ✔ Password-protected Microsoft Word documents
- ✔ Password-protected PDF files
- ✔ QWS on QuickBack forms in QuickBooks software
- ✔ Quicken 2003 Deluxe

Check the "Filling out forms" section in this chapter for specifics on what to do if Norton Password Manager does not automatically fill out basic information in forms.

In the following sections, I show you how passwords get stored through the process and how to modify existing passwords when it's time to set fresh ones on a protected Web site/program and have those reflected in Norton Password Manager. When you understand this process, you'll see how you can use the form-filling features of the software to save you time and keystrokes.

Storing your passwords

The first time you visit a Web site or load a program that requires you to provide a user name and password to access it, Norton Password Manager asks if you want it to record your name and information and to remember it for recall when you visit again. Accept its kind offer, and your user name and password are stored in a small database kept by the program.

At any time, you can go back and view and/or delete passwords stored. To do this:

1. **Right-click on the program icon and select Open Norton Password Manager.**

2. **Click Status & Settings.**

3. **Click Passwords.**

4. **Click Details to see your managed passwords.**

5. **If you want to delete a listed password, select it from the list, and click Remove.**

Changing your passwords

Keep in mind that Norton Password Manager only stores and remembers passwords. To actually change a password used on a Web site or to protect access to a program, you need to visit the site or open the software and modify it there.

After you change a Web site or program password, you run smack into a little issue with Norton Password Manager that makes you feel as though the developers at Symantec didn't quite think this matter through. Norton doesn't allow you to edit your managed passwords directly.

Instead, every time you modify passwords used for sites and programs, you need to delete the former password from Norton Password Manager. Follow the same steps in the "Storing your passwords" section to do this.

After you remove the managed password, the next time you visit the site or launch the software requiring the user name and password and sign in, Norton Password Manager prompts you again asking whether to save and store it. If this seems a little counterintuitive to you, you're not alone. The online help for Norton Password Manager doesn't spell this out very well either.

Filling out forms

Norton Password Manager was designed especially to work with the most common types of forms online, such as those found on popular Web sales sites and online signup programs. It does basically the same thing for forms you might find within Windows programs that require you to provide registration or other personal or work data. Quick Fill is the name of the tool used to help you here.

Go to a Web site or open a program that produces a form you need to fill out, and Norton Password Manager will pop up to give you the option of using Quick Fill. (*Note:* When using Password Manager, you can't turn off Quick Fill.) This features takes the information recorded under your profile and plugs it into the appropriate blanks in the Web or program form.

In practical use, however, expect to do some typing anyway. Password Manager won't magically fill in all forms on all sites or in all programs. Plus, you'll discover that there are nonstandard details you still need to supply yourself.

When you find that your forms are not automatically completed, use the Form Assistant tool, shown in Figure 4-5, to allow you to copy information from Norton Password Manager into the form. With your Web browser loaded, follow these steps:

1. **Go to the Web site where your personal or work information is needed.**

The Form Assistant window with tabs may open automatically. If it doesn't, right-click on the Norton Password Manager icon and choose Form Assistant.

2. **Click on the field containing the information in Form Assistant you want to copy.**

3. **Drag the information into the correct field and release it.**

4. **Repeat as needed to copy additional information.**

These same instructions hold true for Windows programs as well. Just forget the Web browser and launch the program instead.

Don't want Quick Fill to copy your information into a particular Web or program form? If so, when Quick Fill appears, uncheck Disable Quick Fill.

Figure 4-5:
Form
Assistant
lets you
copy data.

Exiting Norton Password Manager

For best results, Norton Password Manager should be open in the Windows System Tray at all times, ready to use. This saves you time over loading and unloading it.

However, you may want to exit the program temporarily — for example, if you normally keep Norton Password Manager at Low or Medium security and someone else needs to use your PC. If you want to exit the program, follow these steps:

1. **Right-click the Norton Password Manager icon.**

2. **Choose Exit.**

Later, when you want to restart the program, choose Start ⇨ All Programs (or My Programs, depending on your Windows version) ⇨ Norton Password Manager ⇨ Norton Password Manager.

Using LiveUpdate

LiveUpdate is a tool known to you through other programs such as Norton AntiVirus. It provides a way of using an available Internet connection to download any needed updates to Password Manager as well as related software.

To access LiveUpdate, it helps to have your Internet connection already established. If you're using cable, DSL, or satellite for broadband Internet access, you should already be connected. If you use a dial-up connection, connect via your modem and phone line before you proceed for best results (meaning less or no delay while LiveUpdate locates the connection and begins to communicate with the Symantec host site).

Then follow these steps:

1. **Right-click on Norton Password Manager.**

2. **If from the submenu you see, Run LiveUpdate, select that. If not, choose Open Norton Password Manager and, when it opens, click on LiveUpdate.**

3. **In the Welcome to LiveUpdate dialog box (see Figure 4-6), click Next.**

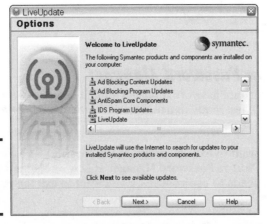

Figure 4-6:
Welcome
to Norton
LiveUpdate.

4. **LiveUpdate then tries to connect with its host servers, search for any needed updates, and download them displaying the progress window shown in Figure 4-7.**

Figure 4-7:
LiveUpdate
retrieves
needed
updates.

Exactly how long this process takes depends both on how standard your Internet connection is and how easily it's found and used by LiveUpdate. Then there is the issue of the speed of your connection for the actual file transfers.

Normally, you can leave the PC unattended, or do work in another window, while this occurs because, if all works well, the download and update will happen automatically.

However, the first time you perform LiveUpdate, you may want to watch the procedure in case LiveUpdate can't work through your connection. You discover this when the LiveUpdate has been going on for several minutes until it finally fails with a `Cannot access the site to get updates` message. There are two major possibilities to explore if this occurs:

✦ **It can't locate or work with your existing Internet connection.** For this, you may want to restart your connection or the entire PC itself (depending on your Internet access type) and try again.

✦ **There's a problem at the Norton update site itself, preventing LiveUpdate from obtaining what it's looking for.** This typically means the servers involved are either down (not operational) or are heavily crowded by other updaters, making it virtually impossible to get in. (If you've been to Microsoft sites right after they release an update, this phenomenon should sound familiar to you.) Usually, there is little you can do except wait anywhere from just a few minutes to a few hours to see if this resolves before you try again.

The use of LiveUpdate is not mandatory, especially in Norton Password Manager. Some people go for very long periods without ever calling upon the tool. However, it can help to take advantage of free product updates that may overcome a problem in Norton Password Manager itself. Other programs that use LiveUpdate, such as Norton AntiVirus, depend far more heavily on the ability to obtain updates like new virus definition files to protect a PC from the latest released forms of infection.

Chapter 5: Employing Password Manager to Keep Prying Eyes off Your Credit Cards

In This Chapter

✔ Understanding how Password Manager helps secure credit-card info

✔ Adding your credit-card details

✔ Using your stored credit card online

✔ Adjusting your security level as needed

✔ Correcting and updating your information

Are you riding the wave of the present and future: online shopping? Or are you one of those holding back because you're worried about how secure the process is? Every day, you hear about credit-card theft and other types of online fraud, and that may discourage you from taking advantage of the convenience of shopping online.

Norton Password Manager is a product designed to try to help you thwart some of that theft. But it does more, because you no longer have to go grab your wallet or purse to retrieve your credit card before you place an online order. Instead, you can store them right in Password Manager for easy, safe retrieval.

Fighting Off the Frauds

Online shopping is a *huge* deal today. You can buy everything on the Web today — from clothes to cars to prescription drugs. But that's just the start. You can also pay bills there using your credit card, or you can buy prepaid postage to place on a package for shipment, taking you out of those long lines at the post office counter.

Unfortunately, however, credit-card and identity fraud is rising at an even faster pace. People actually make their living by trying to steal your financial information.

TIP

The problem with Internet Explorer's AutoComplete

AutoComplete is a tool in the Microsoft Internet Explorer browser that looks at what you're typing into the browser address bar or into a Web form field and then tries to guess the rest for you. The idea is to cut down on the amount you need to type.

Sounds great, right? It is — at least until someone else sits down at your keyboard, goes to an online shopping Web site, orders something, and then suddenly, your credit-card information (such as your number) is automatically added to the payment form.

Whether you're using Norton Password Manager or not, you may want to turn off AutoComplete if anyone else has access to your PC. To do this, within Internet Explorer, choose Tools ➪ Options and select the Content tab. Click AutoComplete, and then uncheck each of the check boxes (as shown in the figure). When you're done, click OK.

For added security, you may want to click the Clear Forms button on the same screen to remove all existing form information stored in your browser history.

AutoComplete Settings [?] [x]

AutoComplete lists possible matches from entries you've typed before.

Use AutoComplete for
- [ ] Web addresses
- [ ] Forms
- [ ] User names and passwords on forms
  - [✓] Prompt me to save passwords

Clear AutoComplete history

[Clear Forms]   [Clear Passwords]

To clear Web address entries, on the General tab in Internet Options, click Clear History.

[OK]   [Cancel]

Norton Password Manager *encrypts* (scrambles in a way that's difficult to sort out without the right key) the credit-card details you store within it. To access those credit cards, somebody has to sign in using your Norton Password Manager profile (sometimes called an *account*).

Also, if more than one person uses your PC, you can each store your own separate credit cards by creating a different profile for each and then adding the credit-card information to each. This helps multiple people in the same office — or even in the same family — keep organized without sharing confidential details.

Even if you're the only one using your PC, you need to create a profile first in which you can store your credit-card information. But if you're one of a few people using the same computer, you'll want to set up additional profiles, one for each person. Chapter 4 shows you how.

Keeping it trim

Although Norton Password Manager will let you store multiple credit cards, consider simply adding just one or two cards per profile. Most people don't use more than that, anyway.

There's a smart reason for this: Just in case you leave yourself signed into Norton Password Manager while you're away from the keyboard, you reduce your risk somewhat if every credit card you own isn't entered there. Also, you're more likely to accidentally choose a card you didn't mean to use if you have several to choose from.

Adding Your Credit-Card Data

Here's how to add your credit-card information to Norton Password Manager:

1. **To open Norton Password Manager, right-click on the icon in the Windows System Tray and choose Sign In User Profile.**

2. **Type your password, and click Sign In.**

If you've forgotten your password and you provided yourself with a hint when you set up your profile, click on the Hint icon at the right of the password dialog box.

3. **Click Password Manager in the left-hand menu.**

4. **Click Credit Cards, and then click Details (see Figure 5-1).**

If you haven't opened Password Manager recently, you'll first see a Profile window with buttons allowing you to restore data or back up data.

5. **Click Credit-Cards in the right-hand pane.**

6. **In the left-hand menu, click Add New Credit Card.**

The Credit Cards screen opens (see Figure 5-2).

7. **In the Card Type drop-down list, select the type of card you want to store.**

8. **In the Card Description field, type a description of the card.**

Choose something that will help you remember which card it is (for example, "My Home Shopping Card").

9. **In the Name on Card field, type your name exactly as it appears on the card.**

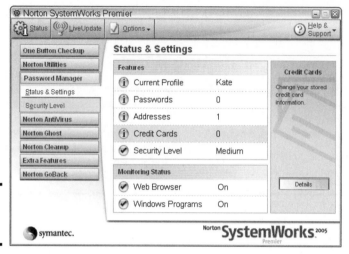

Figure 5-1:
Select
Credit Card.

10. **In the Card Number field, type the account number from your credit card.**

Be sure you've entered it correctly.

11. **In the Expiration Date drop-down lists, select the expiration month and the expiration year.**

12. **In the Card Verification Number field, type the last three digits on the back of your credit card, or, for American Express cards, the four-digit code above your card number on the front of the card.**

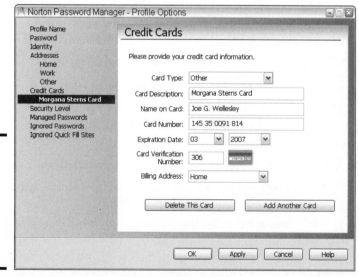

Figure 5-2:
The Credit
Cards
screen is
where you
enter your
card infor-
mation.

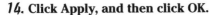

13. **In the Billing Address drop-down list, select Home, Work, or Other.**

14. **Click Apply, and then click OK.**

You can enter more than one card at this time. Just click the Add Another Card button and fill in the card details just as you did for the first one.

If you later want to remove a card, follow these steps:

1. **To open Norton Password Manager, right-click on the icon in the Windows System Tray and choose Sign In User Profile.**

2. **Type your password, and click Sign In.**

If you've forgotten your password and you provided yourself with a hint when you set up your profile, click on the Hint icon at the right of the password dialog box.

3. **Click Password Manager in the left-hand menu.**

4. **Click Credit Cards.**

If you haven't opened Password Manager recently, you'll first see a Profile window with buttons allowing you to restore data or back up data.

5. **Click Credit Cards in the right-hand pane.**

6. **Select the credit card to delete from the left-hand menu.**

7. **Click Delete This Card.**

8. **Click OK.**

To let another person sign in to add a credit card to his own profile, follow these steps:

1. **Right-click the Norton Password Manager icon in the Windows System Tray.**

2. **Choose Sign Out or Switch Profiles.**

3. **Have the other person follow the first set of steps in this section to add his credit-card details.**

Adjusting Your Security Level

After you add credit card details to Norton Password Manager, it's not a bad idea to rethink the level of security with which Password Manager operates. If you make it too automatic (which reduces the security check of asking for your password more than once), you make it easier for someone to use your account if you don't sign out.

Follow these steps to check and adjust your security level:

1. **Open Norton Password Manager and sign into your profile (see Figure 5-3).**

2. **In the left-hand menu (under Password Manager, if you have more than one Norton product installed), click Security Level.**

3. **From the Security Level window, check your security level (see Figure 5-4).**

   If it's set at Low, consider changing it to High. You can also choose Medium, but in the Timeout drop-down list, set a short time between prompts for passwords, such as 5 minutes.

4. **Click OK.**

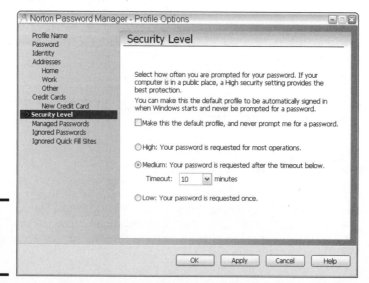

Figure 5-3:
Sign into
your profile.

Figure 5-4:
Increasing
your secu-
rity level.

In Figure 5-4, you'll note that one Security Level option (displayed with a check box), allows you to treat the current profile as the default one and never prompt for a password. Unless you're *really* certain no one else will sit down at your keyboard, be sure to change this to at least Medium security.

Using Your Stored Profile and Credit-Card Details

Although each online store has slightly different steps in the ordering process, here are the basic steps you'll take to use your stored credit-card information to make purchases online:

1. **Sign into Norton Password Manager using your profile.**

2. **Go through the online shopping process and go to the checkout page as you would if you were going to enter your card information manually.**

When you need to supply your first details, such as your name and address, you'll see these form fields highlighted in yellow. The Quick Fill pane opens at the right of your screen, as shown in Figure 5-5.

3. **Click Fill to use your currently stored details for this account, or click Ignore and then type in the details yourself.**

When you reach the screen where you enter your payment details, the Quick Fill pane should appear again.

4. **Click Fill and then complete your order.**

You're done.

5. **Right-click the Norton Password Manager icon in the System Tray and select Form Assistant.**

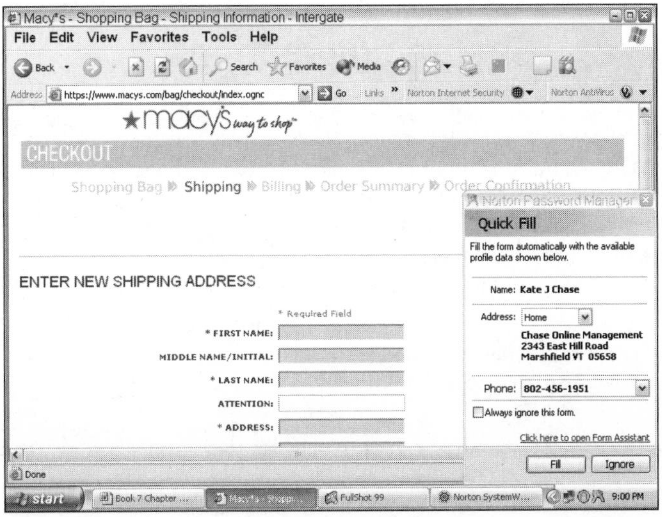

**Book VII
Chapter 5**

Keeping Prying Eyes off Your Credit Cards

Figure 5-5:
Quick Fill.

6. **Select the Credit Cards tab.**

7. **Point to a field of information in your Credit Card details, click within that field and hold your left mouse button. Then drag that field of info and drop it into the corresponding field in the Web form, as shown in Figure 5-6.**

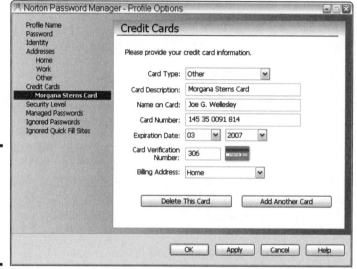

Figure 5-6:
Use Form
Assistant to
fill in your
stored
credit-card
details.

8. **Repeat as needed until all necessary fields are filled in.**

Secure connections

Whenever you're shopping online or using any other kind of Web site where you're interacting with financial data you want to keep private, always look for the Internet Explorer Security Alert warning (see the figure). Other browsers use similar warning windows. The warning advises you that you're entering a secure connection.

This adds a very-much-needed extra layer of protection, ensuring that any data passing from your PC and Norton Password Manager to a Web site won't be intercepted by someone else, like a hacker. Without it, your details are exposed for any enterprising crook to see.

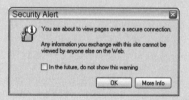

Updating Your Info

Did you get a number wrong when you entered your stored credit card or other information? Or do you need to change your mailing or billing address or update your credit-card expiration date? Norton Password Manager lets you make these changes.

Here's how to do it:

1. **Open Norton Password Manager and sign into your profile.**

2. **To change your profile information, click Current Profile and then click Modify (see Figure 5-7). Make the needed adjustments and click Apply and then OK.**

3. **To change your credit card details, click Credit Cards, and then click Details. From the left-hand menu, select the credit card info you want to modify. Then click inside the appropriate box or drop-down list box. When done, click Apply and then OK.**

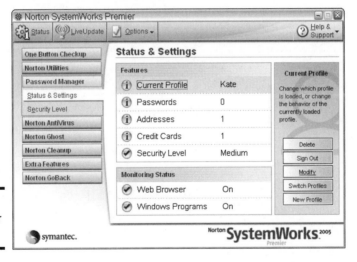

Figure 5-7:
Modify your profile.

Book VII
Chapter 5

Keeping Prying Eyes
off Your Credit Cards

Book VIII

Norton PartitionMagic

The 5th Wave   By Rich Tennant

@RICHTENNANT

FELDMAN
NOVELTY ITEMS

"We can monitor our entire operation from
one central location. We know what the 'Wax
Lips' people are doing; we know what the 'Whoopee
Cushion' people are doing; we know what the 'Fly-
in-the-Ice Cube' people are doing. But we don't
know what the 'Plastic Vomit' people are doing.
We don't want to know what the 'Plastic
Vomit' people are doing."

Contents at a Glance

Chapter 1: Intro to Disk Partitioning

In This Chapter

✔ **Getting the skinny on what disk partitioning does**

✔ **Understanding how it can benefit you**

✔ **Preparing a hard drive for use**

✔ **Knowing the big differences between PartitionMagic and other partitioning tools**

*T*oday's hard drives are H-U-G-E and relatively cheap. For about the cost of taking a whole large family out to a movie and a stop at Mickey D's, you can buy enough hard-drive real estate to keep your basic PC storage needs comfortable for a year or two, at least.

But did you realize that bigger drives need a bit more care? After all, you've got to protect a lot more information stored on them. Just a little thing like poor drive organization — lots of us aren't always so careful how we save files — can turn the simple process of opening a file into a hunt for the proverbial needle in a haystack. You don't need that.

This chapter is all about *disk partitioning,* dividing a single hard drive up into parts. Partitioning is also one of the two routines you need to perform when you're prepping a new hard drive for use. With the basics of partitioning tucked securely within your PC emergency medical bag, you'll be ready to work with PartitionMagic in the following chapters in this book.

What Disk Partitioning Does

Disk partitioning lays the foundation for the physical organization of a hard drive, creating a virtual space to hold all or part of the contents of the data written to platters within the disk itself. Think of a tool or utensil drawer and the way you can divide up the space to hold your smaller items more effectively. This is the same working concept behind disk partitioning.

The actual hard drive is referred to as the *physical drive.* The dividers placed virtually within the drive are called *partitions.* Each partition contains a part of that physical drive, referred to as the *logical drive.* For example, if you have a 60GB hard drive, you might divide it from one physical drive into three logical drives labeled as C:, D:, and E:, each of about 20GB.

One of the problems you see with the wealth of real estate we have with today's drives is that disk partitioning can be so fussy and demands enough skill to do successfully that too many people just leave a big disk as one giant file drawer. As you'll see when I cover FDISK and DISKPART, two disk partitioning tools, one typo can stand between you and a royal mess. Specify the wrong drive letter and you're in deep disk doo-doo.

Even when you avoid dividing up a large drive, you usually don't get to escape disk partitioning because you need to create what's called a DOS partition on every new hard drive to prepare it for installing Windows. That's changing, however. Many hard drives you buy today ship with disk management tools that can prep your drive for you, even if you don't know how. The disk manager steps you through the setup. Likewise, Windows XP lets you use its installation CD to set up a new hard drive for use. You just install the hard drive inside your case, then boot the PC with the Windows CD in your CD or DVD drive. Windows Setup takes care of the rest.

But many people prefer to use PartitionMagic, recently bought by Symantec from its original owner, a company called PowerQuest. PartitionMagic (shown in Figure 1-1) lets you work with either a newly installed or an existing hard drive. Keep reading to discover the serious benefits it offers you.

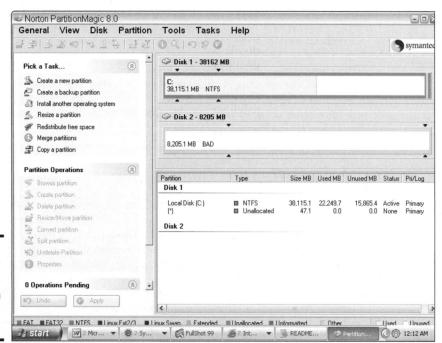

Figure 1-1: Partition Magic is your Norton disk partitioning tool.

Preparing a new drive for use

The most common time to partition a drive is when you're preparing a new hard drive for use. You need to perform two operations before the drive can be used to hold an operating system or store data:

✦ **Create a partition.** You create a DOS partition for disks used to run an operating system or what's called an *extended partition* to store files only.

✦ **Format the drive.** This prepares the drive to run the operating system or receive files.

Only hard drives usually need to be partitioned and formatted in this way. Other types of drives, including CD and DVD drives and most removable storage backup drives like Zip disks and Jaz drives aren't prepped in quite the same way.

If you get an external hard drive that connects through a USB 1.0 or 2.0 serial port or an IEEE 1394 (also called FireWire) port, you usually want to use the drive utilities provided with these drives to prepare them for use. Not all partitioning tools work with these drives.

Organizing with more partitions

Better drive organization is another big reason to partition a large hard drive, whether the disk is brand-new or not. You can take one very large hard drive and divide it into different partitions, or logical drives, where:

✦ One logical drive (your C: drive or primary DOS partition) is used to run Windows and install your applications.

✦ Another logical drive (perhaps your D: drive) is used for all the files you create (like Word documents and Excel workbooks or digital images you take through your Web or handheld electronic camera).

✦ A third logical drive (perhaps your E: drive) stores your backup files or Norton Ghost copies.

Recovering slack space

Besides contributing to poor organization, keeping a large hard drive as just one logical drive makes you lose out on some disk space in the form of lost clusters and space within those clusters.

Want to run two versions of Windows?

You don't have to be a super geek to want to run more than one version of Windows. Sometimes, it's just nice to have a setup where you can use one version of Windows that runs particularly well for your favorite games, while you use a different version to do your normal office-type work and connect to the Internet.

On my main system, I have to do a *lot* of testing of software that isn't always ready for prime-time. If I ran all these still-in-development beta programs while I did my work, I could get myself in a jam. So I have two different copies of Windows XP installed on my main system; one is my usual desktop, while the other has all the beta software. This way I can have my virtual cake and eat it too, without fear of having the cake bite me while I'm on deadline.

Running two versions of Windows — or even Windows and a whole other operating system such as Linux, the PC version of the Unix operating system — doesn't require anything exotic. You just need two operating systems and two DOS partitions. Each operating system needs its own DOS partition.

For this, you can use either two separate hard drives or one physical drive that's been partitioned into two logical drives. Then you install the first operating system on your first logical drive and the second operating system on the other logical drive partition. After the second operating system is installed, you see a special screen called Boot Manager when you restart your system, letting you choose which operating system to load for that session.

Clusters are the tiniest collections of units of information, called *bits,* stored in each drive sector. When you have a huge hard drive, the drive automatically gets set to use the largest possible clusters. But if information written to that cluster doesn't fill the space, you get wasted space also known as *slack space.* Lots of slack space doesn't make for smart drive use.

You want to turn a huge disk into two or three logical drives, so you get smaller clusters and less slack space. Ah, but there's yet one more benefit to partitioning: time.

Saving time with smaller drives

Disk partitioning saves you time. Dividing one big hard drive into two or more partitions produces shorter periods of time required to do disk cleanup and maintenance routines like disk defragmenting or file searches. Figure 1-2 shows Norton Speed Disk working to defragment my under-40GB C: drive; this takes nearly twice as long as defragmenting my 8GB E: drive.

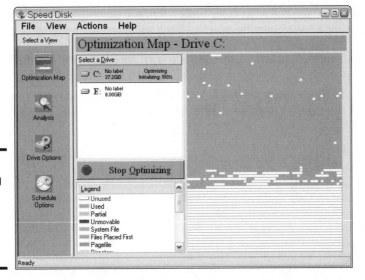

Figure 1-2:
Partitioning
cuts down
on disk
mainten-
ance run
times.

How PartitionMagic Differs from FDISK

Unfortunately, to fully appreciate how much simpler and more straightforward Norton PartitionMagic makes the job of disk partitioning, you almost have to know all that's involved in prepping drives without this great tool.

If you've ever gone online to look for technical support with your hard drives, you've definitely heard about FDISK. If you read any of the instructions, you may have quickly bailed out on the whole idea of partitioning just because it looks so darn much like a combination between geometry and computerese. FDISK has a way of intimidating all but the most hearty or adventuresome souls.

What is FDISK?

FDISK is the MS-DOS command that can be run to partition a hard drive in most versions of Windows. But if you've never used the command prompt or DOS (the predecessor to Windows, in which you need to type everything you do rather than point and click), you won't confuse it with a walk in the park. If you make one typo, or you don't know exactly what to do, you're out of luck.

Although you can run FDISK from Windows, you usually don't want to do that for a few important reasons (including fear of disaster):

✦ **You can't partition the drive you're running Windows from.** So you could only work with a second or third drive that's already installed.

✦ **Windows may crash during the partitioning process.** If that happens, the result is a mess worse than pureeing sardines and blueberries together in the blender with the top off.

Starting with Windows XP, FDISK is no longer included in Windows. Instead, Windows XP has a utility called DISKPART, which runs from the MS-DOS command prompt. Unfortunately, DISKPART is really no easier to use than FDISK, and I don't recommend it for those who faint at the sight of virtual blood.

Instead, here's how Windows XP makes it simpler. Assume you have a single hard disk and it's a new one you just installed. You would insert your Windows XP install CD into your CD or DVD drive and restart your system. When prompted, press any key to boot from the CD. Windows XP Setup starts from the CD, checks the new drive, and steps you through setting it up by partitioning and formatting before the operating system gets installed. *Note:* Windows XP's partitioning also destroys all the files and tidbits sitting on an existing drive.

Thus, when you want a friendlier yet less destructive way of partitioning, it's time to pull out Norton PartitionMagic. In the following section, I show you how PartitionMagic benefits over these other partitioning tools.

How is PartitionMagic better?

There are really good reasons why people go to the trouble and expense to get PartitionMagic when they already have a disk partitioning tool included with Windows for free. Sure, the utility has been around for quite a while and has a very good reputation — but that's just icing on the cake.

PartitionMagic, shown in Figure 1-3, gives you multiple advantages over FDISK, including the following:

✦ It's easier to use (point and click not type and backspace).

✦ It's more forgiving if you make a mistake.

✦ It usually allows you to partition without losing all the existing data on a drive.

✦ It lets you adjust a partition size without making a huge fuss.

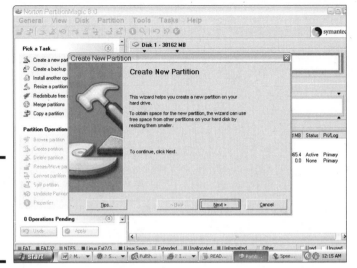

Figure 1-3:
Partition
Magic's
easy
desktop
interface.

Fear of data loss matters a lot when you need to divide up an existing hard drive where you may have oodles of programs installed and a ton of files you've created or added. If you use FDISK or DISKPART to partition that drive, you lose every bit of data on that disk. This is the single greatest benefit of PartitionMagic.

Ah, but even though PartitionMagic is usually perfectly safe, you don't want to risk your data. You'll want to create a backup (discussed in Book 1, Chapter 6) and possibly also a drive image using Norton Ghost (covered in Book 4, Chapter 7). These need to be recorded onto a CD or some drive other than the hard drive you're partitioning.

Book VIII
Chapter 1

Intro to Disk
Partitioning

Chapter 2: Creating a Partition

In This Chapter

✔ Identifying what you have and need

✔ Making your rescue diskettes

✔ Backing up your work

✔ Deciding how to divide the space available

✔ Getting to know the PartitionMagic window

✔ Creating a partition

✔ Knowing what else you may need to do

*N*ow that you have some idea of the pretty important job disk partitioning plays in both preparing a new hard disk for use as well as reorganizing an existing one, you're ready to get down to business.

PartitionMagic makes your work much easier. It's like the difference between the ease of buying sliced bread at the store or having to make your own. If you've had to play with activating yeast, tiring your arms out kneading, and then finding the right knife to slice the finished result, you'll appreciate the analogy.

Here, you're going to see what's needed to create a partition using PartitionMagic. But before you do that, you need to get some protection into place to secure your data. This way, you can leave discussions of chaos theory to science class rather than seeing it in action on your PC.

Launching PartitionMagic

Close all other open programs on your desktop before you launch PartitionMagic. Partitioning and other drive activities aren't really meant to be done with files open and other processes running. You could end up with hopelessly scrambled data as you frequently repeat, "Maybe I shouldn't have done that."

After everything else is closed, choose Start ➪ All Programs ➪ Norton PartitionMagic ➪ PartitionMagic 8.0. If you're in Windows Explorer or My Computer, you can also load PartitionMagic by right-clicking on a drive letter and choosing Norton PartitionMagic 8.0.

Don't forget to close other disk-based programs including Norton Ghost as well as system monitoring programs like the Norton Utilities Windows System Doctor. Right-click on their icons in the Windows System Tray and choose Exit.

Note: Unlike many Norton tools, PartitionMagic doesn't put an icon in your Windows System Tray.

Getting comfortable with the PartitionMagic window

When PartitionMagic opens, it automatically displays any hard disks you have connected to your system (see Figure 2-1). This includes not only hard disks you have installed to the motherboard within your case, but any external hard disks like the newer Universal Serial Bus (USB) or FireWire (IEEE 1394) drives that connect through the external USB and IEEE 1394 ports.

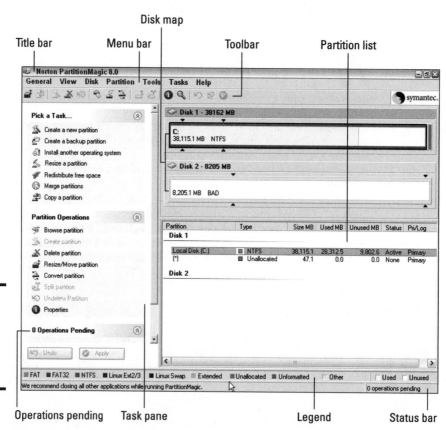

Figure 2-1: Your Partition Magic main work window.

TIP

Approaching with care

PartitionMagic is a serious tool designed to do a serious job: changing the organization structure of a hard disk and helping prepare it for an operating system or data.

Because of this, it's extremely important to only use the tool when you're sure you want to either prepare a new hard disk for use or reorganize an existing hard disk. Don't play with it — and assign a password to protect its use by anyone else with access to your PC.

To set up a password within PartitionMagic, click to open the General menu and select Set Password. Under New Password, type in your password then type it again under Confirm New Password. You can also type a hint if you like (but don't make it too easy or you also make it simple for others to guess).

After a password is set, you'll be prompted to supply the password any time you try to perform an operation in the program.

Just like any Windows program, you have:

✦ A title bar, where the name of the program is displayed

✦ A menu bar, where main menu titles like General, View, Tool, and Partition let you click on them to expand to see major options

✦ A toolbar with the most frequently used operations and needs listed by icon such as Check Partition for Errors

You also see:

✦ A task pane on the left side where operations and helpful wizards are ready for your click

✦ A disk map that shows the recognized drives (choose View ➪ Scale Disk Map to see a rough graphical estimate of size and scale as shown in Figure 2-2)

✦ The partition list that displays information about partitions seen

✦ The operation view (see what's scheduled to happen on the selected partition)

✦ The legend that identifies what the color-coded partition types mean

✦ The status bar and its reports of what is currently happening or how many operations are pending

**Book VIII
Chapter 2**

Creating a Partition

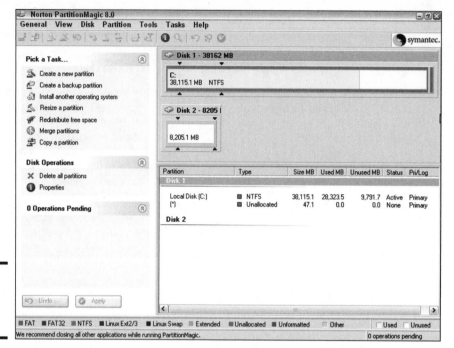

Figure 2-2:
Hard disks
shown to
scale.

Notice the icon near the bottom-left corner of the task pane, beneath the operations status report. The Undo option here lets you undo the most recent action or operation taken so you can reverse course if you did the wrong thing. Remember this!

If you click Undo after you use one of PartitionMagic's wizards, it will vacate any operations taken by that helper.

There's another failsafe built into PartitionMagic. Every operation you select — such as creating a partition or resizing one — actually gets placed in a waiting area, called a *queue,* to be acted on later when you click Apply (located next to Undo). This way, you can cancel an operation before you run it. You can also perform all your operations in one fell swoop rather than one by one, because you set them up in advance. This gives you the freedom to walk away from the screen for a bit after you click Apply and make sure things are starting off okay.

Note: The Undo feature usually isn't available from the PartitionMagic window run from the rescue diskettes.

Calling for extra help

Boy, do you have some choices here.

First, PartitionMagic packs with several wizards to help step you through some of the most common operations you might perform on your hard disks. Then the software is designed to spot certain blunders you may make, so it's going to try to stop you from trying to do anything it knows is wrong.

Choose Help2 ⇨ Flash Tutorial to watch an introduction to the software and what you can do with it. While it's not exactly the dramatic epic you find in a "Lord of the Rings" movie, this animation may boost your comfort level considerably. Also from the Help menu - or by pressing your F1 key on the keyboard - you can load the online help feature to look up keywords like "create" or "resize".

Wait. There's still more, which is great for a product that lets you do as many intricate drive jobs as this. Unlike lots of software these days, Norton PartitionMagic actually comes with pretty extensive documentation that gets into far more details for special situations and advanced functions than a whole book on PartitionMagic would probably cover.

To reach the soup-to-nuts 150-page user manual shown in the figure, choose Start ⇨ All Programs ⇨ Norton PartitionMagic 8.0 ⇨ Documentation. If you can't get into your PC because of a disk or other trouble, you can access this from the setup CD. Just choose PartitionMagic from the first screen, then select Documentation and User Manual.

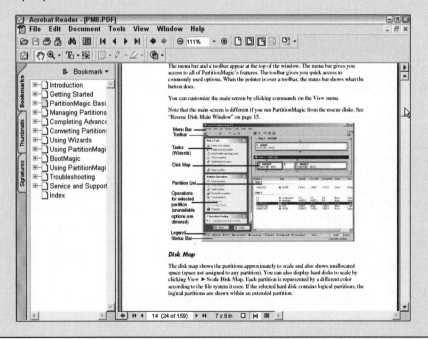

Opening PartitionMagic tools

PartitionMagic comes with a bunch of tools aside from what you see in the main work window. These tools are

+ **Create Rescue Diskettes:** See how to use this in the "Creating Rescue Diskettes" section later in this chapter.

+ **DriveMapper:** A tool that lets you adjust the letters assigned to the drives on your system.

+ **PartitionInfo:** Lets you create a report about your hard disk file structure contents (helpful when getting tech support or trying to understand how things are set up).

+ **PQBoot:** This is a type of boot manager that lets you move between two or more active partitions you may have on your PC but doesn't require the setup of BootMagic, another tool in PartitionMagic.

+ **PQBoot for Windows:** Lets you switch between active partitions and other installed operating systems without installing or making changes to BootMagic.

+ **Tutorial:** This is the same tutorial mentioned in the "Calling for extra help" sidebar.

To see these tools yourself, choose Start ➪ All Programs ➪ Norton PartitionMagic 8.0 ➪ Norton PartitionMagic Tools, and then select the tool you want.

About BootMagic

BootMagic is a tool that falls into the category of utilities called boot managers. This one comes with PartitionMagic and, if you install it, BootMagic allows you to choose between different operating systems you may have installed on different hard disks or partitions on your system.

If you don't have more than one operating system installed, you don't need to worry about BootMagic, or tools like PQBoot or PQBoot for Windows. I don't spend a lot of time on it in this chapter, because most people are running just one operating system.

Just keep in mind that, if you decide to run more than one operating system on your PC, you need different partitions if not entirely different hard disks for each. You'll find that PartitionMagic includes tools directly within it that make it easier for you to work with this kind of situation. The documentation I mention earlier (see the sidebar, "Calling for extra help") has a lot of helpful information on this subject.

Creating Rescue Diskettes

When you've got a brand-spanking-new hard disk, straight from the store shelf, it's not quite ready for prime time. You have no partitions set on the disk, and it's not formatted to prepare it either to accept an operating system like Windows or to store data.

But if you're working with an existing drive, you have at least one partition in place. If you're not sure of your drive setup, you can check it through PartitionMagic, as you see after you get to work in the main work window. Existing details will be listed there and you can reorganize them as needed.

When you installed PartitionMagic, you were prompted to create rescue diskettes. This set of disks is your lifeline if something goes screwy while you're partitioning your drive. They can be used to help get into your system and try to repair things so you can proceed.

If you decided to save yourself time by not making them during the installation, you can prep them now. It doesn't take long and the difference between working with them and working without them is dramatic. This is especially true when you're working with an existing hard disk, one with programs and data.

Even if you've already created a set, I encourage you to make a backup set here, then properly label them and store them so you have them when needed. Having a second set is smart in case the first set becomes damaged, lost, or simply wasn't created right in the first place.

Creating your rescue diskette set

Find two good, blank 1.44MB 3.5" diskettes. You need these to create your rescue set.

Although you can find ways to record a rescue set to a CD or DVD, this is one area where the floppies are usually best unless you don't happen to have a floppy disk drive in your PC. Right now, Symantec warns it may not be able to help you through an emergency if you only store these rescue files on removable media like a CD, but I suspect that policy will change as floppies are used less and less.

You can create your set one of two ways: through PartitionMagic or by using the installation CD you got with the software.

Backing up your work

Excuse me while I kick my soapbox into place before I remind you that even though PartitionMagic should work around any data that is already stored on an existing hard disk partition, don't risk it.

If you can't or won't do a full system backup, copy important files to a different physical hard disk or — better yet — record them to a CD or DVD or other form of removable media that can't be touched through PartitionMagic or its operations. The data life you save will be your own.

I'll just return this soapbox to its corner under my desk next to the foot pedal exerciser I never use.

Follow these steps to do it through PartitionMagic:

1. **Open Norton PartitionMagic.**

2. **Choose Tools ➪ Create Rescue Disks.**

If you can't get into PartitionMagic — or Windows — do this by using the PartitionMagic setup CD. You can even do it from a different PC. Do the following:

1. **Insert the PartitionMagic installation CD into your CD/DVD drive.**

The setup should open automatically. If it doesn't, choose Start ➪ Run, then browse to your CD/DVD drive and double-click on NPMSetup.

2. **Click PartitionMagic and then click Create Rescue Diskettes.**

The rescue disk setup tool launches and asks you to insert the first blank floppy disk. Do this and then click OK. When you're prompted to do so, remove the first floppy, label it, and then insert the second blank floppy disk. Repeat the labeling for the second disk when you see it's done.

Keep these disks somewhere safe in a cool, dry location where they won't be damaged.

Using your rescue diskette set

The rescue diskettes contain everything needed to start your system from a basic configuration, at least enough to get a special version of PartitionMagic running so you can check your drives and operate on them, as needed. The version from rescue is a wee bit different: It's less graphical and doesn't offer all the same tools, but it has enough to help.

Use your rescue disks when:

✦ Your PC locks up while you're using PartitionMagic from Windows.

✦ You convert a partition (from one partition type to another) and it doesn't appear to go well.

✦ You can't start your PC normally or run PartitionMagic from the CD.

✦ You're trying to use PartitionMagic on a particularly elderly version of Windows that won't install the program.

✦ You've chosen to hide the partition that happens to hold PartitionMagic and now you want to make it visible again.

Follow these steps to use the rescue diskettes:

1. **Insert Disk 1 of your rescue set into the floppy drive.**

2. **Start or restart the PC.**

The floppy version of PartitionMagic should load. You can use it much like you use the Windows version.

Return your rescue diskette set to its safe location when you're done with it. You never know when you'll need it again.

Checking Your Drives

Starting out with a good working hard disk always helps when working with a program like PartitionMagic. Reorganizing or setting up a hard disk that is belching black smoke (pretty rare) or is otherwise messed up beyond all redemption (much more likely) is really difficult.

You may want to run Norton Disk Doctor or another disk-checking utility plus Norton AntiVirus or another virus scanner before you use PartitionMagic just to be sure you aren't operating with any nasty surprises onboard.

Yet within PartitionMagic itself you'll find some disk tools, including access to some of the Windows-based tools such as Disk Defragmenter (which works like Norton Speed Disk) to optimize your hard disks and Windows CheckDisk (CHKDSK), which performs an integrity check on a hard disk and can try to fix errors it finds. If you're running an earlier version of Windows, you can also run the Windows ScanDisk tool (available by choosing Start ➪ All Programs ➪ Accessories ➪ System Tools). Note that ScanDisk is not available in Windows XP.

Here's how to perform some checks from within PartitionMagic. Everything is available from the Partition menu. Follow these steps:

1. **From PartitionMagic, click on the disk you want to check in the Disk Map section of the window.**

2. **Open the Tools menu and choose:**

- **Properties:** To see a multitabbed window of information about the currently selected partition, as shown in Figure 2-3. Check this before you run the drive checks or try to partition.

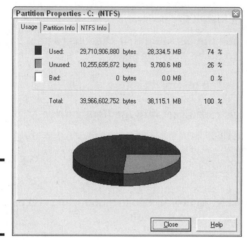

Figure 2-3:
Check
your disk
properties.

- **Check for Errors:** To perform a full integrity check of the selected drive.

- **Windows CHKDSK:** To lock PartitionMagic while the command-line utility shown in Figure 2-4 runs to check the drive for problems.

- **Windows Disk Defragmenter:** To run the disk defragmentation tool similar to Norton Speed Disk (described in Book III, Chapter 3).

```
D:\WINDOWS\System32\cmd.exe                                      _ □ ×

WARNING!  F parameter not specified.
Running CHKDSK in read-only mode.

CHKDSK is verifying files (stage 1 of 3)...
File verification completed.
CHKDSK is verifying indexes (stage 2 of 3)...
Index verification completed.
CHKDSK is verifying security descriptors (stage 3 of 3)...
Security descriptor verification completed.
CHKDSK is verifying Usn Journal...
Usn Journal verification completed.

  39029885 KB total disk space.
  28841684 KB in 65720 files.
     23324 KB in 3709 indexes.
         0 KB in bad sectors.
    149541 KB in use by the system.
     65536 KB occupied by the log file.
  10015336 KB available on disk.

      4096 bytes in each allocation unit.
   9757471 total allocation units on disk.
   2503834 allocation units available on disk.
Press any key to continue . . .
```

Figure 2-4:
Running
Windows
CHKDSK.

Knowing Your Partition Types

PartitionMagic supports partitions for a number of different file systems, with FAT32 and NTFS the type most frequently used by recent versions of Windows. There's also the matter of the status of a partition. Table 2-1 shows some of the partition types you can set under PartitionMagic while Table 2-2 gives you a rundown of status types.

In Figure 2-5, you see that PartitionMagic finds two partitions — one an NTFS-formatted drive for use with Windows XP and the other drive one that PartitionMagic isn't sure about. You can tell the types of partitions by checking the color shown for the partition in the drive map, then looking down at the Legend bar near the bottom of the window.

Here, the darker color tells me Drive 1 is NTFS while the lighter color around the second drive shows in the legend as Other, meaning PartitionMagic doesn't know what it is (a problem I'll probably need to fix after more analysis).

You also need to know about primary versus logical partitions. A primary partition is used to store an operating system. A logical partition is used when you're setting up a partition as a place to store files or serve as a place where the Windows virtual memory is run from. (Remember that virtual memory grabs hard disk real estate and treats it like memory by paging files and programs in and out of your desktop work area.) So when you need to install an operating system, you need a primary, active partition.

**Book VIII
Chapter 2**

Creating a Partition

Figure 2-5:
An NTFS
active
partition and
another
unidentified
partition.

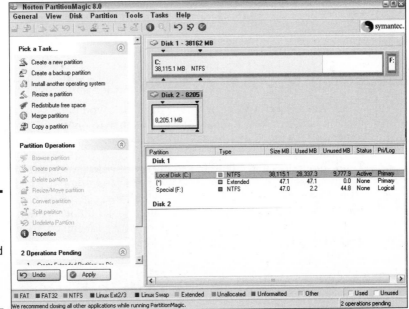

Table 2-1	Partition Types
Partition Name	*How It's Used*
Extended	This can act as a container for other logical drives/partitions (for example, a 60GB extended partition might hold three 20GB logical drives).
Extended*x*	Like an extended partition but without the 8GB extended partition size limit.
FAT	A partition with a file allocation table (FAT) set, for use with older versions of Windows.
FAT32	A partition prepared with the FAT32 file structure for use with later Windows versions such as Windows 98/Me/XP.
FAT32*x*	A partition prepared to accept a special version of FAT32.
Linux	PartitionMagic lets you set different types of Linux-based partitions.
NTFS	Partition prepared for the NT File System (NTFS) used with Windows NT/2000/XP; offers better file security than FAT/FAT32.
Unformatted	Lets you reserve a part of the partition without any file structure, because it isn't formatted.
Unallocated space	Hard disk space not assigned to any partition.

Table 2-2	Types of Partition Status
Type	*What It Means*
Active	A bootable partition such as you see with a drive where an operating system is installed.
Hidden	A partition that has no drive letter and is hidden from view.
None	Any partition that is not set to active or hidden status.

Deciding How to Divide Available Space

When you're faced with a large new hard disk (you poor, poor thing), you have to consider how it makes the most sense to divide up the space. This depends very much on how you intend to use it.

Think about how you intend to use the space before you start the partitioning. PartitionMagic gives you the ability to resize and otherwise change partitions after they're set up. Yet you normally don't want to have to modify your partitions as often as you change your hairstyle, let alone as often as you put on fresh socks. By having some idea beforehand, you can try to make the right decisions to start, requiring less fuss later.

If you have a new 40GB, 60GB, or 80GB hard disk, consider creating both a primary partition and then an extended partition that holds two, three, or four logical partitions. The primary partition needs to be set to active status to accept an operating system like Windows. But if the new hard disk is just acting as a file repository or a backup drive, you probably don't want a primary active partition there. Instead, you create an extended partition divided into subdrives called *logical partitions.*

Here's an example: Think of a pie chart as a view of a 50GB hard disk. You could create just one partition on that disk and make it 50GB in size. But your disk utilities are going to take forever to run because it has to cover all that drive real estate (like trying to do express shopping in a 2- or 3-acre large store).

Instead, you may want to divide that 50GB partition in two or three parts. You could have a main (primary) partition of 25GB where your operating system runs and your programs are installed. Then you could set up an extended partition composed of one 15GB logical partition where your main data files get stored, and another logical partition of 10GB where you keep all your gameware or store backups.

A hard disk can usually accept up to four primary partitions or up to three primary partitions with one extended partition. But within an extended partition, you can have just about as many logical partitions as you want (although common sense probably tells you not to set up 27 of them).

Choosing Your PartitionMagic Operations

PartitionMagic performs a number of different operations on your hard disks, all of which depend on what you're trying to accomplish. These operations include the following:

+ **Creating a partition:** Set up a partition on a hard disk.

+ **Creating a backup partition:** Set up a partition just to store backups.

+ **Setting the status of a partition:** Assign a partition to active or hidden status.

+ **Copying:** Duplicate a partition from one hard disk or logical drive to another.

+ **Resizing:** Change the size of a partition.

+ **Converting:** Change a partition from one type to another.

✦ **Splitting:** Divide a large partition into two or more smaller ones.

✦ **Merging:** Bring two or more smaller partitions together into one partition.

✦ **Removing:** Delete a partition.

✦ **Redistributing free space:** Take free space not assigned to any partition and divide it up between assigned partitions.

In the next few chapters, I cover several of the most frequently used choices. Remember that you can rely on the very extensive user manual documentation in PartitionMagic to find out how to do more exotic things.

Table 2-3 lists some much-needed shortcuts to do — or undo — operations in PartitionMagic.

Table 2-3	Shortcuts for PartitionMagic Operations
Do This . . .	*To Accomplish This . . .*
Choose View ➪ Pending Operations	To see a list of all your pending operations and either apply or undo them.
Choose Partition ➪ Browse	To browse through the contents of a selected partition. You can right-click on a file or folder name to perform standard file functions like copy, delete, rename, create, or move folders.
Choose Partitions ➪ Properties	To view in-depth details about the selected partition.
Press Ctrl+A	To apply all pending operations.
Press Ctrl+D	To delete all changes made.
Press Ctrl+Z	To undo the last change made.
Press the F1 key	To open the PartitionMagic Help window.

Creating Your Partition

The most common operation is creating a partition. For this, I advise you to follow along in PartitionMagic, but don't take any action unless you're working with a freshly-installed blank hard disk or one where you've already stored backups of files residing there.

Use the create operation in PartitionMagic to:

✦ Make a primary partition

✦ Set up an extended or logical partition

Follow these steps to create the partition:

1. **Choose a block of unallocated hard disk space on a drive from the Partition List, as shown in Figure 2-6.**

2. **Choose Partition ⇨ Create.**

   The Create Partition window, shown in Figure 2-7, opens.

3. **In the Create As drop-down list, select either Logical Partition (to store data) or Primary Partition (to house an operating system and programs).**

4. **In the Partition Type drop-down list, select the type of file system you want to use (for Windows XP, NTFS or FAT32; for earlier Windows versions, FAT32).**

5. **Click in the Label box and type a name for this partition to help identify it.**

   Your name can be a maximum of 32 characters for NTFS partitions or 11 characters for FAT32.

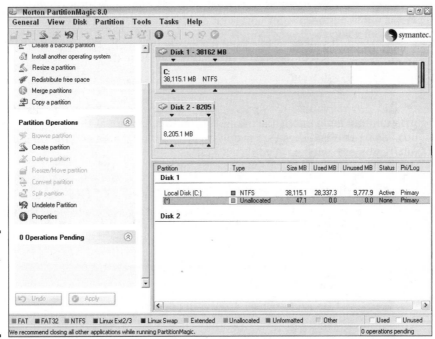

Figure 2-6:
Choose your unallocated space to use for the partition.

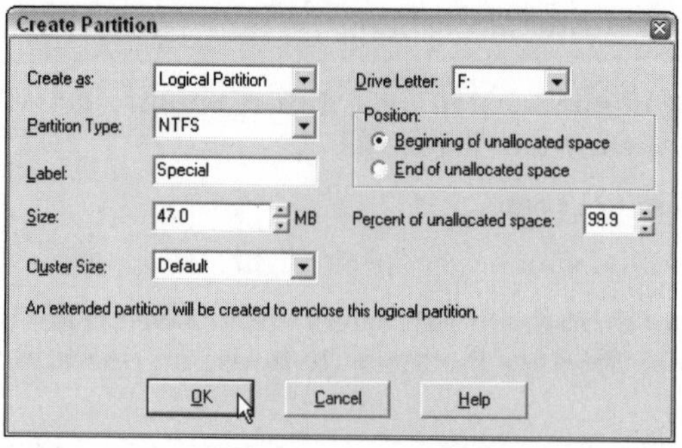

Figure 2-7:
The Create
Partition
window.

6. **To set size, you have two options: Click the up arrow next to the Size box to increase the amount of megabytes assigned to this partition or the down arrow to reduce it (1,000MB roughly equals 1GB, so 8,000MB equals 8GB), or click the arrows next to Percent of Unallocated Space and select a percentage basis for how much space to assign (such as 25 percent).**

7. **To set a cluster size (a *cluster* is the smallest chunk of data that can be written to the drive), click in the Cluster Size drop-down list box to choose what you want or just leave Default listed.**

8. **If you want to assign a specific (unused) drive letter for this partition, click in the Drive Letter box and type it.**

9. **Click OK.**

What you've just done is set up the operation. You'll now see jobs pending as listed on the PartitionMagic status bar and at the bottom of the left task pane. But these operations are in a holding area and the operation won't be performed until you click Apply.

Setting the partition to active status

Before a partition can accept an operating system to boot the disk, the partition must be set to active status.

Follow these steps:

1. **Select the partition.**

2. **Choose Partition ➪ Advanced ➪ Set Active (see Figure 2-8).**

3. **Click OK.**

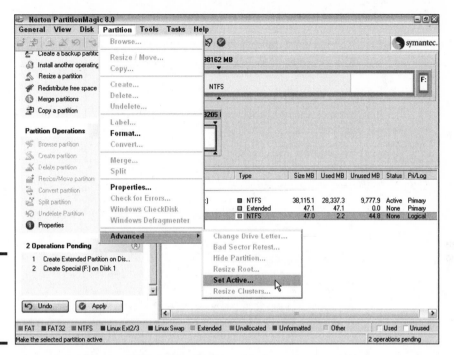

Creating a backup partition

Want to set up a partition as a place to store backups? Here's how to make a backup partition:

1. **Open PartitionMagic.**

2. **Click Create a Backup Partition from the left-sided task pane.**

This opens the Backup Partition Wizard.

3. **Click Next.**

4. **Select the disk to use to create a backup partition, as shown in Figure 2-9, and click Next.**

If needed, the wizard prompts you to ask from which partition it should take room to make space available for the backup partition (see Figure 2-10). Click Next.

The Partition Properties window opens (looking much like you saw it when you created a partition earlier).

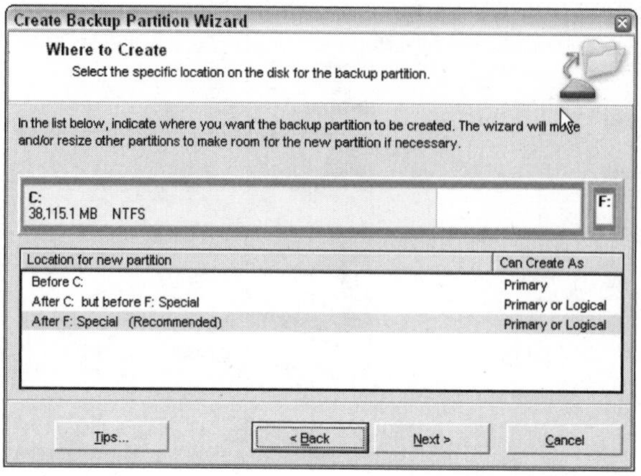

Figure 2-9:
Choose the
drive for the
backup
partition.

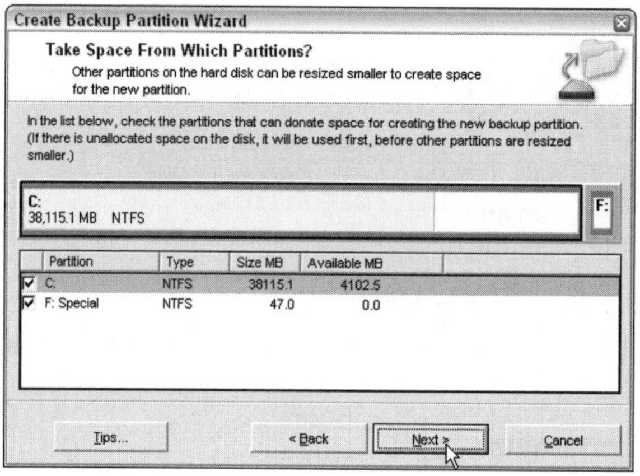

Figure 2-10:
Take space
from which
partition?

5. **Make any desired changes, and click Next.**

6. **From Confirm Your Choices, review your information (see Figure 2-11).
Then:**

- If you need to make a change, click Back until you reach the screen
  where you need to make an adjustment, then click Next until you
  return to the confirm window.

- Click Tips to see a help file with recommendations. (You won't be
  sorry!)

- Click Finish to confirm the backup partition creation as configured.

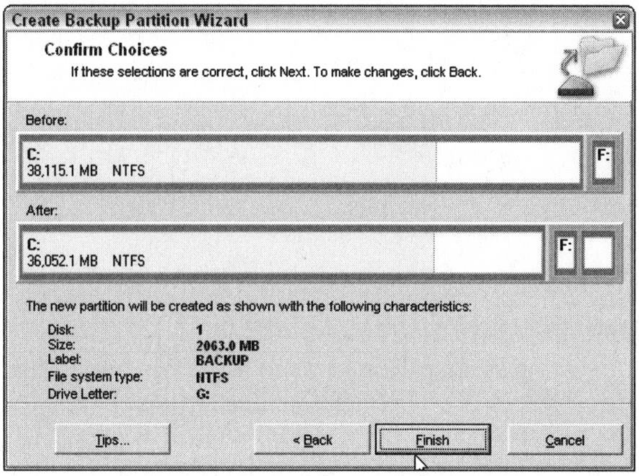

Create Backup Partition Wizard ✕

Confirm Choices
If these selections are correct, click Next. To make changes, click Back.

Before:

| C:
38,115.1 MB NTFS | | F: |

After:

| C:
36,052.1 MB NTFS | | F: | |

The new partition will be created as shown with the following characteristics:

Disk:	1
Size:	2063.0 MB
Label:	BACKUP
File system type:	NTFS
Drive Letter:	G:

[Tips...] [< Back] [Finish] [Cancel]

Figure 2-11:
Confirm
your wizard
selections.

Nothing gets done until you click Apply.

Knowing what else you need to do

Earlier, you created a partition. But any newly created partition usually needs to be formatted to use it. You can also format from PartitionMagic. If you've set an active partition and you need to install an operating system, you need to do that, too, before the disk is ready to use as a bootable hard disk.

Formatting the drive

Although PartitionMagic is designed to try to preserve existing data when you add or modify partitions on your system, the act of formatting wipes a disk clean. This removes any data stored on an existing drive along with any operating system that's been set up. Make sure you've backed up your data on existing drives before you proceed.

Then from PartitionMagic:

1. **Select the disk/partition you want to format from the partition list.**

2. **Choose Partition ⇨ Format.**

The Format window, shown in Figure 2-12, opens, warning you about losing data.

3. **Click the Label box and type a name for this disk/partition.**

4. **To proceed, click OK.**

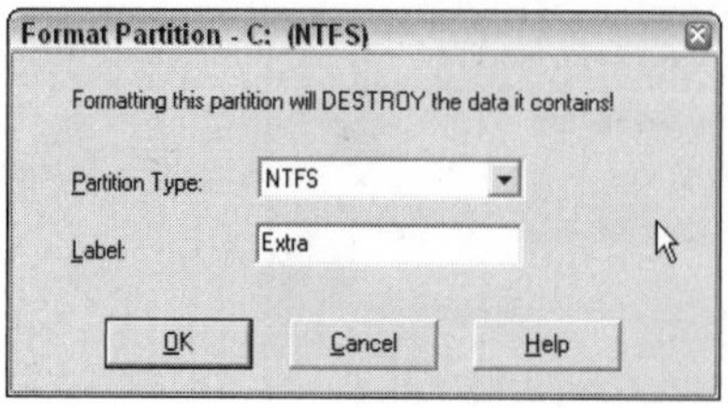

Figure 2-12:
Formatting
a partition/
drive.

> **Format Partition - C: (NTFS)**   ⊠
>
> Formatting this partition will DESTROY the data it contains!
>
> Partition Type: | NTFS   ▼ |
>
> Label: | Extra |
>
> [OK]   [Cancel]   [Help]

Installing your operating system (if needed)

To install an operating system, you need to have your Windows (or other operating system) setup CD. Then follow these steps:

1. **Place your install CD into your CD or DVD drive.**

2. **Start/restart your system from the CD.**

3. **Let Windows setup guide you through the installation, being sure to select the partition/drive letter you've created and set active.**

Chapter 3: Resizing a Partition

In This Chapter

✔ **Analyzing your situation**

✔ **Determining how best to adjust a partition for your needs**

✔ **Resizing your partition**

✔ **Accessing your results**

Today's big new hard disks present a big challenge as well as the glory of all that space. If you remember when even very small hard disks were expensive, you got used to making do with less. When you got lots of space, you may have felt overwhelmed by it.

The problem is that when you're overwhelmed with anything — including PC hardware — you don't make the best choices. Ever try to ace an exam or go through an important job interview when you're sparring with someone? Trying to do well is really tough.

Yet in reality, hard disk space isn't a lot different than planning how to use the space in a large room or a new dresser with lots of drawers. You'd want to organize that space to get the most out of it, right? That's the same basic idea with a highly capacious hard disk — lots of room that needs to be used to your best advantage.

So this chapter turns to how you can resize a partition on your disk so that you can better organize it to suit how you use your PC. Just like in planning the big room or the big dresser, you want to give it a bit of thought and set it up right. If you wait until you begin to fill up that space with tons of treasures and junk, you'll avoid dealing with it.

Analyzing Your Situation

Look at PartitionMagic's drive list (shown in Figure 3-1) and see what you have to work with. Then ask yourself these questions:

✦ How do I use my PC?

✦ Do I create a lot of files?

✦ Do I sometimes have difficulty finding them in the mess of files and folders?

✦ Are my disk utilities (like Windows Disk Defragmenter or Norton Speed Disk) taking half of forever to complete because my drives are too large?

✦ Is that slow performance making me hesitate before running disk utilities, causing my drive(s) to suffer and my PC to slow down still further?

✦ If my hard disk were a file drawer, how would I want to set it up so it makes sense for me?

✦ Do I have one or more very large hard disks connected that only have one partition each? If so, if this were a file cabinet, would it work for organization?

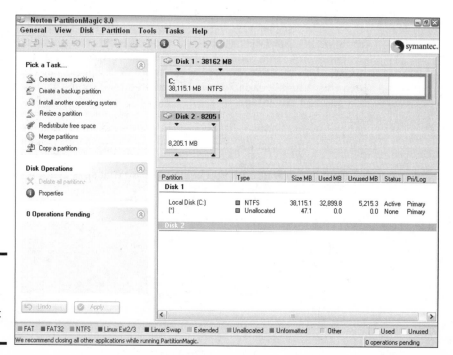

Figure 3-1:
Looking at
Partition
Magic's list
of drives.

Nah, you're not doing PC psychotherapy here. You just need to make sense of the space you have and how you want to organize it better. What you discover here can help when you get a new hard disk, because you're more apt to set it up for the way you work and want to store files rather than just to get the disk running fast.

If, when reviewing your partition sizes, you find just one partition per drive and these partitions are very large, it's time to consider resizing those partitions. One smart way to do this is to take some free space from one partition to create a new one. PartitionMagic gives you some flexibility for this, through the resizing option, through splitting, and through a technique where you can redistribute free space among the drives/partitions.

Consider resizing or otherwise changing your hard disk/partition space when:

✦ A single large partition takes far too long to back up or otherwise complicates the backup procedure because you need so many recordable disks or don't have enough room on other hard disks to store a backup of that size.

✦ You have a partition so small that you're constantly having to clean out files and folders just to keep away from the dreaded "Low Disk Space" warning you get when less than 200MB is available on a drive.

✦ Your disk utilities can run for 30 minutes or an hour or more. (I have one disk that's so large that I have to leave Windows Disk Defragmenter running overnight.)

✦ You want better organization.

If any of these situations sound familiar, it's time to get control of your disks by changing them to better work for you.

Determining How to Adjust Drive Space

Look again at your partition list in PartitionMagic. Exactly what do you see? Identify the following:

✦ Which partitions appear very large (20GB or 30GB or more) with lots of unused space

✦ Which partitions are very small with little if any unused space

✦ Whether you have areas of unallocated space not assigned to a partition (a waste if you need it — you probably will at some point, if not now)

To get a better picture (literally) of your partitions, look up the information for each. You see this basically represented in the partition list under the Used MB and Unused MB columns shown in Figure 3-2. But you can also find a more graphical representation. To do this:

1. **Select the partition in the list.**

2. **Choose Partition ⇨ Properties.**

The Partition Properties window, shown in Figure 3-3, opens.

How should you divide up a large hard drive? Well, probably any physical hard disk larger than 25GB to 30GB should be divided into at two partitions (or more, depending on the drive size), where the first partition should usually be the largest because you're apt to install your operating system and applications there.

You can't make a partition that is smaller than the space occupied by its used area. So if your drive shows you have 4GB of used space in the partition, you can't resize that partition to be 2GB or 3GB.

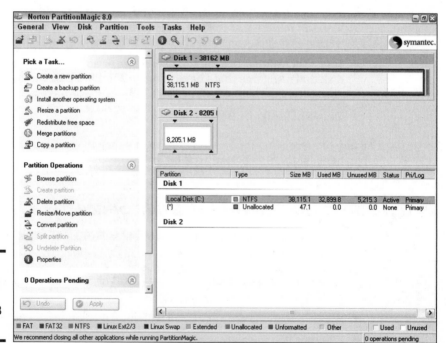

Figure 3-2: Check the Used and Unused MB columns.

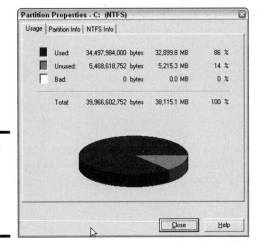

Figure 3-3:
The properties of a drive from Partition Magic.

Never resize a partition in a way that eliminates all its free unused space. You need room to grow. If you reduce a partition to just the current size of used space, you'll be hit with slow disk speed and "Low Disk Space" warnings that will make you wish you had never resized.

To increase the size of a partition, you have to have unallocated space available on the drive either before or behind the partition you want to adjust. If another partition is on the same drive, you could reduce the size of that second partition, which creates unallocated space not assigned to another partition, and then resize that first partition to take over the unallocated space.

A FAT partition — the type used by older versions of Windows like the original Windows 95 — are limited to 2GB (or 2048MB) in size. Anything larger probably won't be seen and recognized for use. But something much worse could befall you, too. If you make a FAT partition larger than 2GB, the drive could become unbootable, a real problem if your operating system is installed there: You won't be able to start your PC to load Windows.

Try to get your partitions right the first time. You can go back and adjust later, but you're usually better off if you don't fiddle frequently. In this way, it's a little like surgery. So much of the tools and technology we have today make it far more likely the patient will survive a surgical procedure; but every time you land on the operating table you're at risk. So too is your drive, its partitions, and the integrity of the data they hold when you surgically adjust them through PartitionMagic.

**Book VIII
Chapter 3**

Resizing a Partition

Resizing and Moving Your Partitions

PartitionMagic allows you to resize your partitions as well as move them to a new location on your hard disk. By moving a partition, you're determining whether that partition sits at the beginning of the hard disk space, in the middle, or at the end. However, except for usually being sure that a partition where an operating system is installed is at the beginning of the disk, there aren't many typical advantages to moving partitions around.

When you have an idea of how you want to adjust the size of a partition, you're ready to proceed. ***Remember:*** Be sure to make a backup of your system or at least key files before proceeding.

Then follow these steps:

1. **Open PartitionMagic.**

2. **Select the partition you want to resize from the Partition list.**

3. **Choose Partition ⇨ Resize/Move.**

The Resize/Move Partition window opens. Be sure it's pointed to the correct partition (the one you selected in Step 2).

At the top of the window (see Figure 3-4), you see a disk map showing the following:

- • Used space

- • Unused space (none shown in this figure)

Left partition handle   Right partition handle

Used space   Unallocated space

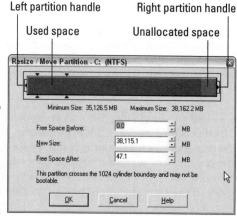

Figure 3-4:
The disk
map on the
Resize/Move
Partition
window.

- Unallocated space on the drive that is not part of this partition

- Handles on the far left and far right that allow you to point and drag them to adjust the space in the partition

4. **Point to either the left or right partition handle and hold your left mouse button, then drag the handle (see Figure 3-5) until you've adjusted the space as you want it, to increase or decrease its size.**

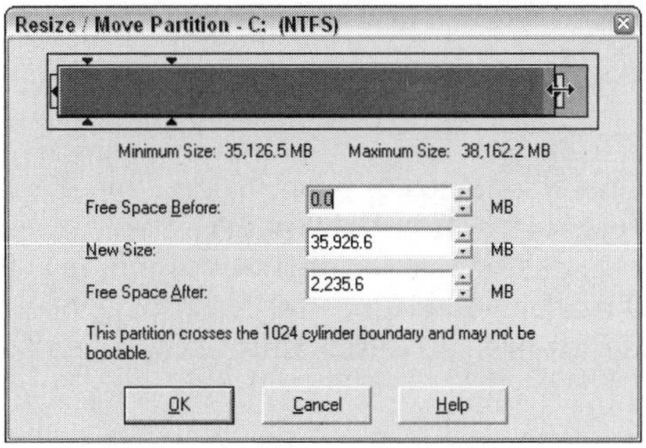

Figure 3-5:
Drag your
handle to
resize the
drive.

You may not work so well graphically or feel that your mouse-pointing abilities are that sensitive when dragging and positioning. If either of those fit you, you may prefer to use the boxes below the disk map.

Here's how to do it this way:

1. **Click in the Free Space Before box (see Figure 3-6) and either type the amount of space (in MB) you want before this partition or use the up/down arrows at the right of the box to adjust it.**

    If you want this drive to remain at the beginning of the partition, this box should read 0.

2. **Click in the New Size box and type the size in MB you want the partition to contain.**

    Remember that 1,000 MB roughly equals 1GB.

3. **Click in the Free Space After box to set the empty space (suitable for another partition) to appear after this partition on the drive.**

4. **If desired, click in the Cluster Size drop-down list to choose a different cluster size.**

    I normally leave the cluster size alone because Windows and Partition Manager usually set cluster size to the best one for most circumstances.

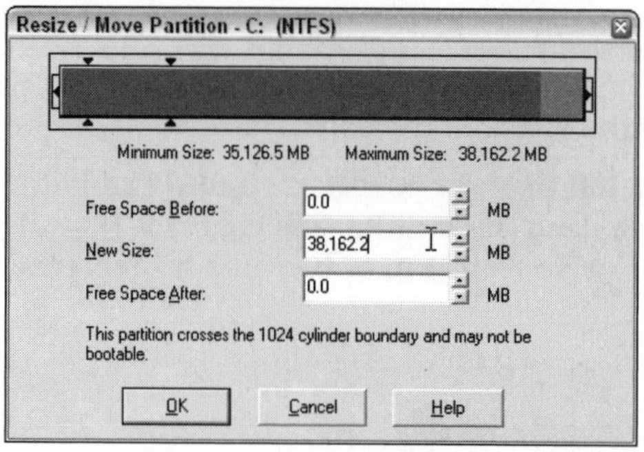

Figure 3-6:
Adjust the
Free Space
Before.

If you don't see a Cluster Size box in your Resize/Move Partition window (note that the Cluster Size box is not shown in Figure 3-6), and you want to look at or adjust your cluster size (again, not something I tend to recommend without good reason and even better backups), choose Partition ➪ Advanced ➪ Resize Clusters; the Resize Clusters window (shown in Figure 3-7) opens.

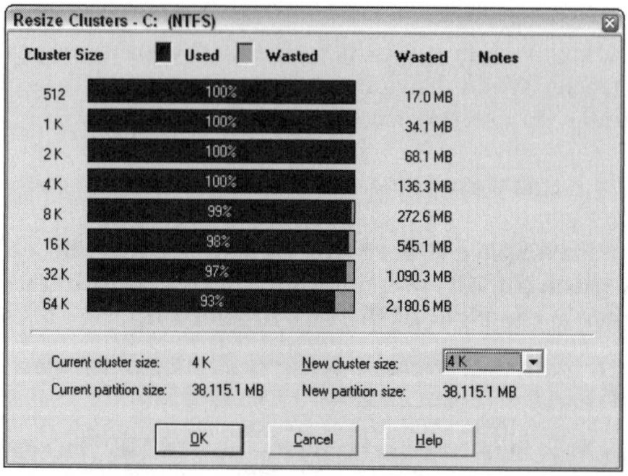

Figure 3-7:
Viewing
your drive
cluster
information.

If you're using a file type other than FAT or FAT32, you won't be able to adjust Cluster Size at all (see the next Tip to see how to do this for NTFS partitions). To adjust the cluster size on NTFS partitions, choose Partition ➪ Advanced ➪ Resize Clusters.

5. **After you're done with your adjustments, review your choices and notice that the disk map has changed above to reflect the adjustments you made below.**

6. **When you feel sure with your choices, click OK.**

Redistributing Free Space

PartitionMagic has a tool that lets you distribute unallocated space not currently assigned to any partitions set up on a physical hard disk. This isn't a bad way to correct a situation where you have a chunk of unallocated space that's really too small to turn into a separate partition yet you don't want it to go to waste.

Follow these steps to perform the redistribution:

1. **In the left-hand task pane in PartitionMagic, click Redistribute Free Space (see Figure 3-8).**

A wizard appears.

2. **Click Next.**

3. **Select the drive you want to involve in the redistribution, and click Next.**

4. **Select the partition(s) on the drive to use as part of this redistribution and click Next (see Figure 3-9).**

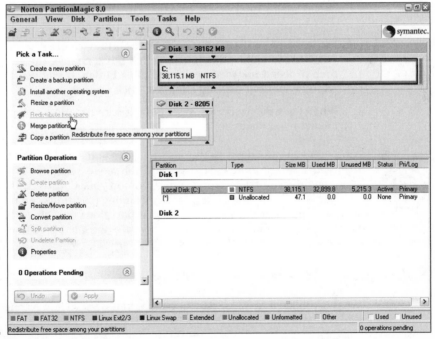

Figure 3-8:
Click
Redistribute
Free Space.

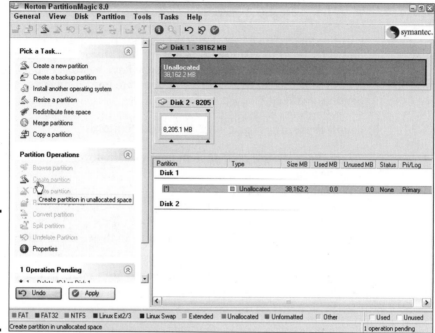

Figure 3-9:
Choose the
partition(s)
to involve in
the space
redistri-
bution.

5. **Review and confirm your selections. If they're okay, click Finish. If you want to make adjustments, click Back, change the selection, and then proceed forward again and click Finish. If you want to close the window without making changes, click Cancel.**

   When the window closes, your partition information will reflect the changes you made.

Although you can adjust partitions, there are some limits. Don't assume that if you have two or more hard disks you can move partitions around between physical drives or try to merge a partition on your C: drive with a partition on your D: drive. It won't happen. Work among partitions can only occur within a single hard disk. You can adjust partitions on a single hard disk, but you can't try to join hard disks together into one giant partition.

Splitting or Merging Partitions

What if you have two tiny partitions that you want to join or one humongous one you want to divide? You operate on them, that's what.

PartitionMagic makes it possible to modify the partitions on your drive(s) in two additional ways:

✦ Split a single partition in two.

✦ Merge two partitions on the same drive into a single larger partition.

When you split a partition, you create two partitions from one. Both of those partitions — like the single one they're made from — must exist on the same hard disk. You can't move them to another disk.

Think about this before you split a partition, however, especially if that single partition you want to divide doesn't have much available free space. Filling a partition full won't be helped by dividing it in two. You want to clean the partition of unneeded files and folders. Then you can reevaluate whether the drive should be split.

Do not try to split partitions that contain your operating system. Also do not try to split partitions that are only 100MB in size or smaller.

If the Split partition option is grayed out in the left-hand task pane, PartitionMagic does not deem any of your partitions good candidates for being split.

Follow these steps to split a partition:

1. **Choose the drive you want to split from the Partition list.**

2. **Click Split Partition in the left-hand task pane.**

   This opens a wizard to help you do that.

3. **Click Next.**

4. **Select the Data tab.**

5. **In the Original Partition list, select the files and folders you want to move into the new partition that will be created when you split the current one.**

   Don't move everything — at least one file and folder should be left behind.

6. **Click in the Label box and type a name for the new partition to help you identify it.**

7. **Click in the Partition Type drop-down list and choose the type of file structure you want.**

   Choose NTFS or FAT32 for Windows XP or FAT32 for earlier versions like Windows Me or Windows 98.

**Book VIII
Chapter 3**

Resizing a Partition

8. **Select the Size tab.**

9. **Click and drag the right-side handle to adjust the estimated size of the new partition, or click in the Maximum Size box and type the size (in megabytes) for the new partition.**

10. **Click OK.**

Your new partition should be established and ready for duty.

Merging two partitions into one — as you might expect — requires that you already have at least two partitions on a single hard disk. Remember that you can't join a partition from C: and one from D:.

To merge two partitions, follow these steps:

1. **Click Merge Partition in the left-hand task pane.**

The Merge Partition Wizard (shown in Figure 3-10) appears.

Figure 3-10: Your Merge Partition Wizard.

2. **Click Next.**

3. **Select the disk that contains at two or more partitions, and click Next.**

4. **Select the merge option you want and click Next.**

5. **Type a name for the folder that will appear in the final merged partition containing the contents of the partition that was merged into it.**

6. **Choose the partition file system to use for the partition you're keeping, and click OK.**

When you're done, you'll receive a message telling you your operation was a success.

Whenever you change your partitions around like this, be sure to run the DriveMapper tool so that PartitionMagic and your system can redetect what's what. (See the following section for more information on the DriveMapper.)

Using DriveMapper

PartitionMagic packs a tool called DriveMapper that is designed to look at the changes you make using PartitionMagic and make sure your PC, Windows, and PartitionMagic itself all recognize these adjustments. Normally, you need to run Drive Mapper whenever you make key changes like splitting or merging or even adding a partition or rearranging your drive letters. Think of this as the finishing touch in making sure that the changes updated throughout your system.

Here's what to do:

1. **From Partition Magic, choose Tools ➪ Drive Mapper.**

An Introduction window opens.

2. **Read the information and click Next.**

3. **Choose the task that applies for the reason you're running the Mapper (Split Operation or Merge Operation — or choose Typical Operation for anything else, as shown in Figure 3-11).**

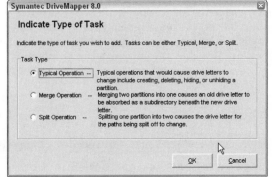

Figure 3-11:
Choose your
task type.

4. **In the Create Typical Task window, select the drive letter for a partition before it was changed in the first box, then the drive letter after the change in the second (see Figure 3-12), and click OK.**

5. **Confirm your tasks in the final window and then click Finish.**

A processing window appears while the changes are being applied. When DriveMapper runs, it will update all drive references just as you've specified them. Nice work!

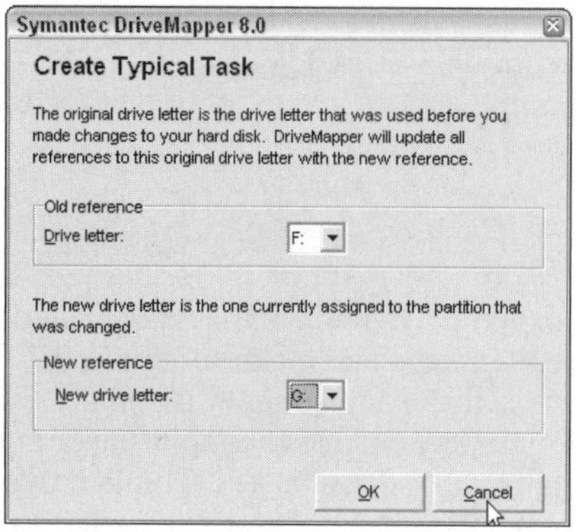

Symantec DriveMapper 8.0

Create Typical Task

The original drive letter is the drive letter that was used before you made changes to your hard disk. DriveMapper will update all references to this original drive letter with the new reference.

Old reference

Drive letter: F:

The new drive letter is the one currently assigned to the partition that was changed.

New reference

New drive letter: G:

OK   Cancel

Figure 3-12:
Specify your
drive letter
changes.

Changing Drive Letters

Don't like the way your drive letters were assigned automatically? You can change them — with care, of course.

You usually don't want to change letters for partitions that contain a booting operating system, such as you usually find with your C: drive. Doing so could cause serious booting errors and other problems you just don't want to experience.

A good example of when to use the drive-letter-changing tool is when your removable external hard drive has suddenly picked up a letter somewhere between the standard hard disks installed on your system. For example, you have two hard disks that are now referenced with letters C: and E:, respectively, and your removable hard disk is letter D: which is a little counterintuitive, because you're more apt to install programs and load files from your main hard disks.

Here's what you do to change this:

1. **In PartitionMagic, choose Partition ➪ Advanced ➪ Change Drive Letter.**

2. **When the Change Drive Letter box opens, click in the drop-down list box and specify the drive letter you want to use.**

3. **Click OK.**

A processing window appears again letting you know the status as it makes changes to references to your old partition letter so that those references reflect the new letter. Then you're done.

Chapter 4: Copying a Partition

In This Chapter

✔ **Knowing how you can use copies of partitions you make**

✔ **Suggestions for finding room**

✔ **Copying a partition**

✔ **Converting a partition from one type to another**

Yes, Virginia, you can even copy partitions so you have an exact duplicate that you can store on a wholly different hard disk. Sweet!

Can you even imagine how many ways that can come in handy? Maybe you wouldn't have to cross your fingers when installing that new game everyone keeps warning you about, yet you really, truly want to give a spin. Think about being able to copy a whole partition from your old hard disk onto a new one.

How much time could that save? How many disasters could you gracefully sidestep with time to spare and not the slightest sweat on your brow (or your PC)?

Knowing How You Can Use a Partition Copy

A partition copy is exactly what its name implies: a 100 percent absolute duplicate copy of a partition on a hard disk. This means every file, every folder, any operating system setup, and even every little failing and questionable setting.

Having a copy can come in terrifically useful in certain situations. Here are just a few of them; see if any apply to you:

+ You're testing flaky software or want to make some type of massive change to your setup. For this, you want an exact copy of your partition as it was, so if bedlam reigns supreme, you can rely on the partition copy to get you back to work.

+ You're preparing to retire a small, older hard disk and want to move its setup and files to a newer, larger hard disk.

+ You're about to upgrade or change your operating system but want a copy of the current setup just in case (not every upgrade goes well).

+ You want to reorder your partitions on a drive.

You need to have available space on the drive where you want to create the copy. You won't be able to store a copy of a 20GB partition on a 40GB hard disk already filled with 25GB to 30GB of data.

I recommend getting a removable USB or IEEE 1394 hard disk. As of this writing, you can get a very fast external one for about $1 a gigabyte or $150 for 160GB of space. Then use the removable drive to store copies of the partitions from your main installed hard disk(s).

Creating a Partition Copy

When you're sure you have the room to create a copy of the partition, I suggest you do the usual disk maintenance on the partition before you copy it. No sense sending along a gigabyte of temporary and leftover Internet files and infinite saved games from that game of Sims 2 that you haven't played in months.

At the very least, you should:

+ Run a virus scanner.

+ Use a disk integrity scanner like Windows ScanDisk, Windows Chkdsk, or Norton Disk Doctor.

+ Dispose of unneeded files with a disk cleanup program.

+ Uninstall any no-longer-desirable programs.

Then, when your disk is so clean and tidy you almost want to throw a party, you can copy the partition to its secondary home. Follow these steps:

1. **Click to select the partition you want to copy in the Partition List.**

2. **Click Copy Partition from the left-hand task pane (see Figure 4-1) or choose Partition ⇨ Copy.**

3. **When the Copy Partition window appears, click the partition you want to copy (see Figure 4-2) and click Next.**

4. **Click to choose an allocated space where you will copy the partition (see Figure 4-3) and click Next.**

5. **If the partition you're copying is smaller in size that the unallocated spaces it's been duplicated into, you need to specify whether PartitionMagic should position the copy at the beginning or the end of the unallocated space.**

   Unless you have a specific reason to copy the partition elsewhere, aim for the beginning of the unallocated space.

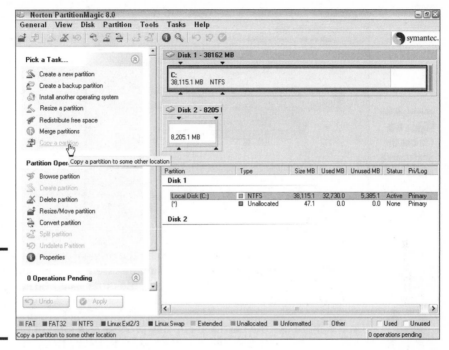

Figure 4-1:
Start the
Copy a
Partition
Wizard.

6. **Click Finish.**

Congratulations! You've got your copy.

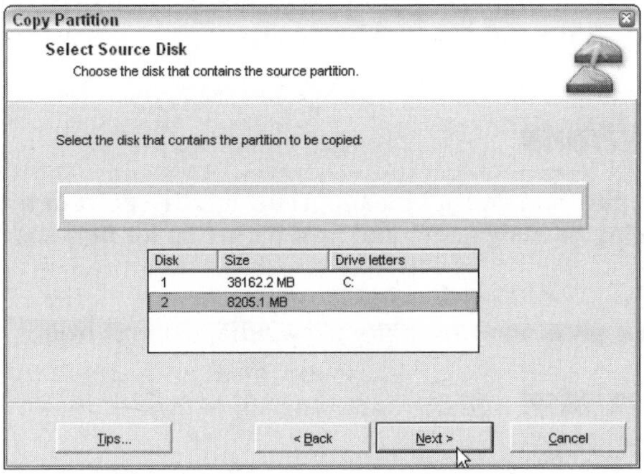

Figure 4-2:
Select the
partition
to copy.

**Book VIII
Chapter 4**

Copying a Partition

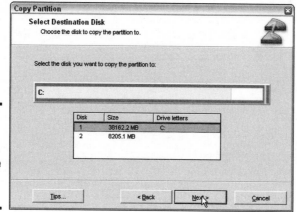

Figure 4-3: Choose the unallocated space to use as the copy destination.

 There is no dynamic kind of link between the original partition and the copy. If you add or change files and folders and installed programs or operating systems stored on the original (or copy), the other won't be affected or automatically updated to reflect the changes.

 If you want to use the partition-copying process as a form of backing up to another drive (not a bad idea!), make a point to follow this procedure every week or so:

1. **Delete the partition copy from the other drive.**

   Chapter 5 shows you how to delete partitions.

2. **Copy the updated original partition from the first drive to the other drive just as you did the first time.**

Converting Partitions

Converting a partition doesn't mean turning it into a newt or a Jaguar. It means changing its assignment and how it's set up for files and the operating system.

PartitionMagic gives you the ability to switch partitions from:

✦ Primary to logical

✦ Logical to primary

✦ FAT to FAT32

+ FAT32 to FAT

+ FAT to NTFS

+ NTFS to FAT

+ FAT32 to NTFS

+ NTFS to FAT32

You could decide to convert a FAT32 disk under Windows XP to NTFS because the latter gives you much better security for your files and folders than FAT32, for example. Or you might try to run a second operating system on a second partition on your system, only to decide later you want to go back to your usual single operating system; as part of the process, you might want to convert the drive from primary (with active status) to a logical partition where it will now just store files and folders.

Follow these steps to convert a primary partition to a logical one:

1. **Select the partition you want to convert from the disk map.**

2. **Choose Partition ⇨ Convert or click Convert Partition in the left-hand pane.**

3. **In the Convert partition window, select Logical Partition, as shown in Figure 4-4.**

Figure 4-4: Choose the new partition type.

4. **Click OK.**

PartitionMagic has a two-step operation process. Nothing you select is actually performed until you click Apply in the bottom of the left-hand pane. To reverse a set conversion, either click Undo in the left-hand task pane (see Figure 4-5) or press Ctrl+D (which discards all changes).

**Book VIII
Chapter 4**

Copying a Partition

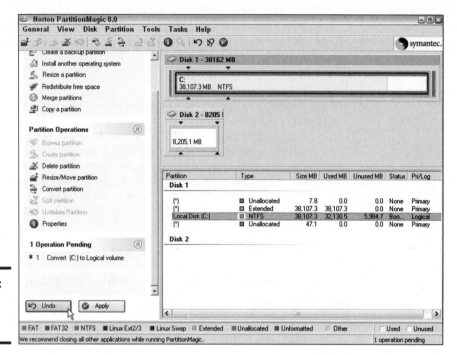

Figure 4-5:
Undo the disk conversion.

Chapter 5: Removing a Partition

*P*artitions aren't something to remove lightly, especially when they live on hard disks you've been using. Even if the only thing you ever do on your PC is send and receive e-mail and browse the Web, there are files stored on your hard disk that you likely don't want to lose.

However — thank you, Norton! — PartitionMagic allows you not only to delete partitions but to recall the decision and try to regain that partition and its data after you thought all hope — and data — were lost. Still, not deleting it at all if that's not exactly what you want to do or should do is easier than trying to recover it. So in this chapter, I fill you in on the right and wrong reasons and times.

Here, you also explore the secrets of hiding partitions. In case you're curious, I fill you in on the reasons you may want to hide a partition. And I also tell you how to make them visible again when needed.

Deleting for the Right Reasons

So why would you want to delete a partition? If you can't answer that question, don't delete.

Almost every day I hear of someone trying to delete a partition or reformat a hard disk for reasons that make no sense. In way too many of these cases, these people got tips from friends at work or family members who didn't bother to tell these unsuspecting help-seekers that wiping the partition erases all the data along with it.

Deleting a partition fixes very little except specific disk-organization issues.

When to delete a partition

You may be the ideal candidate for deleting a partition if any of the following statements apply to your situation:

✦ You want to start completely fresh, wiping everything off a disk, even the file structure and original setup.

✦ You've already copied the partition to a different hard disk and you don't need a duplicate here.

✦ You've already backed up because you're having problems with this hard disk. Now you want to see if a past virus did something to your setup so you want to completely reorganize the whole thing from the ground up.

✦ When you called your hard-disk manufacturer to report a problem, they suggested you wipe the drive and create a fresh partition and then format.

✦ You're about to give this hard disk to someone else so you can get a new one. But you want to make it difficult for the next person to try to retrieve any of the data you had on the drive.

TIP

"Trust me, this will fix anything!"

A woman I know — and I won't give her the delight of identifying her by name — loves to pretend she's a super-duper PC guru. Walk into a room, mention the word *computer,* and she'll gravitate over to you, ask you what problems you may be having, and give you an answer every time.

This woman's solution for everything is to tell you to delete your partition and then format your drive. This is true whether you tell her you have an outdated driver, a problem with your video, or trouble upgrading your Windows version.

You know what? Deleting your partition deletes your partition. That's it. For any of the problems I mention in the last paragraph, there are 10 or 20 better fixes than deleting a partition. If you were wise enough to call this woman on her

strange suggestions, you'd find she couldn't even tell you why her recommendation should work. (I've asked — she can't.)

I shudder to think of how many people have taken her advice. I've chased a number of these folks down to tell them to ignore what she said, though there are always a few that slip away too quickly.

The message here is that there are plenty of people like this woman around. Don't listen in desperation and try the very first thing you hear. Always get a second, third, and maybe even a fifth opinion before you take recommendations that require you to start from scratch. Sometimes, wiping the slate clean is good or great. But when it's not necessary, you'll want to kick somebody for making all that new busywork for you.

Do not remove a partition when you have not backed up the files and folders on your partition. See "Moving Your Data Elsewhere" for suggestions.

When not to delete a partition

Here's the absolute number-one rule in PCs and life as well as in the specific issue of deleting a partition:

If you're not sure why you're doing it, *don't!*

Moving Your Data Elsewhere

If you have another hard disk installed on your PC and it has enough room (or can be adjusted through PartitionMagic to provide the space), you can copy the partition from the current disk to the other one before you delete it. To do this, simply follow the instructions for copying partitions in Chapter 4.

If you can't copy the partition in whole to another physical hard disk, you need to back up the files and folders on the partition you're about to remove. If you want to retain a full copy of everything, use Windows Backup or Norton Ghost (discussed in Book IV). If you only want select files and folders and you're happy to let anything else go, you can burn a CD or DVD with only the items you want to keep before you remove the partition.

Removing Your Partition

Looks like you're committed to deleting that old partition. So let's boogie.

Extended partitions can act as containers for logical partitions or drives within it. So an 80GB hard disk might have one extended partition that holds three logical partitions. If you wanted to delete that extended partition, you would first have to kill off each and every one of those three logical partitions therein.

If you've installed the BootMagic tool with PartitionMagic, you can't remove the partition where that software is installed until you remove the software. To remove BootMagic:

1. **Go to the Control Panel and double-click Add or Remove Programs.**

2. **Select BootMagic from the list and then click Remove.**

3. **Follow the on-screen prompts to complete the removal (you usually have to reboot).**

The Delete and Secure Erase option: Protection worth having

I don't want you to be paranoid but sometimes people really *are* looking over your shoulder.

If you're inclined to skip over the Secure Erase option — or select it without giving it much thought — reconsider.

This sounds like a silly point, but according to a private detective I know who does investigations for all types of individuals and corporations, hard disks are the new way that people are stealing information from others. This private eye says he knows lawyers who suggest a divorcing spouse claim a hard disk failure so he can replace an existing hard disk with a new one just so he can look through the contents of the other person's hard disk. He also says that some companies routinely scan files on employees'

systems to be sure they're not working on something non-office-related or communicating with competitors. In fact, law-enforcement professionals have been looking for incriminating files and photos on hard disks for several years.

Although we often refer to partitioning and formatting as a way of wiping all data from a hard disk, talented people with advanced data-recovery tools can retrieve an amazing amount of confidential and perhaps incriminating information from disks that have been partitioned and formatted.

So if you're sure you don't want the data on the partition to wind up anywhere else, use the Delete and Secure Erase option.

Okay, enough detail. Let's get that partition outta here. Follow these steps:

1. **Launch PartitionMagic.**

2. **Select the partition from the Partition List.**

3. **Click either the Delete Partition item in the left-hand task pane (see Figure 5-1) or choose Partition ⇨ Delete.**

4. **When the Delete Partition window opens, select your desired delete type.**

   PartitionMagic gives you two different ways to wipe the drive of its data. These are

   • **Delete:** This simply erases the data.

   • **Delete and Secure Erase:** This takes an extra measure in removing the data to make it less possible for someone to mine data from the drive by using special drive-recovery software.

Look back at the PartitionMagic window, shown in Figure 5-2 and you'll see that I now have a lot of Unallocated Space (close to 40GB), where my C: partition was in earlier figures.

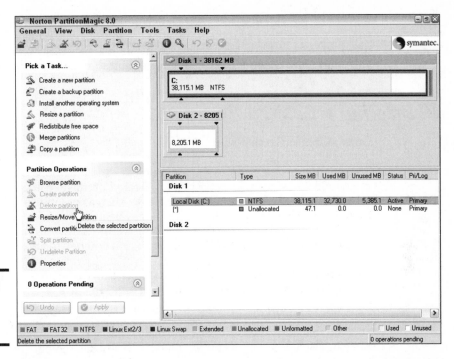

Figure 5-1:
Select
Delete
Partition.

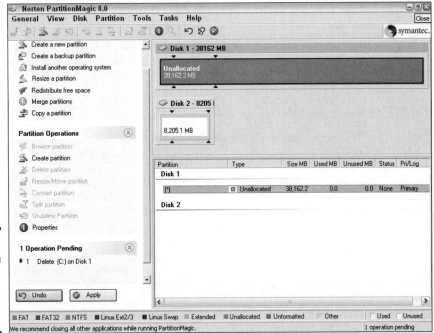

Figure 5-2:
The partition
is gone;
unallocated
space left
in its place.

**Book VIII
Chapter 5**

**Removing a
Partition**

If the partition you delete is set to active at the time you remove it, you need to then set another partition (with an operating system installed) as active or you won't be able to boot your PC without rescue disks. You'll see a message warning you about this when you attempt to delete an active partition.

Recovering a Deleted Partition

Oops! Want to take that back?

Time matters when it comes to recovering deleted partitions. Perform the attempted recovery ASAP after you discover your mistake. If you run any other types of operations in PartitionMagic, such as creating a new partition from that newly unallocated space, you may be out of luck.

Follow these steps to try to recover a partition you deleted erroneously:

1. **Point to the unallocated space that became visible on your disk map in PartitionMagic after deleting the partition earlier.**

2. **Choose Partition ⇨ Undelete.**

   The Undelete window opens and a search begins through your unallocated space trying to find the remains of any deleted partitions. When the search is complete, it will list any recoverable partitions in the window.

3. **If the partition you want is listed, select it and then click OK.**

   Phew! It's recovered and the partition is once again listed in PartitionMagic. Excuse me while I fan myself! That was scary. (Of course, if the partition you're looking for isn't listed, you're out of luck.)

Hiding and Unhiding Partitions

You would only want to hide a partition for one reason, and it doesn't have anything to do with playing a nice game of hide-and-seek with your PC hardware.

That only reason for hiding a partition has to do with computer and data security. By hiding a partition, you can try to keep its contents from the prying eyes of someone who can sit down at your keyboard or can otherwise access your system (such as when a drive is shared over a home or small-office network).

A hidden partition does not get a drive letter (like C:, D:, E:, or F:) assigned to it. If someone had access over a network to your PC with a hidden partition, he could scan your drives but he wouldn't see a drive letter there that lets him open up files on that partition. You can still get to files and folders located there, but the idea is that others won't even know the partition exists so they can't go hunting around in there.

You have a couple of restrictions:

✦ **You may not be able to hide a partition if the partition is where PartitionMagic is installed.** For example, you may not be able to hide your C: partition if you're using PartitionMagic installed on your C: drive to do it.

✦ **If you have more than one operating system on your drives, PartitionMagic usually hides one of the primary partitions automatically if you have a dual-boot system (a system that runs two or more operating systems).**

Follow these steps to hide a partition:

1. **Open PartitionMagic.**

2. **Choose Partition ⇨ Advanced ⇨ Hide Partition.**

You see a warning that your drive letters may change (I'll show you how to try to work around this).

3. **If you want to proceed, click OK.**

Under some versions of Windows — including Windows Me and Windows 95/98 — hiding a partition removes its drive letter and then automatically reorganizes all the remaining drive letters. Say you have one hard disk with two partitions giving you a C: and D: drive and you have a CD or DVD drive marked with the letter E:. If you hide your D: partition, these Windows versions will leave C: alone but move the CD/DVD drive up to letter D:.

To prevent this from happening, run the DriveMapper utility (see Figure 5-3), covered in Chapter 2. Load DriveMapper directly through PartitionMagic by choosing Partition ⇨ Advanced ⇨ Drive Mapper. Or, if you don't want to open PartitionMagic, choose Start ⇨ All Programs ⇨ Norton PartitionMagic 8.0 ⇨ PartitionMagic Tools ⇨ Drive Mapper.

**Book VIII
Chapter 5**

Removing a Partition

Figure 5-3:
Run Drive
Mapper to
recognize
drive
changes on
your system.

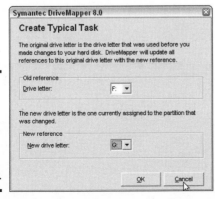

Want to make that hidden drive visible again? In Partition Magic, choose Partition ⇨ Advanced ⇨ Unhide Partition.

Remember to run DriveMapper again.

Book IX

Norton CleanSweep

"A centralized security management system sounds fine, but then what would we do with the dogs?"

Contents at a Glance

Chapter 1: Cleaning Your Drive (s)

In This Chapter

✔ Understanding the pitfalls of having too much junk on your drives

✔ Launching CleanSweep

✔ Choosing what to remove

✔ Archiving unwanted programs

✔ Restoring archived programs

Doing disk maintenance without bothering to clean unwanted, unneeded files and programs from your system is like trying to lose weight by diet alone when you keep ordering a thick milkshake to wash down your salad. If that doesn't sound like a strange lunch mix to you, consider trying to vacuum a room where books and toys litter the floor. Good luck — you'll need it.

Whether you do the kind of work on your computer that requires creating lots of files almost doesn't matter. Web browsing alone can add hundreds of temporary files in a single busy evening. Games leave debris behind, too, as do a bunch of other activities in which you routinely engage.

The result can be a huge, roomy 60GB or 80GB hard disk that's filled with junk. Windows Disk Cleanup can help, but a tool in Norton SystemWorks called CleanSweep has everything you need.

Steering Around the Potholes

Files don't automatically vanish when you delete them. For a period of time, such files go into a holding area either through Windows Recycle Bin or Norton Protected Recycle Bin from which you can recover them. That's great when you make a mistake, but if you don't need them, it's a little like carrying around an extra 20 pounds around your belly.

Because you have this "grace zone" provided by Recycle Bin, deleting a bunch of files manually today doesn't mean you automatically free up the disk space. These files move into Recycle Bin, but they aren't deleted for at least a week, depending on how you may have configured your trash can to work.

Deleting these files one by one is a pain. You can easily spend an hour or two pressing the Delete key while barely making a dent in the mountain of abandoned, orphaned, and otherwise lonely leftovers.

For this reason, having a more disciplined, reasoned approach to the whole concept of keeping your drive free of virtual dust bunnies and other debris makes sense. But before you see how Norton CleanSweep fills the bill in this regard, you also need to know how bad the situation can get if you don't practice good garbage file removal.

Having a disk filled with junk is bad enough. But that's not the worst part. A hard disk congested with unwanted filed and unused programs doesn't operate as quickly and effectively as one that is kept lean and mean, trimmed of all the debris. This congestion makes it harder for drive maintenance programs like Windows Disk Defragmenter and Norton Speed Disk to do their job.

As the mess continues to mount, it can interfere with your *virtual memory,* which is the area of a hard disk that is used by Windows as a form of memory that allows programs and files to sit in a holding area while you work. Leftover files can make it tougher for your Web browser to move back and forth between Web pages.

Over time, your drive slows. As it does, Windows gets sluggish. Opening files and programs becomes something you hate doing. You start to wonder if the PC cops are going to come arrest you for computer abuse.

Consider, too, that hundreds, thousands, and even tens of thousands of junk files can get written to the drive backups that you make. If you have a real problem and have to restore those backups, all those unwanted files get copied right back along with the important stuff. Think of how much extra time and cost can be involved when you're talking about filling backup media like recordable CDs and DVDs with this dreck.

Besides the mind-numbing nature of sitting there manually deleting unneeded files from your system comes the age old question, "Do I need this file?" It's not always easy to tell which files you need and which files you can happily spend the rest of your life without. Even grizzled vets scratch their heads and wonder.

This is another bonus of a program like Norton CleanSweep. It identifies the types of files you're apt to need so it won't accidentally remove them for you. If you delete the wrong file in your Windows folder, for example, you can kiss your next bootup goodbye.

Getting CleanSweep Up and Running

Okay, time to roll up your sleeves and start cleaning.

Here, I zero in on removing general files and unused programs. In the next chapter, I show you the ins and outs of cleaning up all those temporary Internet files.

Before you haul out the vacuum and the yard bags, open Norton SystemWorks. If you have multiple Norton products installed and you're using Norton CleanSweep through Norton SystemWorks, you'll see that the SystemWorks interface, shown in Figure 1-1, gives you both Cleanup and CleanSweep options.

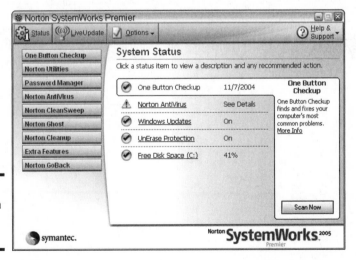

Figure 1-1:
Your Norton
cleaning
choices.

What's the difference between Cleanup and CleanSweep? Cleanup pretty much just focuses on removing old or unnecessary files left over from Web browsing. CleanSweep not only sweeps up some Internet leftovers but also lets you remove and archive unused programs along with unneeded files like temporary files created by running and installing programs.

Installing CleanSweep if you haven't already

Software sometimes is written to pick and choose what gets installed. One of these oddities is seen with CleanSweep which — for a reason that totally escapes me — isn't installed by default as part of Norton SystemWorks or SystemWorks Premier (unless you happened to check CleanSweep from the installation list during the setup process). When I installed SystemWorks, I didn't check CleanSweep in the installation list, and I had to go looking for CleanSweep — so you're not alone.

If you can't find Norton CleanSweep in your program list, you're probably stuck in the same boat I was. So grab a paddle and I'll help you row your way to getting it installed. Just follow these steps:

1. **Insert your Norton SystemWorks CD into your CD or DVD drive.**

   Setup should launch automatically. If it doesn't, choose Start ⇨ Run, click Browse,

and point to your CD or DVD drive. Select the file NCDSTART.EXE and click Open (see the figure).

2. **When the Setup screen appears, choose Install Norton SystemWorks or SystemWorks Premier.**

3. **Click Modify.**

4. **Check Norton CleanSweep and uncheck all the other programs listed, as shown in Figure 1-5.**

5. **Click Next and then Finish.**

Now here's another strange issue I can't explain. This process should work and did on one of my PCs. But on my main PC, I had to take extra measures to get CleanSweep installed; when I didn't, the setup would always fail with a vague, unhelpful error message. The nasty part of the solution is that you remove all of Norton SystemWorks only to install it again more fully.

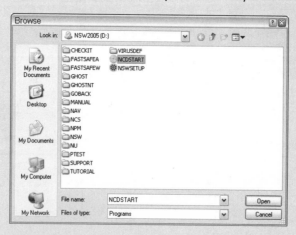

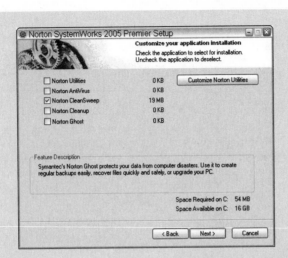

Here's how to proceed if the previous steps don't work for you:

1. **Insert your Norton SystemWorks or SystemWorks Premier installation CD in your CD or DVD drive.**

2. **Go to the Windows Control Panel.**

3. **Double-click Add or Remove Programs.**

4. **Locate and select Norton SystemWorks in your Windows program list and then click Remove (see the figure).**

   Note: At this point, I recommend you take a moment and shut down and restart your system before you move on to Step 5. This isn't mandatory, but it gives you a fresher start between removing and reinstalling.

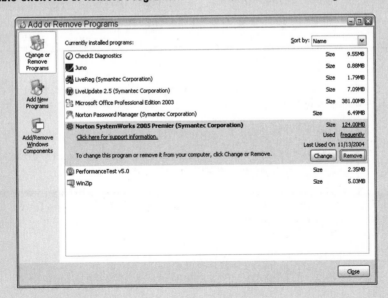

(continued)

(continued)

5. **Choose Start ⇨ Run.**

6. **Click Browse and point to your CD or DVD drive.**

7. **Click on NCDSTART.EXE and then click Open.**

8. **Select Install Norton SystemWorks or SystemWorks Premier.**

9. **Click Modify.**

10. **From the Program List, click to check all the programs listed, as shown in Figure 1-7.**

11. **Click Next and then click Finish.**

You may be prompted to restart your system either after you remove the previous installation or when you finish the improved setup. If so, go ahead and restart.

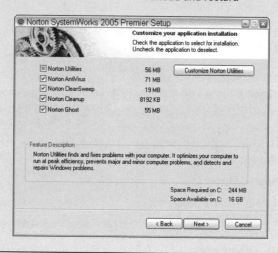

Click Norton Cleanup from Norton SystemWorks and you have the following choices, shown in Figure 1-2:

✦ **Express:** Select this when you want to do a basic, fast disk cleanup.

✦ **Custom:** Choose this when you want to specify exactly what's done during the cleanup and which files are targeted.

✦ **Options:** Click this to configure how cleanup works and where to preserve certain files (like Web cookies you want to keep to use for your favorite Web sites).

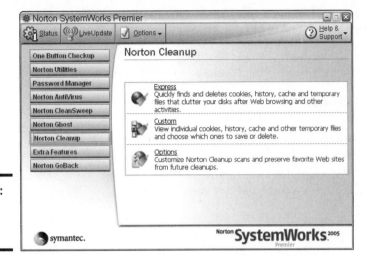

Figure 1-2:
Your
Cleanup
choices.

To launch CleanSweep, choose Start ⇨ All Programs ⇨ Norton SystemWorks ⇨
Norton Utilities ⇨ Norton CleanSweep, or just open Norton SystemWorks
and click Norton CleanSweep in the left-hand menu. Either way, the CleanUp
screen, shown in Figure 1-3, appears (don't confuse this with Norton Cleanup,
which is another utility).

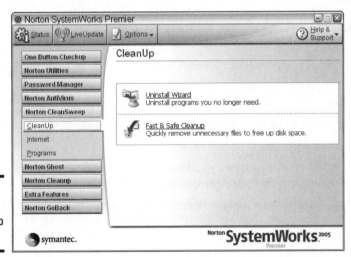

Figure 1-3:
The Norton
CleanSweep
window.

Don't see Norton CleanSweep listed under your program choices? This program may not have been installed as part of Norton SystemWorks. If so, read the following section.

When you open Norton CleanSweep, you see three choices:

✦ **CleanUp:** Your general-use PC vacuum cleaner for sucking up temporary and other unneeded file from your PC.

✦ **Internet:** Specifically targets leftover Internet Web browsing files and cookies.

✦ **Programs:** Removes unused or unwanted programs from your PC while retaining a copy that can later be restored.

Deleting Files You Don't Need

Norton CleanSweep's Fast and Safe Cleanup is the tool to use when you want to remove general types of unneeded files, such as the temporary files left over from running a program and opening files. As its name suggests, this tool is speedy and seems to work slightly more aggressively than the Windows Disk Cleanup tool (available by choosing Start ⇨ All Programs ⇨ Accessories ⇨ System Tools).

Follow these steps to let CleanSweep analyze your system and delete unneeded files:

1. **Open Norton SystemWorks.**

2. **Click CleanSweep and then Cleanup.**

3. **Click Fast and Safe Cleanup.**

CleanSweep then generates a report telling you how much space it expects to be able to recover as part of the cleanup.

4. **Click Settings.**

5. **Select those file types you want removed and/or uncheck those file types you don't want purged (see Figure 1-4).**

6. **If you want to schedule the cleanup to occur at a different time, click Schedule and then specify the time and date on which to do this; then click OK.**

7. **Click Clean Now (see Figure 1-5).**

8. **After CleanSweep reports it's done and how much space was freed, click OK.**

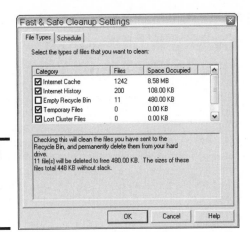

Figure 1-4:
Select
which file
types to
purge.

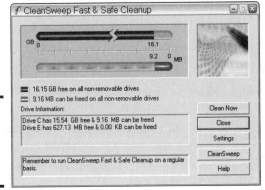

Figure 1-5:
Click Clean
Now to
clean up
your drives.

Clearing Out the Crud Left Over from Programs

Among the files CleanSweep can clear from your system are orphaned
files left over from programs you've already deleted (a no-no) or properly
uninstalled.

But what about programs you installed and have since forgotten about?
Every time you buy a new PC with preloaded software, you're apt to end
up with a laundry list of programs you don't use or rarely load.

The Uninstall Wizard is the part of CleanSweep that can help you remove
programs you either never use or very rarely load. Most people have at least
a few that fit in that category, and if you're one of them, you can use the disk
space better.

Why CleanSweep is better than Add or Remove Programs

I recommend using Norton CleanSweep to remove your unwanted programs rather than Windows' own Uninstalled available in Add or Remove Programs in the Control Panel. The difference between these utilities is big; CleanSweep allows you to save the program as part of an *archive* (a collection of files placed together and compressed to save space) so you can restore it later, if you discover you need it. This means you can keep your program settings and don't have to reinstall the program all over again and reconfigure it. You just restore the archive, which also resurrects all your program settings and any special customization you may have added to it. Because the program is archived, you save space over leaving the unused program installed, while still keeping it close at hand — the best of both worlds.

Follow these steps to use Uninstall Wizard:

1. **Load Norton SystemWorks and select Norton CleanSweep.**

2. **Click Uninstall Wizard.**

3. **In the Uninstall Wizard, locate and select a program you don't use and want to remove as shown in Figure 1-6. When you're done, click Next.**

   To expand listings that start with a plus sign, click on the plus. Click Search if you can't find a program you want to delete.

   The wizard analyzes the program and its associated files and reports this to your screen. This may take a short while.

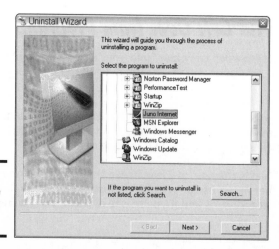

Figure 1-6: Choose the program to remove.

CleanSweep displays the name of the folder where it will store a copy of your archived program. You can click the button with the ellipses (...) next to the location if you want to change the location. Otherwise, click Next to continue.

4. **Specify whether you want CleanSweep to ask to confirm your deletions. Click Yes (for safety sake) and click Next.**

5. **An information screen tells you what's being stored and the basics of getting it back (see Figure 1-7). Click Finish.**

With this done, CleanSweep then proceeds to delete the program you chose to remove. When you're asked to confirm the removal, click Yes.

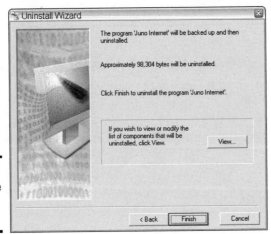

Figure 1-7:
Your archive
information
screen.

Restoring from the Archive

So what do you do when you need to get back a program you removed using CleanSweep? You restore your archive. Here's how:

1. **Load Norton SystemWorks.**

2. **Click Norton CleanSweep and then choose Programs.**

3. **Click Restore Wizard.**

   CleanSweep automatically reports the last program it stored as an archive (see Figure 1-8).

4. **If the last-installed program is the program you want to restore, click Yes and then Next. If it's not the right program, click No and then choose your program before you click Next.**

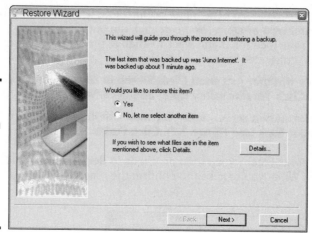

Figure 1-8:
Indicate
whether you
want to
restore
the most
recently
archived
program.

5. **Click Next three times and then click Finish.**

6. **Click Yes when asked if you want to delete the backup of the archive and then click OK.**

   Your program is now restored, exactly where it was installed before. Load the program and you should see that everything looks and works as before.

Storing Program Backups

Norton CleanSweep also includes a Backup Wizard designed to help you protect designated programs on your system by making a copy of them, much as CleanSweep does when you're at least temporarily removing programs from Windows. Follow these steps to create this copy:

1. **Open Norton SystemWorks and choose Norton CleanSweep.**

2. **Click Programs and then Backup Wizard.**

3. **Select the program you want to back up (see Figure 1-9) and then click Next.**

   CleanSweep reports where it will store your backed up files.

4. **Click Next.**

5. **Click Finish and then OK.**

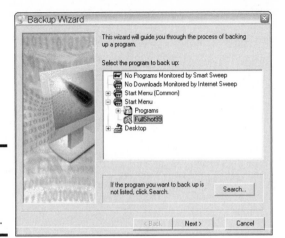

Figure 1-9:
Select the
program to
copy into a
backup file.

If your installed program develops a problem and needs to be reinstalled, use
the same process you used to restore your archive to restore this backup.
Just as with archives, all your program settings remain intact, which is good
because you don't want to have to reset them all anyway.

Chapter 2: When Web Browsing Makes a Mess

In This Chapter

✔ Appreciating the kind of mess left over from Web browsing

✔ Knowing why you need some of these files

✔ Cleaning out your temporary Internet files

✔ Saving special files

✔ Using Smart Sweep and Internet Sweep

✔ Viewing the CleanSweep Master Log

You probably only worry about two things when you're online surfing the Web. First, you wish you could go a lot faster — a fact true even if you're using high-speed access. Then you hope no one's spying on you.

I bet it never occurs to you to wonder exactly what's left behind on your drive from the sites and pages you open in your Web browser. But I'm here to tell you that nearly everything you see in your browser ends up sitting on your hard disk, as cold and unappealing as last night's fish dinner and just about as useful.

If you're a busy browsing Net citizen, you could rack up tens of thousands of leftover Internet files on your drive every single month. Some of these files aren't very large in size, but multiply them by the thousands and you're talking about serious disk space lost to nothing you want to keep.

In this chapter, I show you how to change all that.

Digging a Little Deeper

Think all you do is open your Web browser and visit a Web site, very anonymously without so much as a "hello" exchanged? Well, you may believe you're incognito and off on your own. But you're not.

In the following sections, I show you just some of the ways information gets transferred from a site to your hard disk — and back again — without your permission. Just dig a little deeper into browser and Internet technology, and you'll be amazed at what you don't see.

How's your cache flow?

There's a lot beneath the hood of a Web browser, including a whole truck-load of little tools built in to try to compensate for the overall sluggish speed at which some of us surf. One of those tools is the *browser cache,* a special holding area where Web pages get saved (at least in part) to your hard disk so the browser can call upon the old pages if it's having trouble opening the new ones.

A less-than-sterling side effect is lots of leftover Internet files making up all the photos, drawings, hypertext markup language (HTML), and other assorted goodies that comprise those cached Web pages.

The debris left behind

The browser cache isn't the only way Web leftovers get onto your drive. Most browsers today offer a history feature to let you go back in time to view Web pages you looked at yesterday or two weeks ago Tuesday.

How many days your browser stores this history depends on how it's configured. For example, if you use Microsoft Internet Explorer, you can check your history by following these steps:

1. **Open Microsoft Internet Explorer.**

2. **Choose Tools ⇨ Internet Options.**

3. **From the General tab (shown in Figure 2-1), look in the History section and see what's specified there.**

    You can increase or decrease this by toggling the up/down arrows next to the number of days.

Today, the majority of commercial Web sites transmit a file known as a cookie to you when you visit. This cookie is a small file that stores a certain amount of information; it's exactly what that information contains that often makes cookies controversial (see Book VI for more on cookies).

Some cookies are extremely helpful because they help a site recognize you as a returning guest or member when you return there. Other cookies keep track of where you've been and what you've done on a Web site so you know what you've already looked at when you return. Then there are cookies that can be downright invasive and may report more details back to the mother-ship, er, Web site than you may realize. Many people choose to delete all cookies — even if it causes some inconvenience.

One of the benefits of Norton CleanSweep is that you can pick and choose your cookies — keep the ones you want and toss the rest. This allows you to clear hundreds of cookies while still preserving ones you deem important.

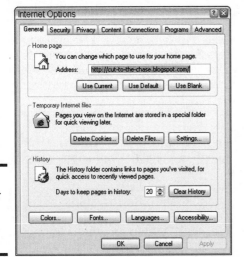

Figure 2-1:
Check your
browser
history
setting.

Cut the nose off your snoops

If you're using CleanSweep as part of Norton SystemWorks, you have Norton
AntiVirus available to you. In Book VI, you discover that Norton AntiVirus
can help kill spyware and adware sent to you while you're browsing the Web
or through attachments to your e-mail.

These files can account for some of the additional ill-gotten booty you get
from some Web sites.

Knowing the performance hit

I can't tell you how many thousands of times I've had someone come to me
asking for help because he's having trouble with going forward or backward
using a Web browser. A number of things can cause this, but the usual cause
is a buildup of temporary Internet files.

Even before you actually have problems using the Back and Forward buttons
in the browser, you usually feel a certain reluctance building as you surf.
People live with this situation for weeks before the browser gives up. Yet the
cure is usually no more exotic than cleaning out all those old files.

Deciding What Needs to Go

Making a decision to clean up your PC is one thing. Knowing exactly what
should get tossed out in the process is another. You can purge every single
little Internet file from your history and Windows Internet temporary folder,
but some of this stuff will be right back tomorrow when you open the same
sites again.

CleanSweep has a tool specifically designed to help you determine which files are safe to delete and which are not. Called Safety Sweep, it literally gives you a green light when it's okay to remove a file or file type as part of the cleanup operation. Safety Sweep also helps out in trying to find all files that may be associated with a certain file or program you're removing to aid you in being sure you get rid of everything possible.

A traffic-light icon goes into your Windows System Tray, and when you select a file to remove, a green light from this icon says you're safe. If the traffic light is yellow, you should proceed with caution. However, if the light's showing red, not only is it not safe to delete a file or program, CleanSweep will prevent you from doing so.

Follow these steps to turn on the Safety Sweep feature:

1. **In Norton SystemWorks, click Options and then choose Norton CleanSweep.**

The window opens to the first tab marked Safety Sweep.

2. **Under Fast Analysis, click On and under Safety Sweep, be sure this is also marked On (see Figure 2-2).**

3. **Click OK.**

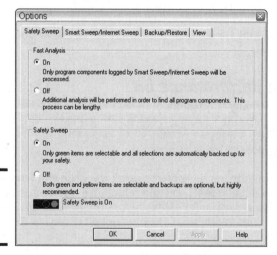

Figure 2-2:
Turn on
Safety
Sweep.

Clearing Out

The Fast and Safe Cleanup tool covered in the previous chapter will take care of many of your Internet leftovers. You can also set up options under Norton Cleanup that help you either purge a broader selection of these temporary Internet files or exclude certain sites from the purge so that you can keep cookies and other files you get from such sites.

Beyond that, there are specific Internet-based tools within CleanSweep that can aid with other issues, including

✦ Removing programs installed to your PC from Web sites

✦ Clearing out Web browser add-ons, also referred to as browser *plug-ins*

✦ Getting rid of unneeded ActiveX controls (ActiveX is one of the technologies that allow you to run Web-based programs directly through your Web browser, such as media players and games)

In the following sections, I take these one at a time.

Doing deeper cleaning

If you use Norton Cleanup or the Fast and Safe Cleanup tool, you get rid of many of your Web-based junk files. However, Norton Cleanup — out of the box — isn't configured to remove cookies. You can change this. Here's how:

1. **Open Norton SystemWorks.**

2. **From the left-sided menu, click Norton Cleanup.**

3. **Click Options.**

4. **From the Cleanup Scans tab (see Figure 2-3), select Cookies.**

5. **Click OK.**

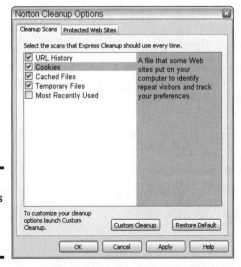

Figure 2-3:
Add cookies
to your
cleanup
routine.

Protecting files from certain sites

Do you regularly visit any Web sites whose cookies and other files you want to keep? If so, you want to add these sites to a protected list in Norton Cleanup and indicate which types of files for these sites you want to keep. Follow these steps:

1. **In Norton SystemWorks, click Norton Cleanup.**

2. **Click Options.**

3. **Select the Protected Web Sites tab.**

4. **Click Add Site.**

5. **Type the domain name (for example, www.symantec.com), and then click to select the file types (such as cookies) you want to keep, as shown in Figure 2-4.**

Your options are

- **Cookies:** The little bits of data such as your name and location on registered Web sites that help identify you to the site when you revisit it

- **Cache:** Files like banners and images transferred to your browser when you visit a site, which can speed up the loading of the page on a revisit because you already have those files

- **History:** Stores the URL and other information related to a Web site and your activity there

- **MRUs:** Short for *Most Recently Used,* this tracks the most recently accessed areas on Web sites you visit

6. **Click OK.**

Removing Internet programs and plug-ins

Time to clean up all the materials you've downloaded off the Web and installed directly into your Web browser or other Internet tool? Help is just a few clicks away. Follow these steps:

1. **From Norton SystemWorks, click Norton CleanSweep.**

2. **Click Internet.**

3. **Click Internet Uninstall (see Figure 2-5).**

4. **Choose the program you want to remove and then click Next.**

5. **Click Next, then Next, and then Finish.**

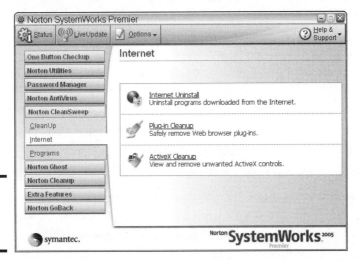

Figure 2-4:
Add a
site name
to your
Protected
Web Sites
list.

Removing Internet programs here allows you to store a backup of the
uninstalled program in an archive that can later be restored.

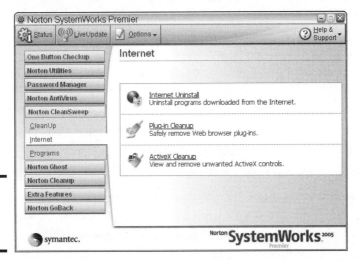

Figure 2-5:
Choose
Internet
Uninstall.

Here's the process for removing those dastardly browser plug-ins we all
seem to acquire:

1. **Click Norton CleanSweep.**

2. **Click Internet and then Plug-in Cleanup.**

3. **Select your plug-in from the list and then click Clean.**

4. **When finished, click Close to exit the utility.**

If you don't see any plug-ins listed even though you know you have them installed, your browser plug-in may be slightly nonstandard. But it's more likely that browser plug-ins you installed prior to adding Norton SystemWorks and/or Norton CleanSweep simply aren't being picked up.

Using Smart Sweep and Internet Sweep

Smart Sweep and Internet Sweep are intelligent monitors that are also part of Norton CleanSweep (if the *Sweep* in the names didn't already give that away). Their job is to watch your system, paying particularly close attention to any new programs you install (the Smart Sweep part) or download from the Internet (the Internet Sweep part).

As you get and install programs, these components record details about what's installed and where it's installed; information it shares with other parts of the CleanSweep tool like the Backup Wizard and the Internet Uninstall Wizard. The idea here is to help CleanSweep know more about your system and be able to assist you better in removing (and if needed, restoring) programs you don't use.

If you're using Norton CleanSweep under Windows 98 or Windows Me, Smart Sweep and Internet Sweep probably load automatically whenever you start or restart Windows. If you're using Windows XP or 2000, these tool components don't load automatically — although you can set them to do this if you want to take advantage of these options.

To turn on Smart Sweep and Internet Sweep and have them launch with Windows, follow these steps:

1. **Open Norton SystemWorks.**

2. **Click Options and then Norton CleanSweep.**

3. **Select the Smart Sweep/Internet Sweep tab and then click Load Smart Sweep/Internet Sweep on Startup, as shown in Figure 2-6.**

4. **Click Apply and then OK.**

To turn it off, you follow the same basic steps except that you click to uncheck the load option in Step 3.

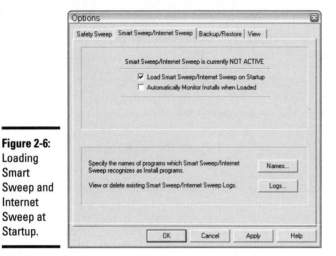

Figure 2-6:
Loading
Smart
Sweep and
Internet
Sweep at
Startup.

Checking Your CleanSweep Log

Norton CleanSweep keeps all the details about the programs you archive
and back up as well as those you restore. At any time, you can go back and
review that log if you have questions about where a missing program is or
whether you've already backed up a program.

Here's how to check the CleanSweep Master Log:

1. **From Norton SystemWorks, click Options and then Norton CleanSweep.**

2. **Select the View tab (see Figure 2-7) and click View Master Log.**

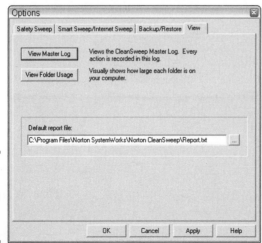

Figure 2-7:
The
CleanSweep
Options
View tab.

The log opens in its own window, as shown in Figure 2-8.

3. When you're done reading, you can click Print to print a hard copy of this log or click Close to shut the window.

4. Click OK.

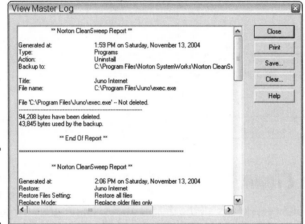

Figure 2-8:
Review your
CleanSweep
log.

Index

E

F

G

H

I

N

O

Notes

Notes

Notes

Notes

Notes

Notes

BUSINESS, CAREERS & PERSONAL FINANCE

0-7645-5307-0

0-7645-5331-3 *†

Also available:

- Accounting For Dummies †
  0-7645-5314-3
- Business Plans Kit For Dummies †
  0-7645-5365-8
- Cover Letters For Dummies
  0-7645-5224-4
- Frugal Living For Dummies
  0-7645-5403-4
- Leadership For Dummies
  0-7645-5176-0
- Managing For Dummies
  0-7645-1771-6

- Marketing For Dummies
  0-7645-5600-2
- Personal Finance For Dummies *
  0-7645-2590-5
- Project Management For Dummies
  0-7645-5283-X
- Resumes For Dummies †
  0-7645-5471-9
- Selling For Dummies
  0-7645-5363-1
- Small Business Kit For Dummies *†
  0-7645-5093-4

HOME & BUSINESS COMPUTER BASICS

0-7645-4074-2

0-7645-3758-X

Also available:

- ACT! 6 For Dummies
  0-7645-2645-6
- iLife '04 All-in-One Desk Reference
  For Dummies
  0-7645-7347-0
- iPAQ For Dummies
  0-7645-6769-1
- Mac OS X Panther Timesaving
  Techniques For Dummies
  0-7645-5812-9
- Macs For Dummies
  0-7645-5656-8

- Microsoft Money 2004 For Dummies
  0-7645-4195-1
- Office 2003 All-in-One Desk Reference
  For Dummies
  0-7645-3883-7
- Outlook 2003 For Dummies
  0-7645-3759-8
- PCs For Dummies
  0-7645-4074-2
- TiVo For Dummies
  0-7645-6923-6
- Upgrading and Fixing PCs For Dummies
  0-7645-1665-5
- Windows XP Timesaving Techniques
  For Dummies
  0-7645-3748-2

FOOD, HOME, GARDEN, HOBBIES, MUSIC & PETS

0-7645-5295-3

0-7645-5232-5

Also available:

- Bass Guitar For Dummies
  0-7645-2487-9
- Diabetes Cookbook For Dummies
  0-7645-5230-9
- Gardening For Dummies *
  0-7645-5130-2
- Guitar For Dummies
  0-7645-5106-X
- Holiday Decorating For Dummies
  0-7645-2570-0
- Home Improvement All-in-One
  For Dummies
  0-7645-5680-0

- Knitting For Dummies
  0-7645-5395-X
- Piano For Dummies
  0-7645-5105-1
- Puppies For Dummies
  0-7645-5255-4
- Scrapbooking For Dummies
  0-7645-7208-3
- Senior Dogs For Dummies
  0-7645-5818-8
- Singing For Dummies
  0-7645-2475-5
- 30-Minute Meals For Dummies
  0-7645-2589-1

INTERNET & DIGITAL MEDIA

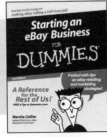

0-7645-1664-7

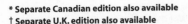

0-7645-6924-4

Also available:

- 2005 Online Shopping Directory
  For Dummies
  0-7645-7495-7
- CD & DVD Recording For Dummies
  0-7645-5956-7
- eBay For Dummies
  0-7645-5654-1
- Fighting Spam For Dummies
  0-7645-5965-6
- Genealogy Online For Dummies
  0-7645-5964-8
- Google For Dummies
  0-7645-4420-9

- Home Recording For Musicians
  For Dummies
  0-7645-1634-5
- The Internet For Dummies
  0-7645-4173-0
- iPod & iTunes For Dummies
  0-7645-7772-7
- Preventing Identity Theft For Dummies
  0-7645-7336-5
- Pro Tools All-in-One Desk Reference
  For Dummies
  0-7645-5714-9
- Roxio Easy Media Creator For Dummies
  0-7645-7131-1

* Separate Canadian edition also available
† Separate U.K. edition also available

Available wherever books are sold. For more information or to order direct: U.S. customers visit www.dummies.com or call 1-877-762-2974.
U.K. customers visit www.wileyeurope.com or call 0800 243407. Canadian customers visit www.wiley.ca or call 1-800-567-4797.

SPORTS, FITNESS, PARENTING, RELIGION & SPIRITUALITY

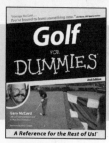

0-7645-5146-9

0-7645-5418-2

Also available:

- Adoption For Dummies
  0-7645-5488-3
- Basketball For Dummies
  0-7645-5248-1
- The Bible For Dummies
  0-7645-5296-1
- Buddhism For Dummies
  0-7645-5359-3
- Catholicism For Dummies
  0-7645-5391-7
- Hockey For Dummies
  0-7645-5228-7

- Judaism For Dummies
  0-7645-5299-6
- Martial Arts For Dummies
  0-7645-5358-5
- Pilates For Dummies
  0-7645-5397-6
- Religion For Dummies
  0-7645-5264-3
- Teaching Kids to Read For Dummies
  0-7645-4043-2
- Weight Training For Dummies
  0-7645-5168-X
- Yoga For Dummies
  0-7645-5117-5

TRAVEL

0-7645-5438-7

0-7645-5453-0

Also available:

- Alaska For Dummies
  0-7645-1761-9
- Arizona For Dummies
  0-7645-6938-4
- Cancún and the Yucatán For Dummies
  0-7645-2437-2
- Cruise Vacations For Dummies
  0-7645-6941-4
- Europe For Dummies
  0-7645-5456-5
- Ireland For Dummies
  0-7645-5455-7

- Las Vegas For Dummies
  0-7645-5448-4
- London For Dummies
  0-7645-4277-X
- New York City For Dummies
  0-7645-6945-7
- Paris For Dummies
  0-7645-5494-8
- RV Vacations For Dummies
  0-7645-5443-3
- Walt Disney World & Orlando For Dummies
  0-7645-6943-0

GRAPHICS, DESIGN & WEB DEVELOPMENT

0-7645-4345-8

0-7645-5589-8

Also available:

- Adobe Acrobat 6 PDF For Dummies
  0-7645-3760-1
- Building a Web Site For Dummies
  0-7645-7144-3
- Dreamweaver MX 2004 For Dummies
  0-7645-4342-3
- FrontPage 2003 For Dummies
  0-7645-3882-9
- HTML 4 For Dummies
  0-7645-1995-6
- Illustrator CS For Dummies
  0-7645-4084-X

- Macromedia Flash MX 2004 For Dummies
  0-7645-4358-X
- Photoshop 7 All-in-One Desk Reference For Dummies
  0-7645-1667-1
- Photoshop CS Timesaving Techniques For Dummies
  0-7645-6782-9
- PHP 5 For Dummies
  0-7645-4166-8
- PowerPoint 2003 For Dummies
  0-7645-3908-6
- QuarkXPress 6 For Dummies
  0-7645-2593-X

NETWORKING, SECURITY, PROGRAMMING & DATABASES

0-7645-6852-3

0-7645-5784-X

Also available:

- A+ Certification For Dummies
  0-7645-4187-0
- Access 2003 All-in-One Desk Reference For Dummies
  0-7645-3988-4
- Beginning Programming For Dummies
  0-7645-4997-9
- C For Dummies
  0-7645-7068-4
- Firewalls For Dummies
  0-7645-4048-3
- Home Networking For Dummies
  0-7645-42796

- Network Security For Dummies
  0-7645-1679-5
- Networking For Dummies
  0-7645-1677-9
- TCP/IP For Dummies
  0-7645-1760-0
- VBA For Dummies
  0-7645-3989-2
- Wireless All In-One Desk Reference For Dummies
  0-7645-7496-5
- Wireless Home Networking For Dummies
  0-7645-3910-8